SAMUEL PALMER

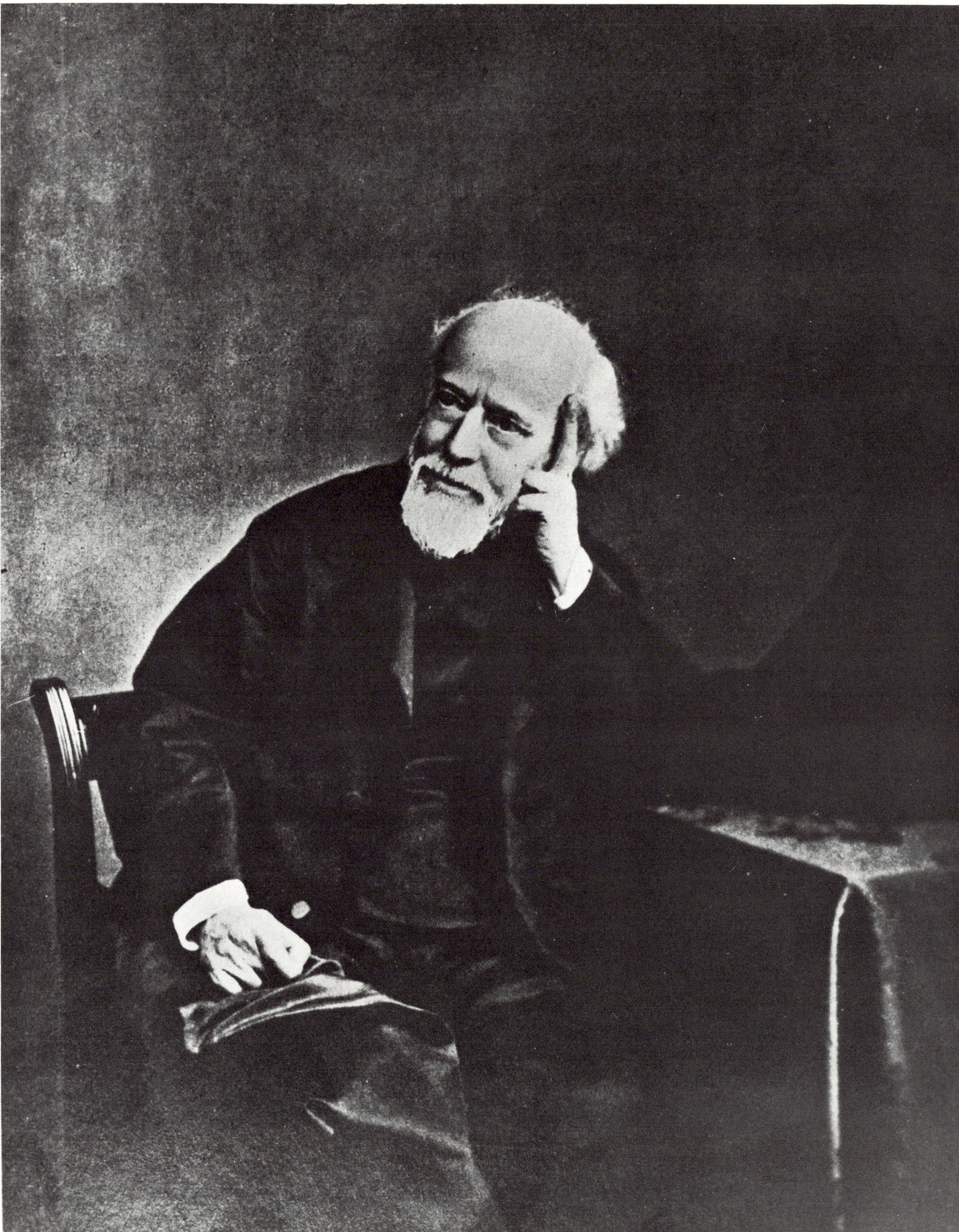

SAMUEL PALMER

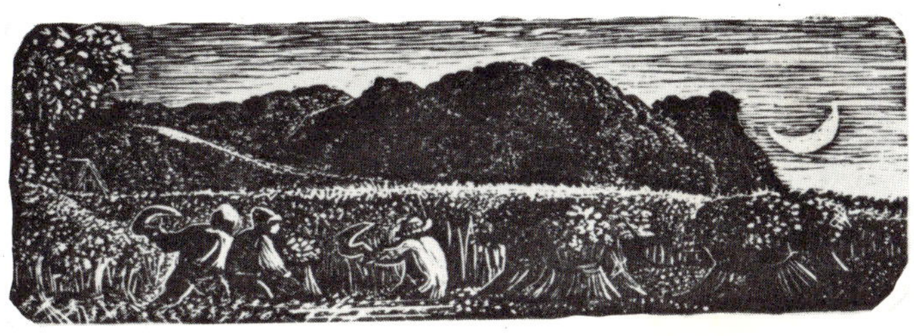

James Sellars

ST. MARTIN'S PRESS · NEW YORK

FRONTISPIECE: Samuel Palmer in Old Age. (A. H. Palmer, *A Memoir*)

TITLE PAGE: *Harvest under a Crescent Moon c.*1826 (Ashmolean Museum)

OPPOSITE: Page 13, Sketchbook, 1824 (British Museum)

The illustrations in the check-list and the bibliography are details from Samuel Palmers' paintings, drawings and etchings illustrated in the text.

ACKNOWLEDGEMENTS
For permission to reproduce works from their collections, the author and publishers wish to thank the Trustees of the Tate Gallery, Victoria and Albert Museum, British Museum and the Courtauld Institute; the National Gallery of Canada, the National Portrait Gallery, the Ashmolean Museum, the Syndics of the Fitzwilliam Museum, Carlisle Museum and Art Gallery, Lord Clark, Mr. and Mrs. Paul Mellon and the many private collectors who have also helped in so many ways; David Posnett of the Leger Galleries for making so much information available, and Graham Bush for his photographs.

First published in Great Britain in 1974 by Academy Editions 7 Holland Street London W8
SBN 85670 148 3

First published in the U.S.A. in 1974 by St. Martin's Press Inc.
175 Fifth Avenue New York N.Y. 10010
Library of Congress Catalog Number 74–81700
Printed and bound in Great Britain by Lund Humphries

CONTENTS

THE EARLY YEARS

1805–1827

Samuel Palmer was born in 1805 at Surrey Square in the Parish of St. Mary's Newington on the outskirts of London. London had not yet absorbed Newington. From the upper windows of the Palmers' house the village of Dulwich, surrounded by woods, could be seen and the air was still fresh with country smells. His father, Samuel Palmer senior, was a bookseller, dealing in books because he liked them rather than because of any success at the trade. His mother, Martha Giles, was the daughter of a banker, William Giles, who, on his death in 1825, left Palmer enough money to allow him seven years in which to practise his art without the tyranny of having to earn his living by it. The Giles were Baptists and upon marrying Martha, Palmer's father also became a Baptist – an important occurrence for Palmer as he reacted strongly against Baptism while still a child, and, perhaps as Geoffrey Grigson suggested, it was 'in part, maybe, the reaction, the impulse, to a high church archaism which made him paint to the Glory of God'.[1]

It was through William Giles, however, that he made his first contact with artists. Giles was the author of several books and Martha had been a model for a drawing by Thomas Stothard which was engraved for the frontispiece of Giles' *The Refuge*. He was also acquainted with Thomas Uwins who later became a Royal Academician and there can be little doubt that these relationships made things easier for Palmer when he later decided to become an artist especially as his maternal grandfather was held in some awe by the rest of the family.

On the paternal side it seems the family were all in business, prosperous and Church of England. His grandfather was a hatter, one uncle a city druggist, the other a wealthy corn factor and the family could claim descent from William Wake, Archbishop of Canterbury, Sir Stephen Fox and Richard Hooker, the sixteenth-century theologian, and was entitled to bear arms. Samuel Palmer was very conscious of this and when at Shoreham used to seal his letters with an armorial signet ring.

Palmer was considered delicate as a child and a nurse, Mary Ward, who was engaged for him and who 'found him pining on pap and other baby diet', boldly substituted more substantial and unusual treatment. She it was moreover who, though uneducated, was deeply read in her Bible and in *Paradise Lost* and imbued Palmer with a lifelong love of poetry. It is probably due to Mary that Palmer became an artist. There is a much-quoted passage in his son's biography of him, which is of great importance to an understanding of his development: 'Mary and he stood watching at a window while the full moon, rising behind the branches of a great elm cast a maze of shadows

1 John Flaxman, *Thomas Stothart* (National Portrait Gallery)

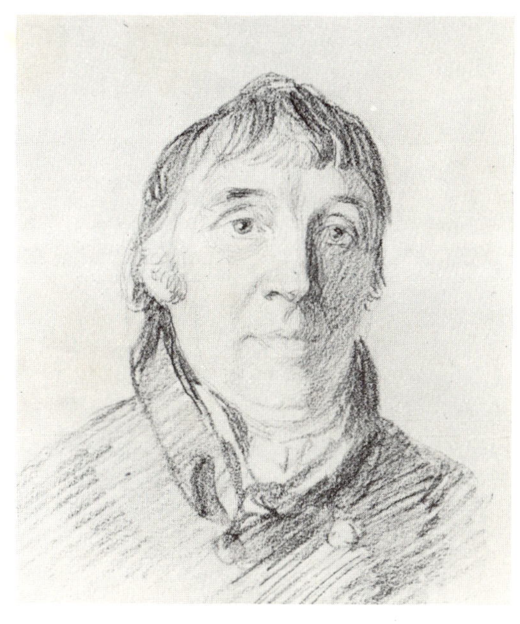

on the opposite wall. As the shadows changed the girl repeated this couplet

> Fond man! the vision of a moment made!
> Dream of a dream, and shadow of a shade!

My father never forgot those shadows and often tried to reproduce them with his pencil.' This was before Palmer was four years old.

Had she remained silent or made only some commonplace remark Palmer could very easily have become a poet for his education, directed by his father, had a strong literary bias. But Mary quoted poetry and the child, who is nothing if not creative, had this line of action temporarily blocked. Palmer could not better the couplet nor could he build upon it but impressed as he seems to have been, he had recourse only to another more obvious alternative – the visual. It is significant that the moonlight, the great elm and the shadows, not to mention the young nurse, were all to figure time and again throughout the 'visionary years' and the time he spent at Shoreham. It was probable that this safety, this warmth, was one of the things he was striving to recapture throughout those years.

Palmer's education was left largely in the hands of his father who appears to have been a very capable teacher. He was later to teach Latin, French grammar and arithmetic to John Linnell's children. At a very early age Palmer was encouraged to learn Greek and Latin and at the same time allowed to read widely in English literature. To judge from his reading, his son recorded, bigotry was not one of Samuel Palmer senior's failings. He was also expected to learn by heart a passage of the Bible daily and every day before his lessons these words were repeated 'Custom is the plague of wise men and the idols of fools'. A maxim which, judging by his eccentric behaviour, he was to carry through in his art when at Shoreham and in his life throughout the later years.

In the spring of 1817 he was sent to the Merchant Taylors school in Suffolk Lane but was quickly taken away, possibly in December of the same year. His upbringing had not been designed to suit him to the rigours of British Public School life and indeed he was very unhappy there. It was also at this time that his mother died after a short illness. The shock of her death was to affect him for a number of years and, according to his son, may have contributed to the intermittent attacks of melancholia which were to affect him later in life for 'His capability of suffering in this and other calamities cannot be gauged by his age or by the usual standard of susceptibility, but only by his own abnormally sensitive temperament'. However this may be, it is possible that the death of his mother can, in the long run, be considered as beneficient. Palmer's extreme sensitivity had been nurtured by his home background, a sensitivity, according to his son, which bordered on effeminacy. The extent to which his mother's continuing influence could have affected him can be imagined and although it may seem callous we, the recipients of Palmer's gifts, could have much to be thankful for in his mother's death when he was only thirteen years old. Certainly father and son were now thrown together more, the father from whom he received his liberal education. But we do not know, unfortunately, to what extent he was thrown into a closer relationship with his nurse, Mary Ward, who was still relatively young. However, it is certain that the symbols that occur in his Shoreham paintings are not of a nature that would occur had he been dominated in whatever degree by his mother.

Shortly after the death of his mother it was agreed that he should attempt to become a painter – he had been drawing long before he went to school –

and he was sent to a Mr. Wate for instruction, an obscure artist but one who seems to have been fitted to the role of teacher by his 'sterling and unostentatious character, together with his methodical habits', at any rate Palmer was considerably impressed by him. By the time he was fourteen he was showing at the British Institution and the Royal Academy where he exhibited *Landscape with ruins*, *Cottage Scene* and *A Study*. These are now all lost. Possibly they owed something to Wate who was also a landscape painter but more than likely were influenced to greater degree by David Cox whose book *A Treatise on Landscape Painting* strongly affected Palmer. In this year, 1819, he sold a picture for seven guineas to a Mr. Wilkinson of 4 Beaumont Street; this was either *Bridge Scene Composition* or *Landscape Composition.* From their titles it would appear that even at this early stage he was already painting from his imagination.

By this time he had become acquainted with two of the artists who were to become members of the group calling themselves 'The Ancients' during the years he spent at Shoreham; these were Frances Oliver Finch and Henry Walter. Finch was three years older than Palmer and a pupil of John Varley. Walter, perhaps less talented than the others, painted landscapes and did animal drawings for Ackermann, he was already twenty-nine.

Palmer visited the Academy Exhibition in 1819, the first he had seen, and was deeply impressed by J. M. W. Turner's *The Orange Merchantman* (*3*). 'The first exhibition I saw is fixed in my memory by the first Turner, "The

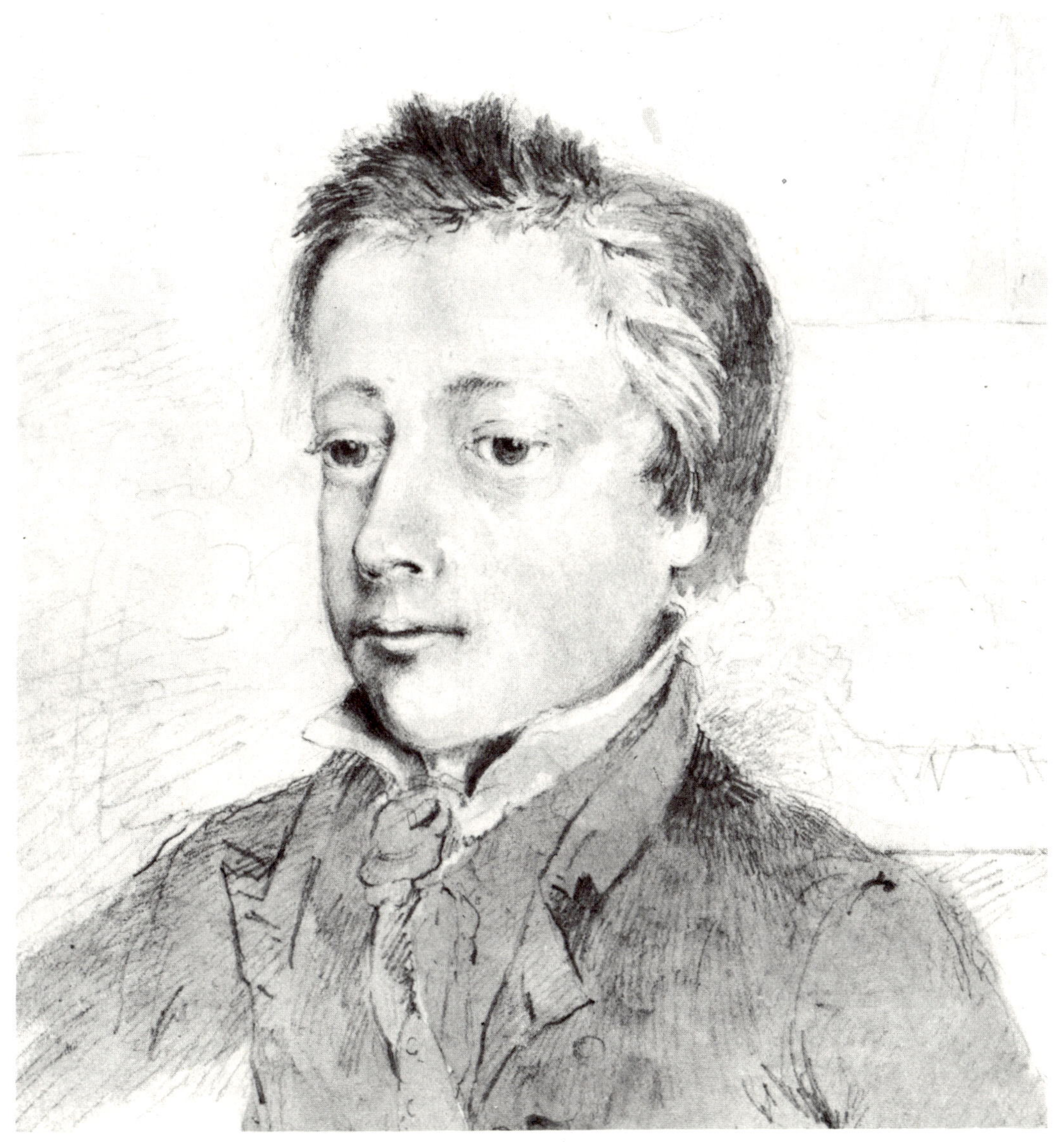

2 Henry Walter, *Samuel Palmer* aged 14, 1819 (British Museum)

Orange Merchantman at the Bar" and being by nature a lover of smudginess, I have revelled in him from that day to this. May not half the art be learned from the gradations in coffee grounds.' This was in a letter to Mrs. Robinson (formerly Miss Julia Richmond) written in 1872. It is a very curious remark for him to make for the very nature of his work at Shoreham as a visionary, seer or mystic, was exactly the opposite of Turner's 'smudginess'. Visionaries such as Palmer and Blake work very precisely, using a clean incised line and in fact the terms visionary, mystic, mean to see clearly. Is this not why Blake was so excellent an exponent of engraving and the bulk of Palmer's work at Shoreham in the exacting medium of pen and ink? When on the rare occasions he used tempera or oil it is handled in a draughtsman's manner rather than a painter's. His use of 'smudginess' may have been true in 1819 but this was written in 1872 – and none of his later work could be described as smudgy – which leads one to the belief that Palmer was unaware of what he was doing, or had done, at any time, certainly had he been conscious of the blatant sexual symbols in his Shoreham paintings, he would have been horrified. The coffee grounds, of course, are an exact counterpart of the shadows on the wall cast by the great elm of his childhood and can be seen in the flattening of foliage and tree shapes in his later Shoreham paintings. A. H. Palmer appositely writes 'The frame of mind which forced the lad of fourteen to stop before the "Orange Merchantman" and to carry away with him such a vivid impression of that picture was

3 J. M. W. Turner, *The Orange Merchantman* (The Tate Gallery)

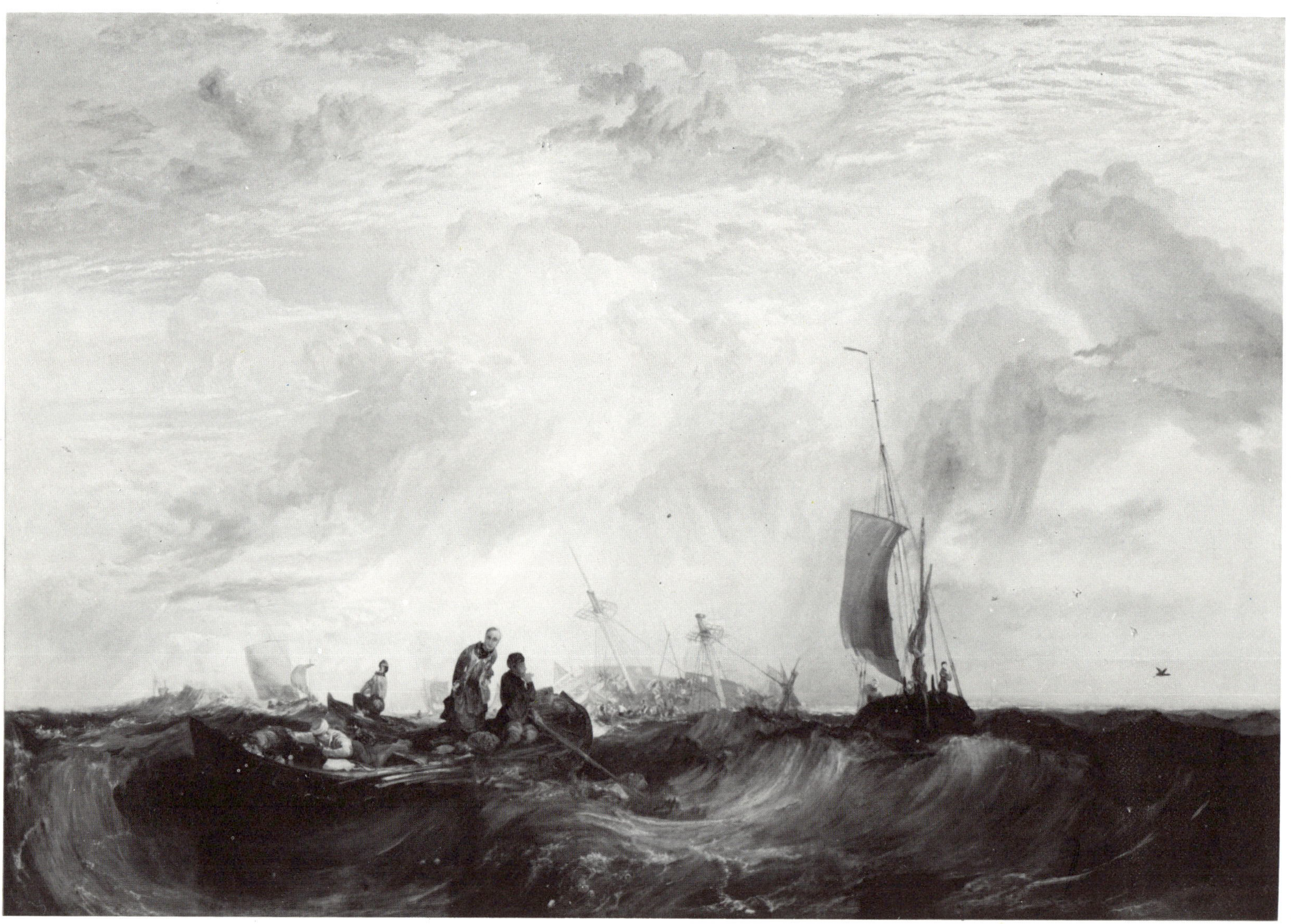

probably due partly to the kind of literature in which he had enjoyed "free pasture", and partly to the same predisposition which fixed moon-cast shadows in his memory. Faculties, which at that age are generally rudimentary, appear to have been already fairly developed.'

In 1820 he had another picture accepted by the Royal Academy and, according to the catalogue index, we find that the family had moved to 10 Broad Street, Bloomsbury. For the next few years Palmer was to 'flounder into the deep waters of his profession', continuing to be accepted by the Royal Academy and the British Institution showing works which seem to have been of little originality, mainly influenced by Turner, Cox and his teacher, Wate. He received advice from Stothard and tickets of admission to Flaxman's lectures at the Royal Academy but much of this, fortunately, had little real effect upon him. 'As far as art was concerned he continued to misuse his days, but at the same time, be it remembered, to exercise very diligently his mental facilities, till he became acquainted with Mr. John Linnell.' This was in September of 1822 when Palmer was seventeen and Linnell, his senior by twelve years, already a well known artist. Here was the 'Good Angel' as Palmer called him who 'plucked him from the pit of modern art'.

Linnell, son of a frame maker, was born in 1792. Forceful and energetic, he had from an early age shown a talent for painting. He was competent at landscape and portrait, had painted a number of subject pictures and had a wide acquaintance with other artists of his day. He was also a very domineering and grasping person who was in the habit of being rude to anyone who disagreed with his views. It was his religious beliefs, however, which could have influenced Palmer. He had joined the Baptists and Plymouth Brethren but left them when he found they required him to conform too much to the will of others, he had contemplated the Quaker movement but found even this too constraining for a person of his character. Eventually he evolved his own version of Christianity which he allowed no one to question. He was opposed, amongst other things, to Sunday Observance, fox hunting, marrying in church and even Christmas decorations. A radical in religious and political matters who it is not hard to imagine would be readily accepted by someone of Palmer's susceptible temperament and unconventional education at this time.

But Linnell was also a gifted painter with a highly individual feeling for English landscape and one who trusted his own intuitions. While he was still young he was almost the only person to appreciate William Blake, the one to 'discover' Palmer and perhaps the first English painter to look at his native landscape through English eyes. It is certain that Palmer owed the style, if not the inspiration, of the early visionary works to Linnell. Here was a man who, perhaps because of his idiosyncratic character, was able to eschew the Italian and French Renaissance paintings and the 'effects' the moderns theoretically derived from them. Something which not even Turner or Constable had been able to do. And begin to develop a rapport with the English landscape that had been lost since the brief flowering of the Romanesque sculpture by such artists as those of the Herefordshire School.

The meeting of the two men – or rather man and boy – was a success and Linnel quickly became Palmer's mentor. He took Palmer to galleries showing him the works of early Italian, German, and Flemish masters, Breughel and Dürer, especially Dürer. 'Look at Dürer' Linnell was to say to Palmer again and again. 'A new world opened itself to Palmer's young eyes; and a world much more akin to that of his own private vision. These old artists observed nature closely; in exact detail they portray hills and cities and clouds. But they also wonderfully suggest the spiritual and the supernatural. The angels and saints in their pictures are more convincing than those of later artists; largely because they are drawn in a different pictorial convention stylised and intensified, with pure vivid colours and sharp outlines. The firmness of their creator's faith was expressed in the firm outline with which they draw these figures. The impression made by them on Palmer can be imagined.'[2]

He was also encouraged to study figure drawing which he did in the antique galleries of the British Museum. Drawing from these marbles was the usual course before trying for admission to the Royal Academy Schools. Students were left entirely to themselves receiving no instruction but each one doing what appeared useful to them. With Palmer studied George Richmond, Sydney Cooper, Solomon Hart and a number of others who, with the exception of Palmer, all gained entrance to the Royal Academy Schools. It is not known why he failed but this failure was perhaps fortunate even though Fuseli, who was much admired by Palmer, was tutor at the time. It was while studying at the British Museum that Palmer saw the Greco-Roman figure of *The Sleeping Mercury*. In a letter to George Richmond in 1834 he writes 'one of the deepest sayings I have met with in Lord Bacon seems to me to be "There is no excellent beauty that hath not some strangeness in the proportion".' *The Sleeping Mercury* – which he misnamed *Endymion the Shepherd Boy asleep on Mt. Latmos* – 'has this hard-to-be-defined, but most delicious quality to perfection'. He not only carried the figure of this sleeping shepherd into his Kentish countryside, where it appears in different guises over and over again, but also the strangeness of proportion which appears in

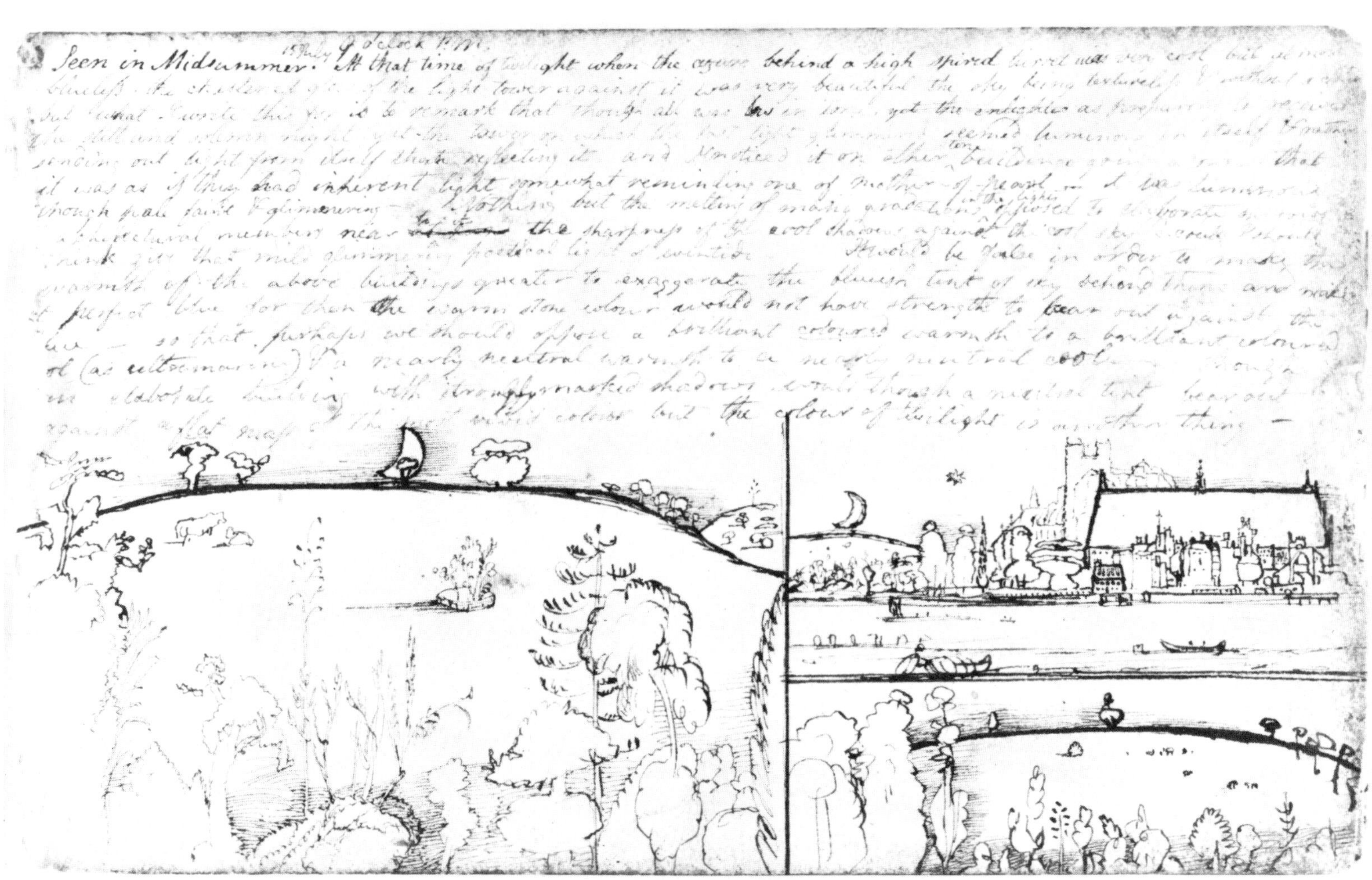

4 Page 1, Sketchbook, 1824 (British Museum)

the hills and groins, cottages and trees of his landscape for the next ten years.

Palmer himself best sums up these years until 1823. 'As it seems reasonable to divide the soul's journey into stages and starting-points, and to stop and look back at certain intervals, and at each fresh stage to go back to the primitive and infantine feeling with which we set out; and to lay in such store of humility, simple anxiety to get on, and diligence in the great, nay stupendous pursuit of grand art as may stand us in stead for a year's journey or so, I divide my life with respect to art into two parts. First, my very early years, in which I distinctly remember that I felt the finest scenery and the country in general with a very strong and pure feeling; so that had I then seen the works of the very ancient Italian and German masters I should have admired and imitated them, and wondered what the moderns could mean by what they call their "effects". Then, when I gradually learnt arithmetic and grammar, my feeling and taste left me, but I was not then completely spoilt for art. But when I had learned to paint a little, by the time I had practised for about five years I entirely lost all feeling for art, nor did I see the greatest beauties of even the Dutch masters, Cuyp, Ruysdael and etc; so that I not only learnt nothing in this space of time that related to high art, but I was nearly disqualified from ever learning to paint. But it pleased God to send Mr. Linnell as a good angel from Heaven to pluck me from the pit of modern art; and after struggling to get out for the space of a year and a half, I have just enough cleared my eyes from the slime of the pit to see what a miserable state I am now in . . . I have now made my first struggle – alas, with how little success. I shall now begin a new sketch book, and I hope, try to work with a child's simple feeling and with the industry of humility . . . '

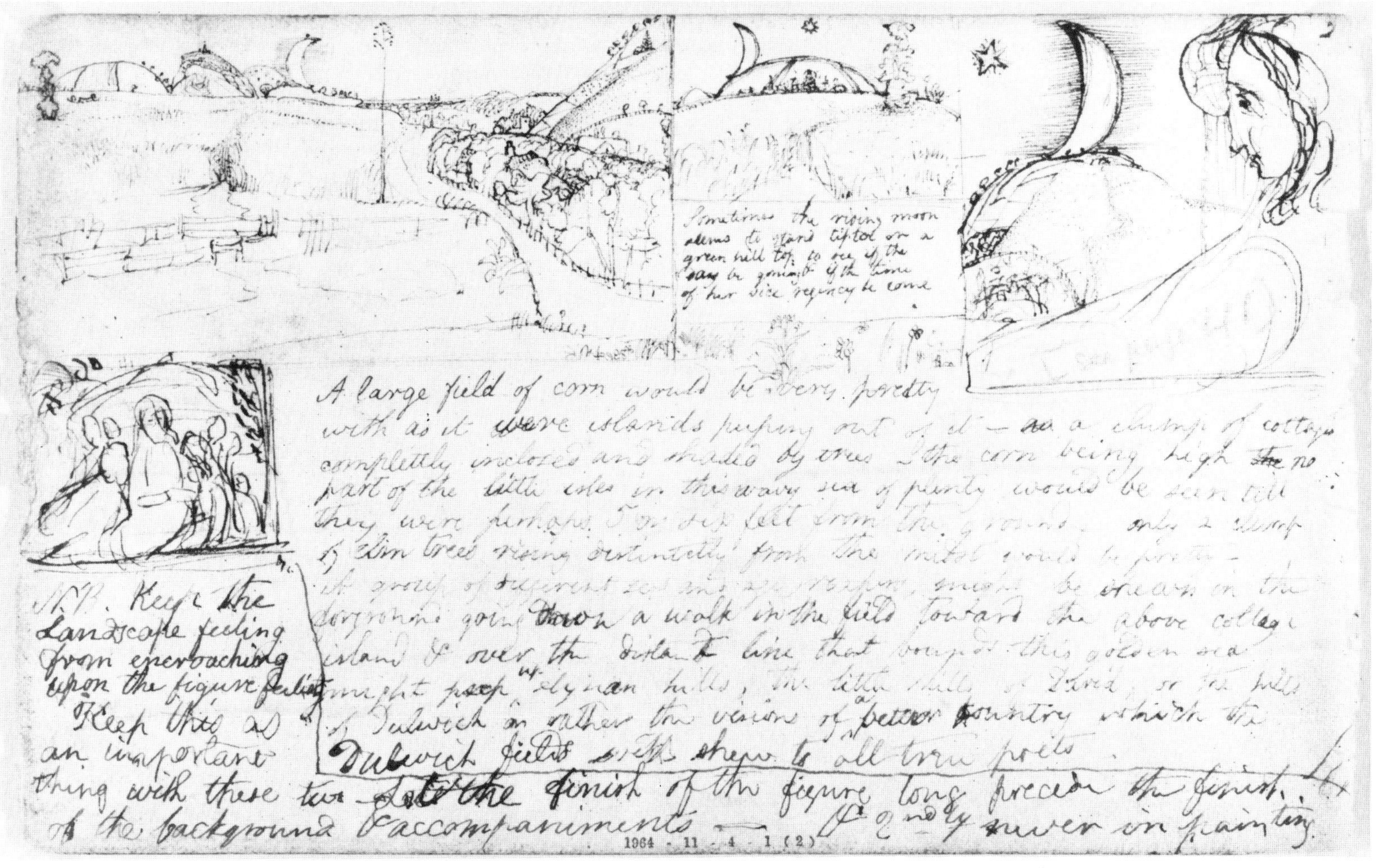

5 Page 2, Sketchbook, 1824 (British Museum)

The sketch-book he refers to is the one now in the British Museum. Apart from five leaves in the Victoria and Albert Museum and eleven pages, now lost, it is complete. It is one of many notebooks and sketch-books 'more than twenty' that Palmer kept, all of which, with the exception of this one, were burnt by his son, Albert Herbert, on his emigration to Canada in 1910. A. H. Palmer gave his reason: 'Sooner than that multitude of slight sketches, blots, designs etc. which my father valued so much . . . should be scattered to the winds, I burnt them, and so much more before we sailed that the fire lasted for days!'

Before discussing this surviving sketch-book in which we see the beginnings of Palmer's visionary period it is worth reading what he wrote about the same time. 'In my attempts to copy the Antique statues to try and draw most severely: and to cry out for more and more form; and then I shall find in the Antique more than I can copy, if I look and look and pry into it earnestly for form. I shall not be easy till I have drawn one Antique statue most severely. I cannot execute at all. The least bit of natural scenery reflected from one of my spectacle glasses laughs me to scorn, and hisses at me. I feel, ten minutes a day, the most ardent love for art, and spend the rest of my time in stupid apathy, negligence, ignorance, and restless despondency; without any of those delicious visions which are the only joys of my life – such as Christ at Emmaus; the repenting thief on the cross; the promise of Abraham; and secondary visions of the ages of chivalry, which are toned down with deep gold to distinguish them from the flashy, distracted present.' It is these reflections in his spectacles that became the vehicles for Palmer's visions.

Palmer was nineteen when he began this sketch-book in 1824. It is not known at what age he reached puberty but, given his delicate constitution, there is a strong presumption that it was later than in most boys. This, coupled with his intense religious feelings had, until now, retarded his sexual impulses. There is no trace of sexual imagery recorded in his previous work and there seems to be no other explanation for the extraordinary erotic landscapes that Palmer suddenly finds before him and with which he fills the sketch-book, than that he was growing up and that his religious beliefs were no longer spiritually satisfying nor were they strong enough now to retain the tide of puberty. The situation Palmer found himself in, albeit unconsciously, at the time he began the sketch-book seems accurately described in a passage from George Wingfield Digby's *Meaning and Symbol In Three Modern Artists*. Writing about the medieval monks' fascination with the grotesque carving of Romanesque sculptures he remarks 'however fundamental the teaching, however elaborate and comprehensive the philosophy, the dogma and the ritual, unless the individual can himself find the way not only to experience and understanding, but to integration as well, he will go spiritually hungry; which means that his phantasy life will be active, unsatisfied. He will be searching however unwittingly, for the symbol which will help him and which will open up the paths of release and development for that within which is still unrealised. Moreover, he will tend to seek it in the very opposite to that which is offered him for the sustenance of his spiritual or civilised being. He will have an appetite for the strange, the exotic, the recondite.'

Pen and ink is the medium usually employed throughout the book with occasionally some under drawing in pencil, a very few pages are in pencil only, some have water-colour washes applied to them and in one case gold was used for a sun, there are also a few sketches in black chalk with black and grey washes. From the employment of pen and ink it would appear Palmer wanted his statements to be read clearly, none of the lover of smudginess

6 Page 5, Sketchbook, 1824 (British Museum)

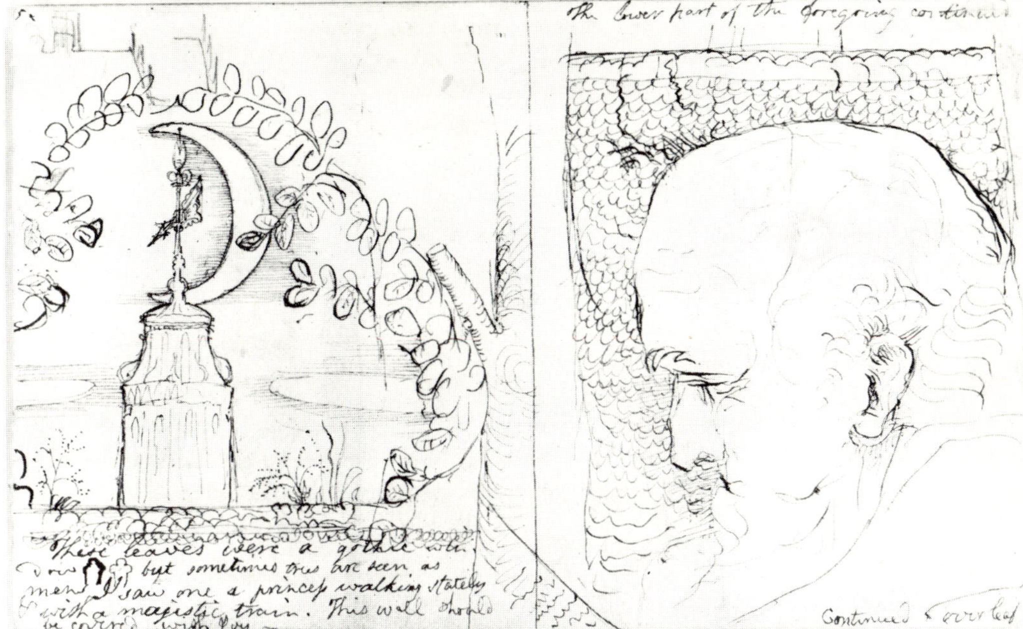

7 Page 7, Sketchbook, 1824 (British Museum)

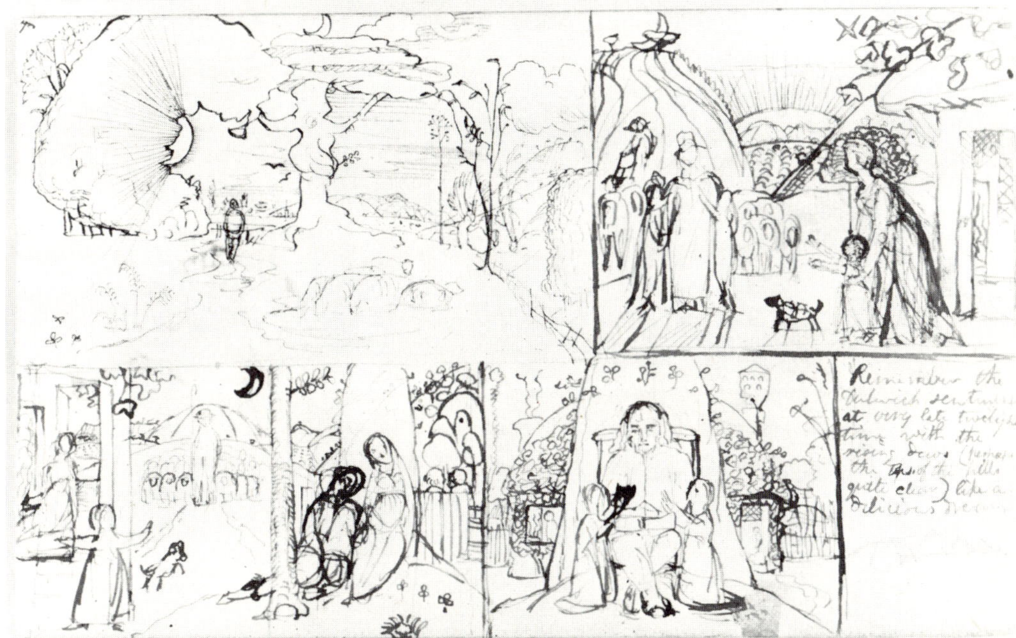

8 Page 8, Sketchbook, 1824 (British Museum)

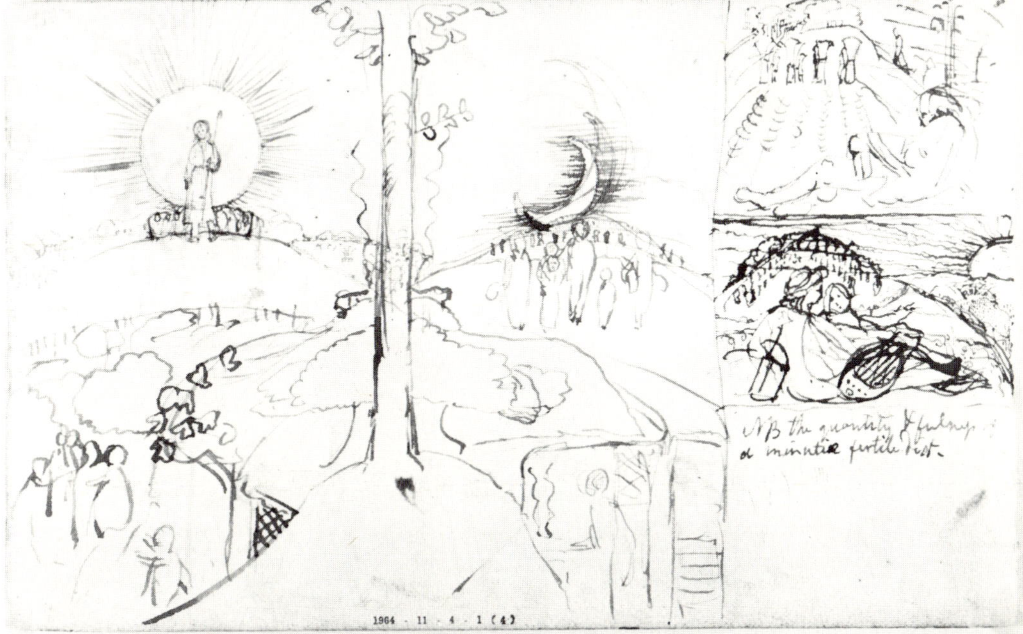

here, but it was also essential to employ such a medium in order to allow himself to depict minutiæ and the rich textural quality of this new world which he was beginning to discover and the pen was the ideal tool for his language. On seeing these drawings for the first time one is impressed by the extraordinary tactile qualities that they possess. This is closely bound to the sketch-book's greatest appeal, its air of sensuality, a sensuality that is created by his insight into the landscape of southern England with its rolling downs, its fecundity and the close, intimate, almost breathless quality it can achieve on a summer's day. Whoever has sat for an hour in a secluded corner of the English landscape in late spring will know what Palmer was about. This sensuality is enhanced by his use of symbols. There are pages and pages of 'horned' moons – very few harvest ones, time enough later for these – and they perch on top of a hill or have just begun to rise above it. In one case a moon rests atop a phallic, Gothic monument which is garlanded by leaves.

Here the artist's new-found vision and the virility to express it are depicted, and his passion expressed in the torrid suns which blaze out upon his landscapes. But the lover cannot help but dote upon the loved one and we find him delineating with infinite care details of shrub and leaf, texturing the hills and fields with lines and dots, garlanding the tree trunks with leaves and ivy, a symbol which D. H. Lawrence was to adopt in *Lady Chatterley's Lover* a century later. For Palmer here is seeing not with a male eye but a universal one which is at once male or female. He is excited by the forms of tree trunks and these are not just phallic but the phallus metamorphosed into trees, so closely does Palmer identify with his landscape. When he shows the whole tree it is frequently soft and breastlike as are his hills, foreshadow-

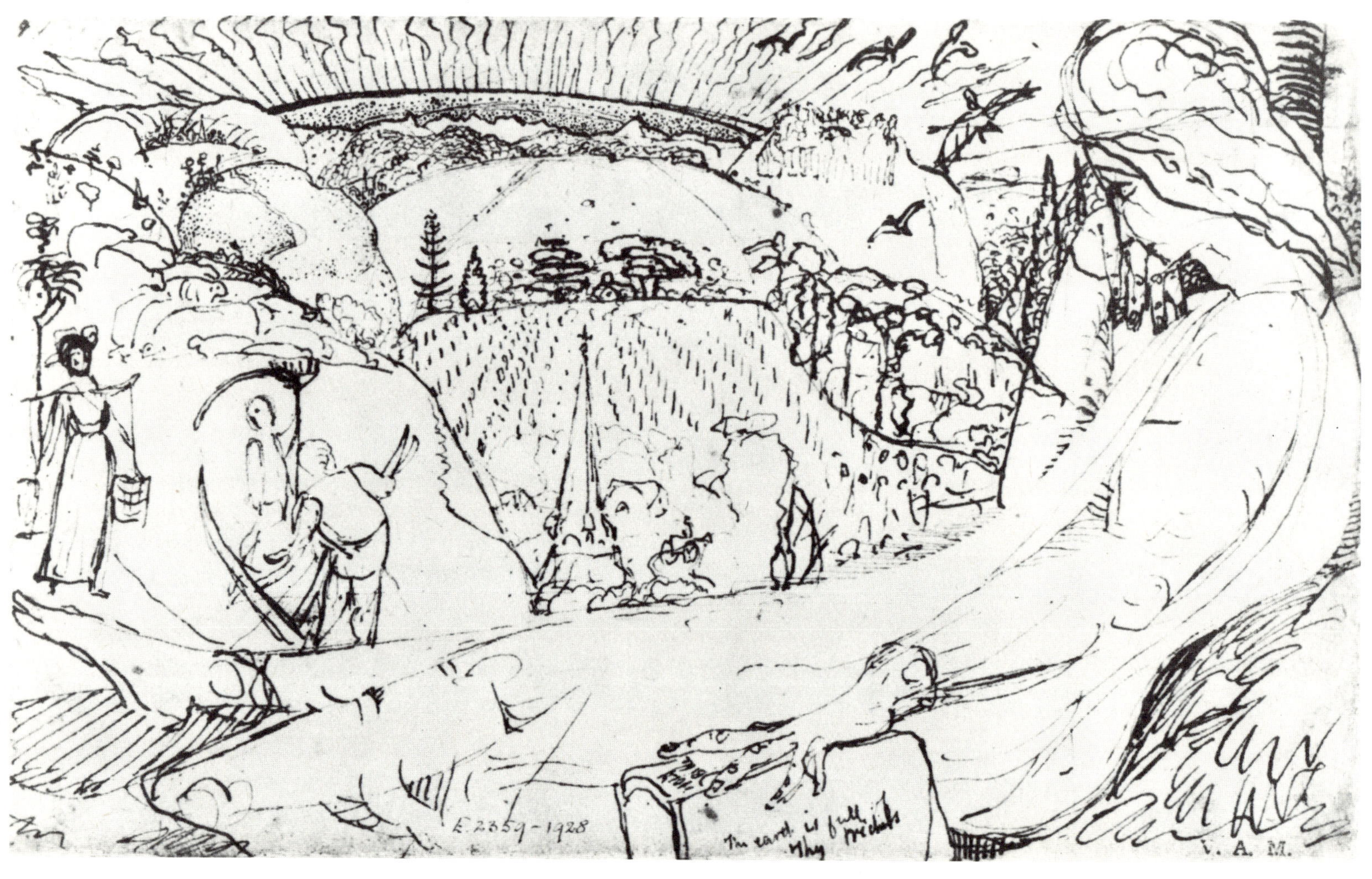

9 Page 9, Sketchbook, 1824 (British Museum)

ing the paintings of 1825 now in the Ashmolean Museum.

Palmer must have made his first visit to Shoreham at the time of this sketch-book, although there is no documentary evidence that he had been there before 1826 when he stayed for the summer. But the book certainly suggests that he knew the district in 1824, as did many others as it was a favourite sketching location for a number of artists. Much of the work in the book however is notes made in the studio and less detailed topographical descriptions than the effects of landscape upon his imagination. This can be seen in the exaggerated forms of the hills, the cliffs and rocky prominences which are reminiscent of the German and Flemish primitive paintings to which Linnell had introduced him. An excellent example of this is the exotic tree on page seven of the sketch-book which is an almost exact counterpart of the tree on the left hand side of Dürer's woodcut of *The Flight into Egypt* in the British Museum; the sheep in the same drawing may also be compared with Blake's wood engravings for the Thornton Virgil. But the richness and lushness of the Shoreham area is all here and very likely a few of the drawings were executed from nature, as the beautifully free study of a group of trees on page twenty-three (*17*) and the rhythms of the ploughed fields on page twelve (*16*). Even when making notes direct from nature he was quick to portray anything that would enhance his newly found paganism: the phallic spires of the little Kent churches, two trees merging into one on page eleven (*15*), the ladder leaning against a rick on page twenty-three, projections and scars on trees as on page thirty-three (*21*). All these he sees with the excitement of discovering affirmation of his unconscious beliefs. Besides these there are a few figure studies strongly influenced by Blake (with

10 Page 10, Sketchbook, 1824 (British Museum)

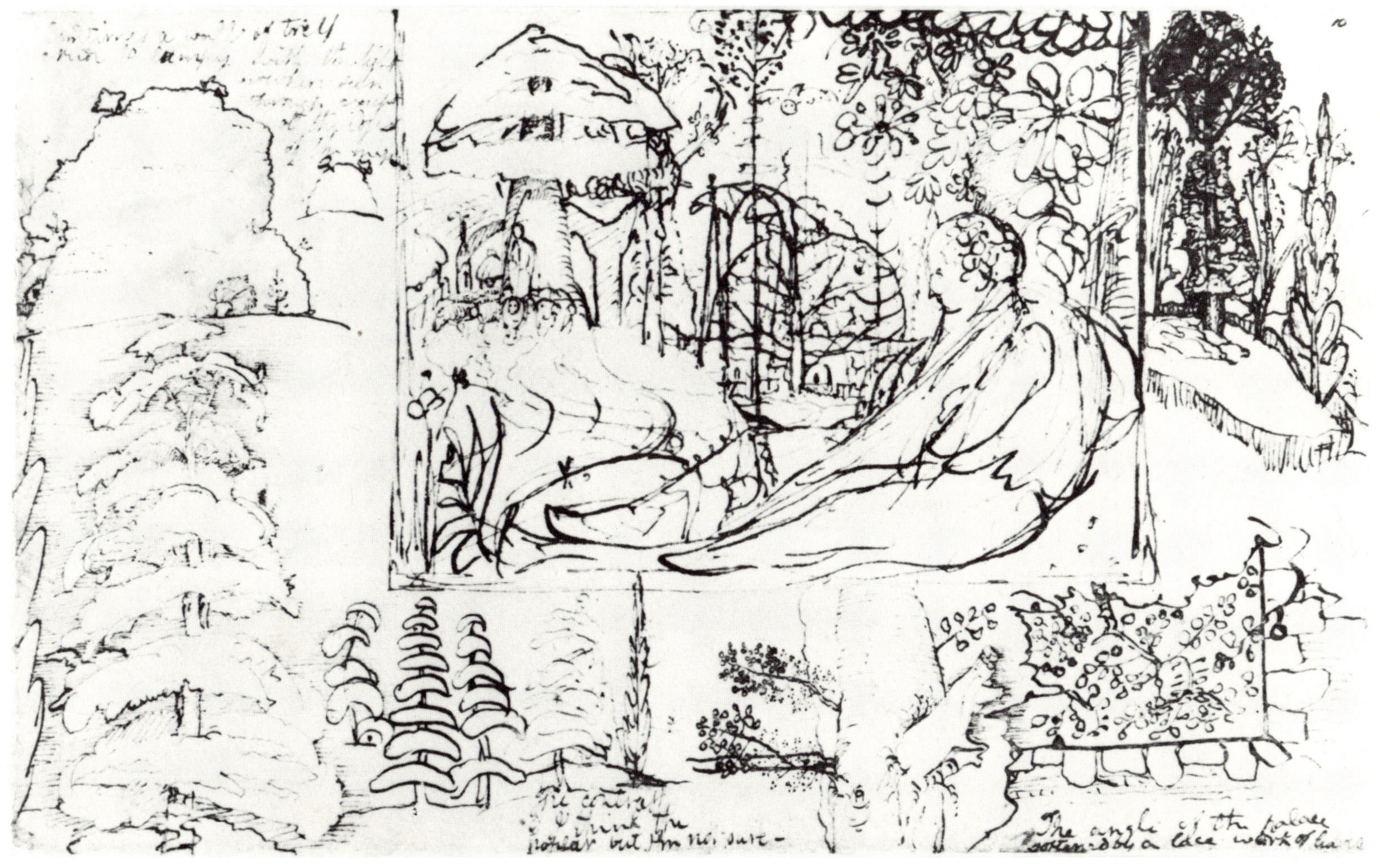

the exceptions of reclining forms related to *The Sleeping Mercury*) and a drawing of two little girls on page twenty-nine (*19*) which it is tempting to describe as drawings from life inserted into an imagined landscape. Of the other studies the male figures are full of vigour, not only in their actions but in the manner in which they are drawn, no doubt a reflection of his own feelings of metaphorically flexed muscles, curiously however they have an air of effeminacy about them. The female figures in contrast are beautifully tender and wear diaphanous gowns which delightfully reveal their sex, a feature totally lacking in the males although they are depicted nude. This may be a convention dictated by the times perhaps but we must remember this was a private sketch-book. The answer is more likely to be found in the fact that all the symbols he needed 'for the sustenance of his spiritual or civilised being' were here in the landscape around him. For he was primarily a landscape painter and it is in landscape that he found his images. It is our own close environment that influences our emotions and this need not be the place where we happen to live but the one we would gravitate to, given the opportunity and the knowledge of its situation. Palmer eventually gravitated to Shoreham and here he found all he needed for his finest work and indeed some of the greatest English landscapes ever to be painted. In these the human figure, when used, is subordinate to the forces of nature, not the incidental forces of weather, the melodramatic clash of thunder of a John Martin or even the profound drama of a Turner storm but the far more powerful one of procreation, of the loaded boughs of apple trees, of fields rich with corn, of trees bursting with blossom. Even had he been able to, it would have been superfluous to show the male figures in all their virility, but he was unable because it would have been too conscious an action, Palmer's intuitions were far stronger than Linnell's. Palmer would probably have produced the work he did at Shoreham had he never gone further afield than Dulwich, for, everything he subsequently did is in the sketch-book in embryo, even the style is developed to an extraordinary degree and much of his work between 1826 and 1834 could be described as no more than elaboration and development on themes he had already established.

When he met Blake in October of 1824 he had laid his foundations and although Blake's influence upon him is of great importance it would be mistaken to regard Palmer as a mere disciple or follower. Geoffrey Grigson states the case clearly by quoting Blake's remarks on Raphael in answer to Joshua Reynolds 'I do not believe Raphael taught Mich Angelo, or that Mich Angelo taught Raphael, any more than I believe that the Rose teaches the Lilly how to grow, or the Apple tree teaches the Pear tree how to bear fruit. I do not believe the tales of Anecdote writers when they militate against individual character'.[3] Palmer described in one of his notebooks the actual meeting with Blake on Saturday, 9 October 1824. 'Mr. Linnell called and went with me to Mr. Blake. We found him lame in bed, of a scalded foot (or leg). There, not inactive, though sixty-seven years old, but hand-working on a bed covered with books sat he up like one of the Antique patriarchs, or a dying Michel Angelo. Thus and there was he making in the leaves of a great book (folio) the sublimest designs from his (not superior) Dante. He said he began them with fear and trembling. I said "O! I have enough of fear and trembling". "Then", said he, "you'll do." He designed them (100 I think) during a fortnight's illness in bed! And there, first with fearfulness (which had been the more, but that his designs from Dante had wound me up to forget myself), did I show him some of my first essays in design; and the sweet encouragement he gave me (for Christ blessed little children) did not tend basely to presumption and idleness, but made me work harder and better

OPPOSITE

11 *The Repose of the Holy Family*, 1824/5 (Ashmolean Museum)

12 *Cornfield by Moonlight with the Evening Star*, *c.*1830 (Collection Lord Clark)

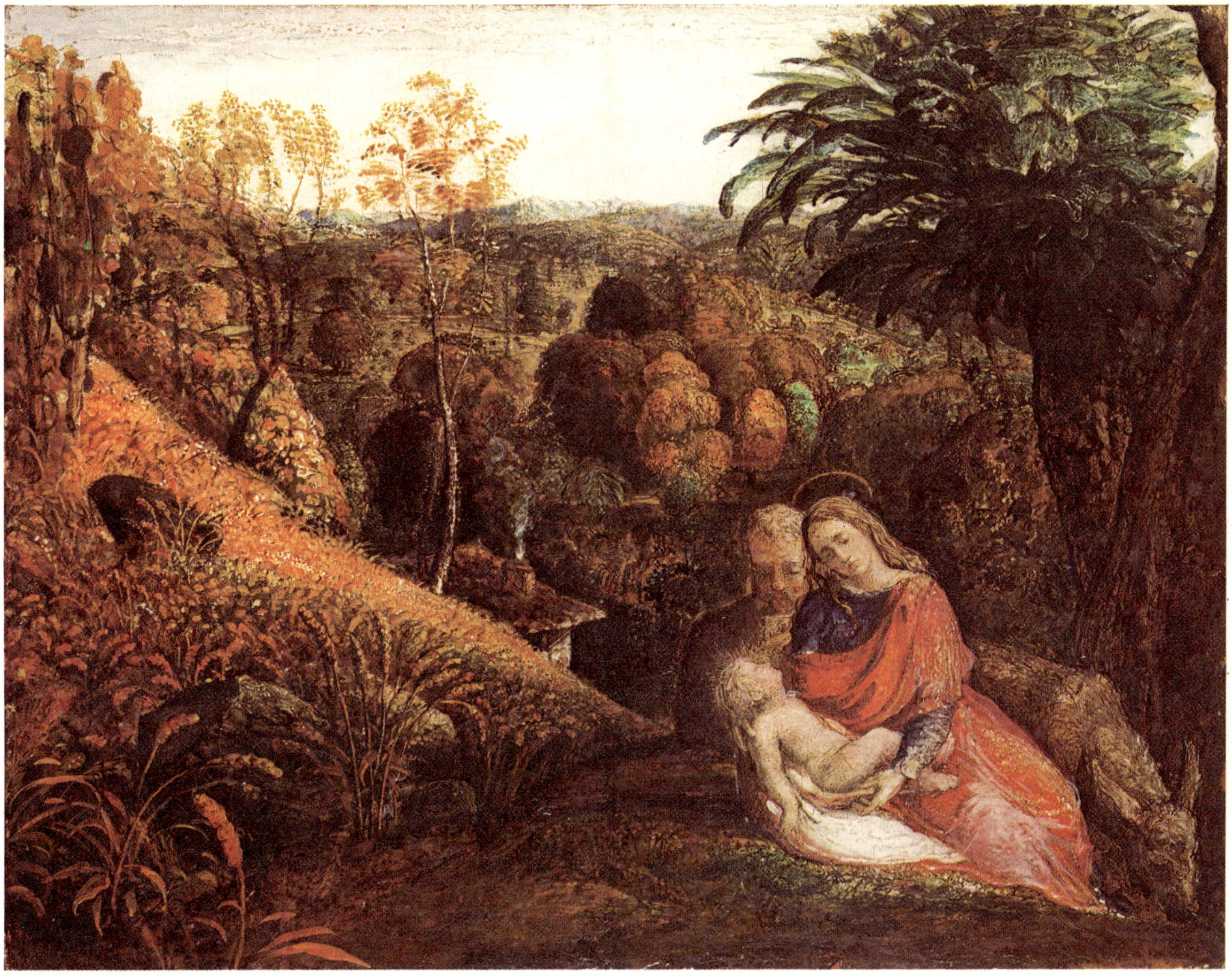

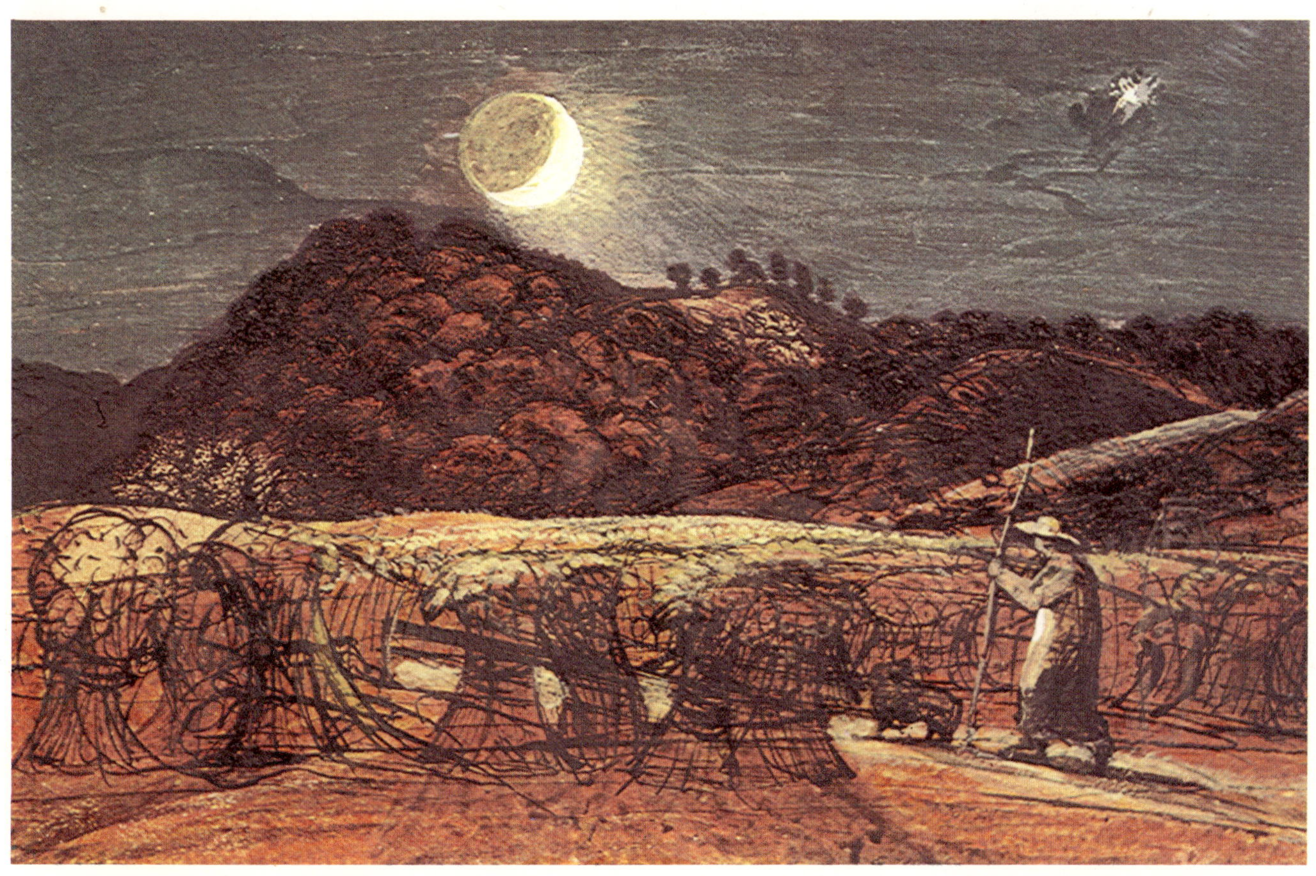

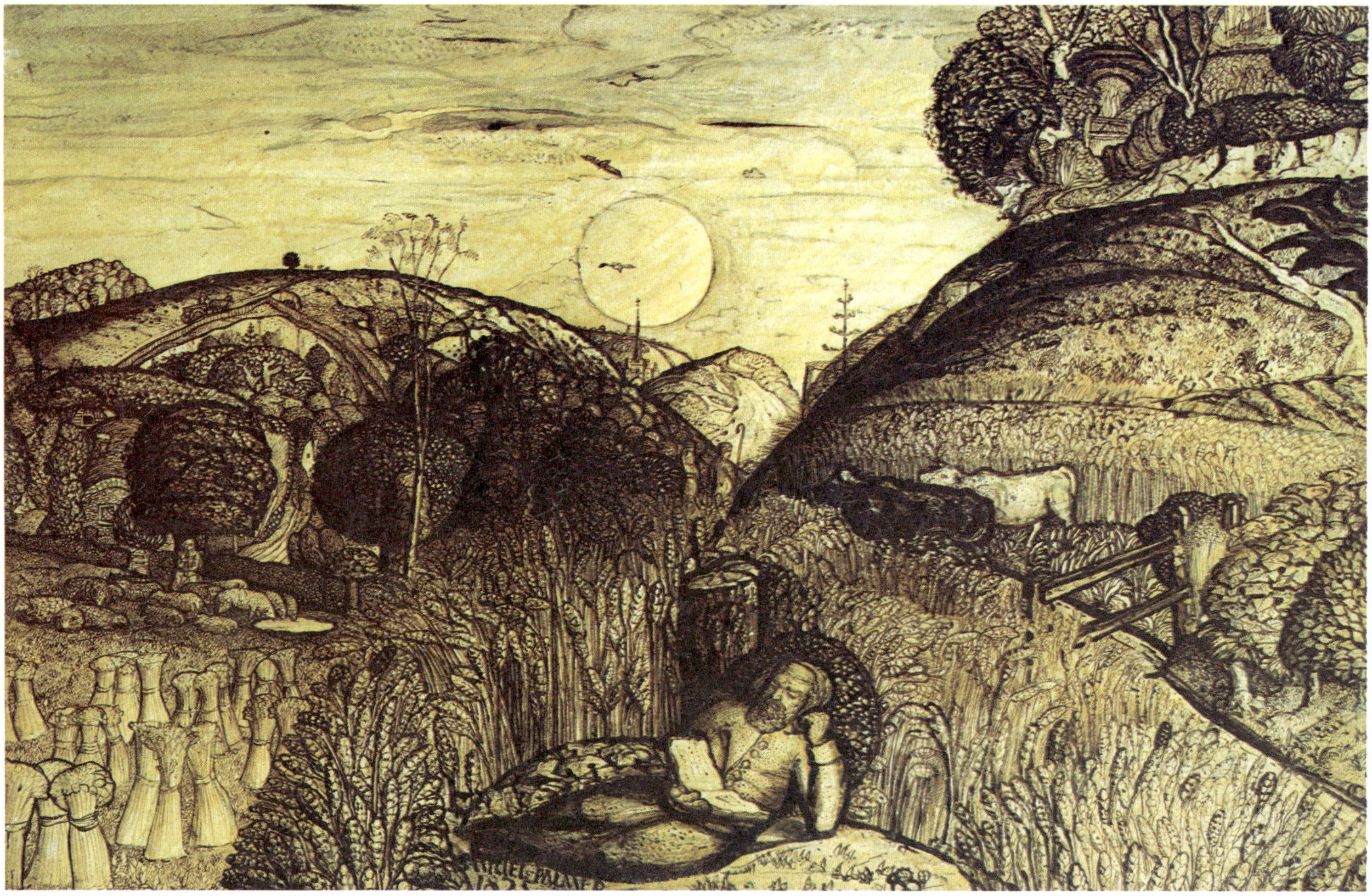

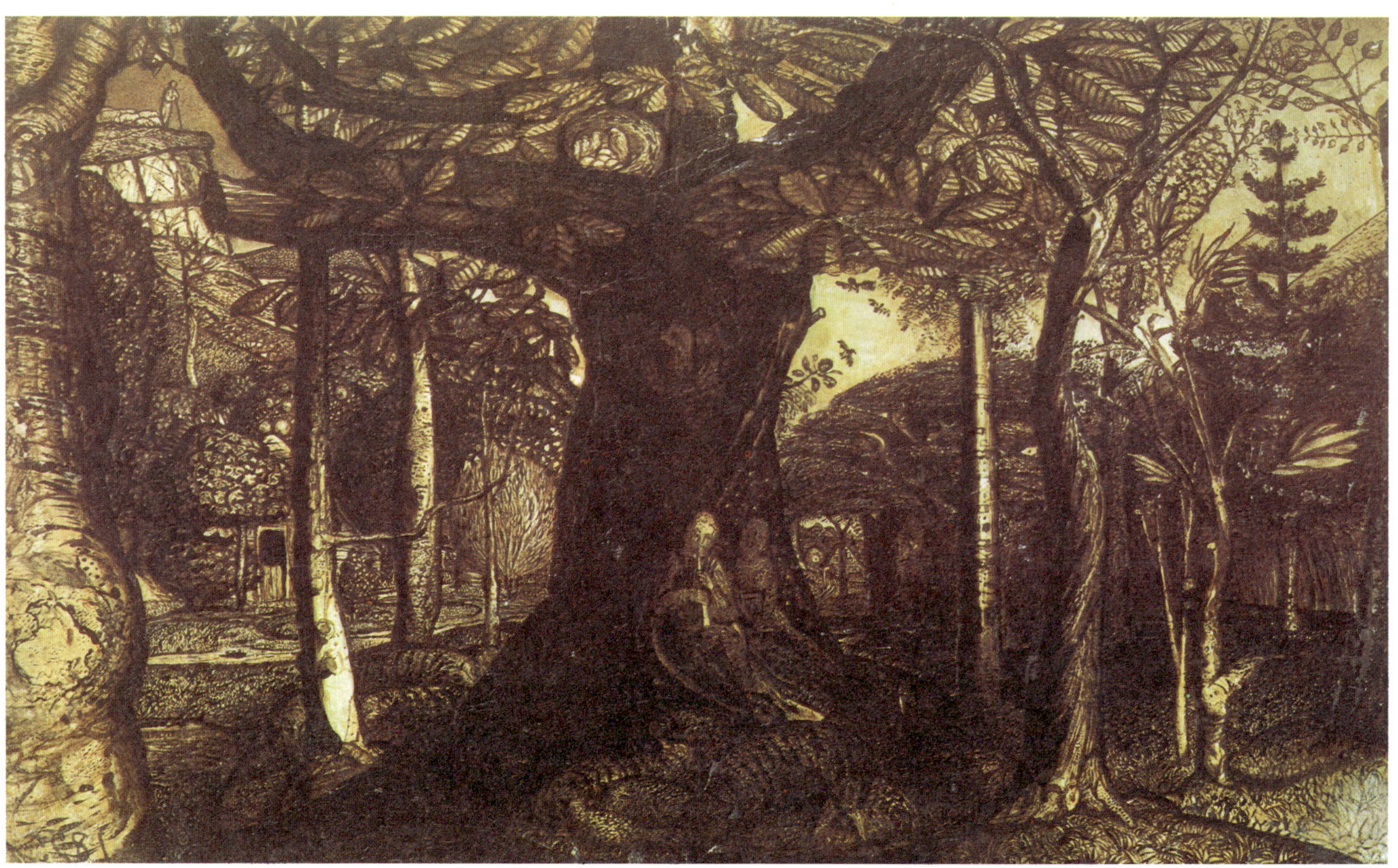

OPPOSITE
13 *The Valley thick with Corn*, 1825 (Ashmolean Museum)

14 *The Skirts of a Wood*, 1825 (Ashmolean Museum)

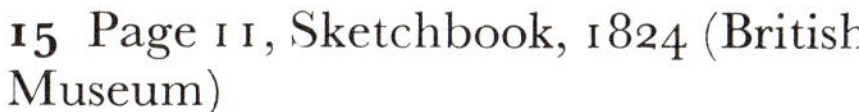
15 Page 11, Sketchbook, 1824 (British Museum)

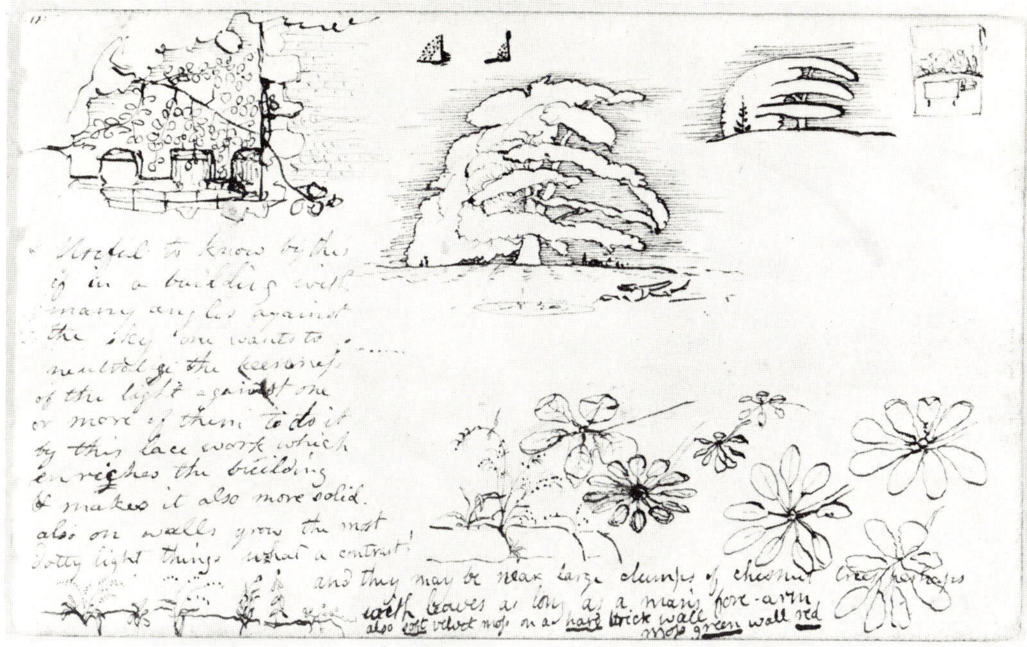

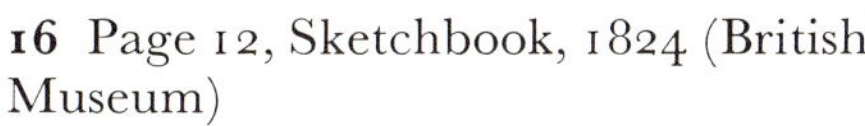
16 Page 12, Sketchbook, 1824 (British Museum)

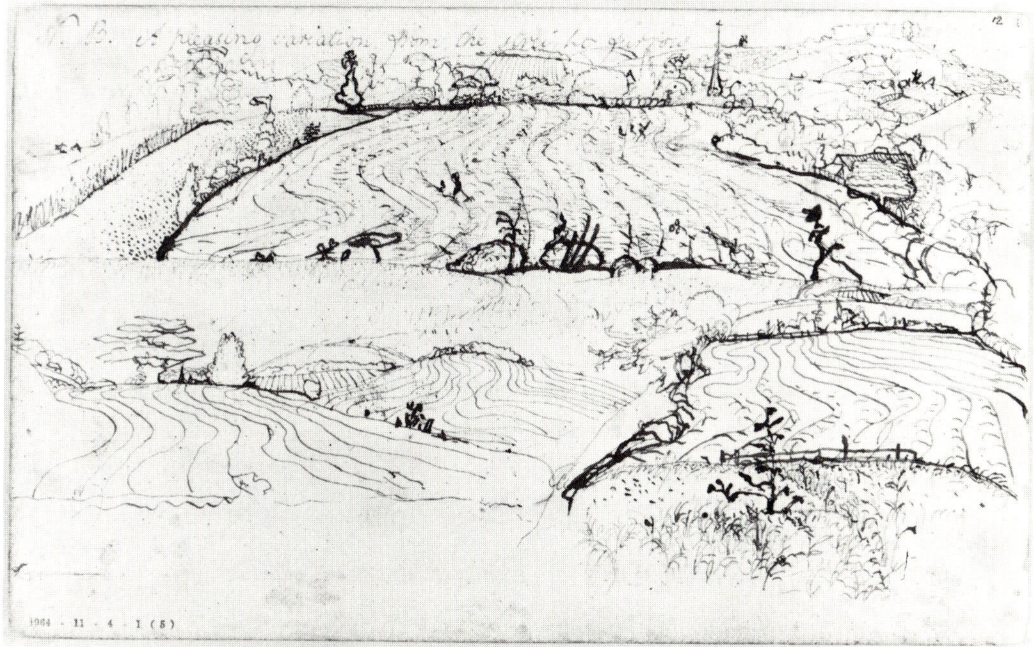

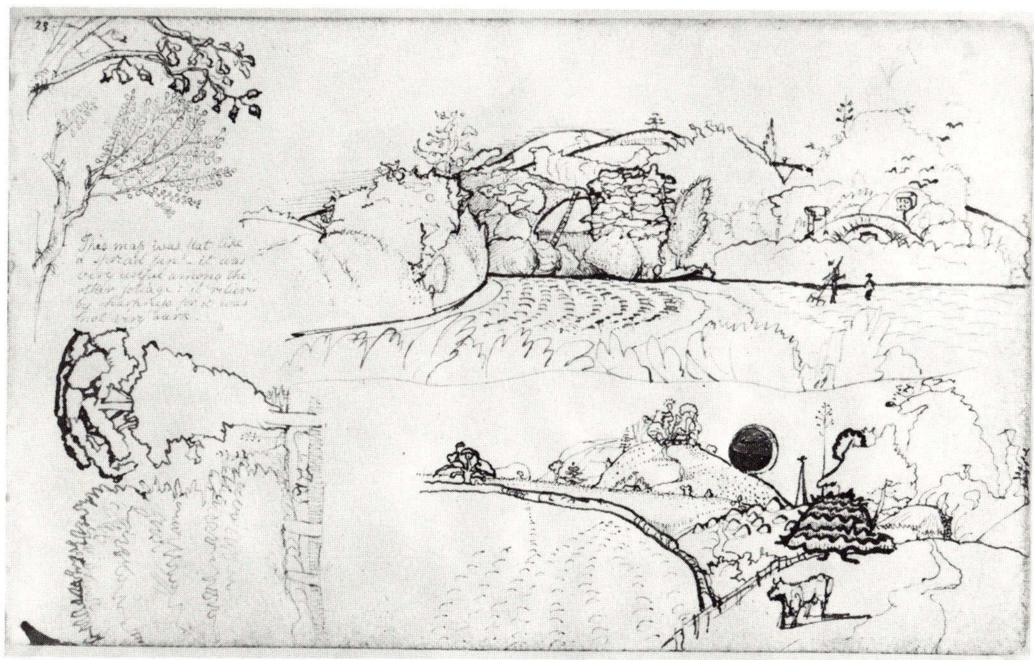

17 Page 23, Sketchbook, 1824 (British Museum)

that afternoon and night. And, after visiting him, the scene recurs to me afterwards in a kind of vision; and in the most false, corrupt, and genteelly stupid form my spirit sees his dwelling (the chariot of the sun), as it were an island in the midst of the sea – such a place is it for primitive grandeur, whether in the persons of Mr. and Mrs. Blake, or in the things hanging on the walls . . . '

Blake's influence upon Palmer was twofold, upon his art and his life the greater effect being upon his spiritual life, for, like his art, his everyday way of living had already been formed. There are stylistic similarities in Blake's and Palmer's work: the sheep and the fields of corn in Blake's Virgil wood engravings (*23*) and certain fragments in the Job engravings. But these are of minor importance compared to the effect of the confidence that Blake instilled in him, enabling him to pursue the course he had already set for himself. It must have been an enormous relief to Palmer to find a man like Blake existing in the climate of the times and one who could so clearly expound the facts of the spiritual life necessary for such an existence – a life divorced from material considerations. But in making this assumption Palmer was mistaken for Blake was already an old man, he had less than three years to live when they met and perhaps it was only possible for a man such as Blake to function during the time that he did. Palmer was very young, life was changing rapidly and he was unable to achieve such an equilibrium, had he been he could not have produced the incredibly beautiful paintings – in content and execution – that he created over the next ten years. For, when the life of the early nineteenth-century was forced more rudely upon his consciousness, he escaped, in marriage and to Italy, but to

18 Page 27, Sketchbook, 1824 (British Museum)

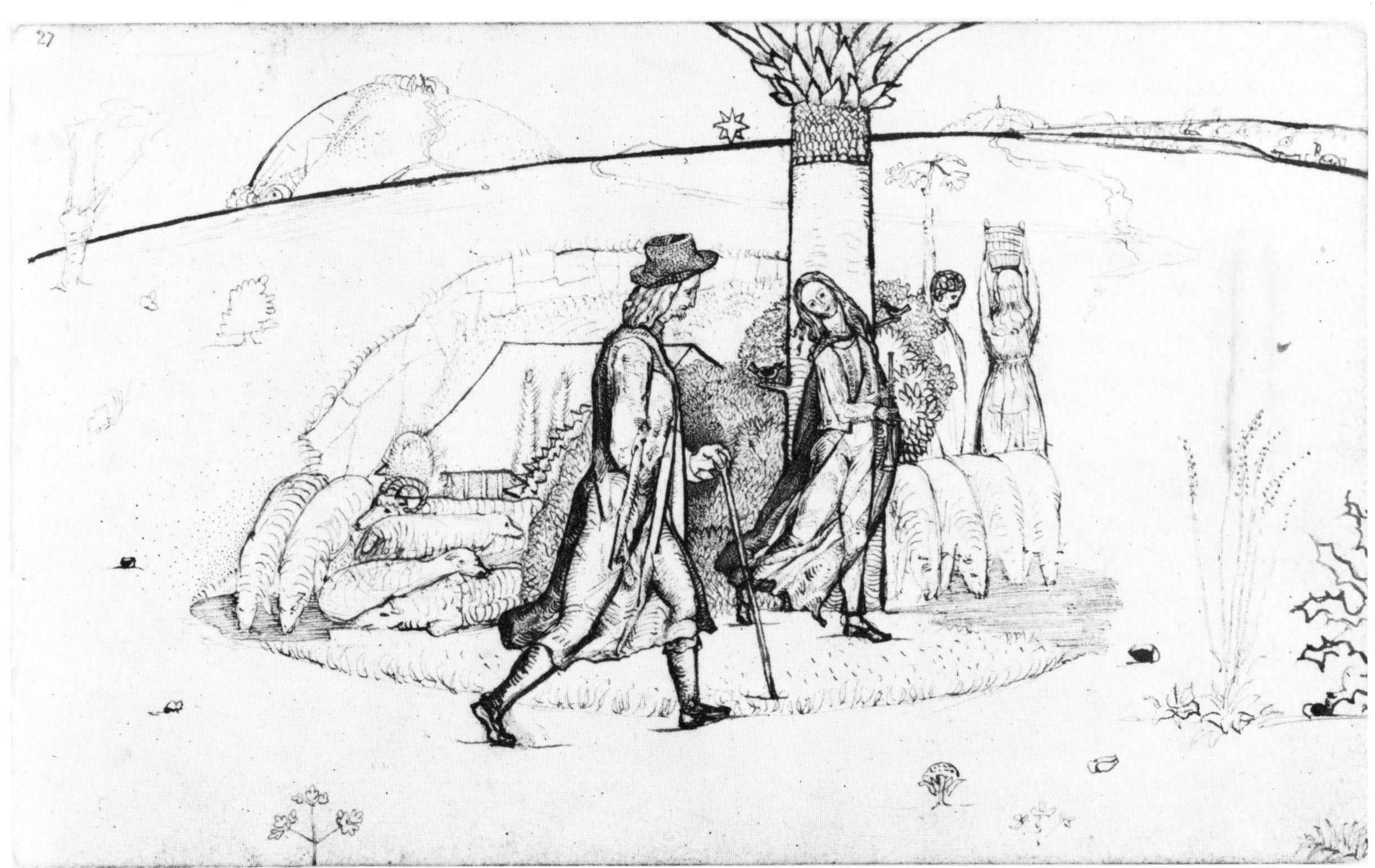

escape meant he had to leave much behind. Blake was absolutely essential to him in 1824. To Palmer and his friends his rooms were known as the 'House of the Interpreter'. In *Pilgrim's Progress*, Christian came to the House of the Interpreter and knocked '"Sir," said Christian, "I am a Man that am come from the City of Destruction, and am going to the Mount Zion, and I was told by the Man that stands at the gate, at the head of this way; that if I called here, you would shew me excellent things. Such as would be a help to me in my journey".'

Palmer himself shows how Blake became the prop to support him through his visionary years. In a notebook, one of the ones destroyed by his son, he wrote, 'I sat down with Mr. Blake's Thornton's Virgil woodcuts before me, thinking to give to their merits my feeble testimony. I happened first to think of their sentiment. They are visions of little dells, and nooks, and corners of Paradise; models of the exquisite pitch of intense poetry. I thought of their light and shade, and looking upon them I found no word to describe it. Intense depth, solemnity, and vivid brilliancy only coldly and partially describe them. There is in all such a mystic and dreamy glimmer as penetrates and kindles the inmost soul, and gives complete and unreserved delight, unlike the gaudy daylight of this world. They are like all that wonderful artist's works, the drawing aside of the fleshy curtain, and the glimpse which all the most holy, studious saints and sages have enjoyed, of that rest which remaineth to the people of God. The figures of Mr. Blake have that intense soul – evidencing attitude and action, and that elastic, nervous spring which belongs to uncaged, immortal spirits . . . Excess is the essential vivifying spirit, vital spark, embalming spice . . . of the finest art. Be ever saying to yourself

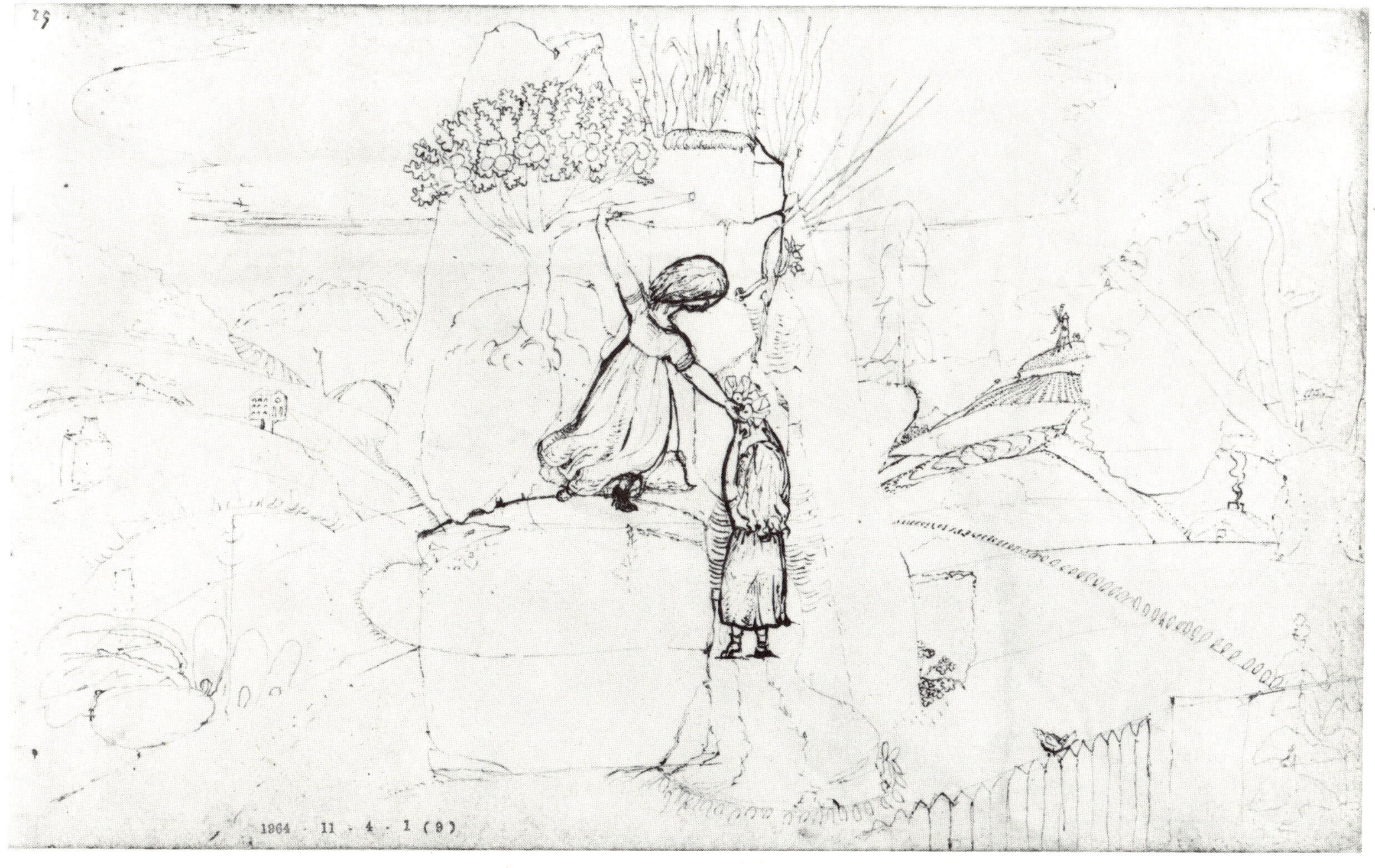

19 Page 29, Sketchbook, 1824 (British Museum)

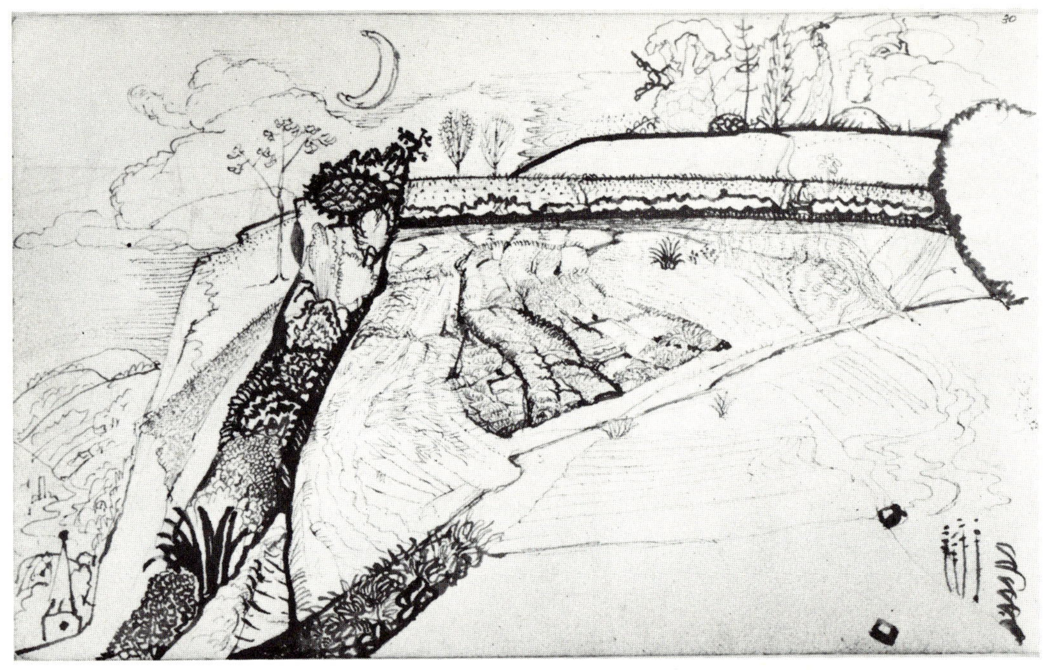

20 Page 30, Sketchbook, 1824 (British Museum)

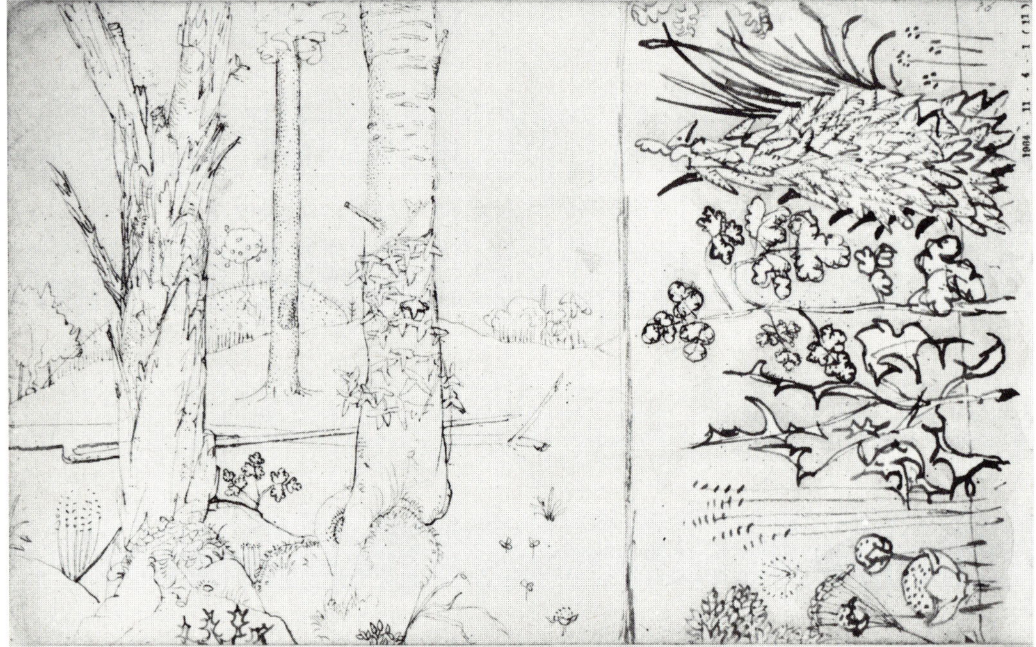

21 Page 33, Sketchbook, 1824 (British Museum)

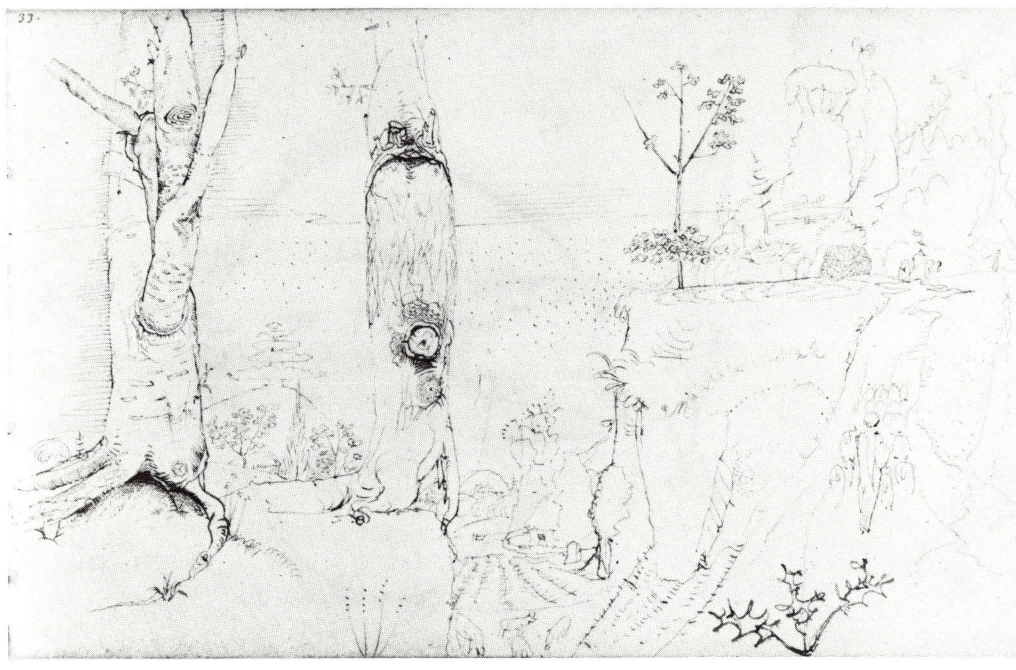

22 Page 36, Sketchbook, 1824 (British Museum)

"Labour after the excess of excellence".'

In a letter to Alexander Gilchrist which he wrote when he was fifty he shows in retrospect even more clearly the benefits, the confidence in his own ability, so necessary to him at this time, endowed upon him by this contact with Blake (it is also a very fine portrait of Blake): 'In him you saw at once the Maker, the Inventor; one of the few in any age: a fitting companion for Dante. He was energy itself, and shed around him a kindling influence; an atmosphere of life, full of the ideal. To walk with him in the country was to perceive the soul of beauty through the forms of matter . . . He was a man without a mask; his aim single, his path straight-forwards, and his wants few; so he was free, noble, and happy . . . Declining like Socrates, whom in many respects he resembled, the common objects of ambition, and pitying the scuffle to obtain them, he thought that no one could be truly great who had not humbled himself "even as a little child" . . . His eye was the finest I ever saw: brilliant, but not roving, clear and intent, yet susceptible; it flashed with genius, or melted in tenderness. It could be terrible . . . such was Blake, as I remember him. He was one of the few to be met with in our passage through life, who are not in some way or other, "double-minded" and inconsistent with themselves; one of the very few who cannot be depressed by neglect, and to whose name rank and station could add no lustre. Moving apart, in a sphere above the attraction of worldly honours, he did not accept greatness but confer it.'[4] As Geoffrey Grigson pointed out 'This overwhelming example, a revelation of the possibilities of a man, gave Palmer the additional strength that he needed to resist the world for the few authentically creative years of his life.'[5]

Palmer's contacts with Blake appear to have been frequent. Blake would call for him on his way to visiting the Linnells on Hampstead Heath; they visited the Royal Academy in each other's company and later Blake went at least once to Shoreham. Palmer was also used to calling on Blake once a month at his rooms in Fountain's Court, even when he stayed for the summer with Tatham in Shoreham, walking to London to do so. They talked of Ovid and Milton, examined early Italian prints and antique gems, discussed the works of St. Theresa and Jakob Boehme and the ideas in *The Marriage of Heaven and Hell*, which it is unlikely Palmer was able to understand at this time. Blake spoke to him of 'precision', and exhorted him to 'draw anything we want to master a hundred times from nature till we have learned it by heart', at first sight a curious remark for Blake to make for he was above all an artist of the imagination, but the operative part of the statement is 'till we have learned it by heart'. Palmer in fact was to absorb rather than merely learn. Blake is also reported to have advised a young painter, very probably Palmer, 'you have only to work up imagination to the state of vision and the thing is done' and 'he who does not imagine in stronger and better lineaments, and in stronger and better light, than his perishing mortal eye can see, does not imagine at all'. The next three years under Blake's energizing influence were to produce what are perhaps the most remarkable and possibly the greatest works of his whole career, the six sepia works of 1825 now in the Ashmolean Museum, and their culmination, *A Hilly Scene* (*28*) of 1826 now in the Tate Gallery.

One of the earliest works of this period and the earliest work extant painted in oil and tempera is the *Repose of the Holy Family* (*11*). It is very warm and rich in colour but apart from the corn on the left-hand side with its characteristic figure stooped amongst it, it is rather derivative. The palm tree on the right is from Dürer and not yet digested into Palmer's scheme of things to come; the figures, particularly Mary, are also from Dürer, and the landscape

23 William Blake, Four Illustrations for Virgil's *Pastorals*

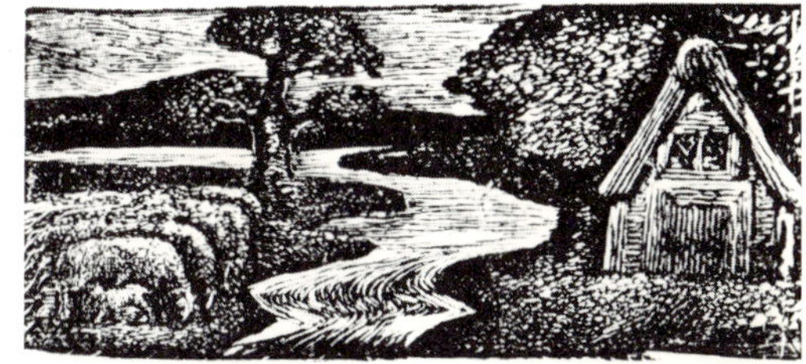

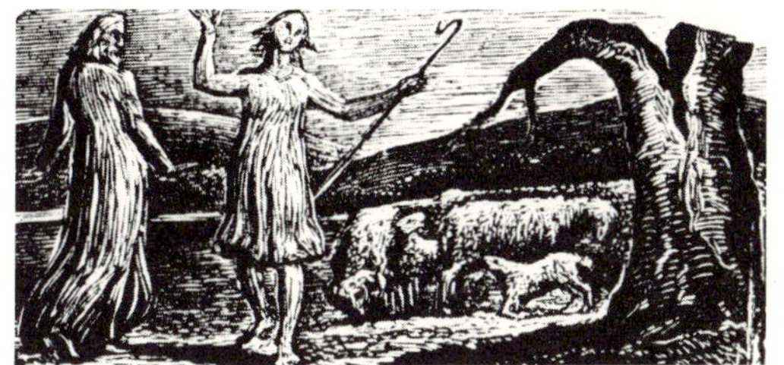

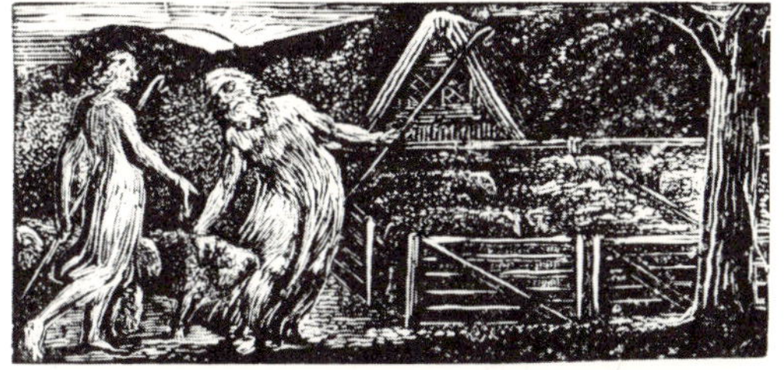

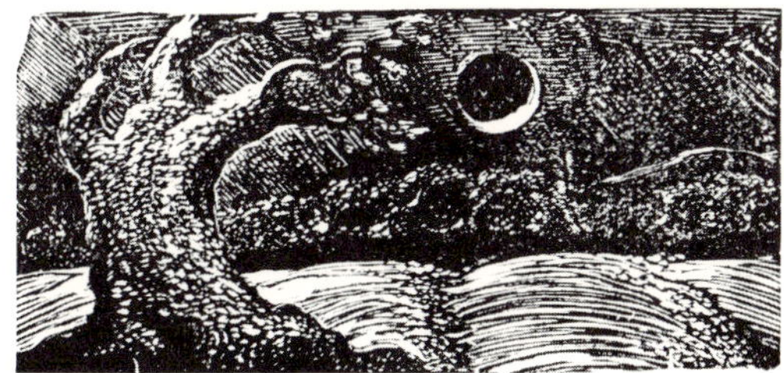

in the middle distance and hills in the background are strongly influenced by early German and Flemish painters; the donkey is from Blake. The manner of painting is very reminiscent of Linnell, thin glazes, giving a beautiful glow to the painting, over quite heavily-applied impasto, and the whole very glossy. It is the corn field and the richness of colouring that lend this picture the weight and scent of summer that lifts it from the rut. There is little, if any, of the symbolism of the 1824 sketch-book embodied here and it is as if he was unconsciously afraid to make these statements in a painting intended for exhibition. This is probably the picture he laid by 'in much distress, anxiety and fear in 1824'.

About this time, early in 1825, he accepted a commission from a Mr. Bennett to produce some drawings. When the work was finished he wrote to Mr. Bennett, begging to state that 'the pictures and drawings now delivered were somewhat different in style from those he used to paint when Mr. Bennett gave the commission'. Very soon afterwards he writes, however, 'it was given me this morning (16 October 1825) to see that I had done wrong in seeking for Mr. Bennett's pictures, visions more consonant with common nature than those I received, at my first regeneration, from the Lord. I will no more, by God's grace, seek to moderate for the sake of pleasing men.' And no more did he, if we are to judge by the six highly finished sepia works completed in 1825. In these paintings, there are 'echoes' of Blake, the sheep in *Late Twilight* (*29*) and *The Skirts of a Wood* (*14*) and the man and the oxen in *A Rustic Scene* (*34*). The design of *The Skirts of a Wood* is based on *Homer and the Ancient Poets* in Blake's Dante series, but the symbolism, the medium, the handling and selection of the forms, the intensity and quality of emotion produced by these landscapes are entirely Palmer's.

They are painted in a brownish sepia that has been mixed with gum and the finished work then varnished giving the whole a glossy appearance not unlike the finish in his oil and tempera paintings, no doubt an attempt to achieve the same translucency and depth to the medium that can be produced in an oil painting by glazes applied with varnish used as a vehicle. The outlines of the objects depicted have been raised up by constant application of the gum and sepia mixture, in contrast to the detailed passages where it would have been impracticable to do this and at the same time create the extraordinarily rich textures produced by the minutely observed qualities of bark and herbage, leaves and rocks of the natural landscape. An excellent example of this is in the swelling tree trunk on the extreme right-hand side of *The Skirts of a Wood*. Throughout the whole of this series everything had been painstakingly drawn, there are no contrived textures, no slick applications of wash, each portion has been lovingly pored over with pen and brush.

It is impossible to establish Palmer's exact state of mind when he painted these pictures but it must have been of a very high order of excitement indeed to sustain him through these six works which must have required incredible powers of concentration and application in an artist so young. We find evidence of this excitement in the symbolism used in each one, revealing the root of the energies he directed into his work. The overriding theme of the paintings is fecundity and, since there is no effect without cause, he defines the origins as well as revealing the consequence, the satiety, which he was denied. The time of day in the works ranges from *Early Morning* (*26*) to *Late Twilight*, two of the titles, but the season is always high summer and full of excess. Everywhere the land burgeons with growing things, the hills are encrusted with trees, the valleys thick with corn. In the one painting, *The Skirts of a Wood*, which could be regarded as an exception to the theme of everlasting summer, for he depicts a bird with both eggs and fledglings in its nest in the horse-chestnut and, just above the cottage, a tree laden with apples, the atmosphere is unmistakably summer, hot and ennervating, even the sheep are asleep. Birds occur frequently in Palmer's works, usually in flight, a symbol of the artist's soaring spirit, and these paintings of the early visionary period are no exception. But in two of this series, *Early Morning* and *Valley with a Bright Cloud* (*27*), they are shown paired, in the one on a branch and the other on the ground, a symbol often employed by the Indian miniaturists in erotic paintings. Felled trees occur in four out of the six works, *Valley with Bright Cloud*, *Early Morning*, *Late Twilight* and *The Valley Thick with Corn* (*13*), in the latter appearing only as an upright tree stump behind the

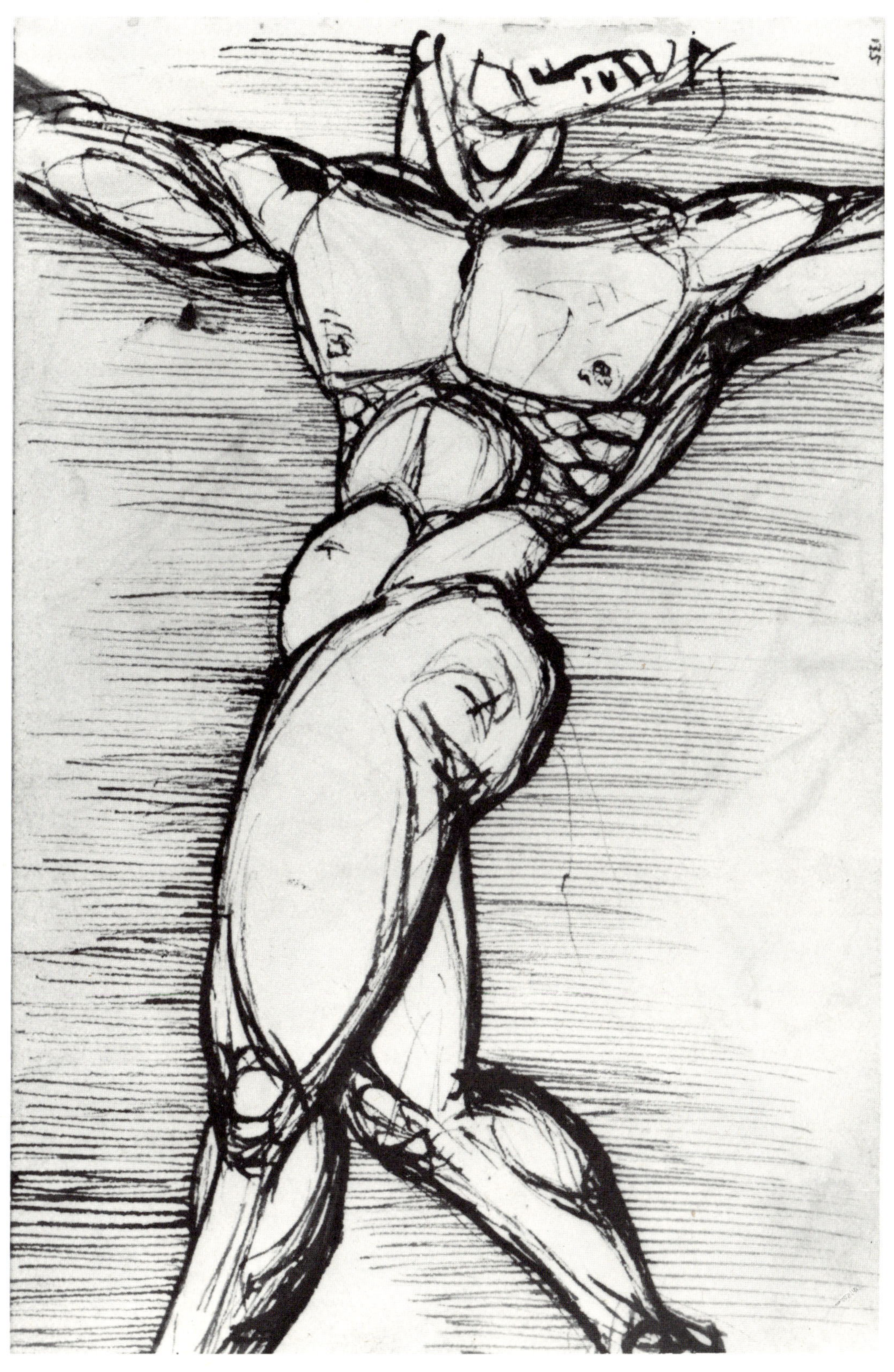

24 Page 135, Sketchbook, 1824 (British Museum)

Old Testament God-like figure with his halo of leaves or corn, reminding us that His principal activity is creation. In the other pictures they recline as if Palmer had at last contained his sexual drive only for them to rear up again in *Valley with a Bright Cloud* and *Early Morning*, in the one pointing to a stream the source of life, in the other to a thatched cottage, his haven, his Mary Ward. And in *Late Twilight* the tree lies adjacent to a pool of water.

Early Morning is perhaps the most interesting if not the most satisfying or accomplished of the series. It owes much in detail, the leaves in the bottom right-hand corner and foliage of some of the trees for example, to notes made in the 1824 sketch-book but with the difference that here there are cast shadows. There is not one cast shadow in the whole of the sketch-book. It is a measure of Palmer's new confidence that these paintings are no longer mere imaginings but visions, vital and real. Apart from the phallic log, the remainder of which still stands in affirmation of its virility on the far left, all the trees have a litheness and vitality that could only exist through Palmer's complete identification of himself with his landscape. He identifies to the extent of depicting himself in the form of a hare making its way up the rutted track, its eye warily upon us, and it is no accident that the hare's back takes on the same curve as his signature to which it is adjacent.

In the *Valley with a Bright Cloud* groups of toadstools appear, small soft symbols of energy, that will force their way through the hardest ground, pushing aside obstacles many times their size and weight to scatter their spores. *Early Morning* has the one enormous mushroom-like tree with vast trunk under which, overwhelmed, is seated a group of people backed by a field of heavy-eared corn waiting for harvest; cause and effect side by side. It is interesting how accurate Palmer was with his titles. In *Early Morning* everything is vital and alert, the figures staring back at the spectator as if aware of an intrusion, the hare ready to bolt, the trees, corn, herbage, urgent and alive. In *Late Twilight* all is stilled, the corn is stooked, the gate has been closed, the figure in the field turns its back on us and the shepherdess lies across her sheep satiated, even the hare has become a rabbit which takes no notice of our presence. The felled tree has lost its spring and points only to its origins. Even so, one feels it is only an interlude, the horned moon has risen and the church spire points straight at her, bats flit and the 'dodman', snail, emerges from the puddle by the log.

25 *Study of a Hand holding a knobbed stick*, 1825 (Victoria and Albert Museum)

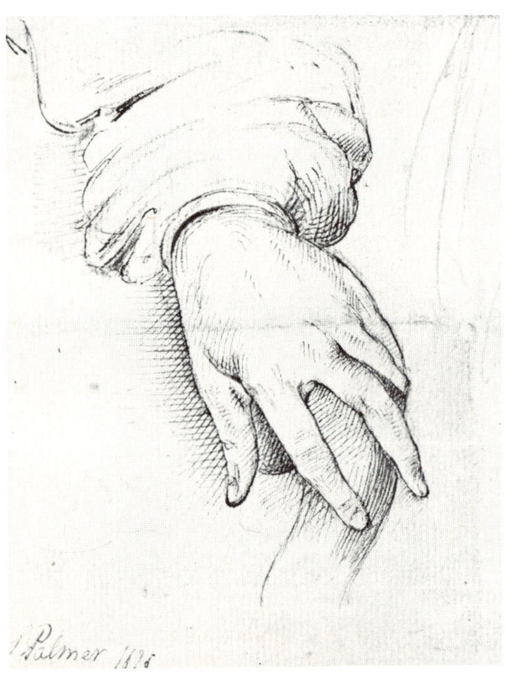

The same church spire occurs in *A Hilly Scene*, this time with one angle of its roof towards the moon, hanging cradle-like as if supported by the trees on either side, the other pointing at a star, the guiding light, shining between the branches. The trees also support the picture, reaching from just above the base and disappearing out of the top, giving tremendous stability to the whole. It is the tree on the left, a horse-chestnut, which is the most interesting. Near the top a branch arches over which has split open and beneath it a 'candle', quite out of season for the corn below is ready for reaping, points to the centre of the wound. Below again, on the horizon, thrust two white pointed hills. This must be one of the most extraordinary examples of unconscious symbolism produced by any artist. The gate to the field is now open and the wheat with its exaggeratedly large ripe ears points invitingly to allow passage, at first sight, to the church but the path turns unerringly towards the cottages as the log did in *Early Morning*.

It was in 1826 that Palmer made a protracted visit to Shoreham in the company of Frederick Tatham, ostensibly to 'design for Ruth' but perhaps from reasons of health as he suffered from bronchitis and possibly asthma. In a notebook, since destroyed, he kept a cash account of his expenses while he was there, the cost of board and lodging for the two of them amounting to

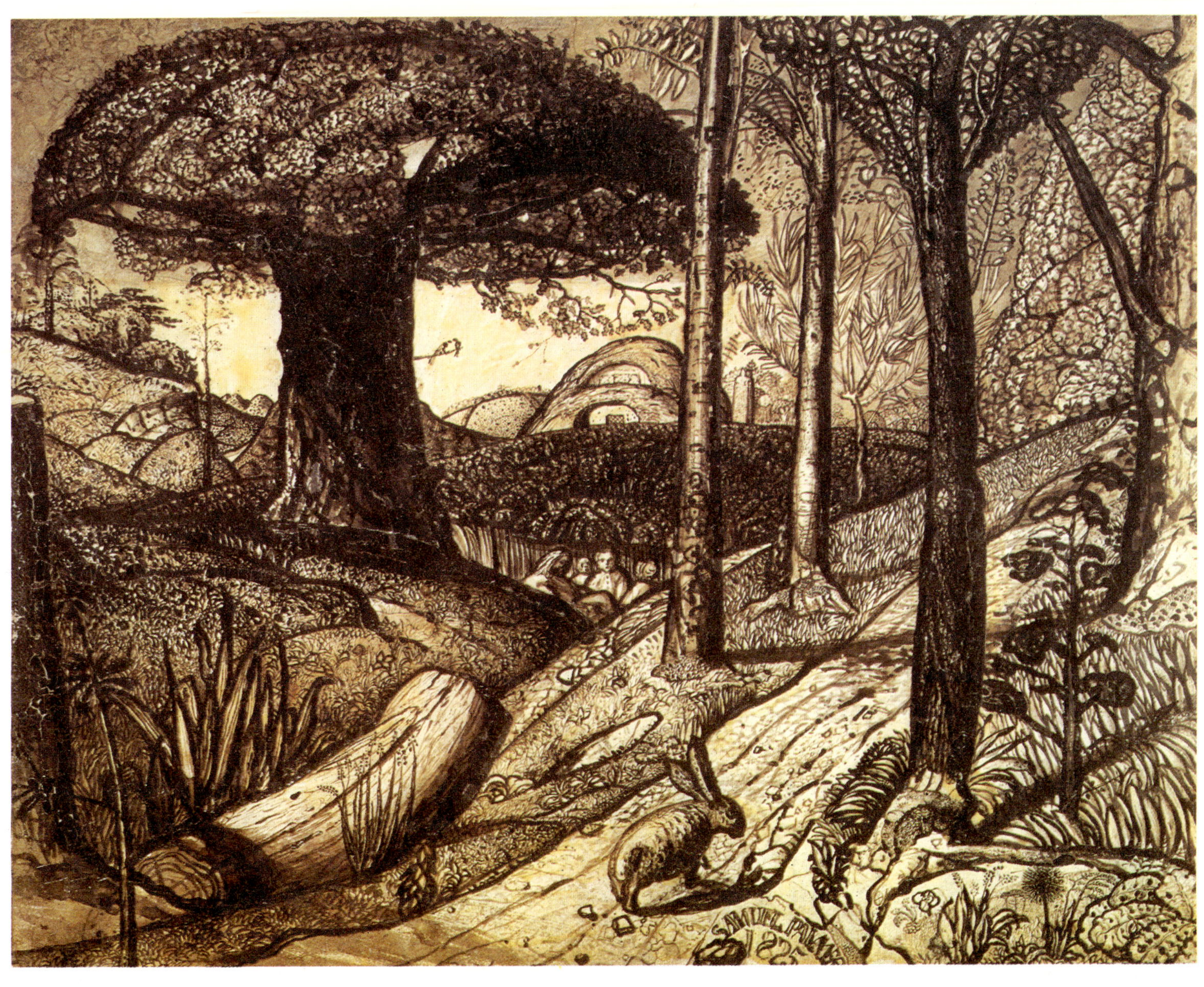

26 *Early Morning*, 1825 (Ashmolean Museum)

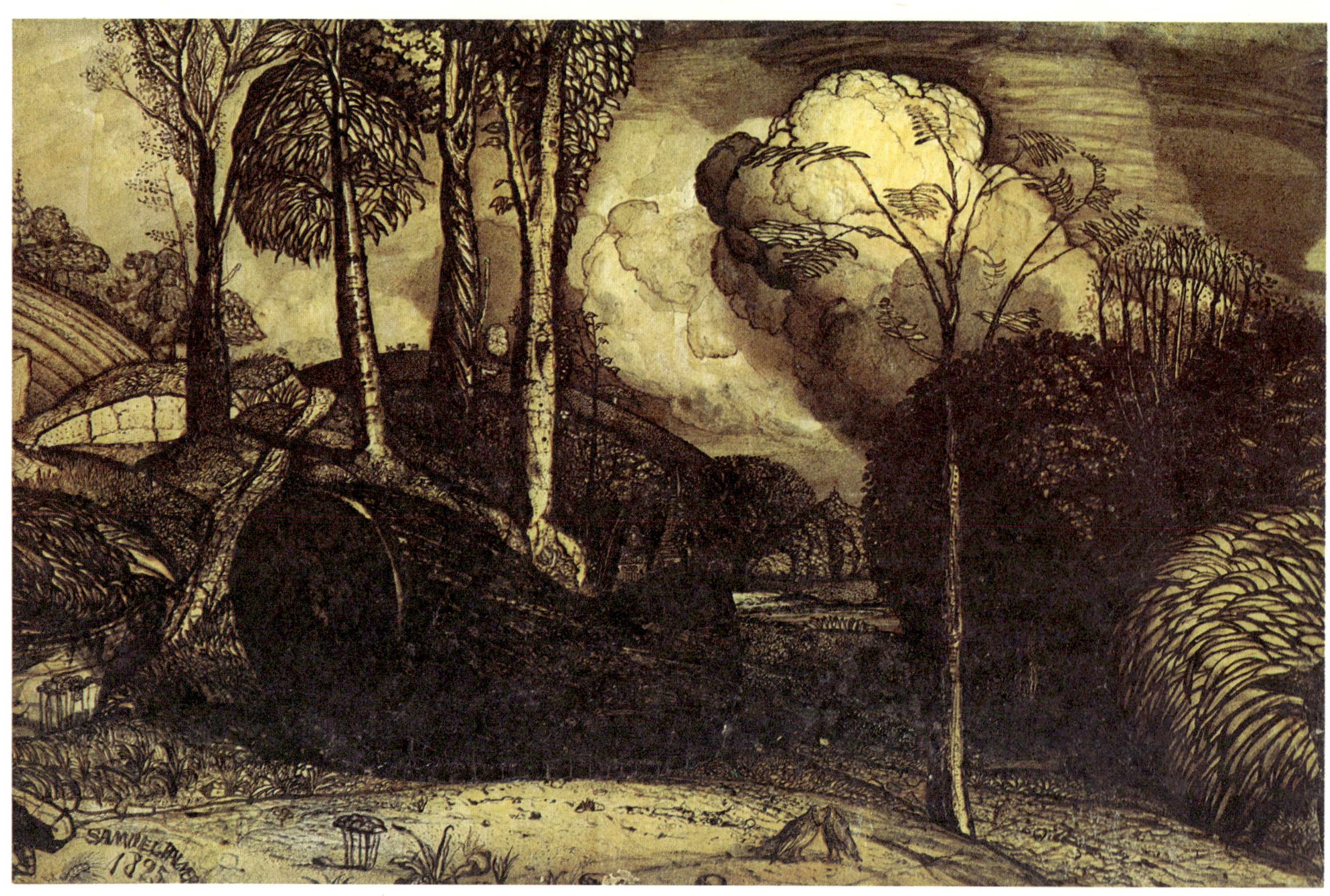

27 *Valley with a Bright Cloud*, 1825
(Ashmolean Museum)

28 *A Hilly Scene*, *c.*1826 (The Tate Gallery)

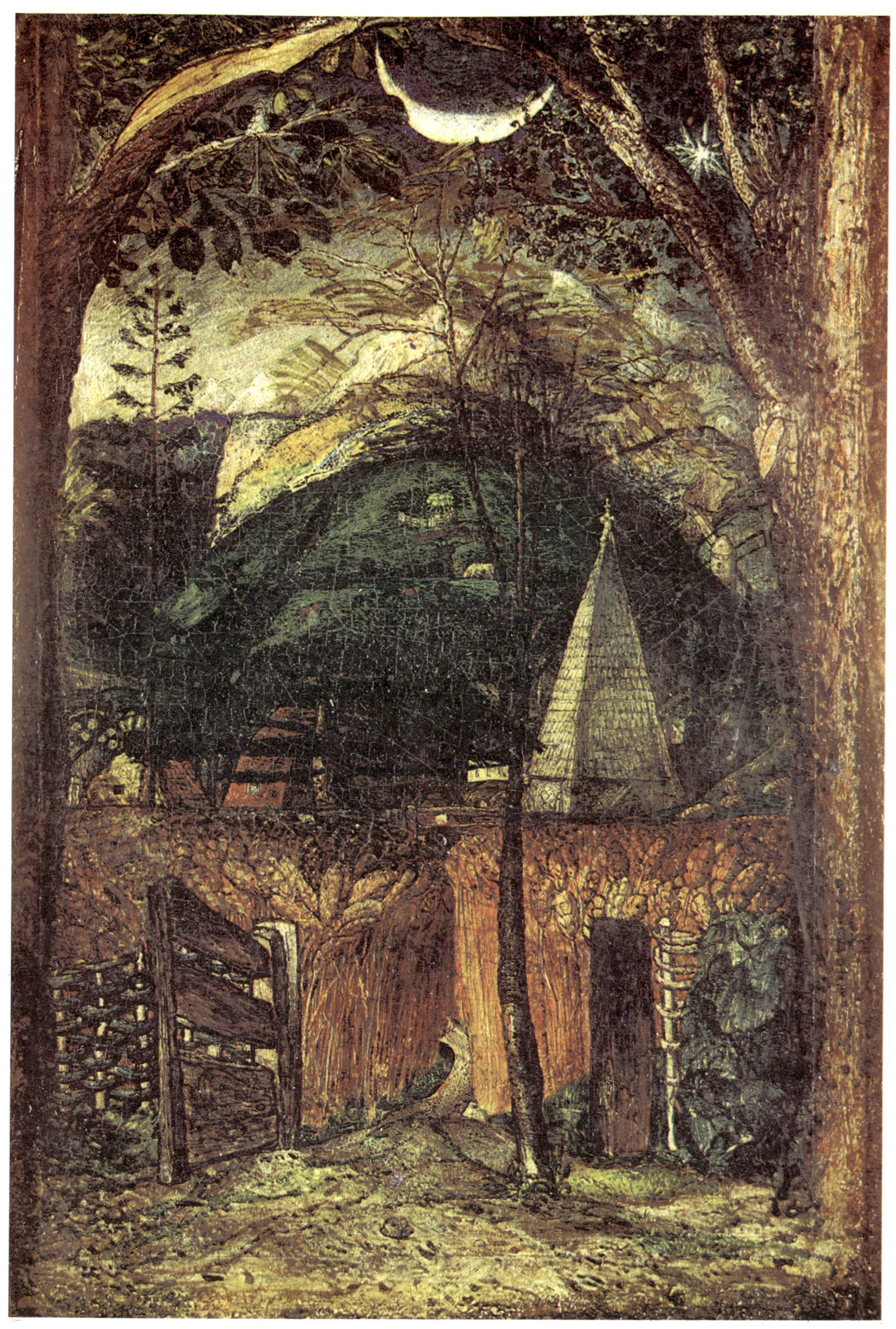

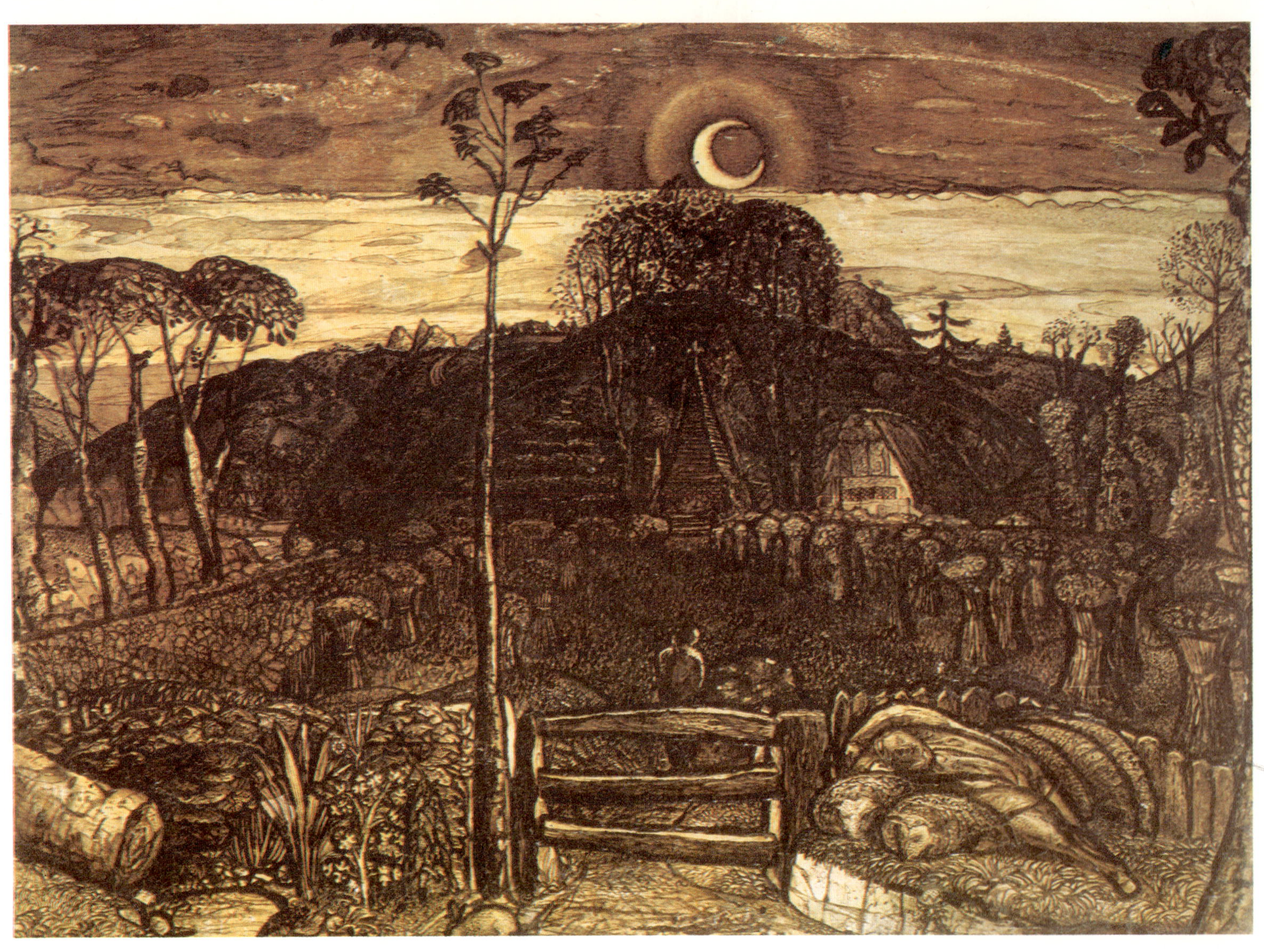

29 *Late Twilight*, 1825 (Ashmolean Museum)

eight shillings per week. Palmer, it seemed, lived almost entirely on milk, eggs, bread and butter, so frugal a diet could not but be a contributing factor to the state of the visionary heights he attained during this period. But apart from the physical inconveniences, he described in a journal he kept at the same time the mental sufferings he endured: 'At Shoreham, Kent, August 30 1826, God worked in great love with my spirit last night, giving me founded hope that I might finish my "Naomi before Bethlehem" and (to me) in a short time . . . That night, when I hoped and sighed to complete the above subject well (it will be my maiden finished figure drawing), I hoped only in God, and determined next morning to attempt working on it in God's strength . . . Now I go out to draw some hops that their fruitful sentiment may be infused into my fingers . . . August 31. We do or think nothing good but it has its reward. I worked with but little faith on my "Naomi before Bethlehem" this morning and succeeded in just proportion. After dinner I was helped against the enemy so that I thought one good thought . . . Satan tries violently to make me leave reading the Bible and praying . . . O artful enemy, to keep me, who devote myself entirely to poetic things . . . The last 4 or 5 mornings I thank God that He has mercifully taken off the load of horror which was wont so cruelly to scare my spirits on awaking. Wednesday. Read scripture. In morning ill and incapable, in afternoon really dreadful gloom; toward evening the dawn of some beautiful imaginations, and then some of these strong thoughts given that push the mind (to) a great progress at . . . I had believed and prayed as much or more than my wretched usual, and was near saying "what matter my faith and prayer?", for all day I could do nothing. Thursday. Rose without much horror . . . Began this day with scripture. Friday. So inspired in the morning that I worked on the "Naomi before Bethlehem", which had caused me just before such dreadful suffering, as confidently and certainly as ever did M. Angelo I believe.'

Naomi before Bethlehem and *A Biblical Subject*, painted around the same

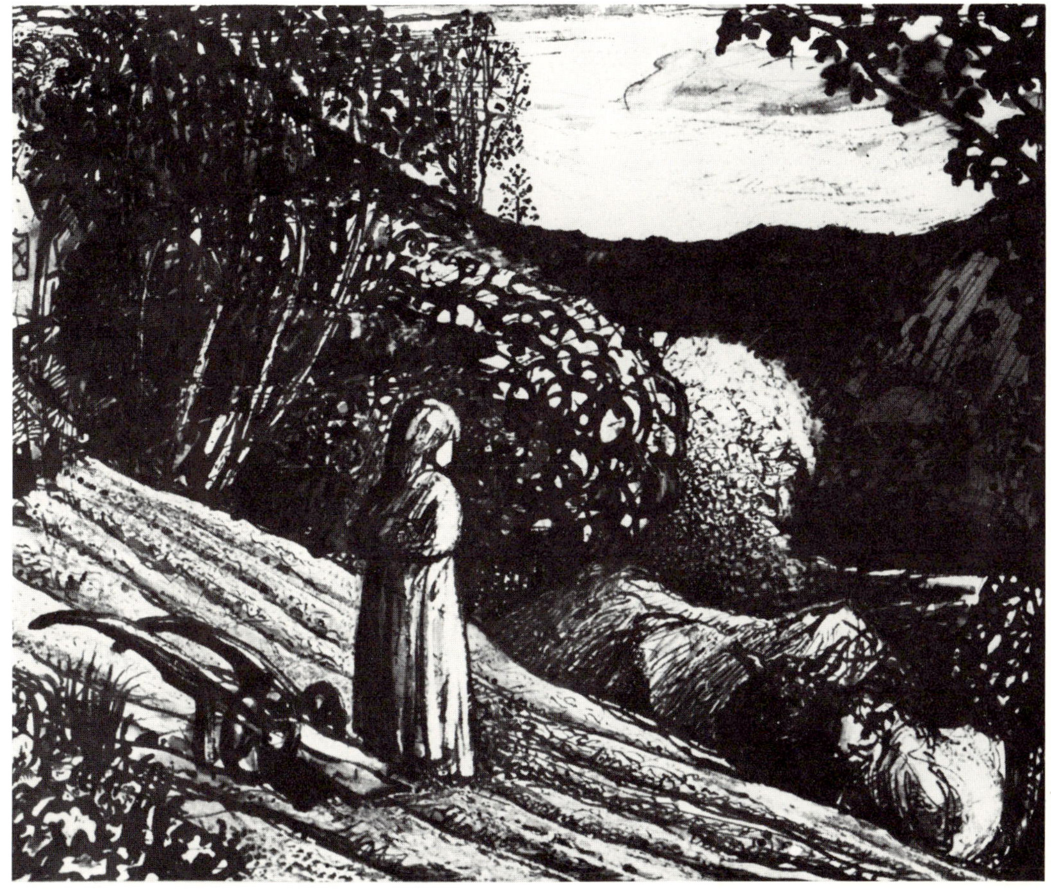

30 *Landscape: A Girl Standing*, *c.*1826 (The Tate Gallery)

time, are now unfortunately missing. They seem to have been the only works in which figures took pride of place and much could probably have been gleaned from them concerning Palmer's state of mind at this time. For from his son's description it is probable that in them his visionary excess was at its height: 'In the first of the examples before me (all of them being in monochrome), two inordinately brawny female figures, one young, the other older, are crammed into the opposite sides of a design measuring about 17 inches by 11½. Between them is a low table bearing some small fruits, and on the sward just beyond the barn or cottage where they sit, dance four men and women in a measure which would do honour to the orgies of any savages correspondingly muscular. A few sheep (in the conventional rows affected by Blake) browse behind, and behind them again is a cottage bosomed in rugged but abnormally fertile country. On one side, an open manuscript shows certain biblical writings. Parts of the figures, such as the extremities, are elaborated with evident pains and show some knowledge. A still more remarkable design is one probably identical with the "Naomi before Bethlehem" which caused so many mental throes. The wildest conceptions of Blake and Fuseli combined with the most extravagant symbolism of early art could not be more wild and extravagant than this. It is of the same size as the drawing last described, but much more elaborate, and there are crowded into it seven or eight figures. Upon the right, staring fearfully and fixedly at the spectator, stands a woman. She points towards a kind of symbolic city which is half concealed by the flaming rays of a portentous sun, and her extended arms separate a heavy shroud-like cloak. Leaning on her bosom in a somewhat graceful attitude, is a girl in classical drapery. On the left and also in the foreground are two old men with limbs so huge, attitudes so contorted, and countenances so forbidding, that it is difficult to associate them in any way with the story of Ruth. They are reapers and one holds in his hand an archaic sickle, his foot resting on bundles of corn. Behind them walks another reaper, and behind him again appear the grotesque heads of two oxen. In the middle of the background a sleeper pillows his head upon the abundant grain, while over him seems to hover a female spirit possessed by some great emotion. Close to the sun and just rising above the horizon, a crescent moon and six stars of astounding size blaze in the sky. Such are the works for which the young painter bestowed his prayers and his energies during the first summer's residence in Kent . . . Although intense of its kind, does not look as if it grew so much from prayer, fasting and thanksgiving, as from inexperience lashed on by an ill-controlled and powerful imagination which in its own turn, was nurtured by some strong and strange influence.'

There are a few other works extant from 1826, notably *The Haunted Stream*, *A Shepherd and his Flock under the Moon and Stars*, and a wood engraving *Harvest Under a Crescent Moon*. In the *Shepherd and his Flock* the moon to which the shepherd's crook directly points has grown enormously and the stars have multiplied, become huge, almost aggressive presences as if Palmer would blind us with their light. But it is Palmer reassuring himself with their multiplicity and the fierceness with which his light now shines. The wood engraving is directly related to Blake's Thornton's Virgil. Palmer, however, is able to infuse it with his knowledge and feeling for the natural world, lifting this tiny work out of the category of mere imitation. Such hills as the one in the background abound at Shoreham, the wooded hillside at Underriver which he was to draw in 1829 is an excellent example, and the light reflected from the corn and glowing behind the hill is pure Palmer. The harvesters appear as if surprised by the rising moon, and one gazes in rapt attention, making them more than just a composition, but a truly integral part of the whole. Paradoxically this little engraving, because of its very similarity in medium and subject to Blake's Virgil, proves the originality and independence of Palmer's mind. However much he needed Blake's spiritual support, what he produced was essentially his own, he was able to absorb information from the outer world, and use it with such telling effect, that not only did it not impair his inward vision but enhanced it.

Landscape: A Girl Standing (*30*), *Cornfield, Windmill and Spire* (*31*) and *A Windmill and Cornfield* can also be attributed to this period. All of them are small and are in sepia and only one, *Landscape: A Girl Standing*, can be said to bear any relationship to the work of preceding years. It is very freely drawn in pen and ink with a sepia wash added and may have been a study for another work which was either not carried out or has since been lost. The little girl stands on the field, now ploughed, beside a plough with handles downturned in contrast to the one in *A Rustic Scene* where they rear up to the breast-shaped hill in the background. She gazes down into a valley, across two oxen and a thatched cottage, where a shining river flows. The relationships between the active participants in the picture are beautifully felt and are very tense. This relationship is further conveyed to us by Palmer for, while one of the oxen directs his attention toward the girl, the other with upward curving horns stares out at us challengingly. The other two works are, in comparison, but charming landscape studies although the *Cornfield Windmill and Spire* contains a number of his recurrent symbols such as the hill, church spire and a lane winding between lush foliage and corn.

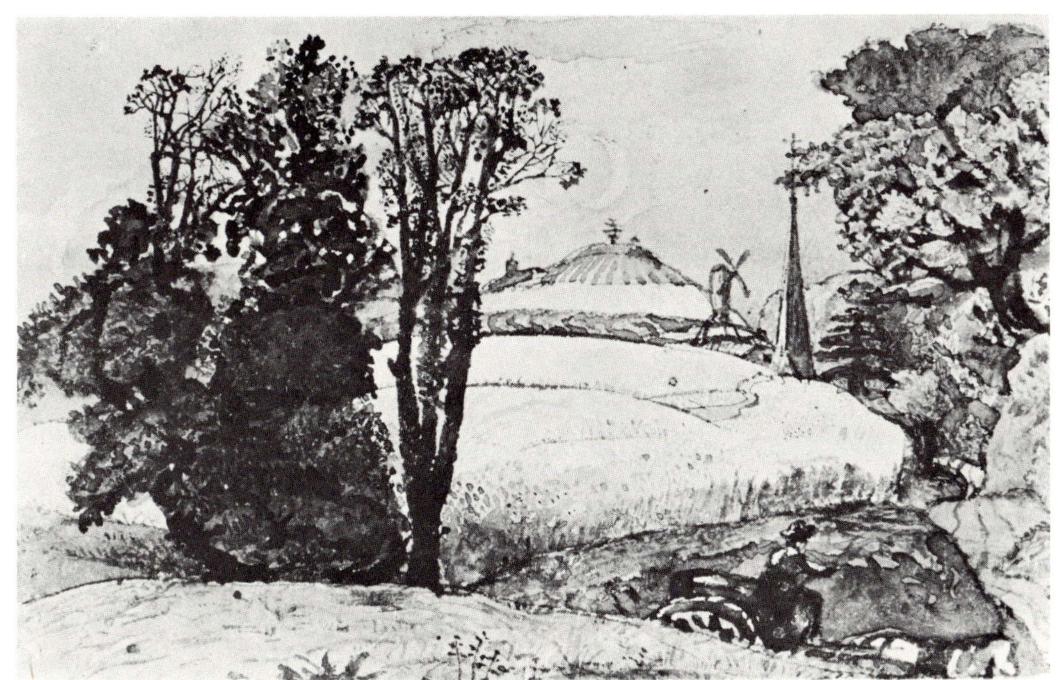

31 *Cornfield, Windmill and Spire*, 1826/7 (Private Collection)

SHOREHAM

1827–1837

Palmer moved to Shoreham, where he was to stay for the next seven years, in 1827. The reason for the move is generally given as illness, Palmer says himself in his autobiographical letter published in *The Portfolio* in 1872: 'Forced into the country by illness I lived afterwards for about seven years at Shoreham in Kent with my father.' It is also possible that at this time he received the legacy, about £3,000, left him by his grandfather on his death in 1825 and with the independence this afforded him he was able to return to the Eden of which he had had a taste the summer before. Another factor may have been that his father was more dependent upon the allowance made him by his brother Nathaniel, the corn factor, than the living he made from the sale of books. 'At last my father's austerely business-like "Uncle Nat" lost patience with his brother. Samuel the bookseller must either live once more the life of a gentleman of leisure, and live a widower or forfeit his allowance.' However, A. H. Palmer continues, 'His son's health grew worse. Even the walks and talks with Blake made no amends for the rumbling roar of traffic, for the stench of graveyards and drains, the dense swarms of flies, or the fogs so dreaded by artists in those days of feeble oil-lamps and tallow dips.'[6]

Shoreham had indeed strong attractions. Father and son were next to be seen exploring the quiet nooks of an old walled garden, and an orchard sloping to the shady banks of one of the loveliest streams in the South of England. With very different ideals in view, they had rented the old place still known as 'Waterhouse' close to the bridge in the Kentish Village of Shoreham. In fact they did not move into 'Waterhouse' until later. In May Palmer wrote to George Richmond offering to engage lodgings for him to stay in Shoreham.

Shoreham, even today, retains much of the qualities that it had when Palmer was there and differs only in that there are a few extra houses on the edge of the village, and a main road and railway which are fortunately over half a mile away. When his son described it, he noted that 'The village is still adorned by much that is ancient and nestles in a hollow between the shapely shoulders of the chalk range near Sevenoaks. It is threaded by the cheery, trout haunted little Darenth winding its way past old Lullingstone to Farningham and Dartford, through old demesnes and water-meadows, while here and there (to make it pay its way as even the gayest rivers should) there rumbles a venerable mill.' With the exception of the venerable mill which has now fallen into disuse a visitor today would still find this a reasonably accurate description.

Blake died the same year that Palmer moved to Shoreham though not before he had paid at least one visit to the village and Palmer had continued

32 Cast of William Blake's head, aged 66 (National Portrait Gallery)

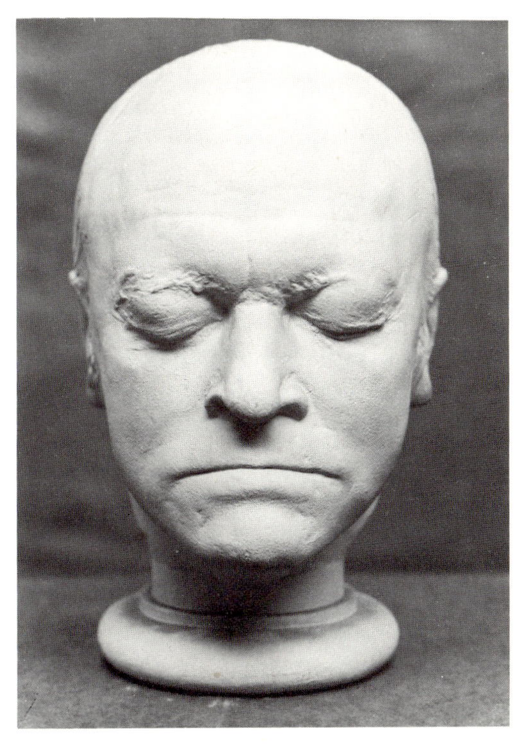

their monthly meetings. Palmer did not go to his funeral although it was attended by a number of his friends, nor watched at Blake's deathbed, he was a victim of his own sensitivities perhaps originating in the death of his mother when he was a child. But for a number of years Blake continued in Palmer's mind to be his spiritual prop and guide. Palmer did not, however, cut himself off from London associations and friends, and no doubt made good use of the frequent passage of carriers' and farmers' wagons that plied between London and Shoreham. He was in any case far from incapable of walking the twenty miles or so as he had the previous summer when he stayed in company with Tatham. He had none of the qualities of the recluse. He enjoyed the company of his friends joining them in friendly argument and debate and he had a finely developed sense of fun. His friends came frequently to visit him, even Linnell who had in a previous letter warned that the 'voluntary secession from artists will end in the withdrawing of art in your mind'. The group that gathered round Palmer at Shoreham called themselves 'The Ancients'. It consisted of six artists, Henry Walter, F. O. Finch, George Richmond, Edward Calvert, Frederick Tatham, and Welby Sherman. Two others, Tatham's brother Arthur and Palmer's cousin John Giles, although not practising artists were very concerned with the visual arts, and it was Giles who originated the name of 'The Ancients' by frequently referring to the superiority of ancient over modern man. None of them, however, with the exception of Palmer, worked continuously at Shoreham but were frequent visitors there, especially in the summer, where they would draw and paint in the surrounding countryside. With his friends Palmer walked, bathed in the river, and read much poetry – Keats, Milton and Shakespeare especially. They even set off at ten o'clock one night to try to obtain a copy of Mrs. Radcliffe's *Mysteries of Udolpho*. Welby Sherman was there in the spring of 1827 and in the summer, Henry Walter, Frederick Tatham and George Richmond were also to arrive, this being Richmond's first stay in the country without his family, Palmer engaging rooms for him at two shillings a week.

Not many works date certainly from the summer and winter of 1827; no

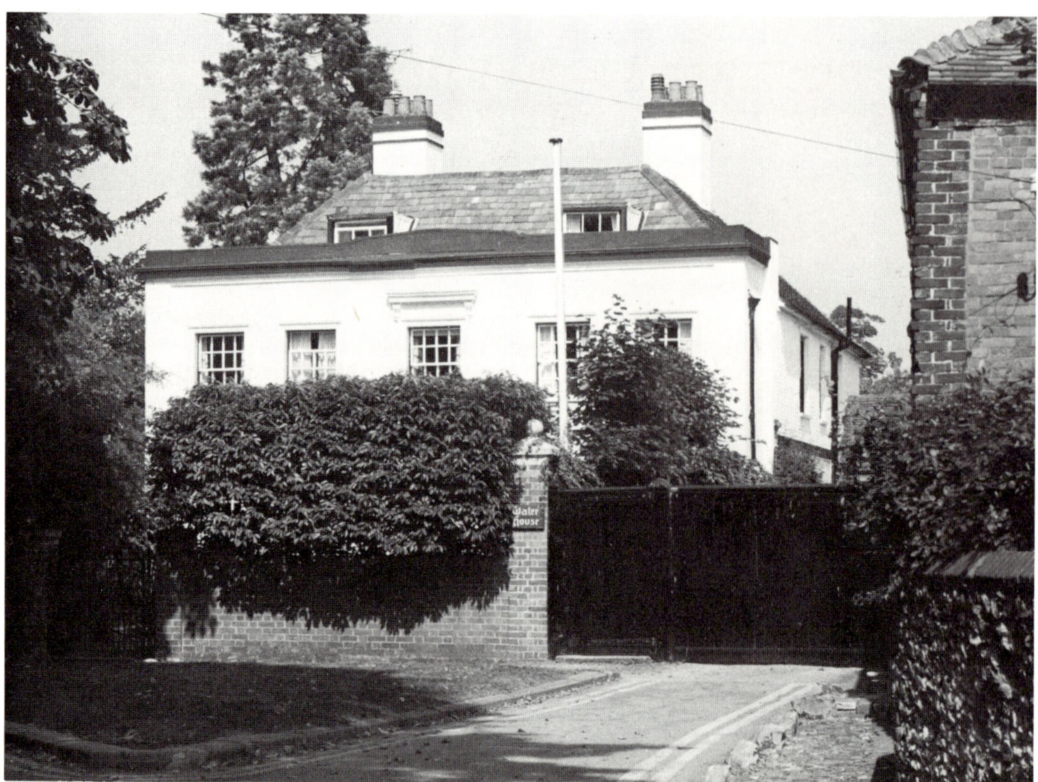

33 The Waterhouse, Shoreham

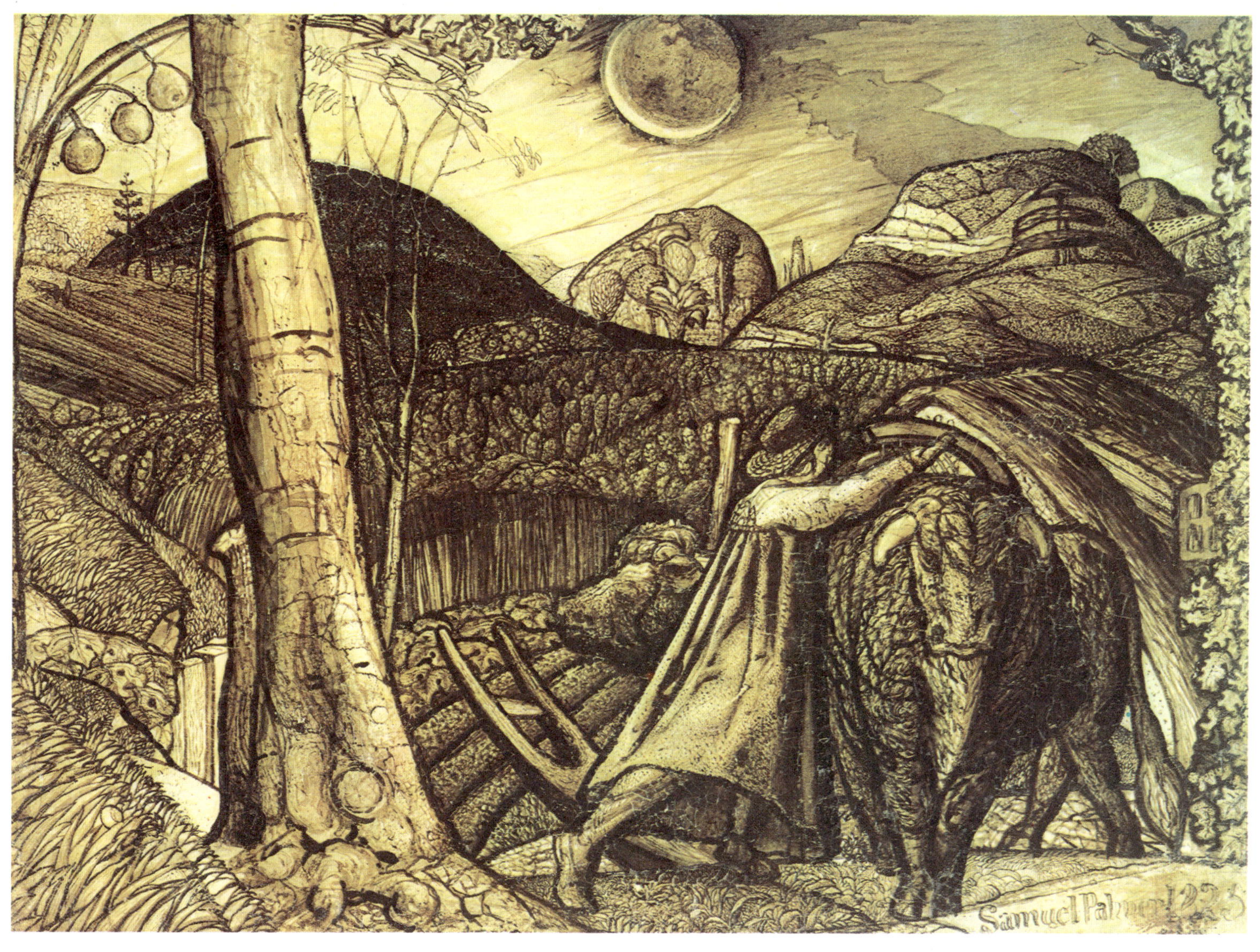

34 *A Rustic Scene*, 1825 (Ashmolean Museum)

OVERLEAF
35 *Lane and Shed, Shoreham*, 1828 (Victoria and Albert Museum)

36 *A Cow Lodge with a Mossy Roof*, 1828/9 (Collection Mr. and Mrs. Paul Mellon)

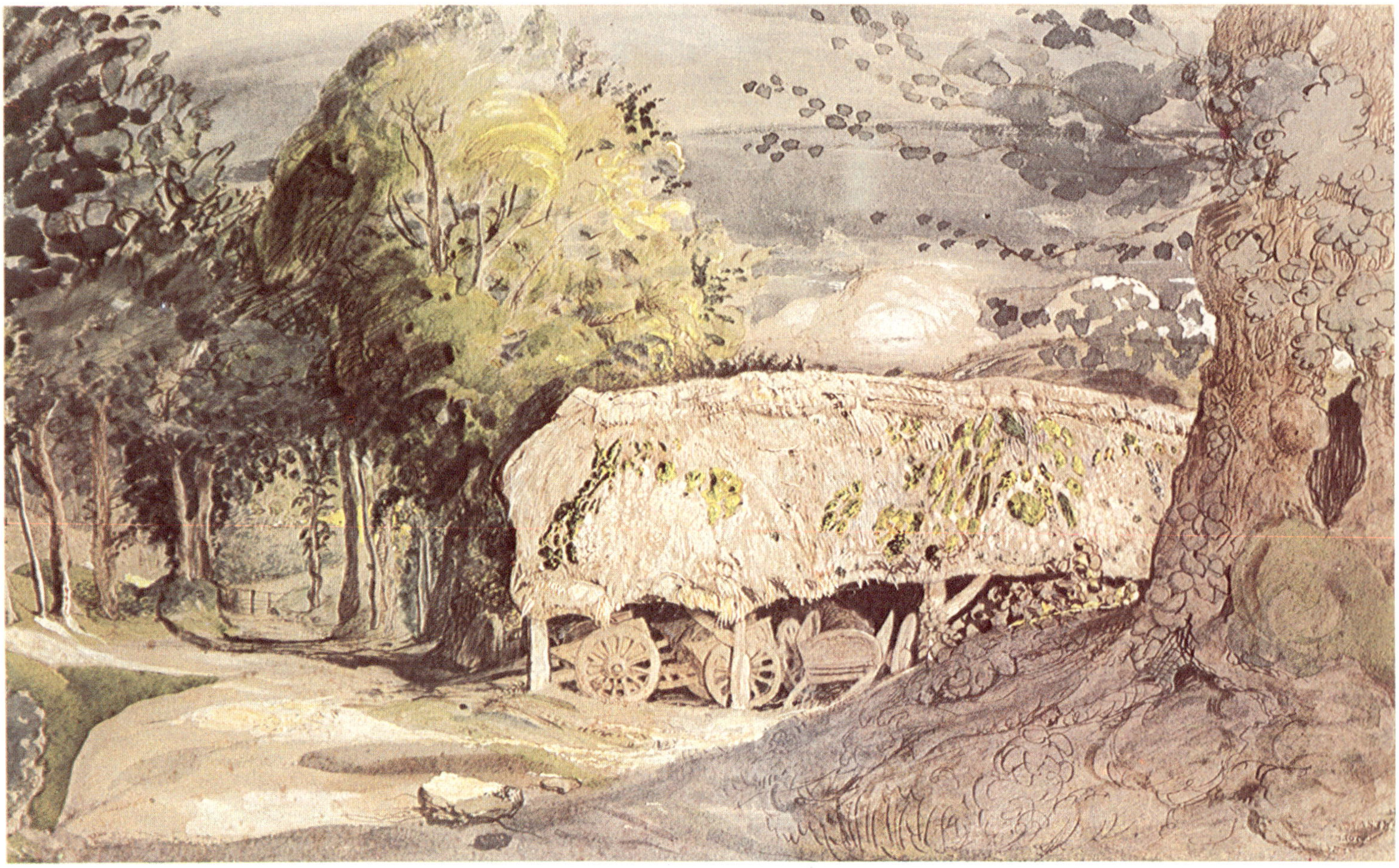

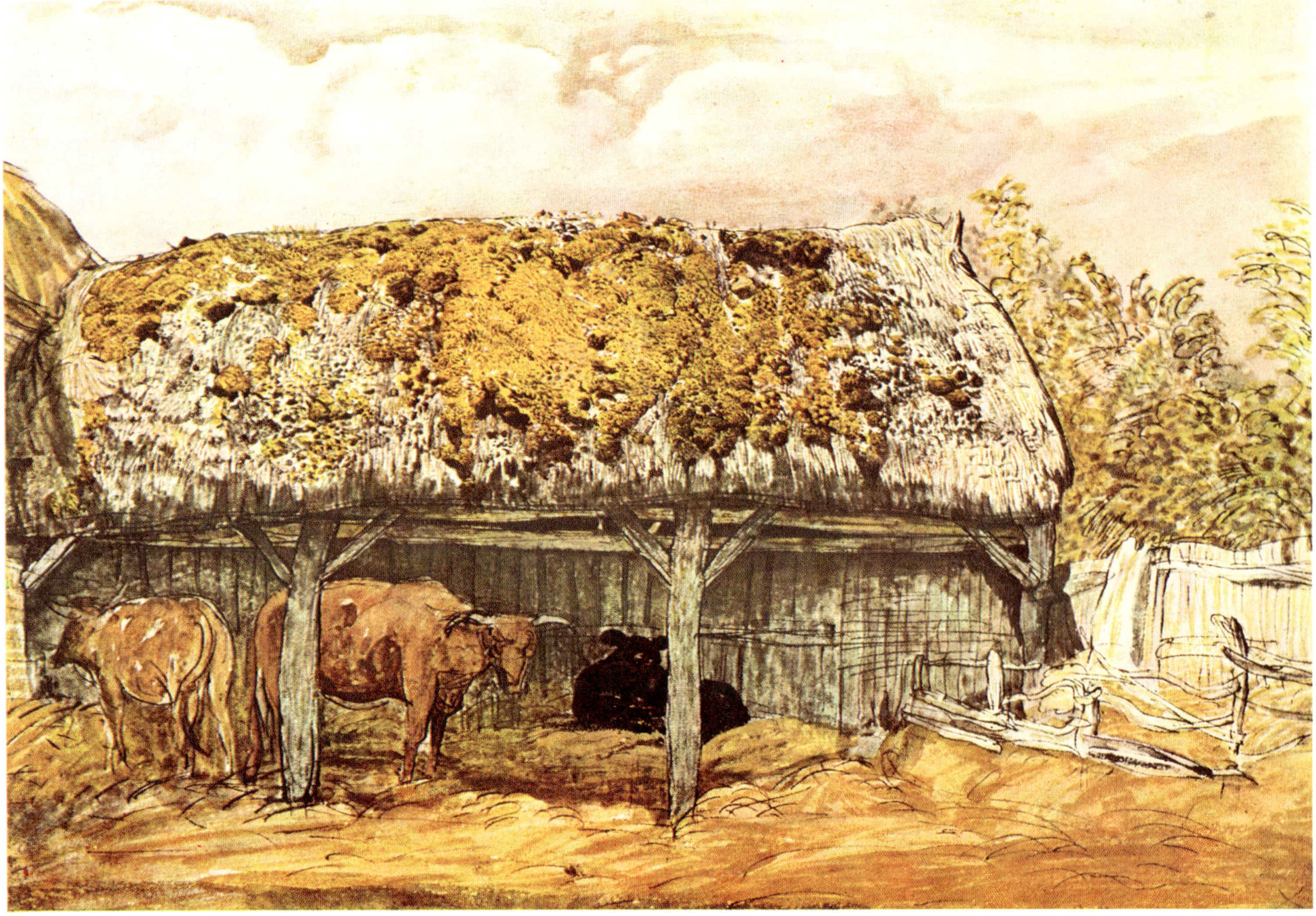

doubt Palmer was unsettled by the move and in finding somewhere for his father, nurse and himself to live. But *Moonlight: The Winding River* (*40*) could well be one of them. It is interesting in harking back in style to 1825, as in the Dürer tree on the right, the treatment of the cottage on the left, the herbage in the foreground and the folded flock on the right but the foliage of the trees through which the moon is shining looks forward in the patterning and flattening of shapes to the paintings of 1830.

Another work, *Shoreham, Moonlight* (*41*) seems to be a study for this picture. Less 'finished' than the *Winding River* it is very similar in composition, but with the addition of a church and a cart shed. The small vigorously handled chalk and wash drawing *Landscape with Figure embracing a Tree* (*42*) is also attributed to the Shoreham period but if so must be very early. It is more than likely that it was made at the time of the 1825 sepias to which it is closely related with its mushroom-shaped tree, the swelling hills in the background and symbolically in the figure embracing the tree trunk and gazing toward the enormous energetic stem of the tree on the right. *Meditation upon the Wonderful Providence of God* (*43*) has also a lot in common with the 1825 series and it could be that it is a study for a projected design that was wisely never undertaken. It is almost as if it were a copy of his earlier style – which he is now beginning to abandon – even to the extent of mixing his paint with gum and giving the picture a final coat of varnish. Compared to the earlier paintings it is a crudely executed work showing a deal of heavy handedness in the handling and, compositionally, it is a little more than a concoction of the elements used in the six Ashmolean designs. Although all the artifacts are there, the shepherd with his crook, the sheep, the heavy-eared corn, the moon, the cottage, the church spire, the mushroom-shaped trees, they are totally unrelated. The overwhelming atmosphere of visionary excess and fecundity produced in the 1825 paintings is totally lost. The parts in themselves are meaningless, and multiplicity only adds confusion. Only in an instinctively controlled juxtaposition of parts can they have value and a structure be created that reveals what the artist has to say.

Palmer's work was to be increasingly affected by the absence of Blake's

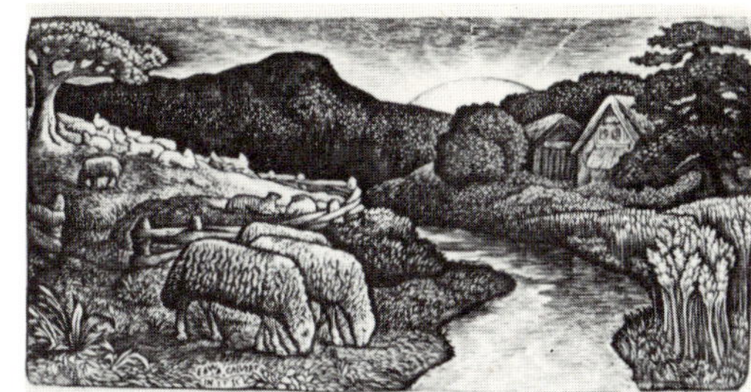

37 Edward Calvert, *The Sheep of his Pasture*, 1828 (The Tate Gallery)

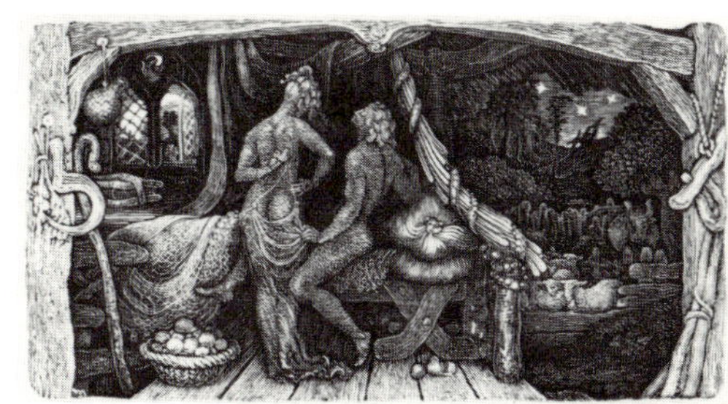

38 Edward Calvert, *The Chamber Idyll*, 1831 (The Tate Gallery)

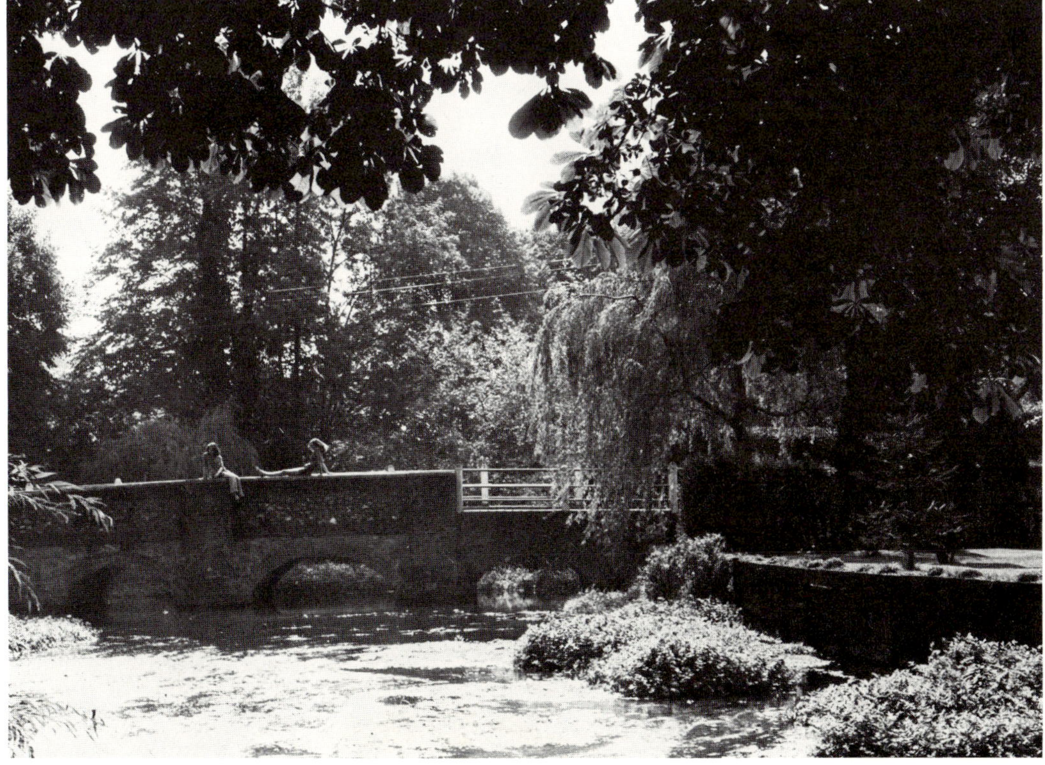

39 The Bridge over the Darenth, Shoreham

strength of purpose. He was still to produce sepias, drawings and paintings of incredible beauty and great insight but with increasing reliance upon the visual world. Without Blake's physical presence to sustain him, the demands of worldly existence were, more and more, to penetrate his inward vision and tax his spirit until he finally capitulated in 1837. Never again was he to produce pictures of the quality of sublime completeness that exists in the six sepias of 1825, not even in the *Ruth Returned from Gleaning* (57) where he makes his nearest approach, nor *Coming from Evening Church* (77), clumsy both in conception and execution in comparison with *A Hilly Scene*. In the *Young Man Yoking an Ox* (88), previously thought to have been a study for *A Rustic Scene* but now considered to date from 1831/2, we have an excellent oppor-

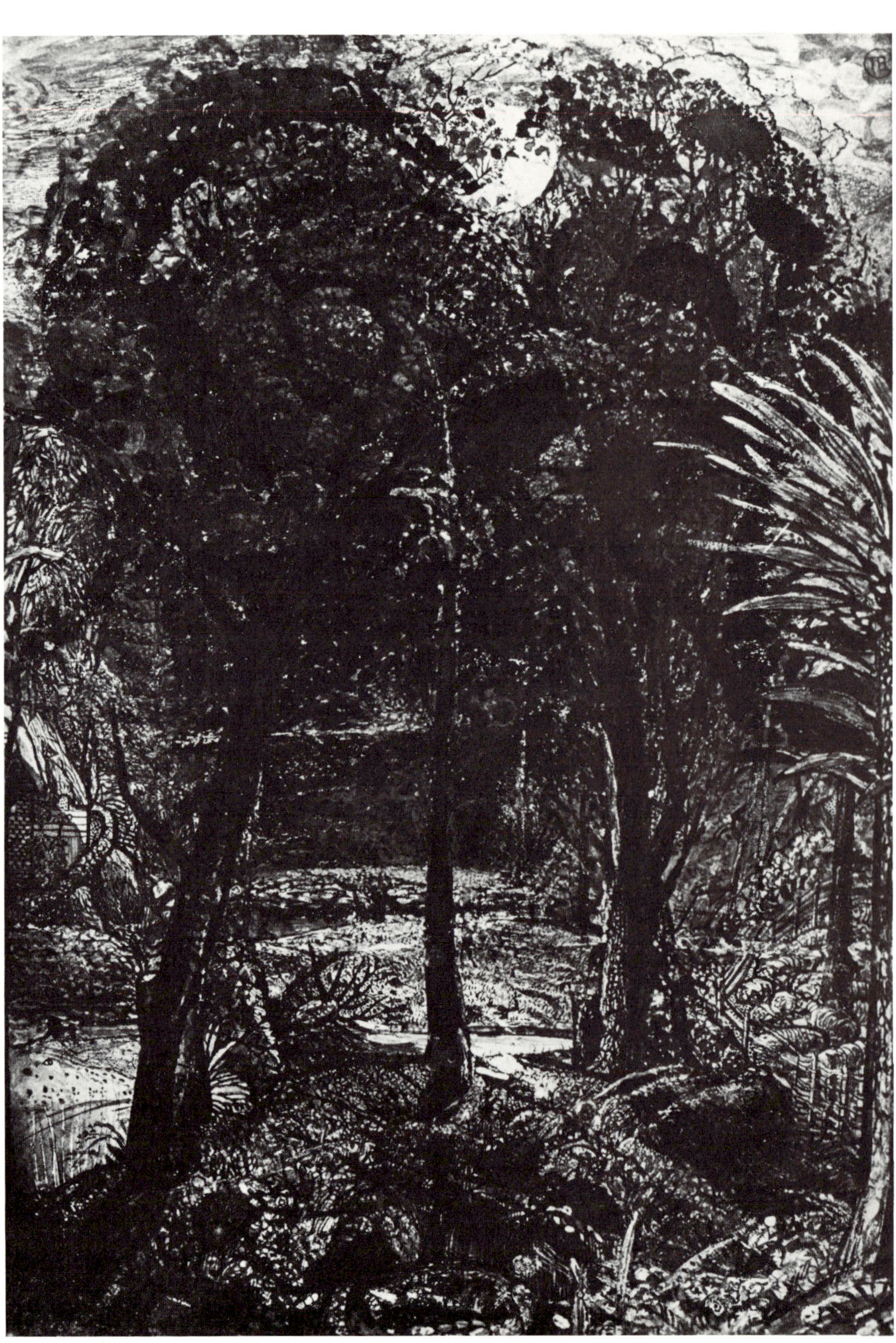

40 *Moonlight: The Winding River*, *c.*1827 (Collection Mr. and Mrs. Paul Mellon)

tunity, through the superficial similarities of the two compositions, to see how far his visionary powers had faded with the cooling of the heat of his youth. The vigour is all there but without the conviction, the intensity and the sure intuitive vision and planning of the forms seen in *A Rustic Scene*. The tautness that exists between the angle of tree and the man has gone; the 'muscles' of the tree have become flaccid; the tension generated between the tightly drawn bows of the branch with its three pears, the moon, the yoke and the plough, themselves circling the cornfield, is no longer there, and the brute beast that had calmly allowed itself to be yoked is beginning to spring in an awareness of what is happening.

In a letter he wrote to George Richmond from Shoreham on 14 November, 1827, there is already a glimpse of the beginnings of his own awareness of a more worldly existence.

'My dear Sir,

Winter, shorn of the pleasure and instruction of your society which brighten'd my summer – a Shoreham midsummer, is a very emission of loss; and this gasping hiatus sucks in many dank and acrid crudities of the gloomiest month: I mean in the jaded halts of intellect tugging up the hill of truth with the sun on her head and the excrescent wen of flesh broiling on her

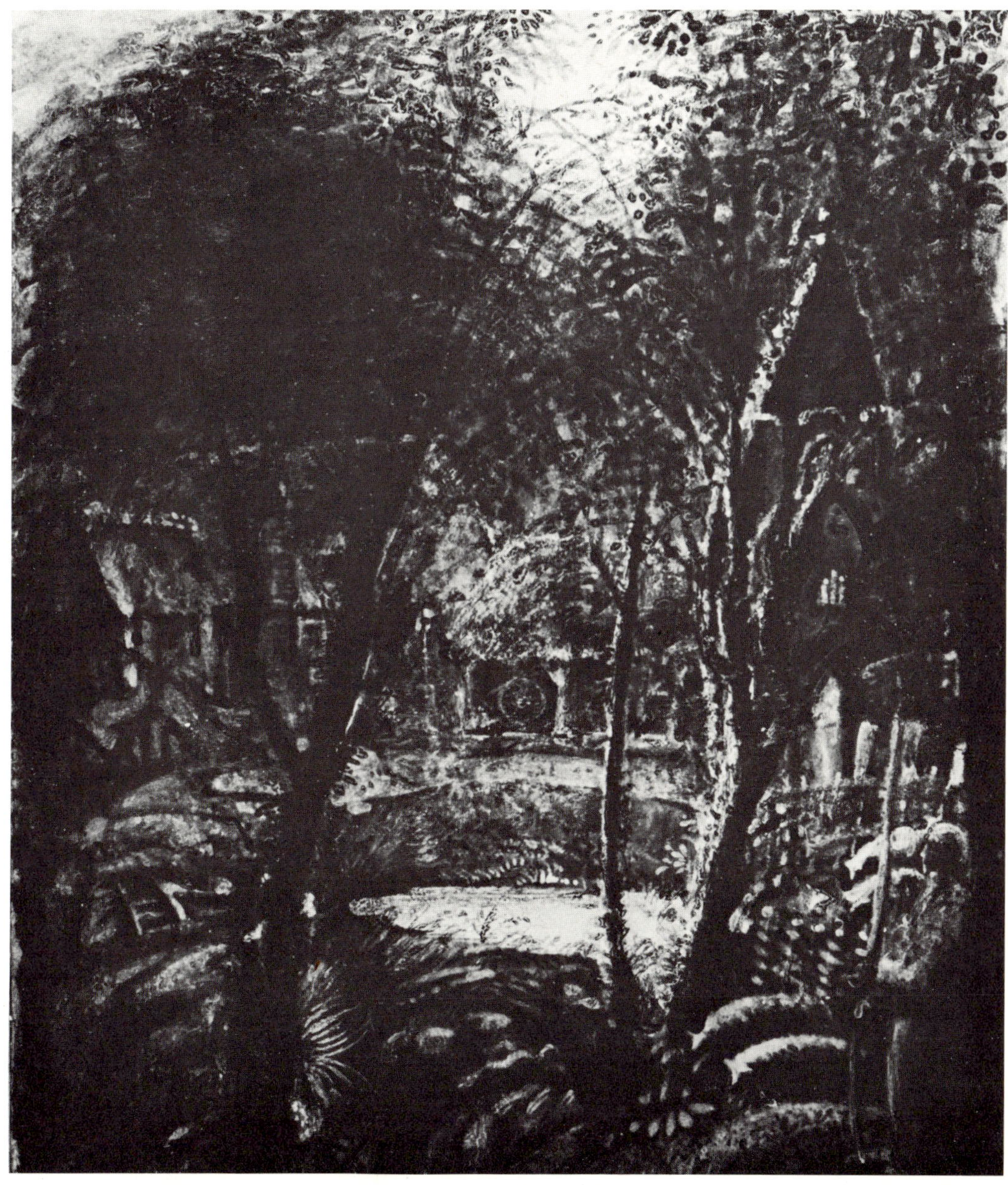

41 *Shoreham, Moonlight*, 1827 (Private Collection)

back: for tho' the eclipses of thought are to me a living inhumement and equal to the dead throes of suffocation, turning this valley of vision into a den of scorpions and stripes and agonies, yet I protest, and glory in it for the sake of its evidence of the strength of spirit that when inspir'd for art I am quite insensible to cold, hunger and bodily fatigue, and have often been surprised, on turning from work to find the fingers aching and nearly motionless with intense cold. Nor can the outward sense govern thus in turn; it is a tyranny of those brothers cruelty and weakness for whom the rear of spiritual thoughts is found too much; the recollections of happy enlighten'd hours, spiriting up to resistance the whole territory of man, till all his energies and desires break chains – march out and rush to prevent half way, with hymns, triumphs, acclamations, the majesty of their returning Freedom.

I want so much to be talking with you that you see I cannot wait till next coming to town, but use (would I could as it deserves) that choice device, that wing of lovers' thoughts which "Wafts a sigh from Indus to the Pole"; but not to baulk Montesquieu's too true notion of an Englishman – he says had he been British he had been a merchant – head and shoulders will I shove in mine own secular interest, and beg the favour that if in your ivory researches, you meet with three or four morsels of very fine ivory, size and proportion not very particular so they be from about 1 inch by $1\frac{1}{2}$ inch up to about 3 inches by 2 inches, you would buy them for me. Some thoughts have

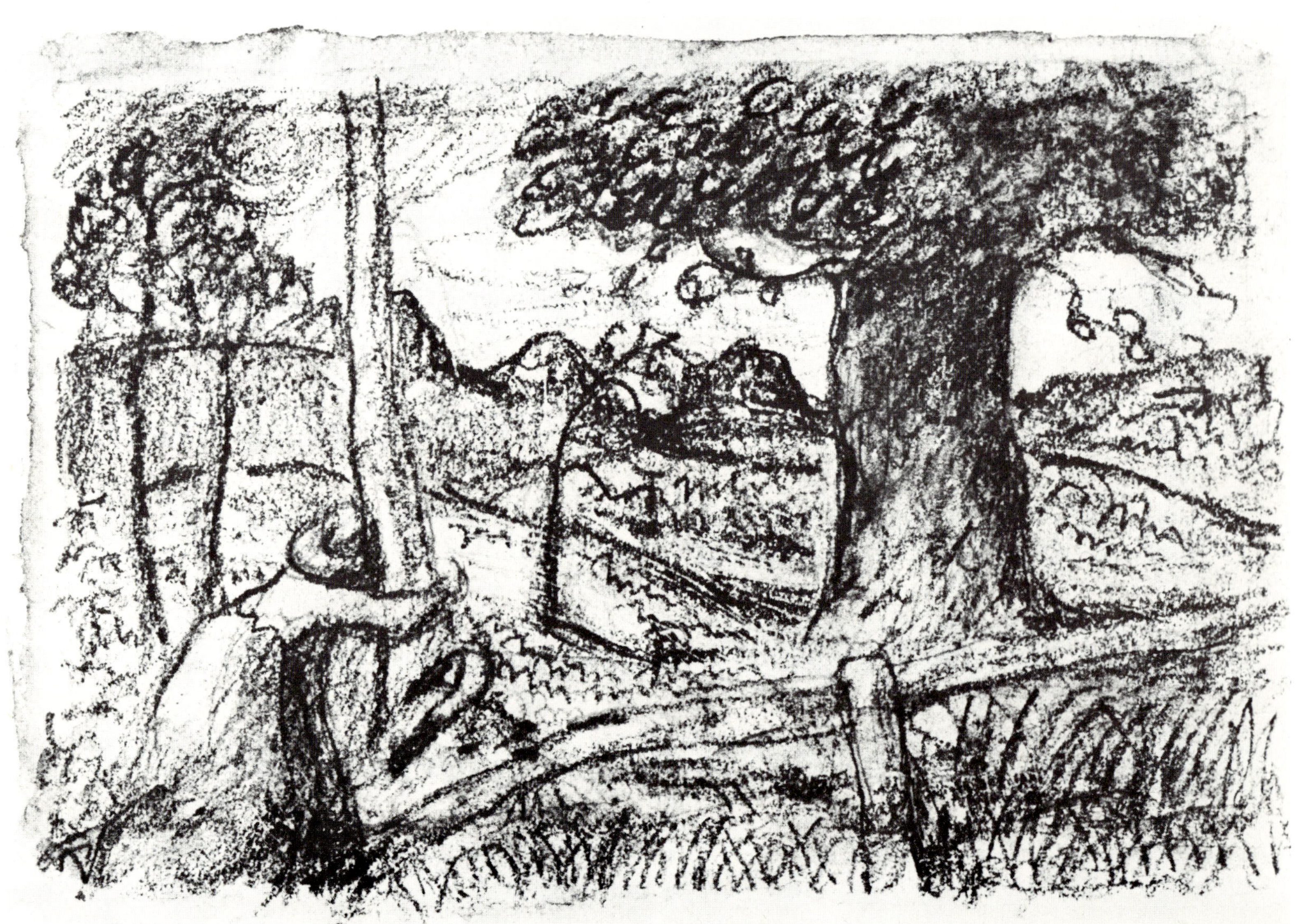

42 *Landscape with Figure embracing a Tree*, 1827? (Private Collection)

concocted and condensed in my mind of what I have seen walking about in midsummer eves and I should not care if I got a few of the subjects on ivory now, to study upon with fresh recollections of similar appearances next midsummer if God spare me; I prefer doing them very small, for they are not things by themselves, but wings, terraces or outbuildings to the great edifice of the divine human form – otherwise snares. But I have beheld as in the spirit, such nooks, caught such glimpses of the perfumed and enchanted twilight – of natural midsummer, as well as, at some other times of day, other scenes, as passed thro' the intense purifying separating transmuting heat of the soul's infabulous alchimy, would divinely consist with the severe and stately port of the human, as with the moon thron'd among constellations, and varieties of lesser glories, the regal pomp and glistening brilliance and solemn attendance of her starry train. Remembering me kindly to all friends you may see, if you think of it, would you, Sir, do me this kindness in particular to present Mrs. Blake with my most affectionate and respectful rememberances; only the having nothing to shew prevented my going to Mr. Linnell's when I was last in town. You will perhaps also, giving the same to Mr. Frederick Tatham and best respects to Mr. and Mrs. Tatham and Mr. Waters if he be there, most adoringly, vehemently and kissingly present my quaint but true knightly devotion to the young ladies One and All, collectively ador'd and individually belov'd – telling them, imploring them sometimes to think on me (for is it not an honour for fair ladies to think on me, tho'd it be only to set their pretty mouths a-giggle at the rememberance of my spectacles?)

Tell them that herein is my disadvantage – whereas mine eyes are dim save when I look at lady fair – and whereas I can only see their lustre thro'

43 *Meditation upon the Wonderful Providence of God*, *c.*1827/8 (Private Collection)

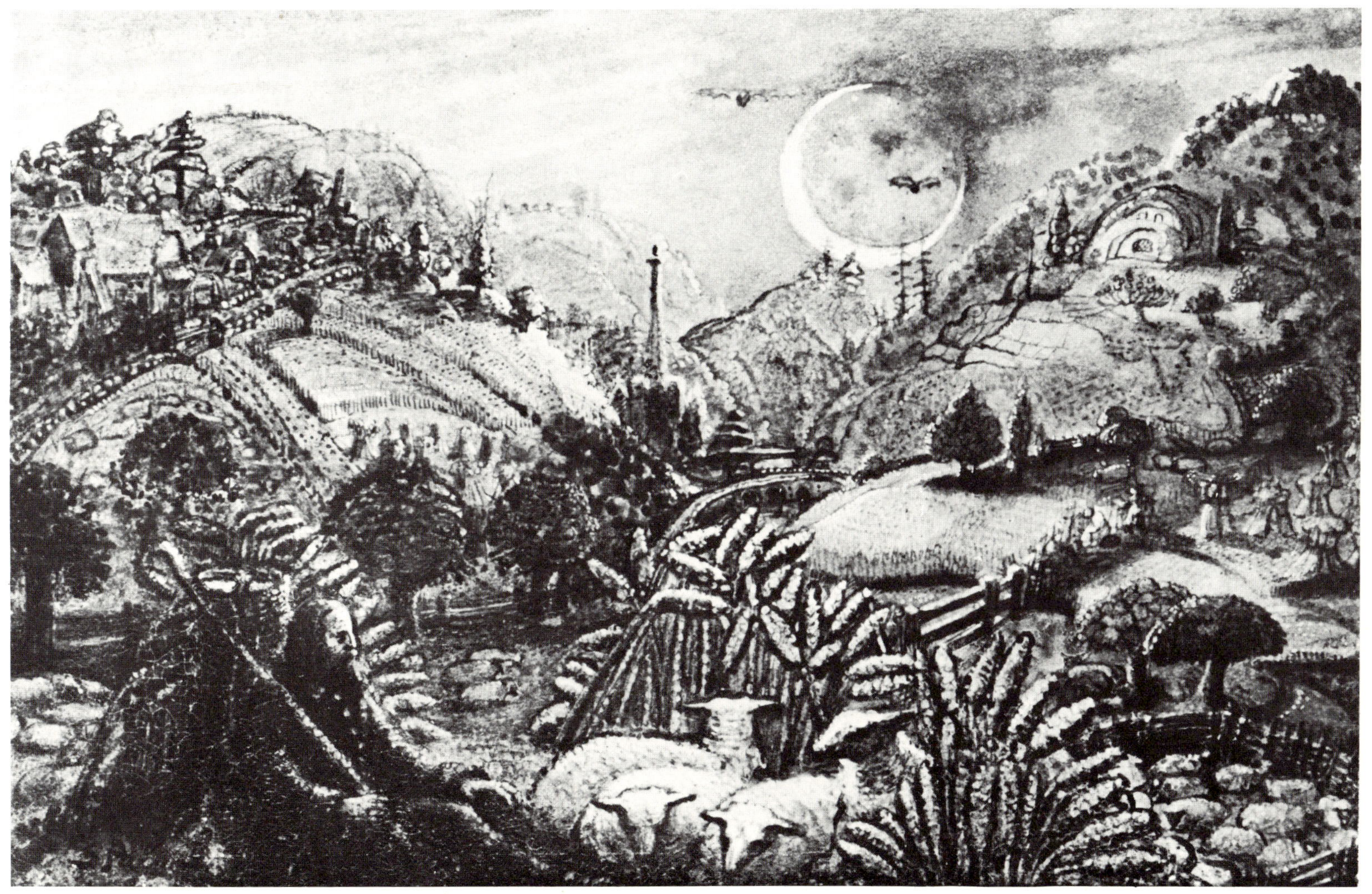

OPPOSITE
45 *Oak Tree and Beech, Lullingstone Park*, 1828 (Private Collection)

46 *Oak Trees in Lullingstone Park*, 1828 (National Gallery of Canada)

my goggles; those said unlucky goggles are so scratch'd and spoil'd that all the fire of the love darting artillery of my eyes is lost upon them and redounds not to my advantage, the ladies seeing only two huge misty spheres of light scratched and scribbled over like the sun in a fog or dirty dish in a dark pantry, as lustre lacking, as leaden and as lifeless as a lad without a lady. But tell them sometimes to think on me, as I very often think of them, and as in sullen twilight rambles, sweet visions of (their) lovely bright eyes suddenly sparkle round me, (and il)lume my dusky path – double the vigour (of my) pace, rebuild my manhood and renew my y(outh). You see the perfections of the ladies are unsp(aring?) – that is the reason that no sooner do I begin (to) write of them than lo! I scribble nonsense – arrant nonsense. Hervey's Meditations and the heath's of Fingal and the vapours of the hill of storms.

Ought I to send you such a scribble? but I will send it for the ivories' sake, and to speak my hope that you may have the blessing and presence of the Almight for ever, and that absence has not yet rased from the tables of your memory, dear Sir,

Your affectionate Humble Servant
Samuel Palmer.

I must let this note go unpointed, uncorrected, with all its orthographic blunders whether of negligence or ignorance, for if I begin to revise I shall sentence it to the flames very speedily. I am looking for a wife.'

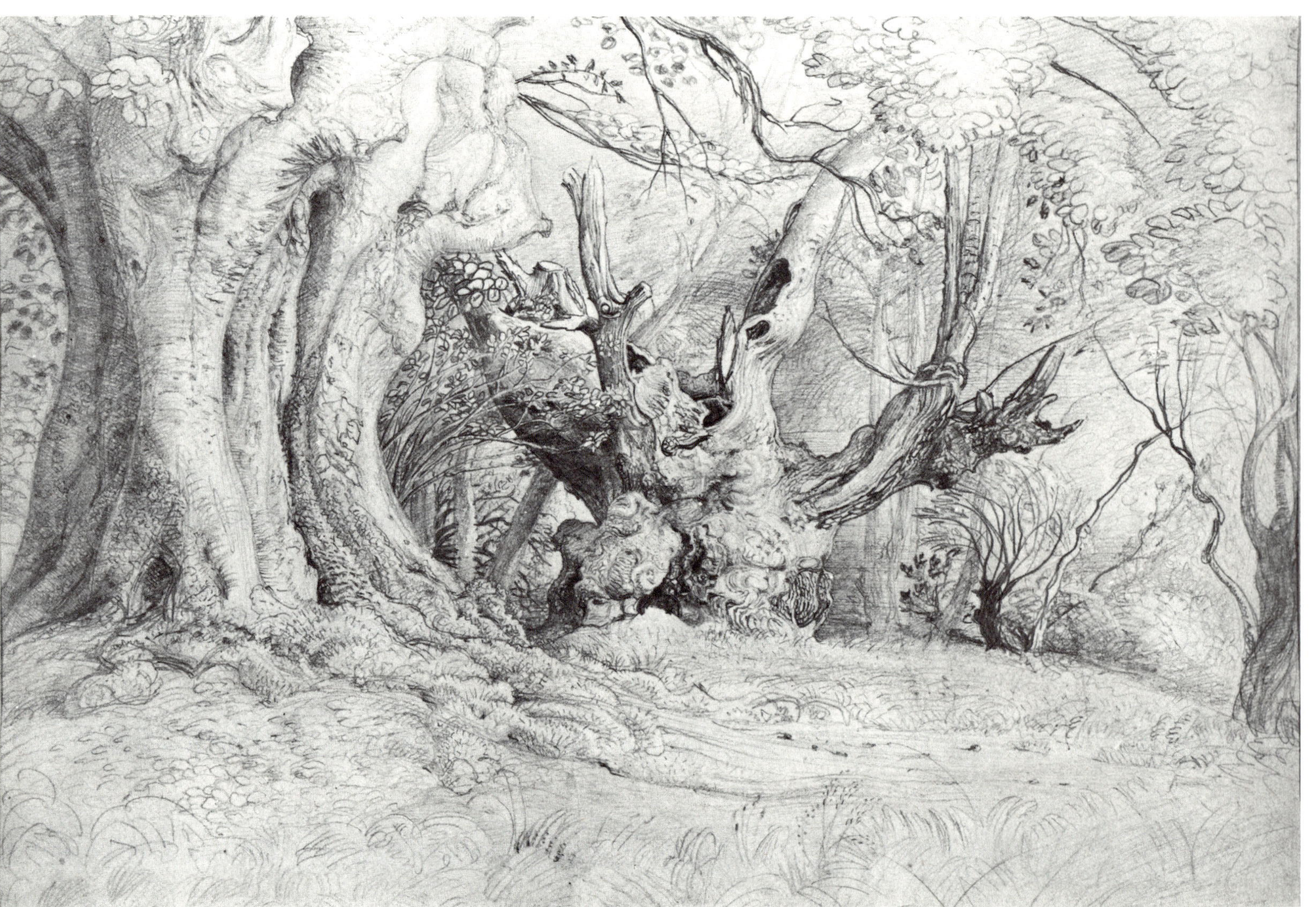

44 *Ancient Trees in Lullingstone Park*, 1828 (Collection Lord Clark)

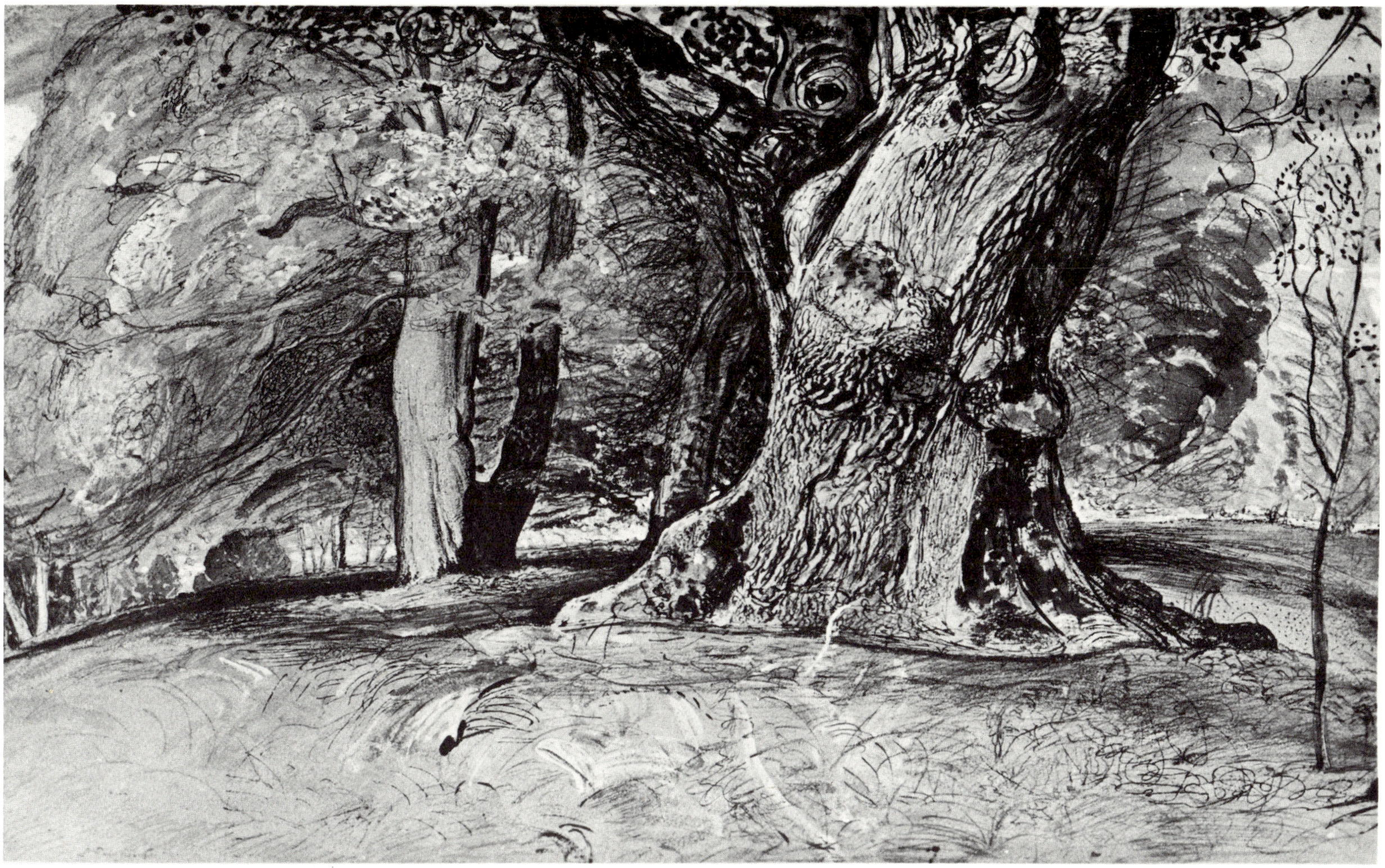

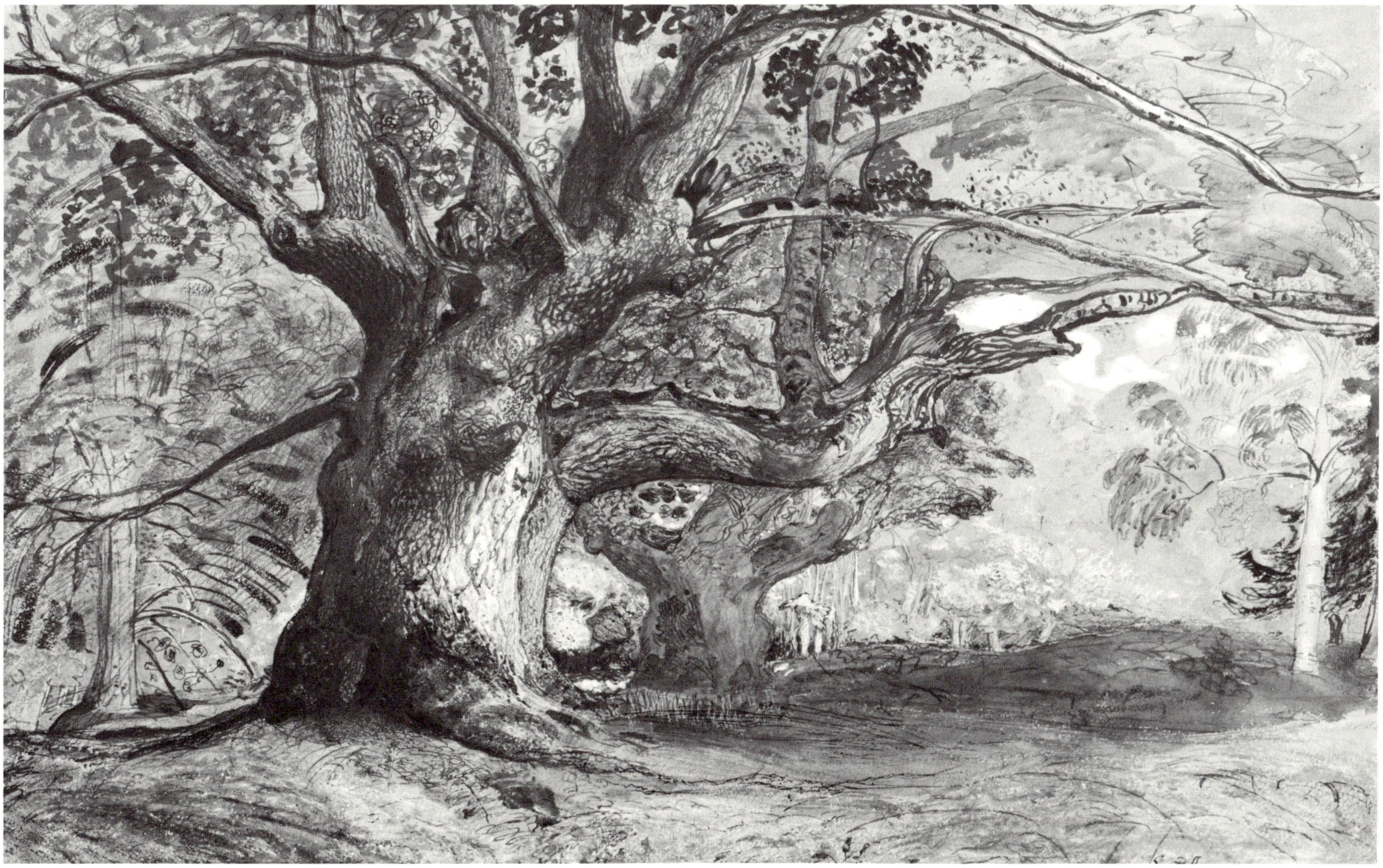

OPPOSITE
49 *In a Shoreham Garden*, *c.*1829 (Victoria and Albert Museum)

OVERLEAF
50 *The Gleaning Field*, 1833 (The Tate Gallery)

But something of the vision of 1825 remained, at least for a while although the heat had gone. In the next few years he was to create some of the most dramatic landscapes to be found in the history of English painting through his insight and sensitivity to the brooding quality of summer in the English countryside. On Linnell's instigation to do some drawings for him from nature he began to transmute his earlier vision through a close study and observation of natural phenomena and he discovered the drama not of light but of shadow. Light, in these drawings only exists to point the contrast. Through Linnell's commission he was to make a series of drawings of the great oak trees in Lullingstone Park (*44–46*) – these trees are still in existence – and in consequence he discovered another type of excess, the excess, the fecundity, that nature specializes in. This discovery led to the series of paintings, *A Cow Lodge with a Mossy Roof* (*36*) and *In a Shoreham Garden* (*49*) among

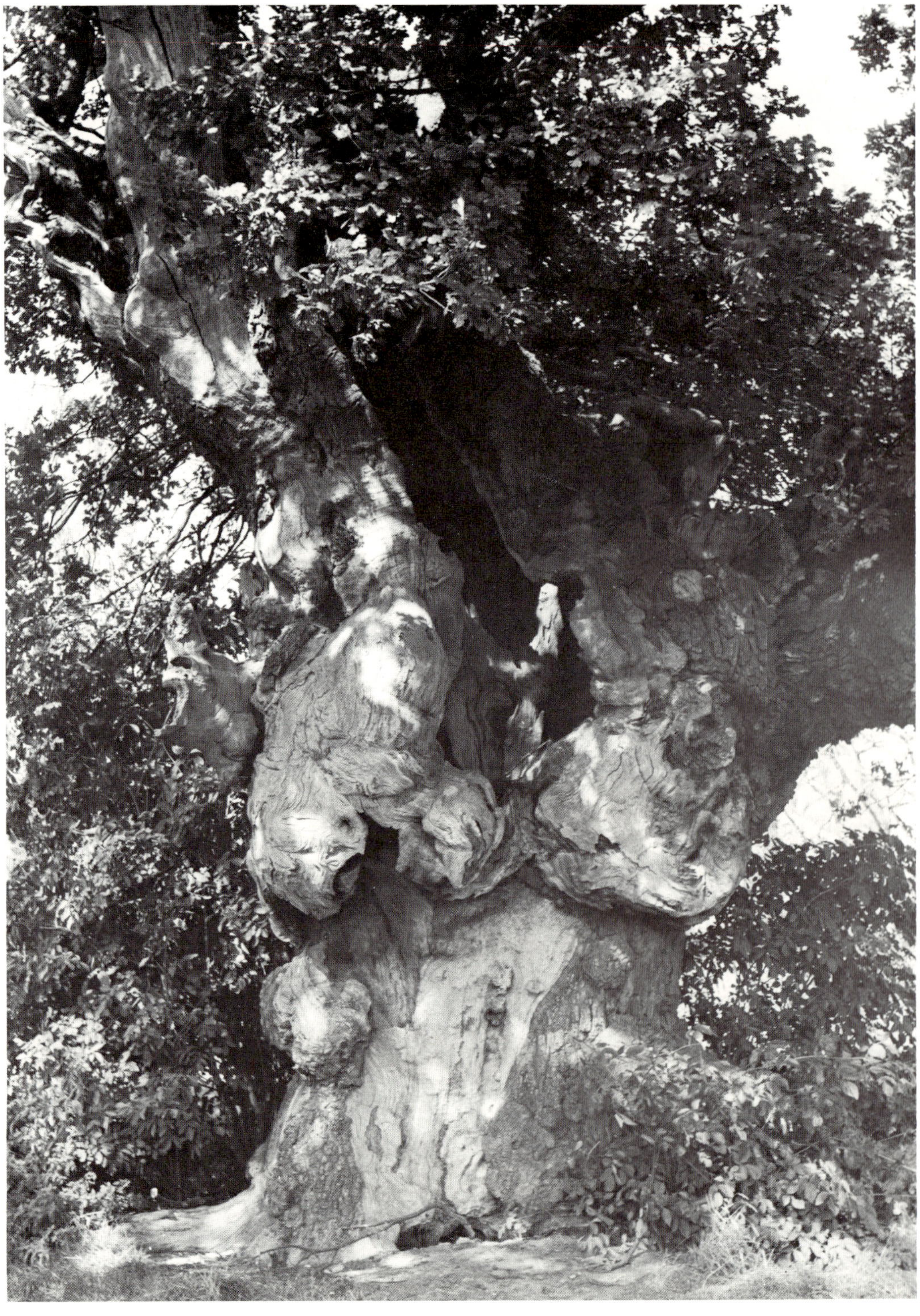

47, 48 Oak Trees, Lullingstone Park

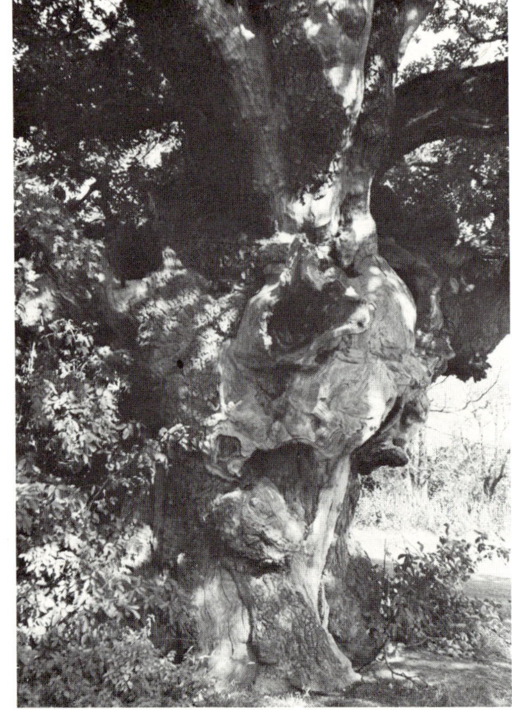

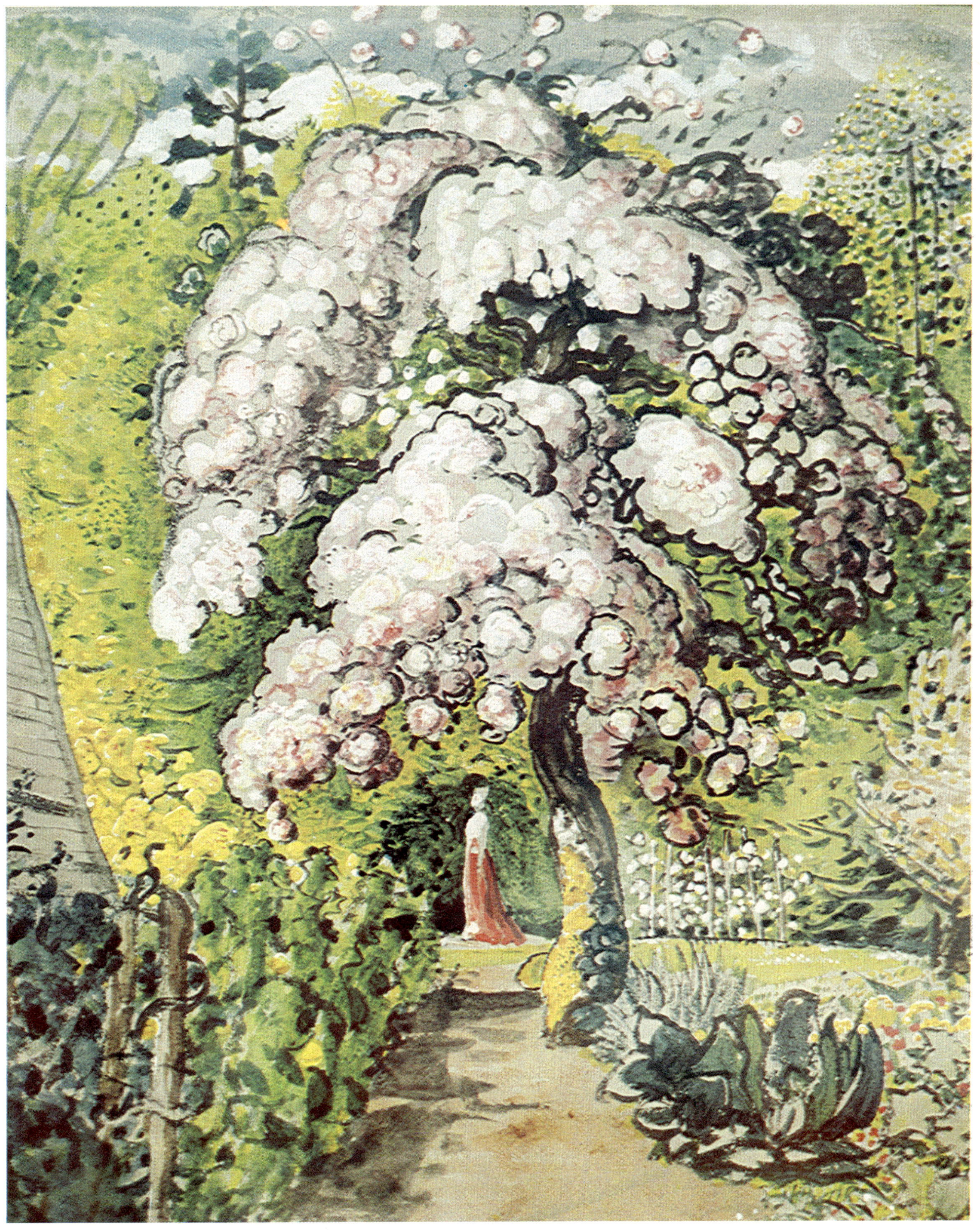

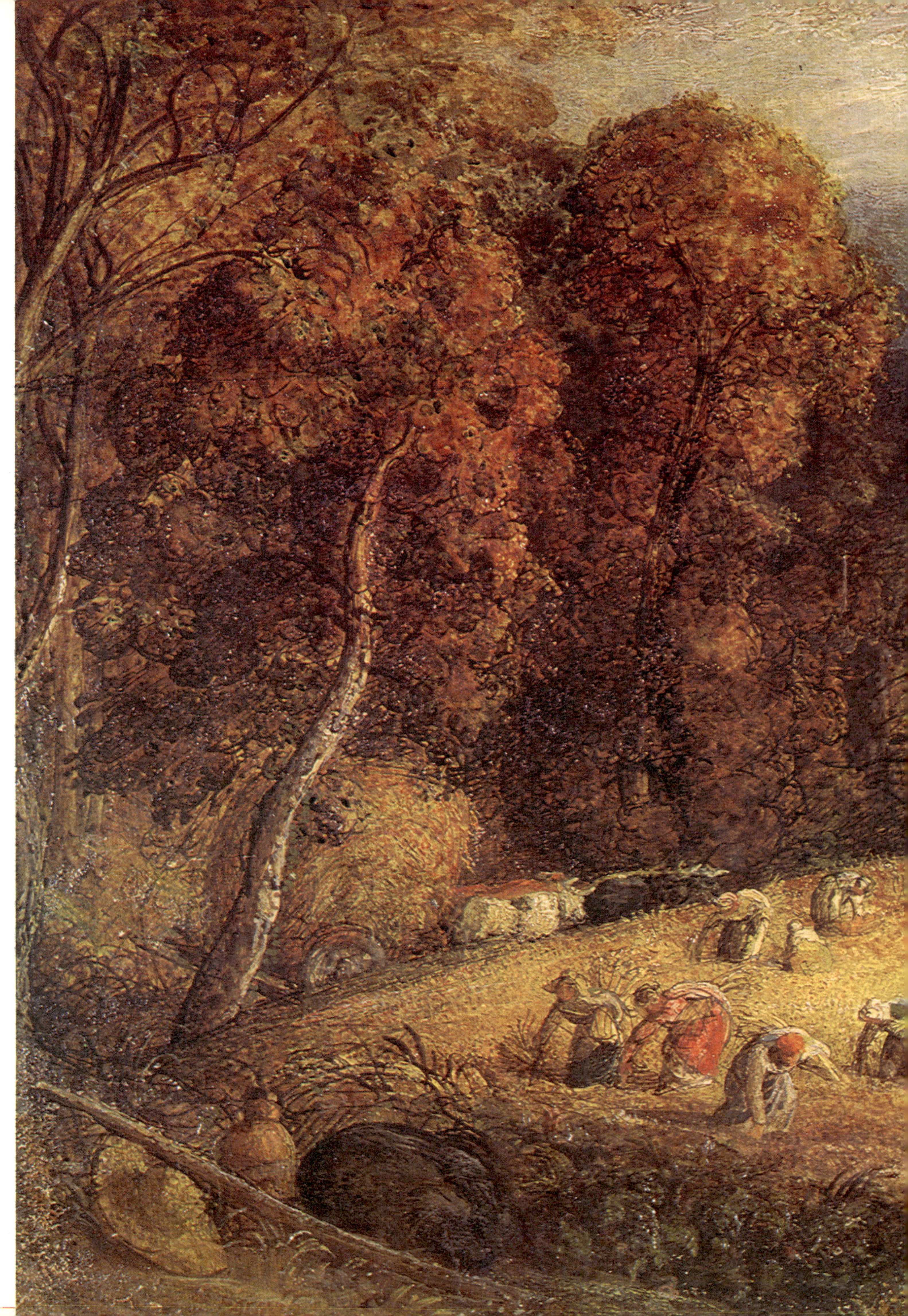

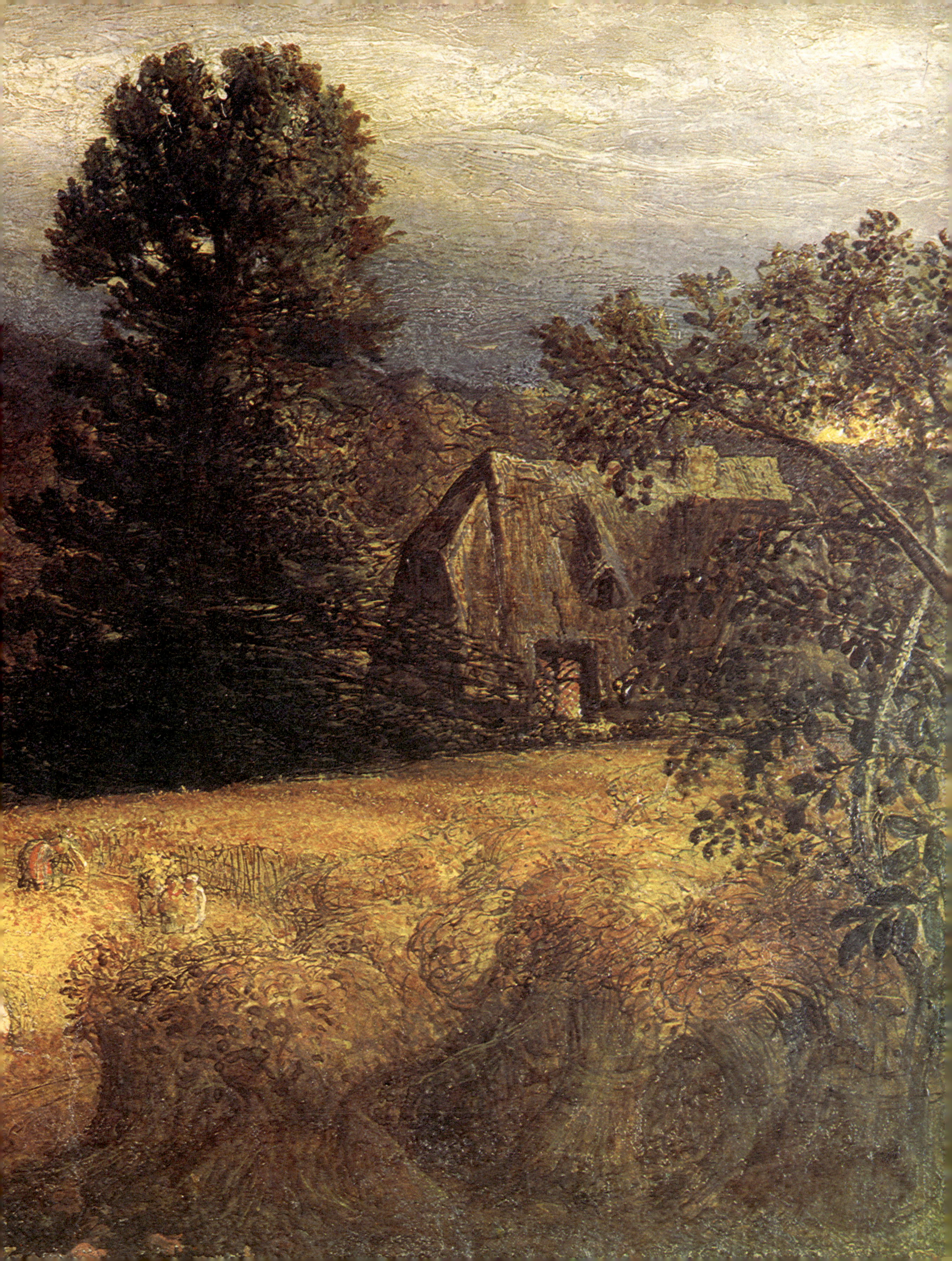

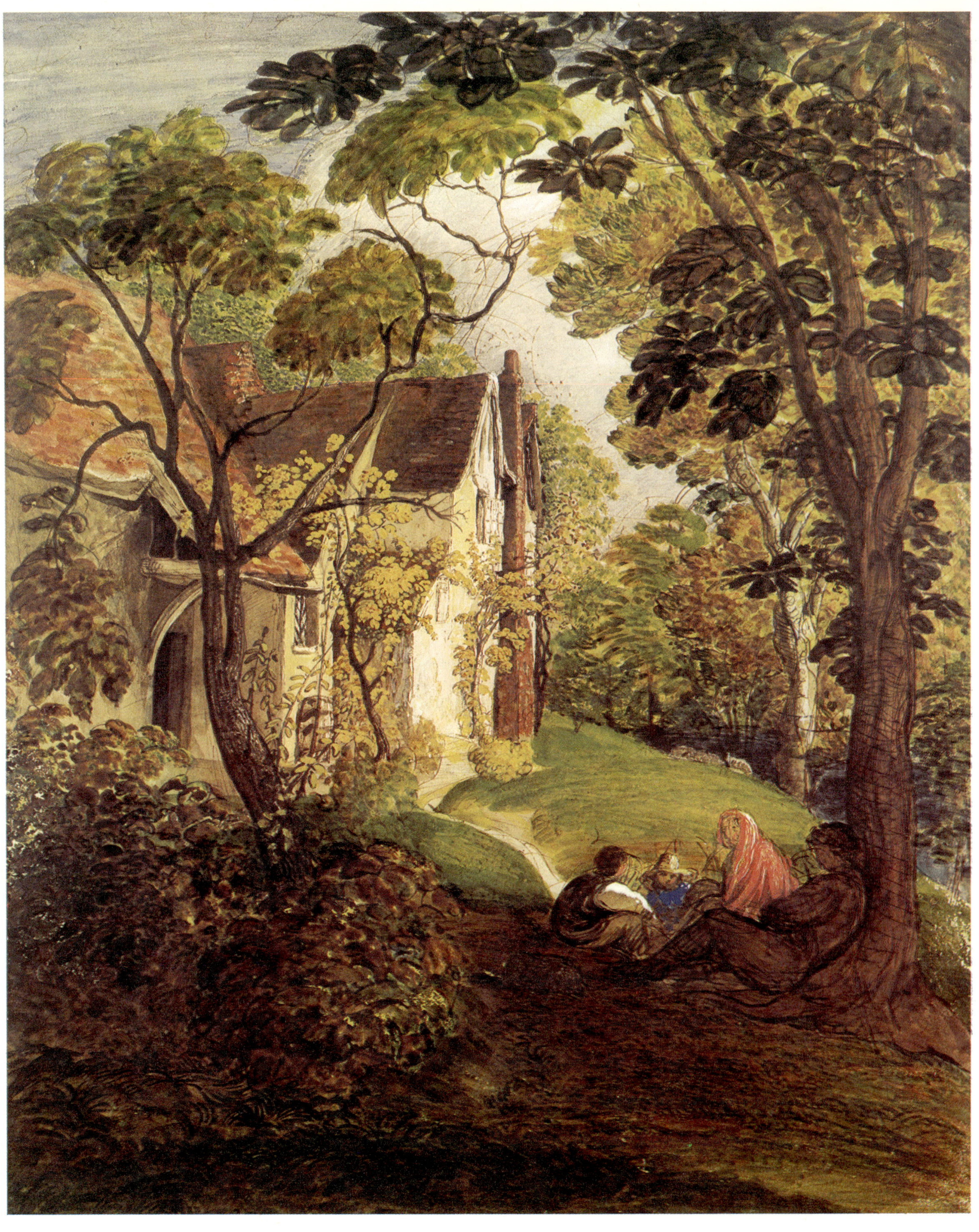

51 *Old House on the Bank of the Darenth, Shoreham*, 1831/2 (Ashmolean Museum)

others, that parallel his dark twilights and full moons and these two qualities, of procreation and fecundity, he never mixes and no wonder, for to imagine *The Valley Thick with Corn* with the overtones of *A Village Church among Trees* (*71*) is an awesome prospect. He approaches close on occasion, as near as he dare, in *The Magic Apple Tree* (*72*) and in the strange harking back to 1826 of *Cornfield by Moonlight with the Evening Star* (*12*), perhaps the most extraordinary painting he did at Shoreham.

In a letter to John Linnell in December, 1828, he wrote 'Nature, with mild reposing breadths of lawn and hill, shadowy glades and meadows, is sprinkled and showered with a thousand pretty eyes, and buds, and spires, and blossoms gemm'd with dew, and is clad in living green. Nor must be forgotten the motley clouding; the fine meshes, the aerial tissues, that dapple the skies of spring; nor the rolling volumes and piled mountains of light; nor the purple sunset blazon'd with gold and the translucent amber. Universal nature wears a lovely gentleness of mild attraction; but the leafy lightness, the thousand repetitions of little forms, which are part of its own genuine perfection (and who would wish them but what they are?), seem hard to be reconciled with the unwinning severity, the awfulness, the ponderous globosity of Art.' Of the Lullingstone drawings he says in the same letter 'Milton, by one epithet, draws an oak of the largest girth I ever saw, "Pine and monumental oak": I have just been trying to draw a large one in Lullingstone; but the poet's tree is huger than any in the park: there, the moss, and rifts, and barky furrows, and the mouldering grey (tho' that adds majesty to the lord of forests) mostly catch the eye, before the grasp and

52 Oak Trees, Lullingstone Park

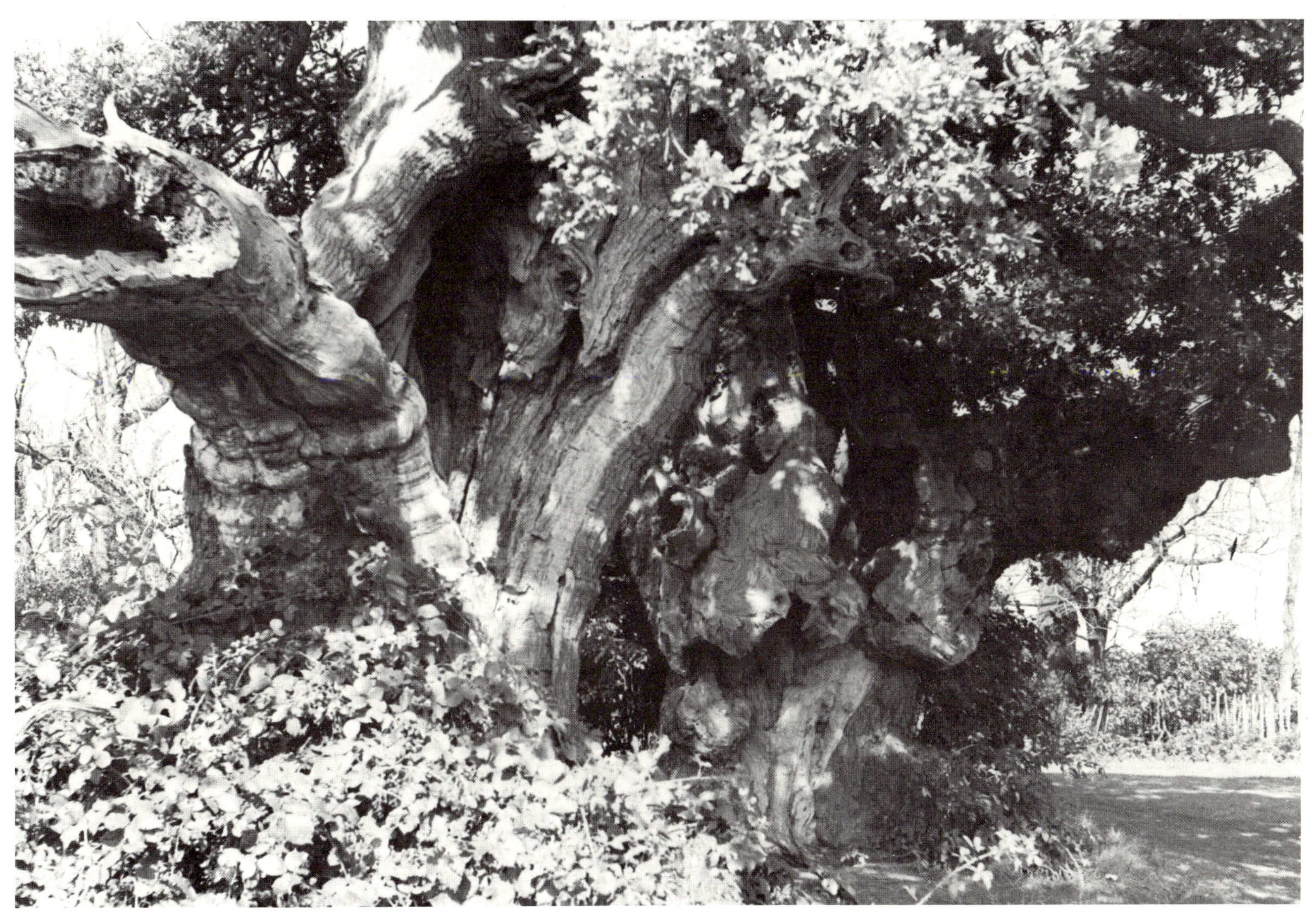

OPPOSITE
55 *Self Portrait*, 1828 (Ashmolean Museum)

grapple of the roots, the muscular belly and shoulders, the twisted sinews.'

He is still able to sense the relationship between himself and the 'muscular belly and shoulders, the twisted sinews' in the *Trees in Lullingstone Park* and *Oak Tree, Shoreham, Kent*, but it is as if he was now seeing for the first time and at first hand, the inexorable force of nature, a quality not apparent in the 1825 paintings because of the exaggerations and formalizations and one that fascinates him. He depicts every furrow of the bark, every encrustation of lichen and moss until in *Ancient Trees in Lullingstone Park* the trees are beginning to be overwhelmed by a tide, of epiphytic growth. Now he goes searching for visual evidence of natural excess and he returns with *Barn with a Mossy Roof* (53), *Pear Tree in a Walled Garden* (54), *A Cow Lodge with a Mossy*

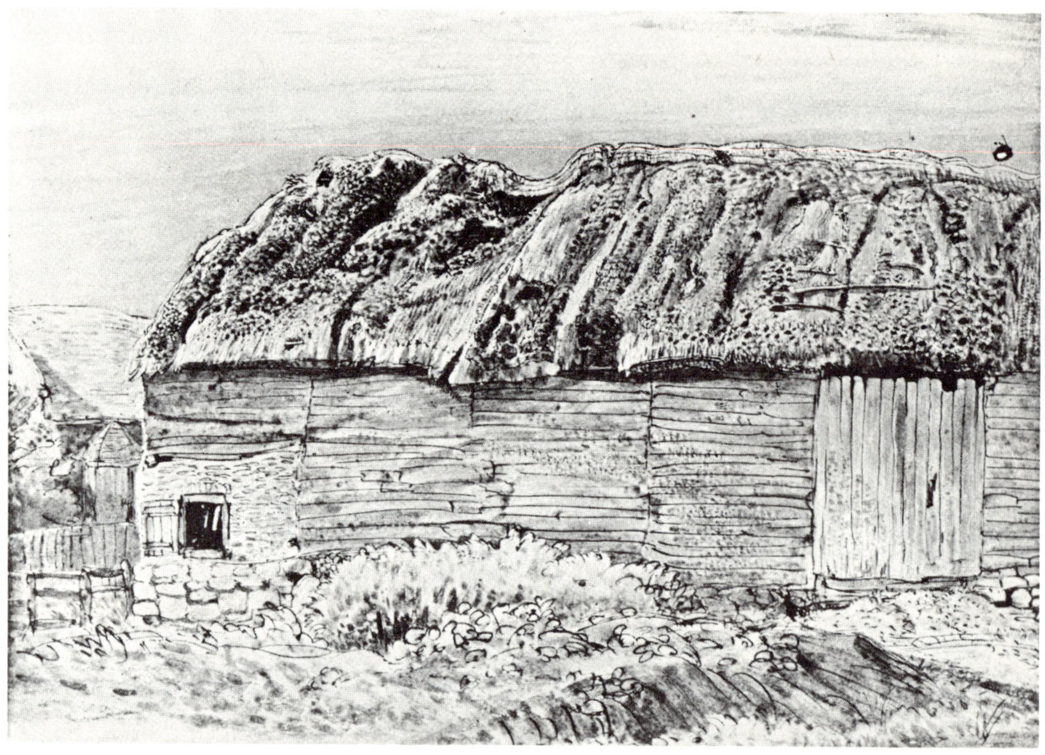

53 *Barn with a Mossy Roof*, 1828/9 (Private Collection)

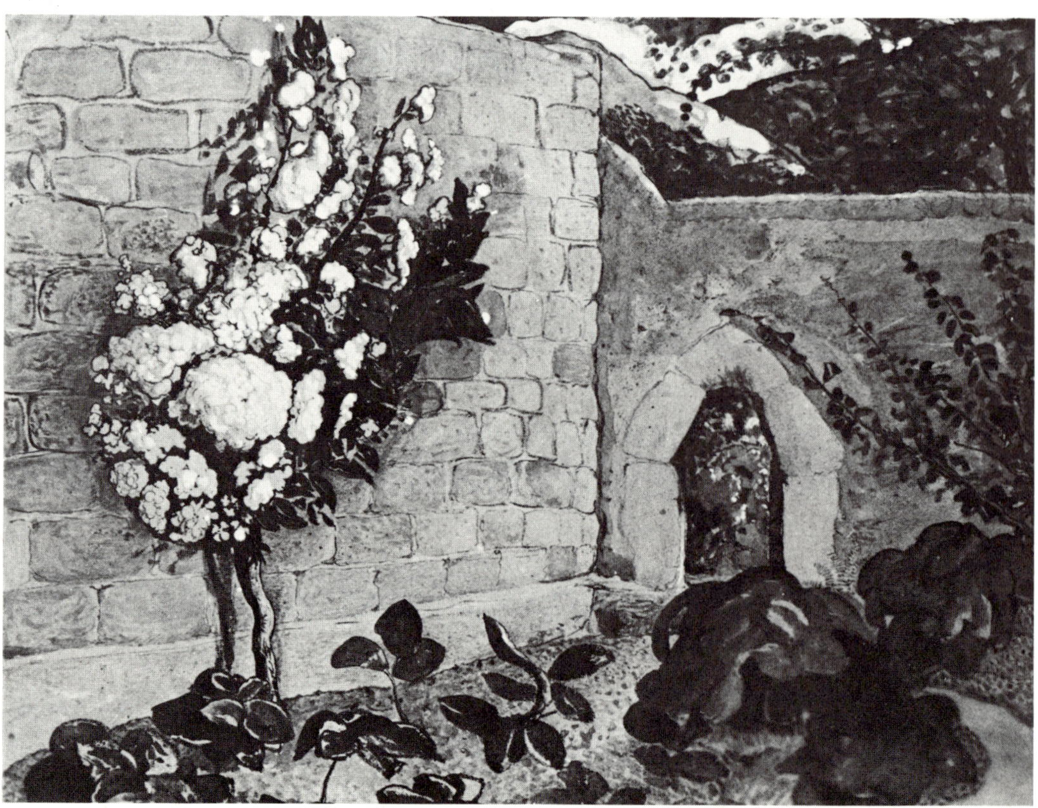

54 *Pear Tree in a Walled Garden*, *c.*1829 (Private Collection)

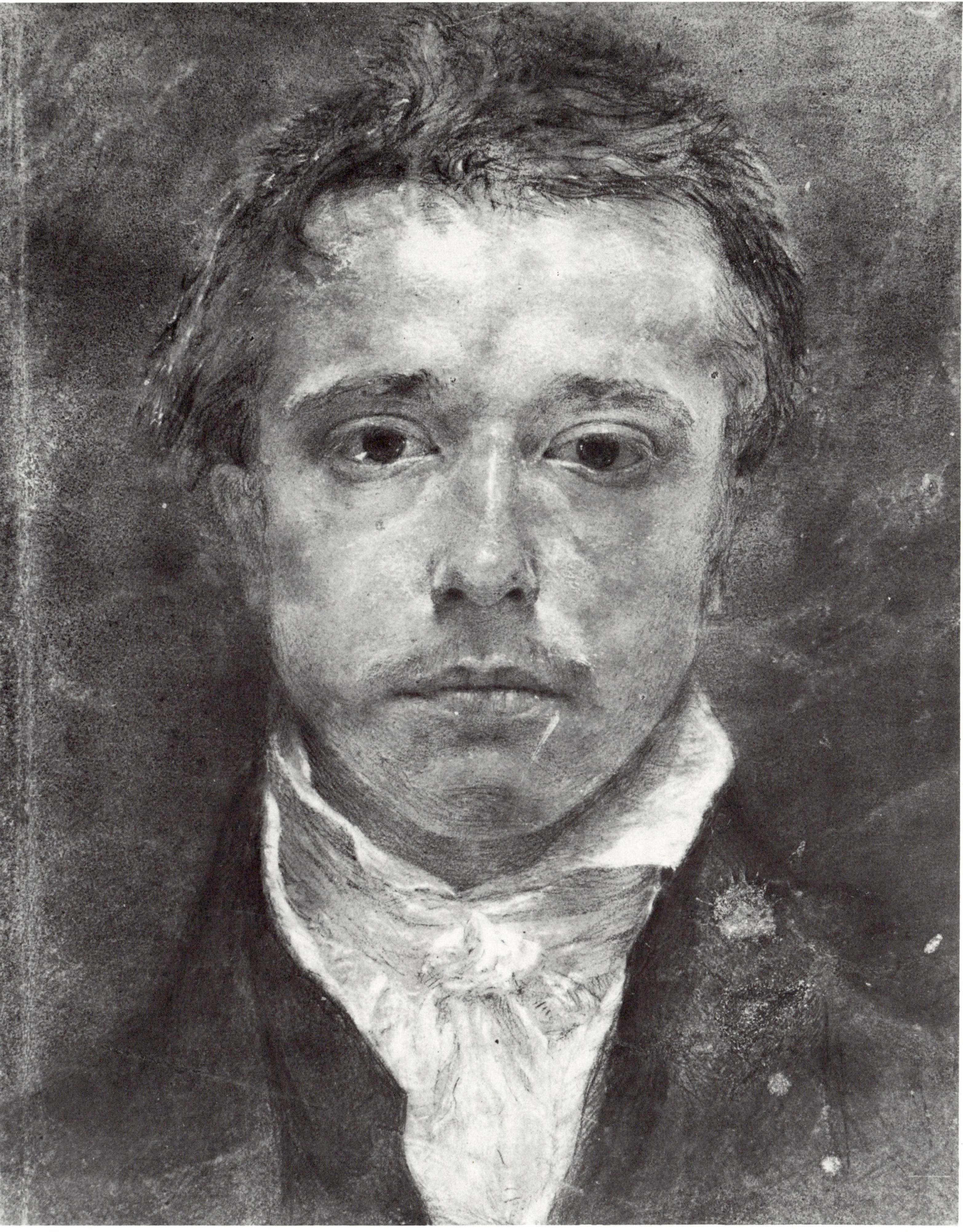

Roof and *In a Shoreham Garden*. He is not content with giving the spectator just a visual impression of the rich textural qualities in these subjects but by building up the paint – probably with Blake's white[7] – and then glazing his colours on top, he attempts to present actual tactile sensations with the secondary, but by no means unimportant, effect, that the light reflected from the under painting of white causes the colour to glow, adding even further to the already abundantly rich qualities of these roofs and trees alive with blossom and the sense of their pregnancy.

It had always been there of course, this excess of nature's, but a changed attitude to nature is apparent in the work of a number of early nineteenth century artists and poets. In place of a certain wariness in face of nature's excess there is a rejoicing in her outpourings. Perhaps the awareness that the classicism of the previous century was leading to sterility prompted the search for a new artistic vocabulary, or the knowledge that drastic technological changes were now threatening natural beauty and creating new misery and squalor led to re-appraisal in place of acceptance. But above all, the power harnessed by the industrial revolution had made it possible to face nature with more confidence, even control some of her excess and suspicion was giving way to analysis. Certainly Palmer was not alone among his contemporaries in his re-examination of man's relationship to the natural world and his reaction against traditional artistic conventions. In a letter to George Richmond he emphasized that he would not consider becoming a conventional topographical artist although Linnell had assured him that thereby he could earn a thousand a year for 'By God's help I will not sell away this gift of art for money; no, not for fame neither, which is far better.'

Among the drawings that John Linnell commissioned Palmer to do in 1828 there is one, *Barn in a Valley* (*58*), that not only shows his reactions against producing mere topographical works but looks forward to the twilight landscapes of 1829–32. It is one of the finest he did for Linnell,

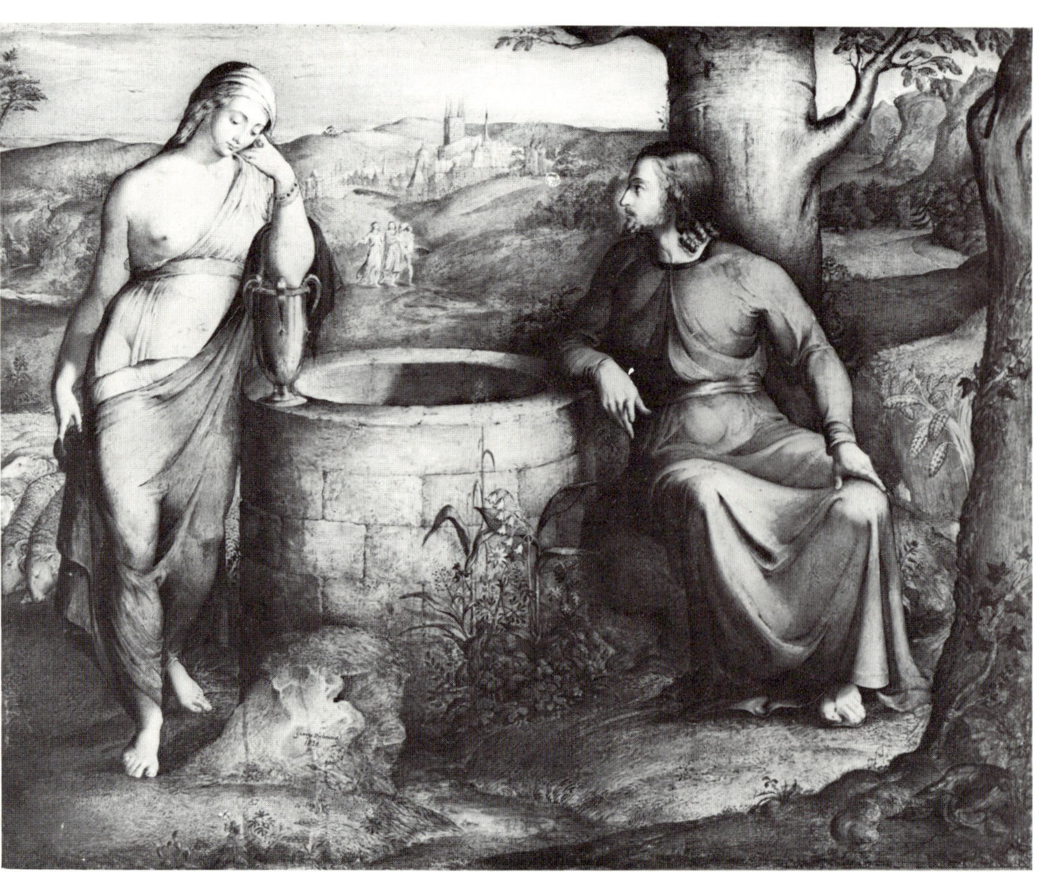

56 George Richmond, *Christ and the Woman of Samaria*, 1828 (The Tate Gallery)

certainly the freest in handling, even compared to *The Primitive Cottage* (*59*) or *Landscape at Shoreham* (*61*).

Barn in a Valley is on brownish paper, drawn with pen and brush with bistre over pencil, with further additions of pencil over the wash and heightened with white on the barn roof and in the foreground. The freedom with which he has drawn the tree on the right – much of it is little more than scribbling with the pen – shows the competence that Palmer had now reached with his draughtsmanship, able to create something with such feeling of life and be entirely convincing in the means he has employed. But it is the hill in the background that lifts this work above the not inconsiderable qualities of the other drawings. The hill is in shadow which has the effect of intensifying the light flooding over the foreground, lending drama to a work which for all its skill would have appeared thin and perhaps even slight in its absence. But the shadow is not so dense as to obscure details of the trees and bushes that cover it, thereby allowing the eye to penetrate into the picture and at the same time create a solidity, by its depiction of form, to what, if an opaque wash had been used, would have been merely a backdrop and as flat. By allowing us to see these vague details of growth on the hill the eye is attracted to the background only to discover, seemingly, a dark chasm below from which it recoils to the light and safety of the foreground. The

57 *Ruth Returned from Gleaning*, 1828/9 (Victoria and Albert Museum)

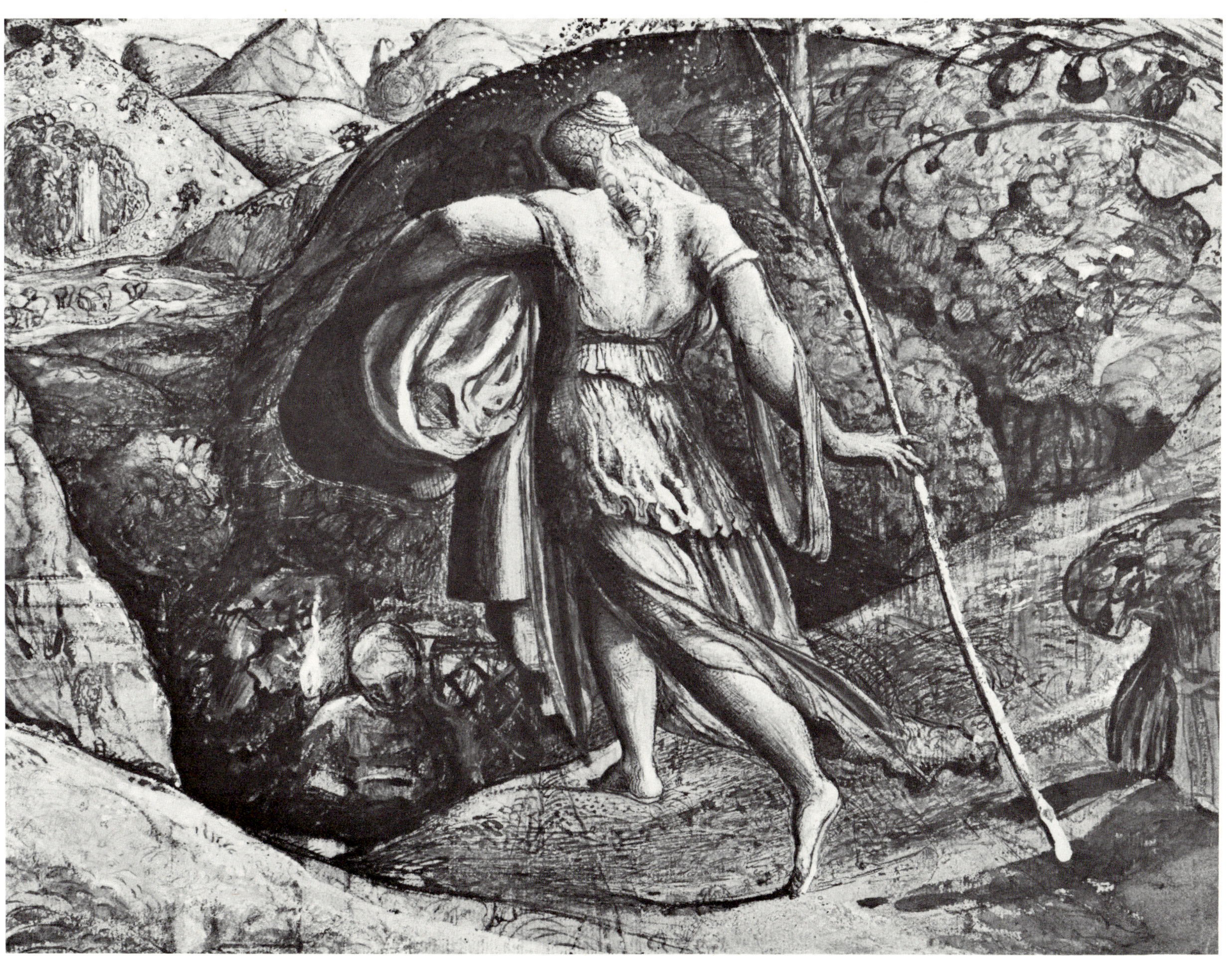

more one looks at the picture the more one finds that there is a strange compulsion for the eye, led in the curve of the field, to return to this dark brooding hillside. This long dark hillside fascinated Palmer for it crops up frequently throughout his visionary period. Making its first appearance in *Late Twilight* where the horizon line is broken by a group of trees, it later turns up in the wood engraving of 1826 *Harvest and a Crescent Moon* the composition of which is repeated with minor alterations and reversed in *Cornfield by Moonlight with the Evening Star* of 1830; it is in the background of *Landscape: A Girl Standing* and behind the trees in *Evening, a Church among Trees* (*75*), also of 1830, and again in the *Folded Flock* of 1831/2 (*84*).

Several reasons can be adduced for the frequent use of this shadowy escarpment and, perhaps, the first is a purely geographical one. Shoreham lies in a valley that is oriented north-south, therefore the sun rises over one bordering hill and descends behind the other, in each case casting the hills into shadow at dawn and again at twilight. From many of the titles like the twilight scenes it appears that the hill featured is the westerly one and it so happens that Shoreham lies closest to this side of the valley. This particular hill became more important to him because of its proximity and probably because, when in Shoreham village, the eastern half of the vale would be obscured by trees to Palmer. Secondly, with the coming of twilight it is but a short step to associate the moon and clearly Palmer felt a close relationship with this dual symbol of the male and female principle, in a horned stage in his earlier work and later in the fullness of maturity. Thirdly, it is possible that the depiction of the hill could have coincided with the attacks of depression mentioned by his son. This is, of course, pure conjecture but cer-

58 *A Barn in a Valley*, 1828 (Ashmolean Museum)

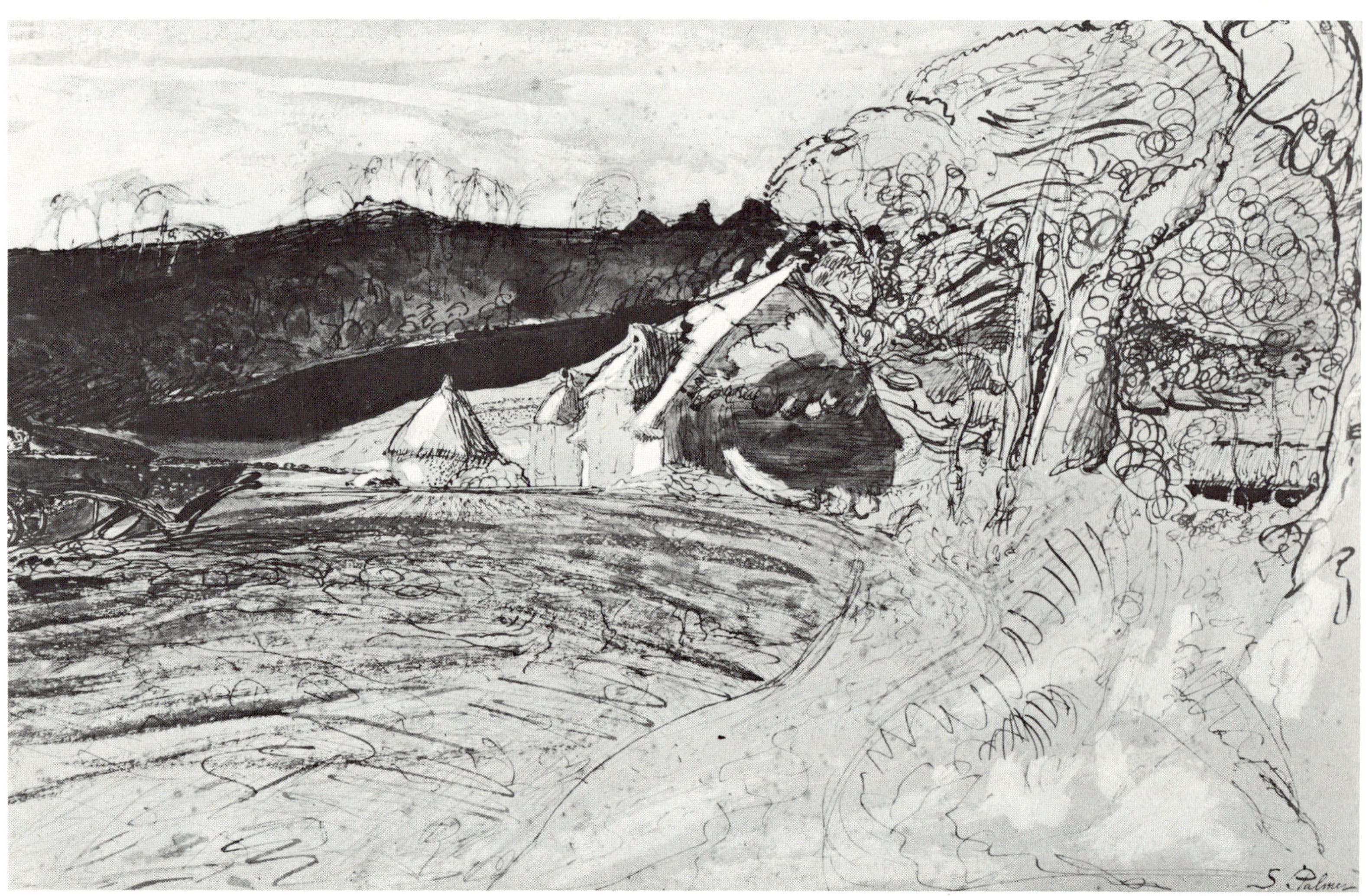

tainly there is an aggressive quality in these landscapes that would suggest that the mind that produced them was highly charged at the time.

Although the first work in which this feature appears was completed before he went to live in Shoreham he had visited the place before 1825 and in a person as sensitive as Palmer it would be immediately apparent that you cannot have vales of Eden without attendant hills. By the time of *Barn in a Valley* it seems probable that he was beginning to associate the valley, however tenuously, with a feeling of being trapped by his situation.

He had been in love, probably with one of Tatham's sisters and he had been refused. It is unlikely that her snobbish father would have agreed to the union in any case as he had opposed the marriage of George Richmond to his other daughter Julia who, however, eloped to Gretna Green. He was also 'looking for a wife' and he must have felt very isolated at Shoreham from time to time, particularly in winter when he would have had only Mary Ward and his father for companionship, neither of whom would have been able to share in his visual excitements. Nor was he selling any of his work, with the exception of Linnell's commission, and most of his pictures were being

59 *The Primitive Cottage*, 1828/9 (Victoria and Albert Museum)

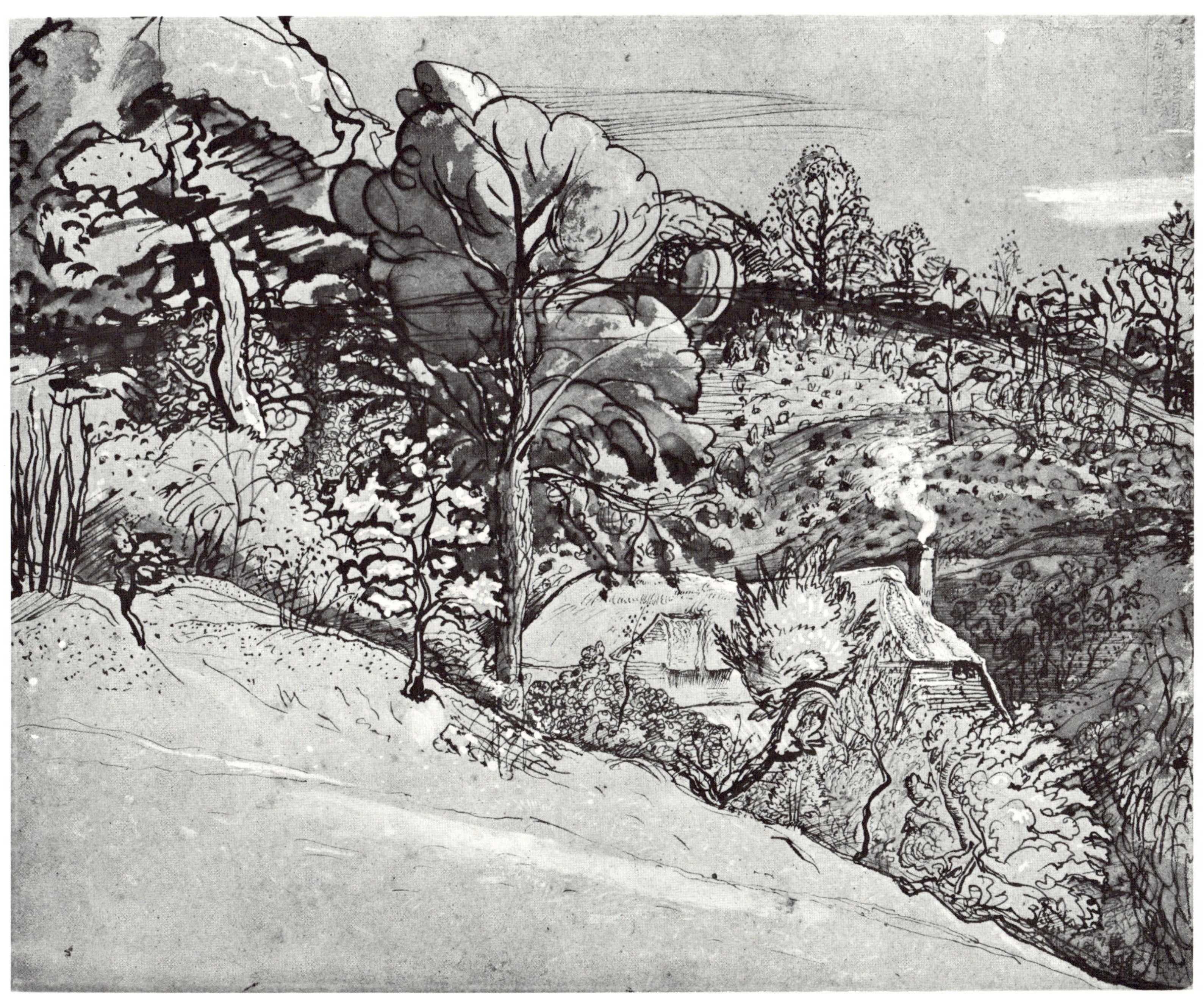

rejected by the Royal Academy.

'The ways of the Royal Academy are to me unaccountable – not that it is unaccountable they should reject six of my drawings; but that they should hang those two which I thought far least likely. I expected they would reject the "Whole kettle and boiling", as they have for these two years, and intended, with the patience of an ox, to prepare eight colour'd pictures for their rejection next season; and if they were refused, a like dose on the year succeeding. As they condescended to receive any, I wonder they did not prefer the nature sketches, and perhaps the two little moonshines, in which, I think, there was more look of light than I got before; and less of my wonted outrageousness than in the "Ruth" or "Deluge".'

Without Blake it is hardly surprising that some of his despair should show in his work. There are superb exceptions however. In *The Magic Apple Tree* we cannot help feeling that Palmer was at the apogee of his innately optimistic nature. The hill now shines in the background with a mystical light, a light not of sunset but dawn and the lane leads us down to the church whose spire leaps joyfully toward this golden revelation dotted and richly textured with sheep and herbage complementing the fruit weighing down the tree below which droop about the spire, for the handling of space and the placing of forms is so ambiguous as to suggest that this is what in fact is happening. The small, dark green tree on the right of the church, for example, which is of a size and placing that convinces us it is actually near

60 *Old Barn*, *c.*1829 (Private Collection)

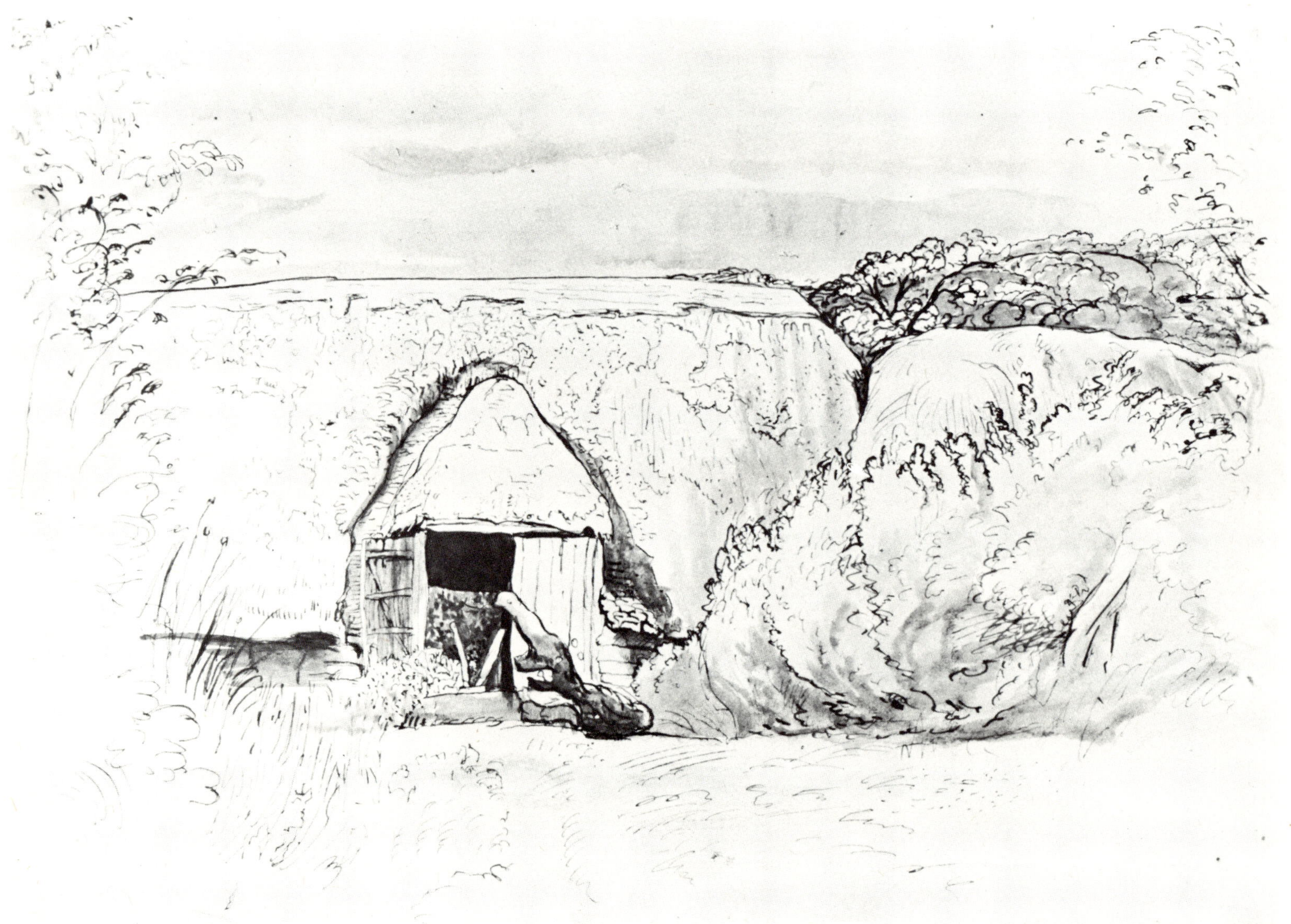

the church, overlaps the lower boughs of the apple tree whose trunk is placed in the middle distance and much nearer than the church to the picture plane. It is only when the fruit is related to the trunk that it becomes apparent that it is not of such a gigantic size as it would be logical to suppose were it actually by the church. So cleverly has Palmer handled the possibilities of the ambiguity of form and colour that the spectator has to make a definite mental effort to disabuse his eyes of the illusion in order to relate what he sees to the normal world.

Consciously he depicts his religious fervency bearing fruit in creative activity but, more important, subconsciously he has arrived at a distillation of his discernment of cause and effect that he had conceived in 1825 and the joy and virility with which he represents his vision is seen in the freedom with which he handles his medium. For though he may spend his mornings in prayer to summon up the courage to create and suppress the 'horrors', he then goes, with sure pagan instinct, 'out to draw some hops that their fruitful sentiment may be infused into my fingers' and the spectator must make the effort to slough off what he believes he knows of the visual world and accept Palmer's visionary one with all its inconsistencies to allow its 'fruitful sentiment to be infused' into them.

That *The Magic Apple Tree* marks the height of Palmer's powers at this time can readily be seen if it is compared to two others *Pastoral with Horse Chestnut* (*74*) – for which *Shoreham at Twilight* (*87*) another of his sepia and gum works may have been a study, although from the medium used it is more likely a variation on the same theme – and *Old House on the Bank of the Darenth, Shoreham,* (*51*) both painted the following year in a similar medium and with a similar subject but completely lacking the other-worldness that

61 *Landscape at Shoreham*, 1829 (Courtauld Institute, Witt Drawings Collection)

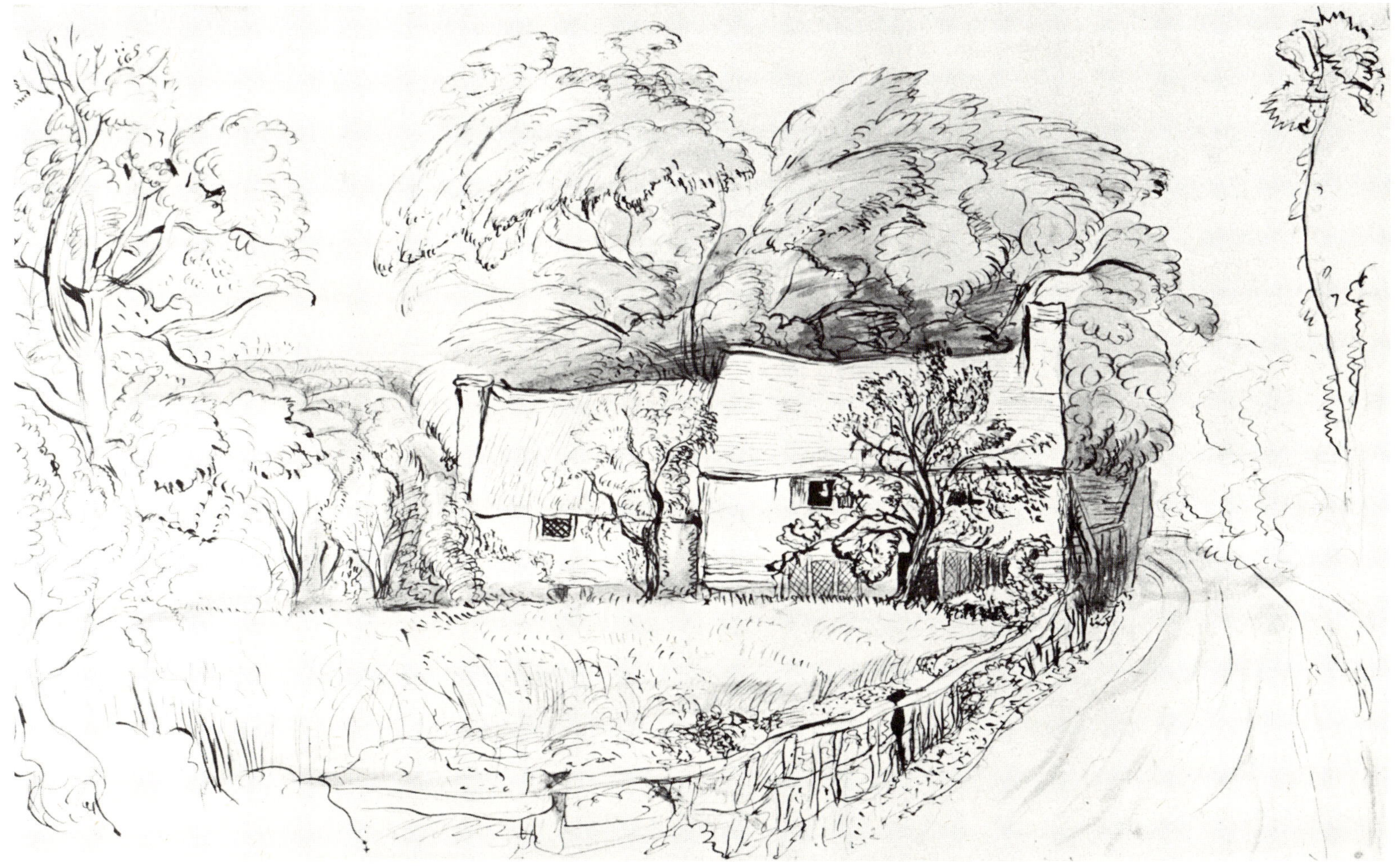

he was able to create in 1830 through his intuitive grasp of the interaction of the parts of a painting.

In the *Old House on the Bank of the Darenth*, although still a beautiful painting especially in its glow of light on the building and through the leaves of the horse-chestnut, can be seen the first real lapse of his visionary powers. The light is purely a representation of what he has observed and the trees have not been passed through 'the intense purifying separating, transmuting heat of the soul's infabulous alchimy'. Neither, in comparison to *Barn in a Valley*, has *The Valley of Vision* (63), one of the drawings done for Linnell, although it contains certain features such as the shadow passing over the hill which helps to retain something of Palmer's intensity. But it is interesting, and may be significant, that it is one of the few drawings in which winter is depicted with snow on the downs in the background. Several other drawings done for Linnell, one of which *The Primitive Cottage* (59) almost rivals *Barn in a Valley*, deserve mention if only for the extremely fine draughtsmanship. They all contain that excess, if only implied, that Palmer loved to portray but in the use of the pen can be detected the impatience that he felt with being bound to a certain naturalism by his patron. Perhaps his impatience is the saving of these drawings for they were obviously done quite quickly and he has not therefore pondered upon the manner of doing but allowed his natural talent for the medium to dictate the result. They have much in common with the style of Van Gogh's drawings that he did in the fervour of his first year at Arles. The corn in *Cornfield* (62) sways with the wind and the roofs of the barns sweep along in unison with the movement. This sympathy for the inanimate and for the furiously growing life around is even more evident in *Landscape at Shoreham* but in *Old Barn* (60) he discovers one of his earlier symbols, the log, which points into the open door of the barn and the movement becomes arrested in cognizance of the event.

62 *Cornfield*, *c.*1829 (Private Collection)

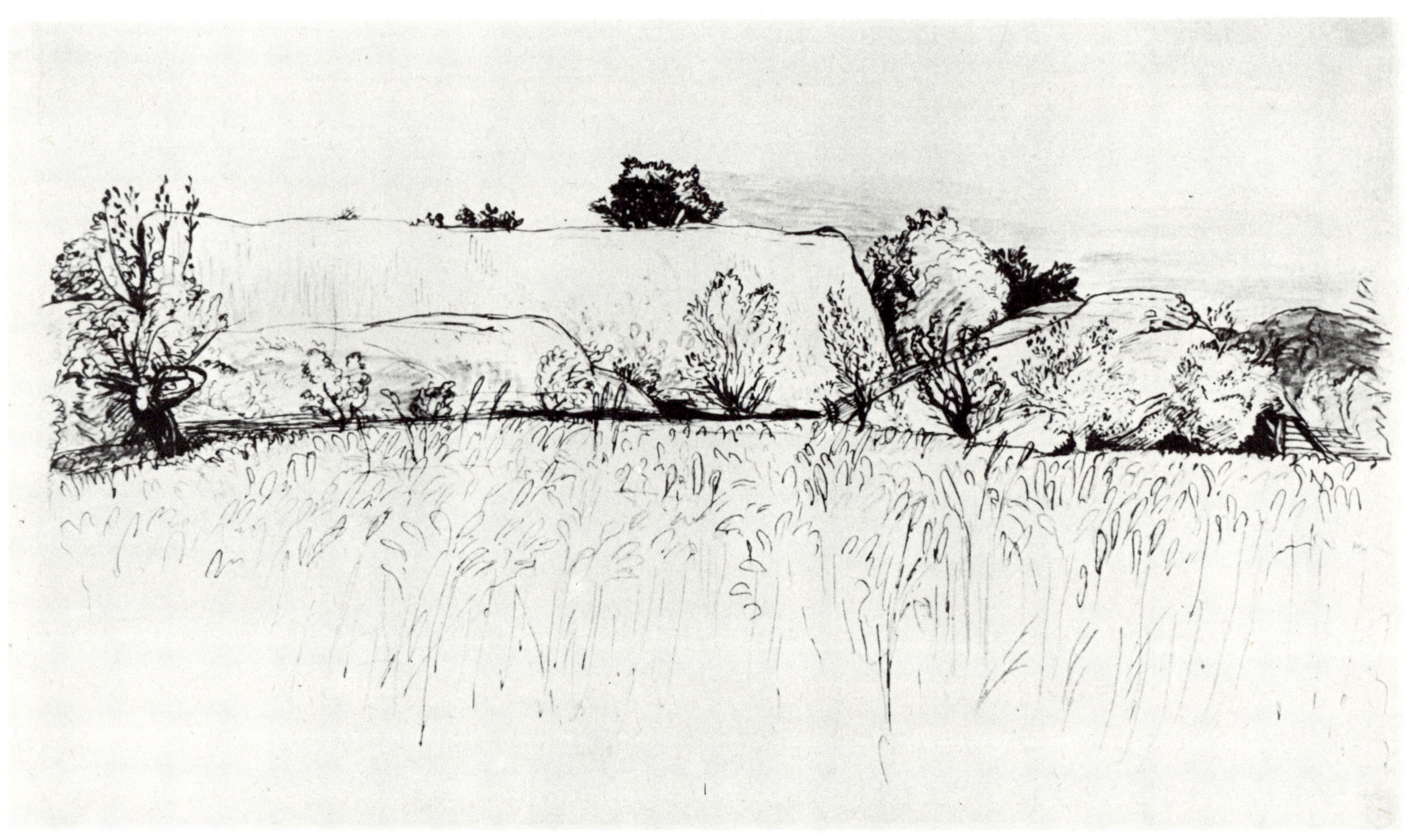

An interesting comparison can be made between the *A Wooded Hillside at Underriver near Sevenoaks, Kent* (*64*) and the same landscape rendered by John Linnell (*65*). It is almost as if their roles had been reversed, with Linnell imparting to Palmer a certain prosaicness while Linnell gains immeasurably from Palmer's adroit execution and use of light, or rather 'darks'. But if the two pictures are examined in more detail it will be realized that, staid as the Palmer appears – for him that is – it betrays none of the slickness that permeates the Linnell, a slickness which becomes in places just shoddy craftsmanship, particularly in the trees clothing the left-hand side of the hill on the left. However, it is just possible that Palmer was influenced to some small extent by Linnell's drawing at this time, perhaps in anxiety to fulfil Linnell's commission to his liking, which may account for the rhythmic quality of some of the work. But how much better Palmer does it, sacrificing none of his integrity as a craftsman.

There is only one painting of these years 1828–29 that bears any true relationship to the works of 1825, *Ruth Returned from Gleaning*, and it is the only one of his extant visionary works where a female figure takes pride of place. The landscape holds many of the ingredients that appear in his earlier work, even to the three pears in *A Rustic Scene*; but in a looser technique. It is the female figure that is the most revealing feature. She is graceful but of monumental stature and carrying an enormous bundle under her left arm she looks down to where a man – Palmer? – in front of a latticed window is reading a book by candlelight. The figure of Ruth has much in common with the female sculptures of Michel Angelo in muscularity and implied physical strength but with the difference that she is much more gentle as shown by the grace of the trailing foot and the manner in which she holds

63 *The Valley of Vision*, 1829/30 (Collection Mr. and Mrs. Paul Mellon)

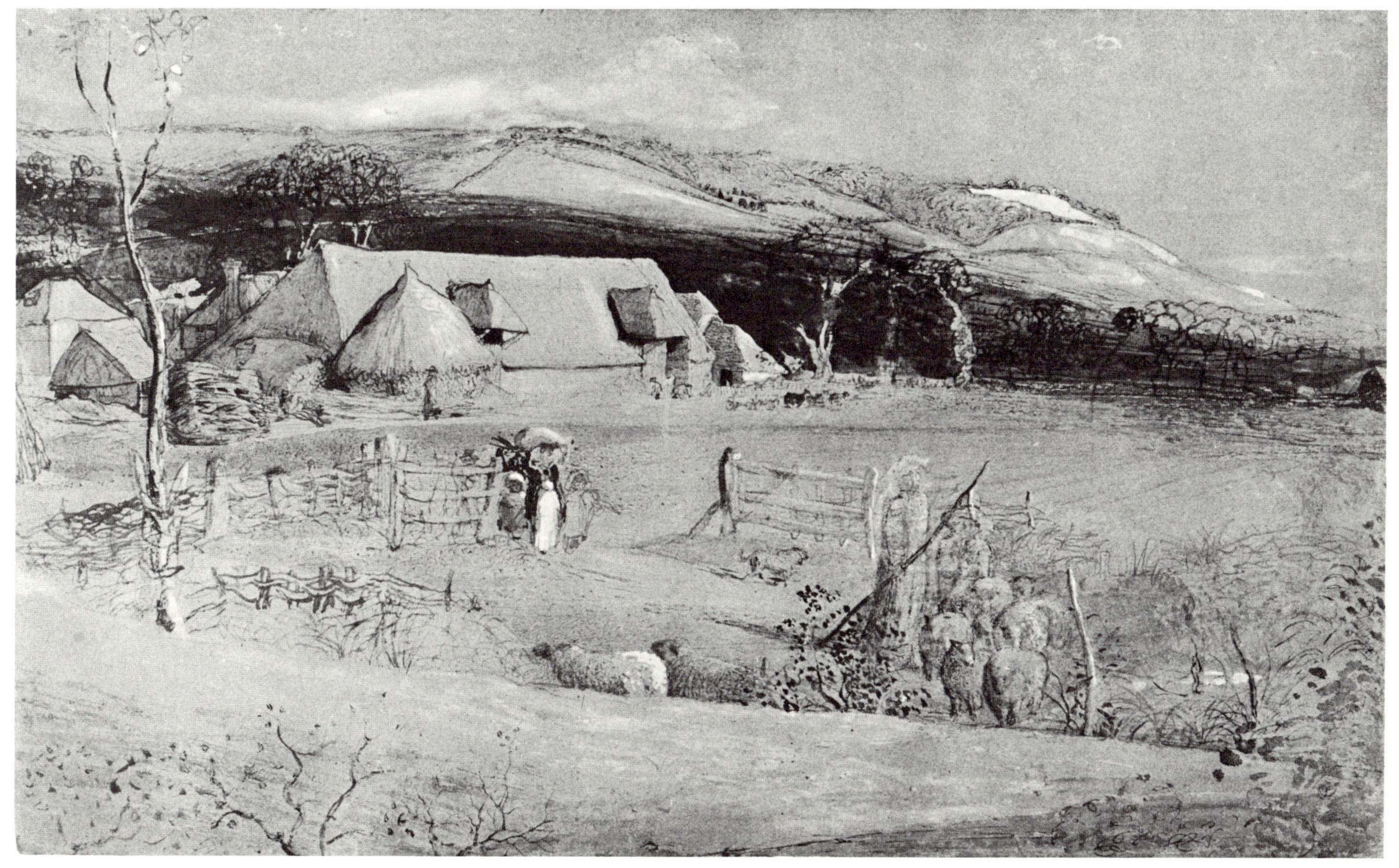

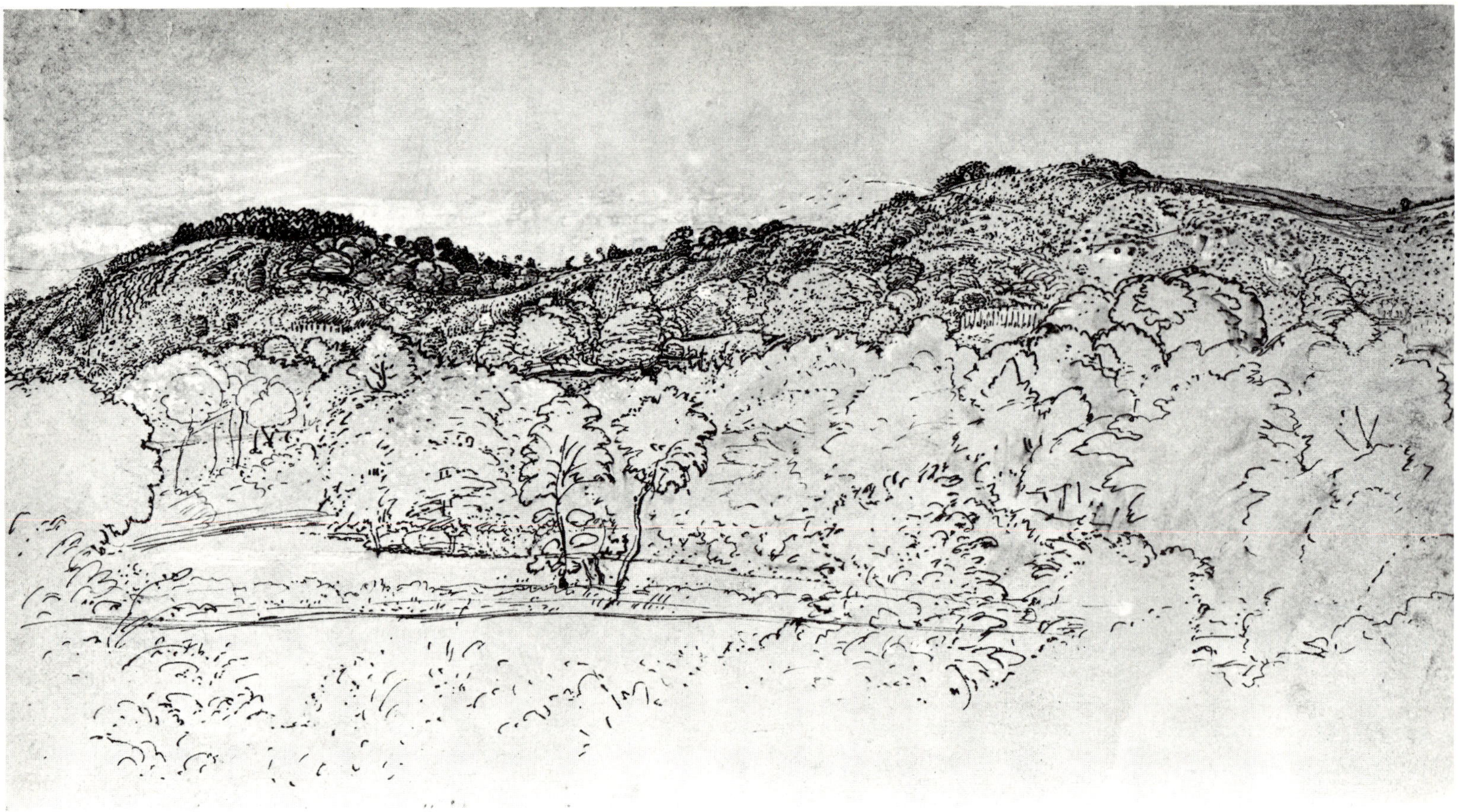

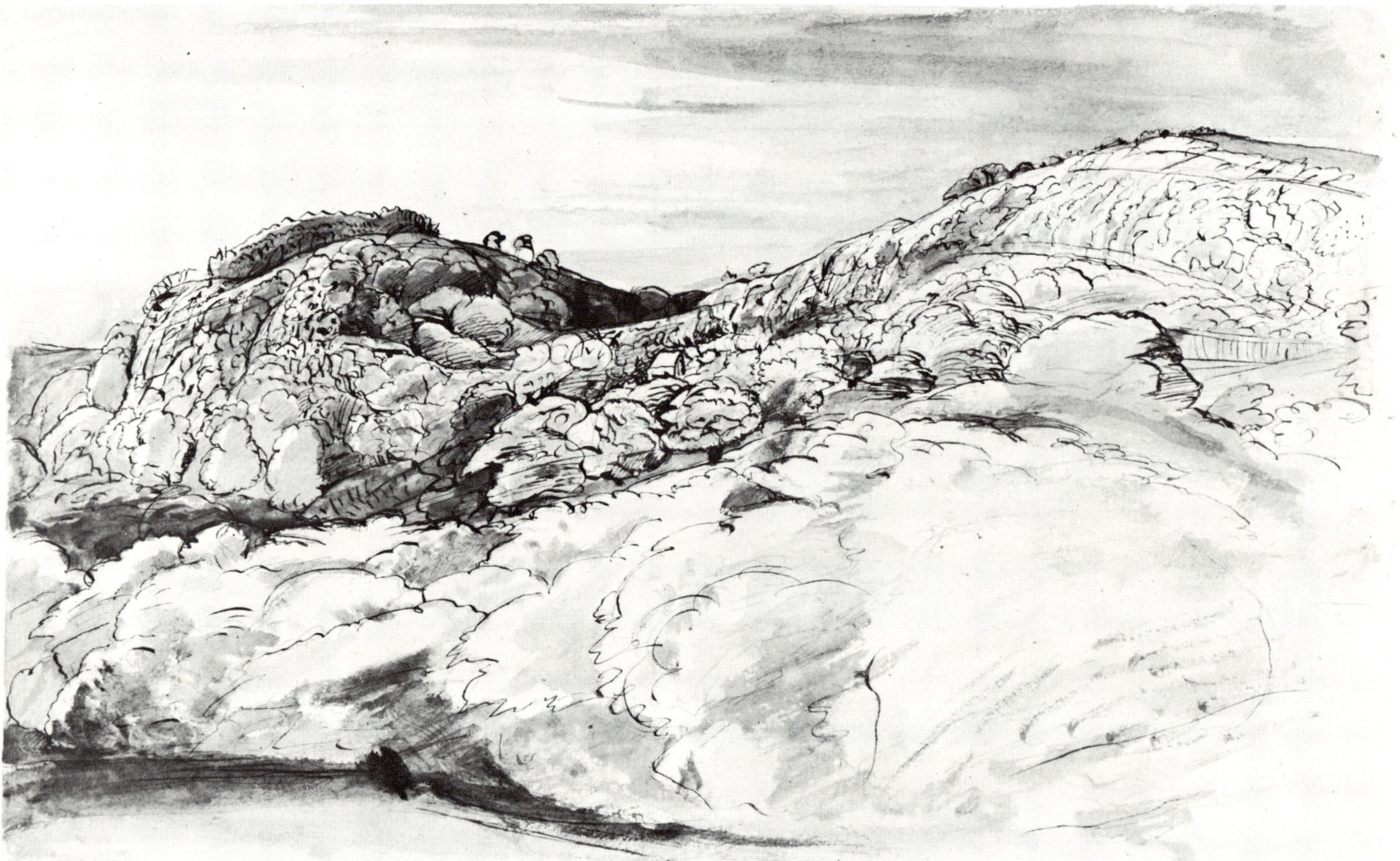

the ash pole in her right hand. The same connotations cannot be applied to Palmer's figure as to Michel Angelo's. Palmer could have been in awe of women to a slight degree but here Ruth signifies the wife he was looking for, who would be able to look after him and be strong enough to relieve him of the burden of everyday existence. The strength with which she is shown does not necessarily denote physical strength but in the visual arts it is a means which may have to be adopted of necessity. It is significant that the small figure of the man has the 'guiding' lighted candle and is reading by it – the intellectual pursuit – while to the woman protectively above falls the lot of the provider.

In the same year as the *Ruth* a small study, possibly for a painting he did

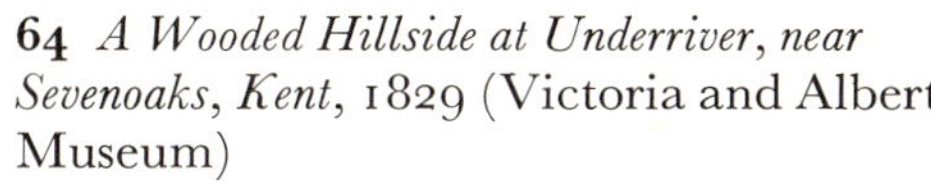

64 *A Wooded Hillside at Underriver, near Sevenoaks, Kent*, 1829 (Victoria and Albert Museum)

65 John Linnell, *At Underriver near Sevenoaks*, 1833 (The Tate Gallery)

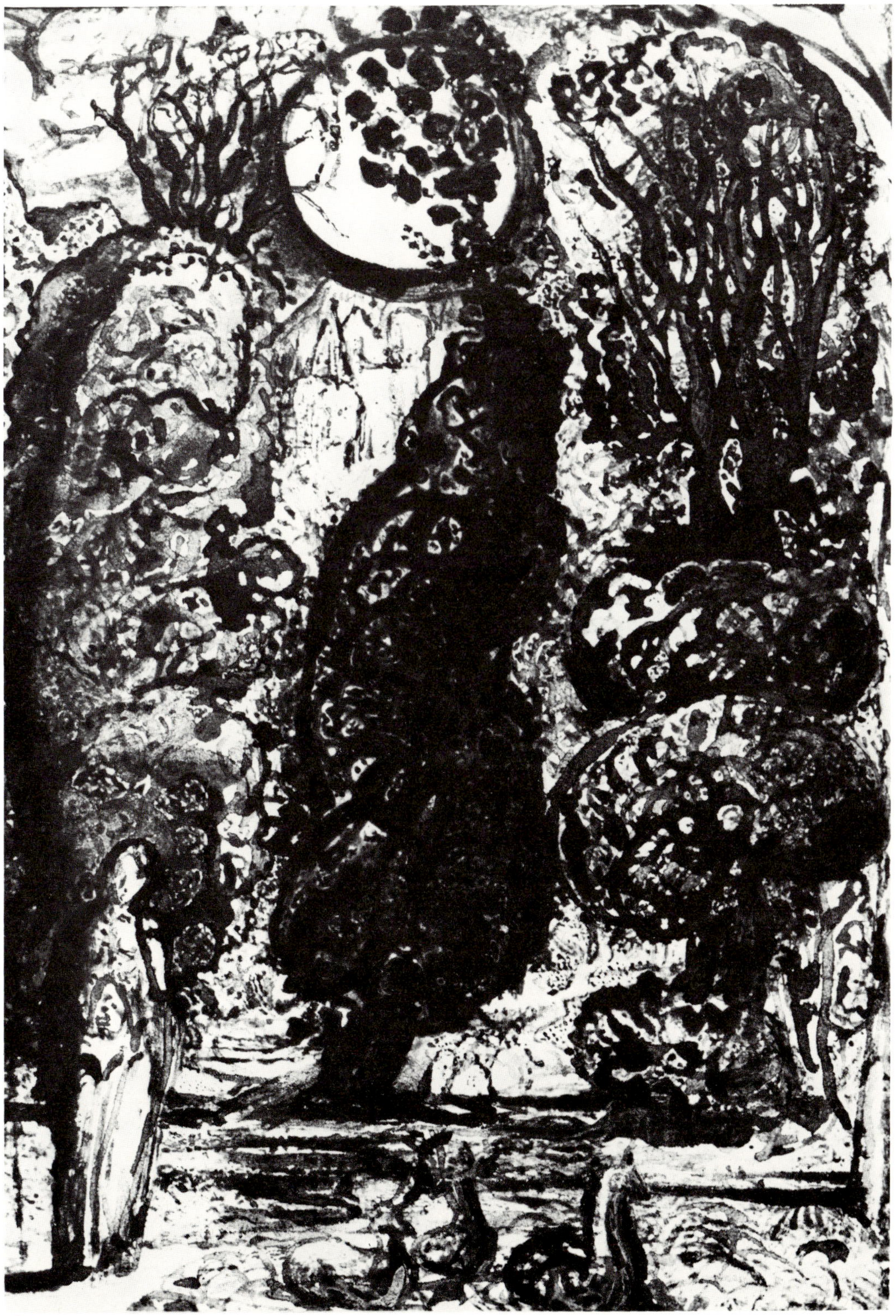

66 *Woman with Full Moon and Deer*, 1829/30 (Victoria and Albert Museum)

not carry out, looks forward to the works of 1830–31. This is the *Woman with Full Moon and Deer* (*66*). The association of the woman with the deer points to Diana and although this cannot be entirely ruled out the real relationship, the pictorial one, is between the figure and the dark tree in the centre, the movement of which she complements in its rhythmic progress toward the full moon which in the last instance it splashes across. The whole work, in spite of its small size, is very intense, far more so than a comparable study *Shepherds under the Full Moon* (*67*) made the following year. Here many of the elements are repeated, the female figure, the mottled sky and the huge full moon. And in the patterning of the foliage across the moon we see the beginnings of his 'blacks' as he later called them, those serene studies of trees spattering a twilight sky.

Although there is little evidence from his letters of what was happening in Palmer's life in 1830, agitation for the Reform Bill was creating a far from untroubled political and social atmosphere and this may have had the effect of causing Palmer to work with greater fervour, accounting for the quality of the work he produced in 1830. Certainly it has an incredible intensity that could only be achieved by bringing to bear great powers of concentration. The pictures are not highly finished; the use of pen and brush has an extraordinary liveliness and they look as if nothing could go wrong, every mark is in just the right place with the correct weight and depth of tone, the right degree of tension and stress in the architecture of the picture and a nicety of balance between areas of hard and soft qualities, texture, pattern and the relieving features of the tranquil, transparent shadows that allow the eye to travel through the carefully controlled space that can only be achieved when an artist is in complete empathy with his creation. One in particular, *A Village Church Among Trees*, exhibits these qualities to the degree that I can

67 *Shepherds under the Full Moon*, *c.*1830 (Ashmolean Museum)

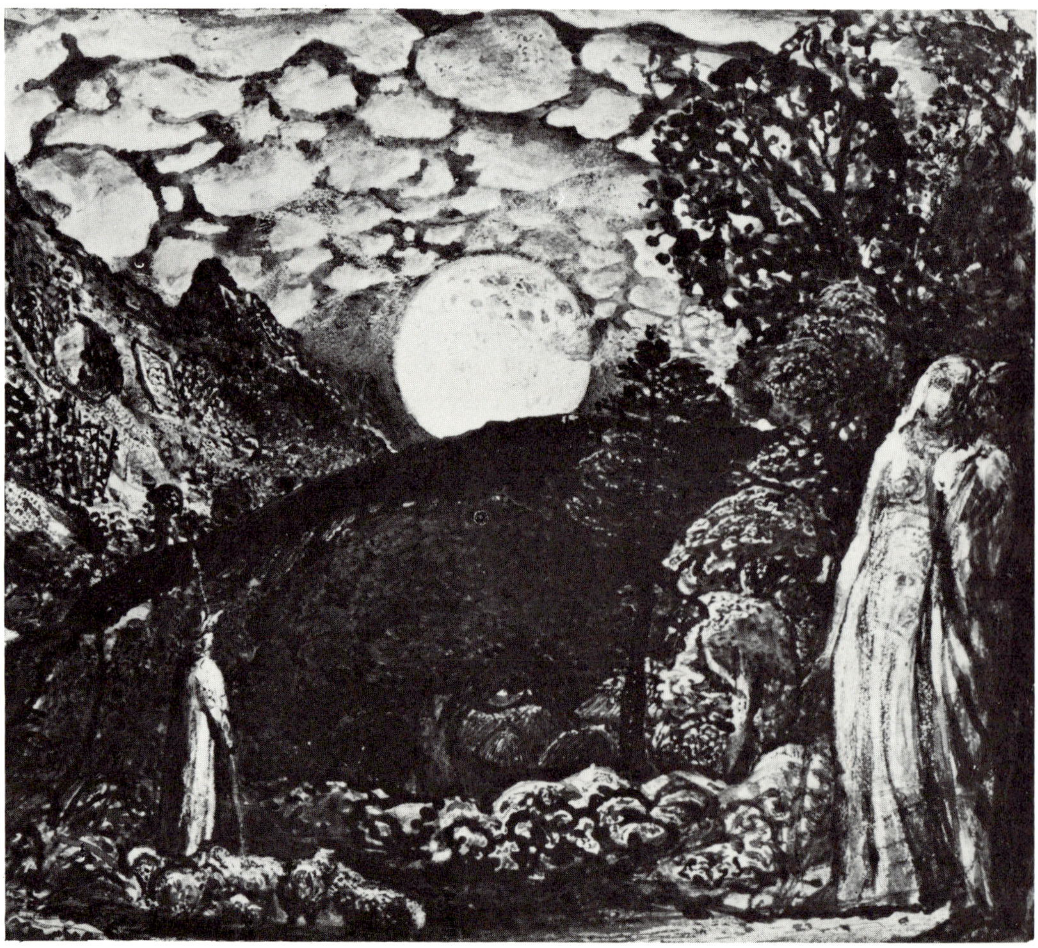

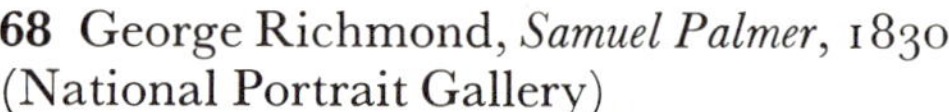

68 George Richmond, *Samuel Palmer*, 1830 (National Portrait Gallery)

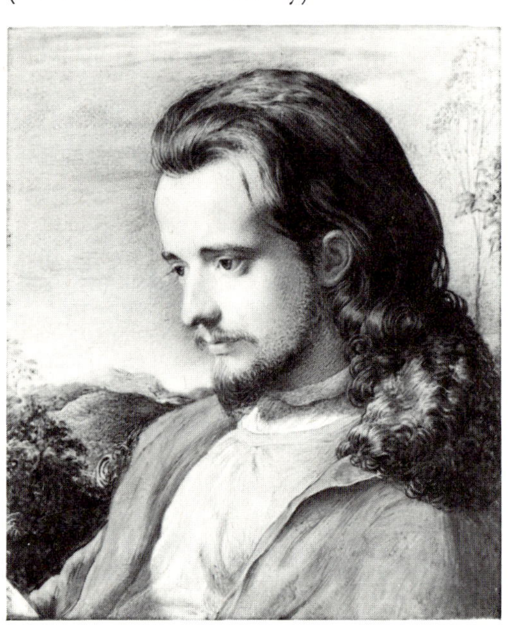

think of no other painter of landscape who has been able to achieve simultaneously so powerful a sense of serenity and excitement. Although very few moons appear in this series of small monochrome paintings, moonlight is evident in both *Cornfield and Church by Moonlight* (69) and *Church Among Trees*, linking them directly with the great elm in moonlight he experienced when he was four years old. Remarkable evidence of how he could hold an image in his mind for many years without dilution of the excitement he originally felt. His symbolism has been reduced to the minimum, apart from the richness and profusion of the trees, we are left with only the corn and church spire. But in *Cornfield and Church by Moonlight* one of the figures, all of whom face the path leading to the church, holds up a sheaf of corn in salutation to the spire.

After this outburst of energy in 1830 a calmer, more sedate series of works ensue, the serenity is still there but the furious growth of the trees which began with the *Woman with Full Moon and Deer* and reached its climax in *A Village Church Among Trees* has been expended. There is an attempt at revival in the water-colour *The Harvest Moon* (79) but even though the figures work furiously, urged on by the enormous moon, it has the appearance of too

69 *Cornfield and Church by Moonlight*, *c.*1830 (Private Collection)

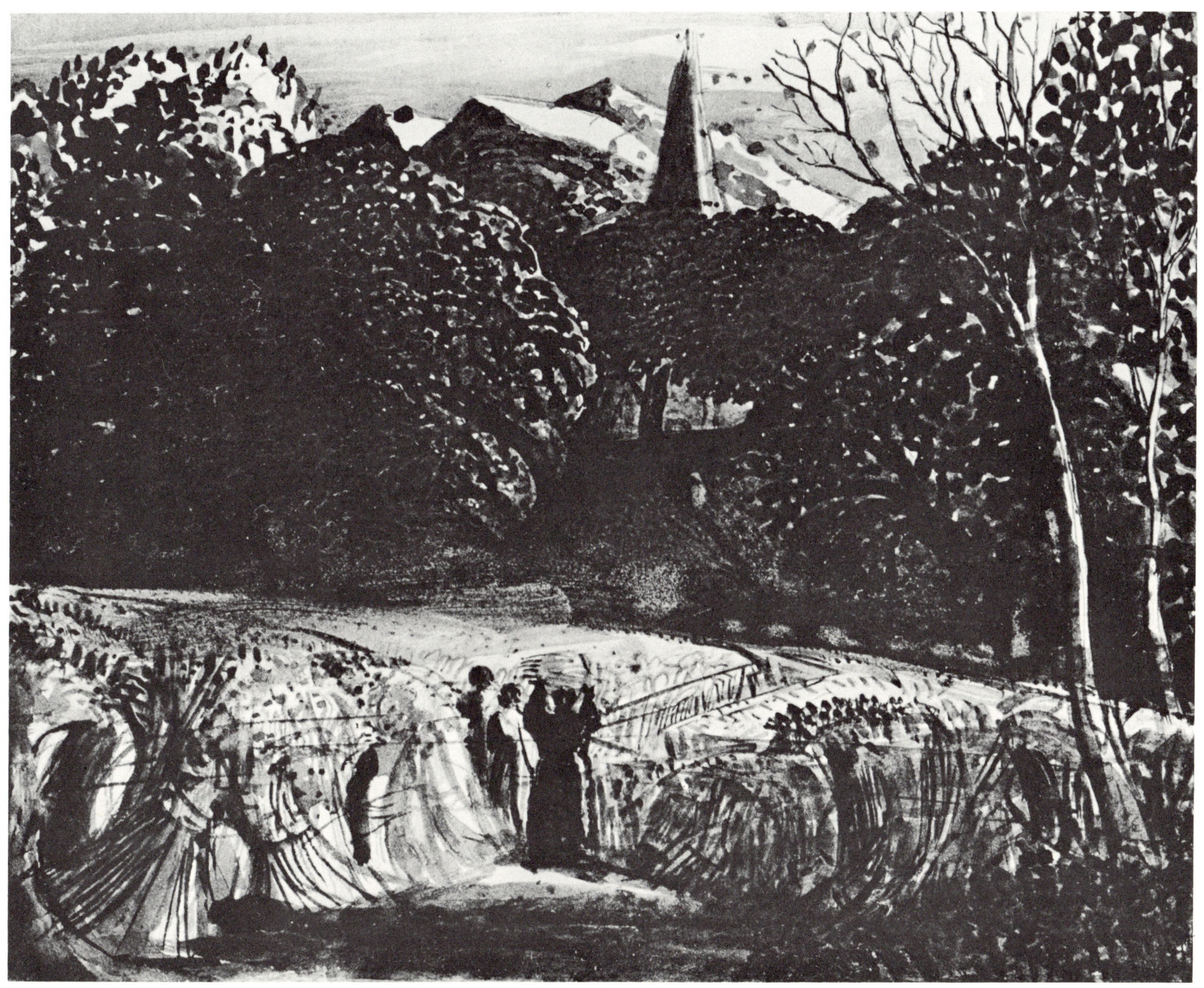

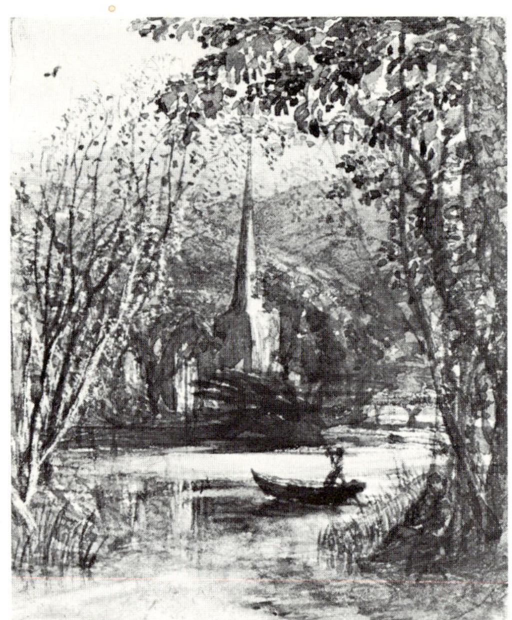

70 *A Church with a Bridge and a Boat*, *c.*1830 (Ashmolean Museum)

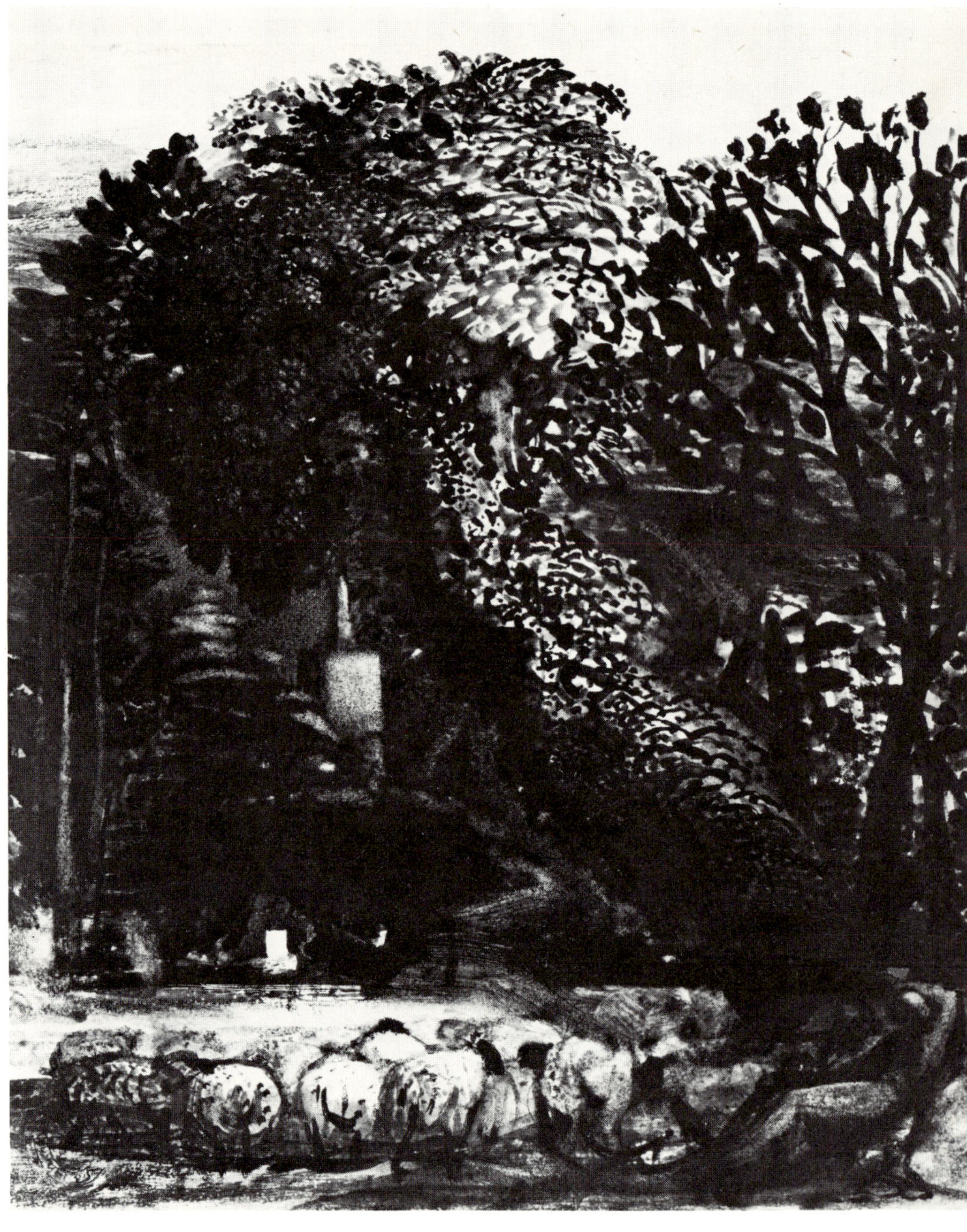

71 *A Village Church among Trees*, 1830 (Victoria and Albert Museum)

conscious an effort. Rather slight and also very small is *A Church with a Bridge and a Boat* (*70*) but it is, nevertheless, imbued with the same innate calm that is the major charm of the work he did in 1831. The soft effulgence of light, the cessation of activity – even the trees seem to be resting – is all there in embryo in this tiny brush drawing. It is in this set of sepia and indian ink drawings that a feature appears that has been seen only once before, in *A Village Church among Trees*. This is the lighted cottage window shining out in *Cornfield*, *Shoreham at Twilight*, *The Folded Flock* and *The Flock and the Star* (*76*), gentle precursors of the dazzling beam in the landscape study (*93*) he was to do in 1834. Palmer's attention has shifted; in none of these three works does the moon appear, and when it does as in *Moonlight, a Landscape with Sheep* (*86*), the cottage light is absent.

He was becoming even lonelier at this time, his father was very rarely at Shoreham and his brother had gone, Arthur Tatham was ordained, and Richmond was busy with a wife and child; he still kept monthly contact with Francis Finch and Edward Calvert, but Welby Sherman and Henry Walter were the only ones of 'The Ancients' who were free to stay any length of time

OPPOSITE
72 *The Magic Apple Tree*, 1830 (Fitzwilliam Museum)

OVERLEAF
73 *A Pastoral Scene*, 1835 (Ashmolean Museum)

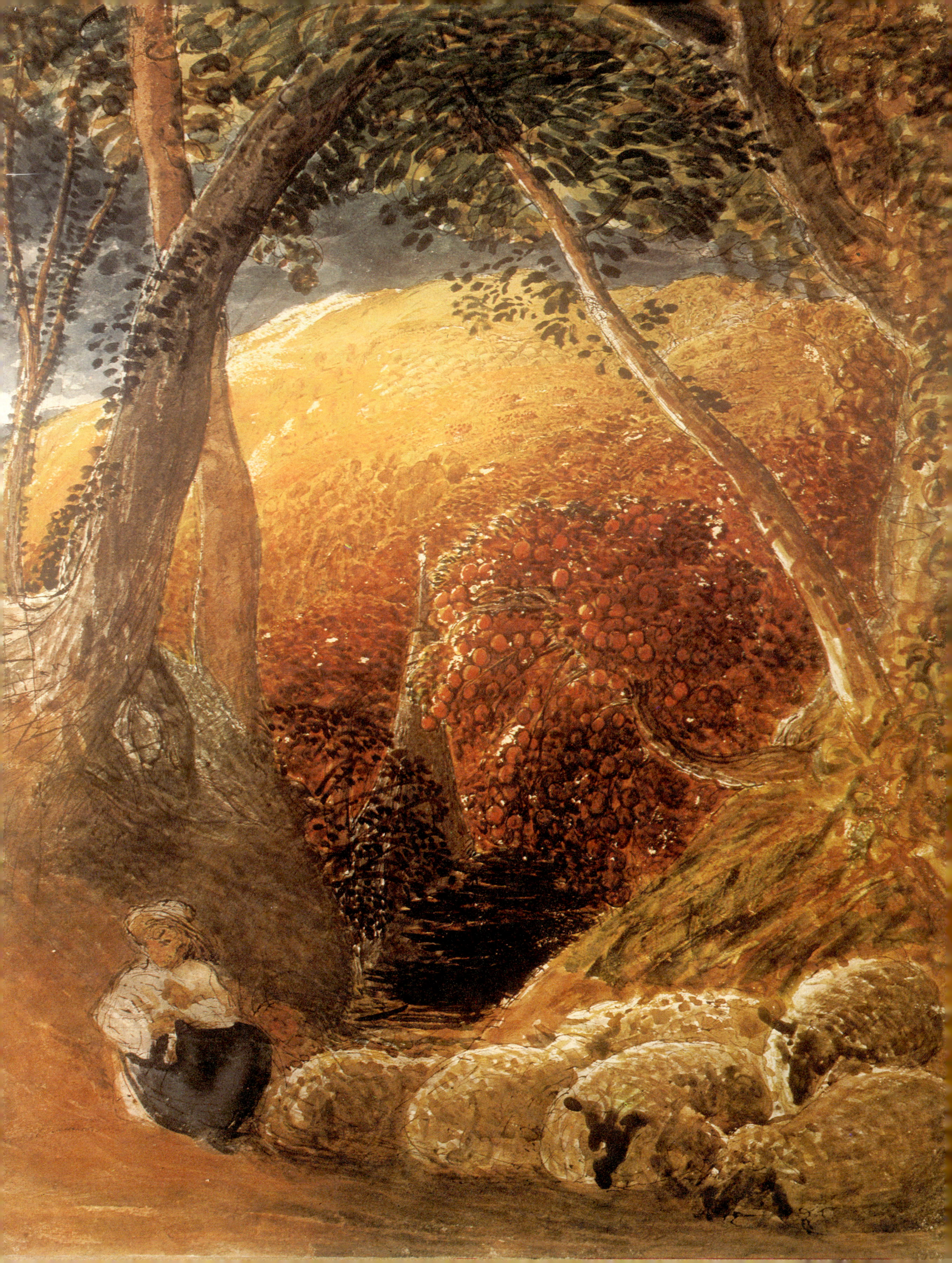

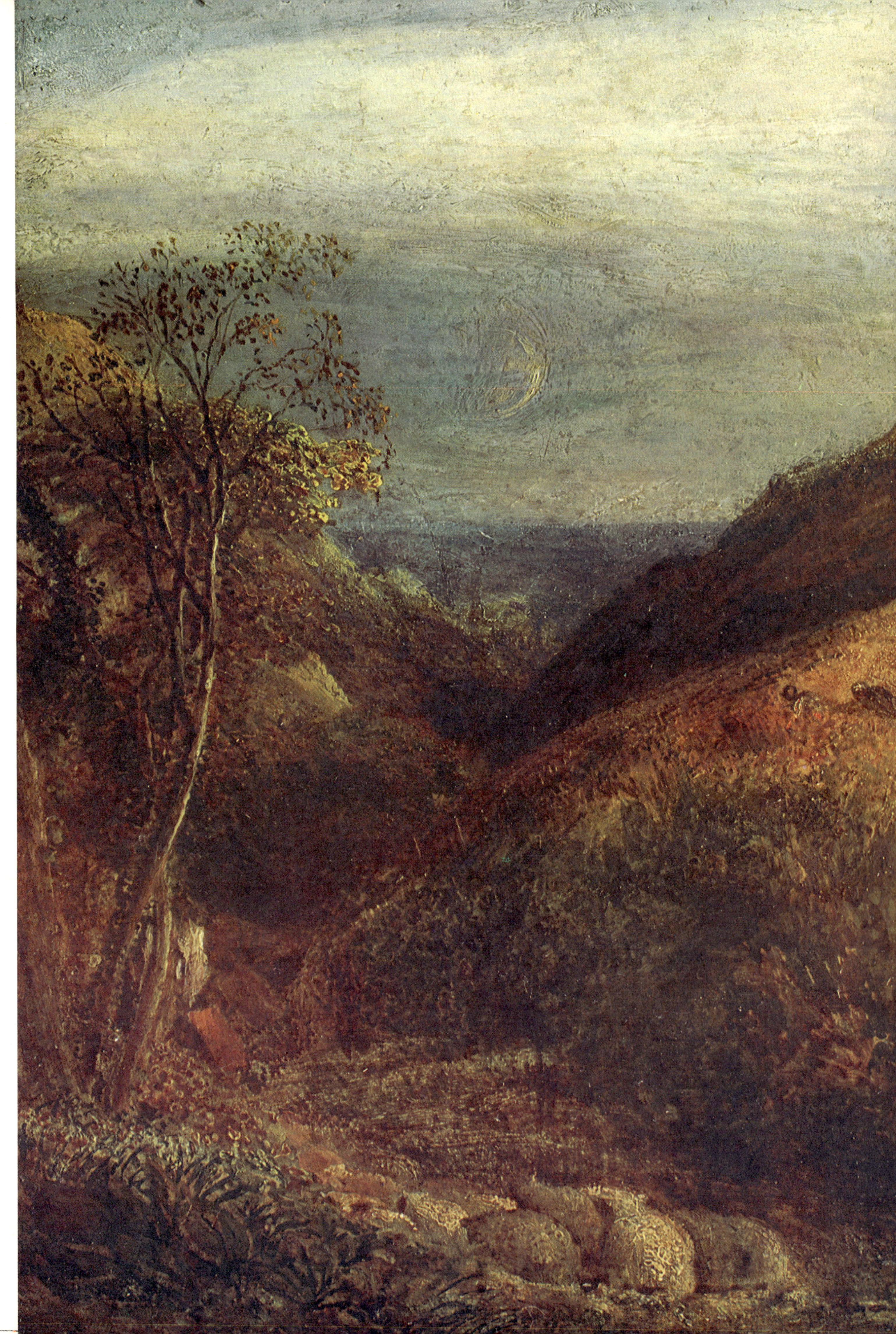

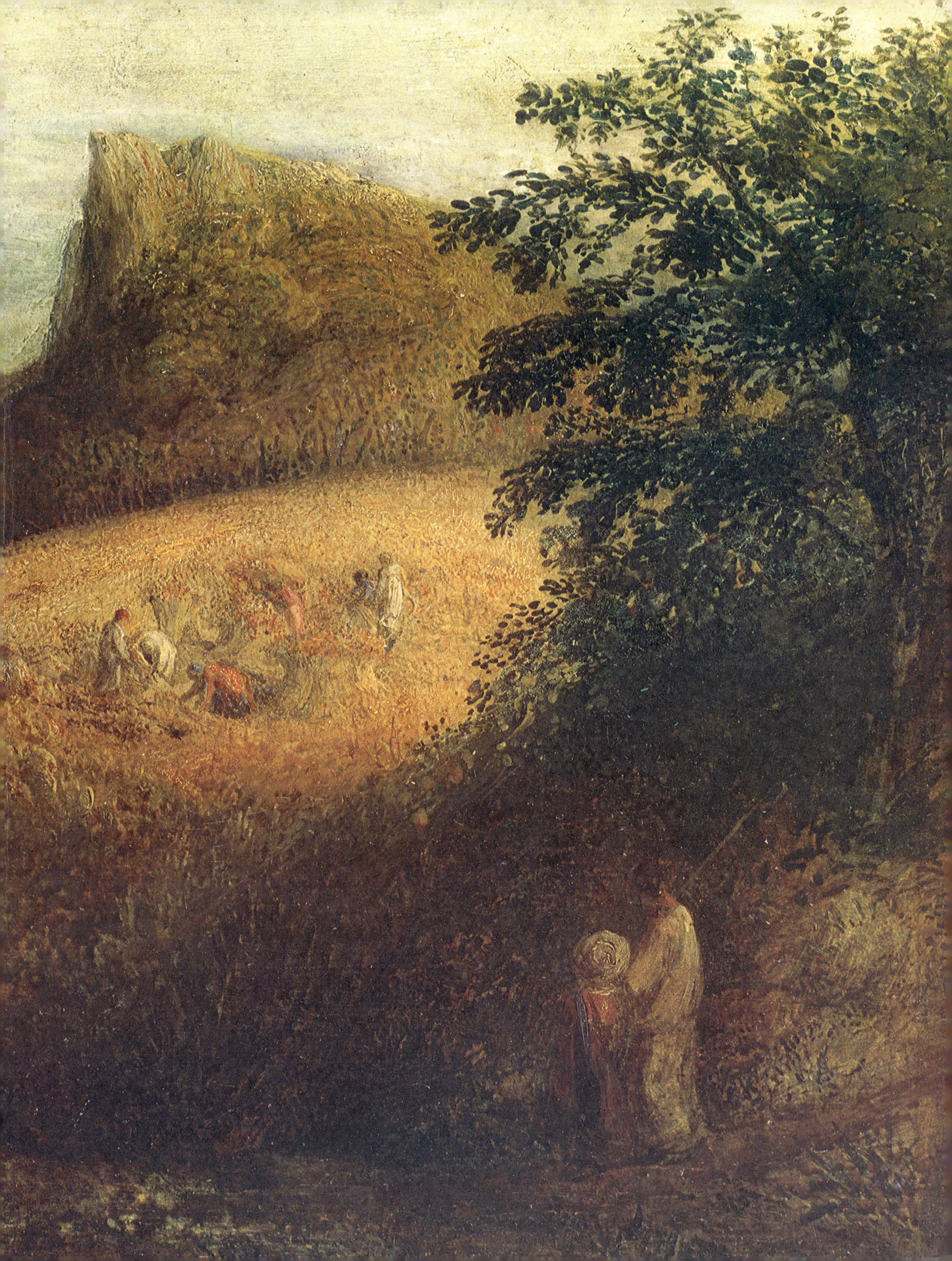

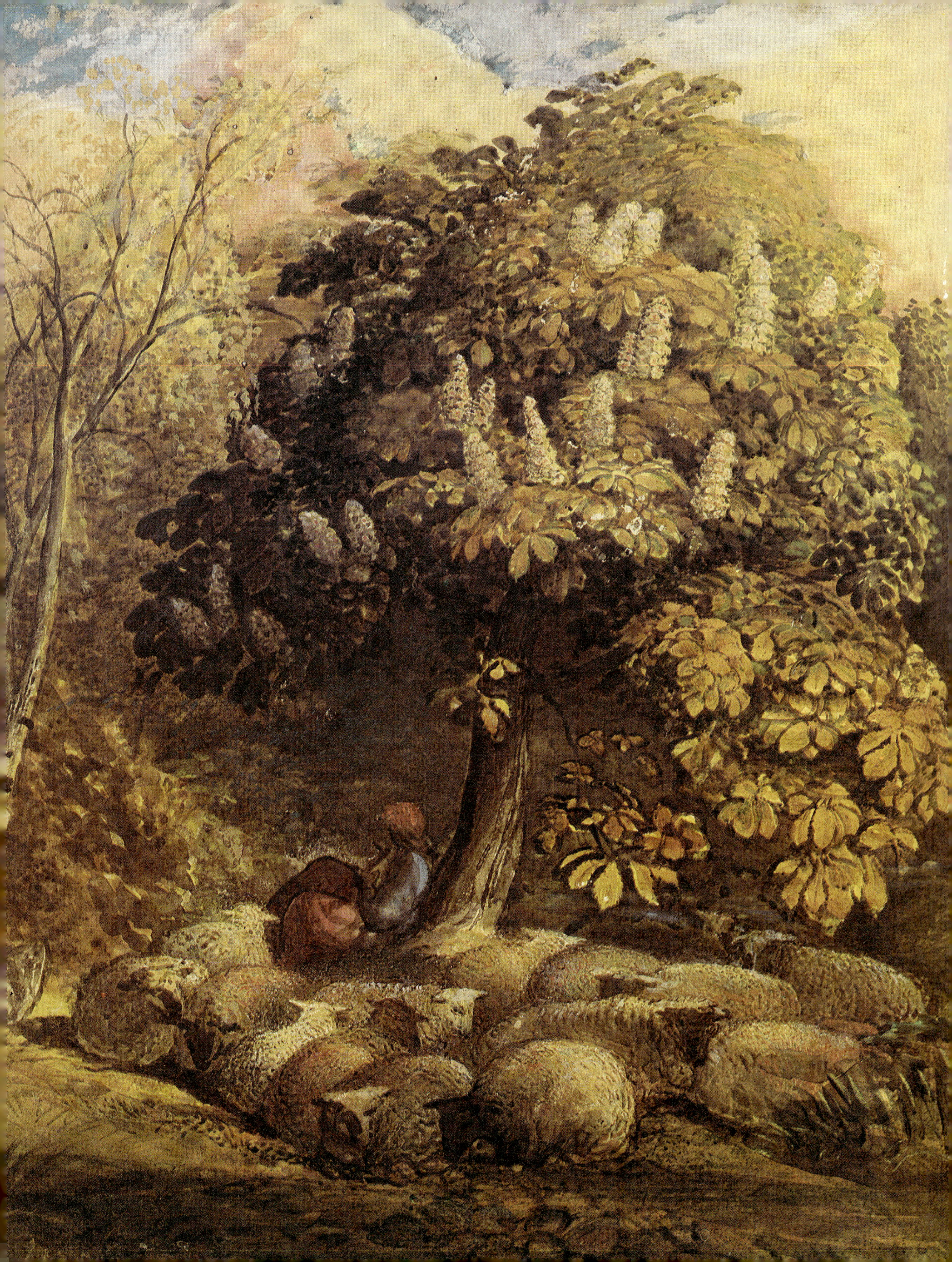

OPPOSITE
74 *Pastoral with Horse Chestnut*, 1831/2 (Ashmolean Museum)

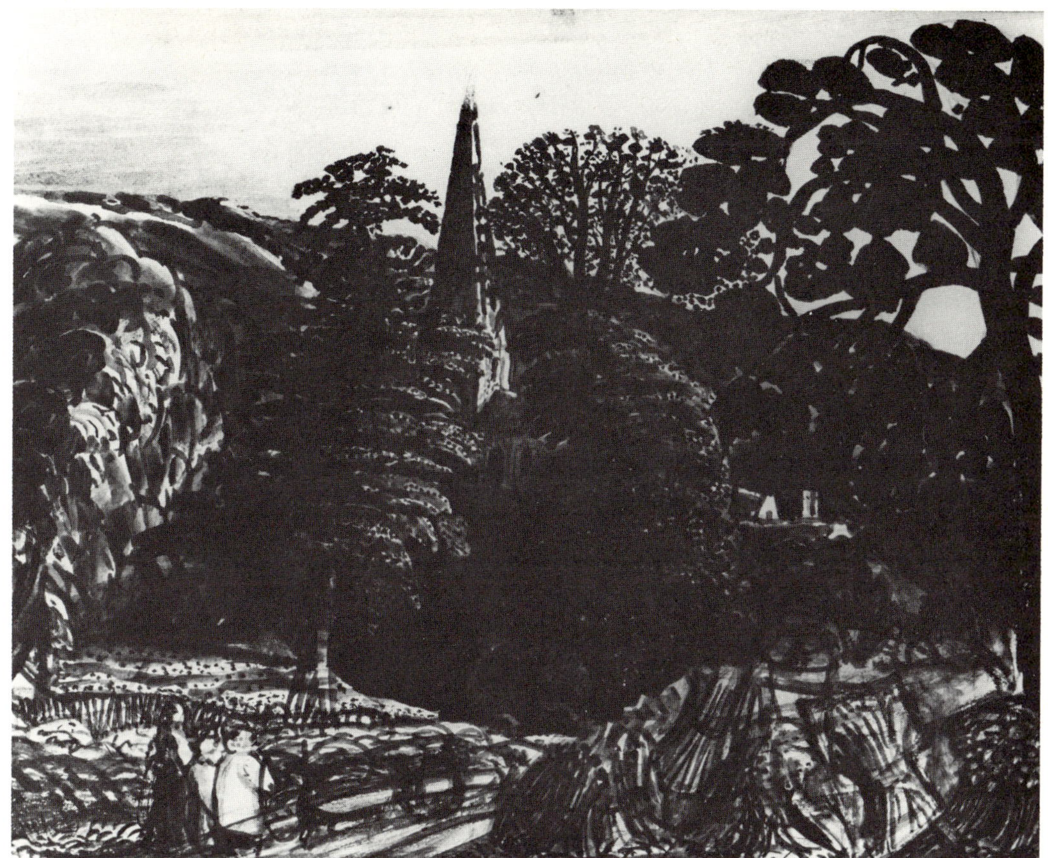

75 *Evening: A Church among Trees*, c.1830 (The Tate Gallery)

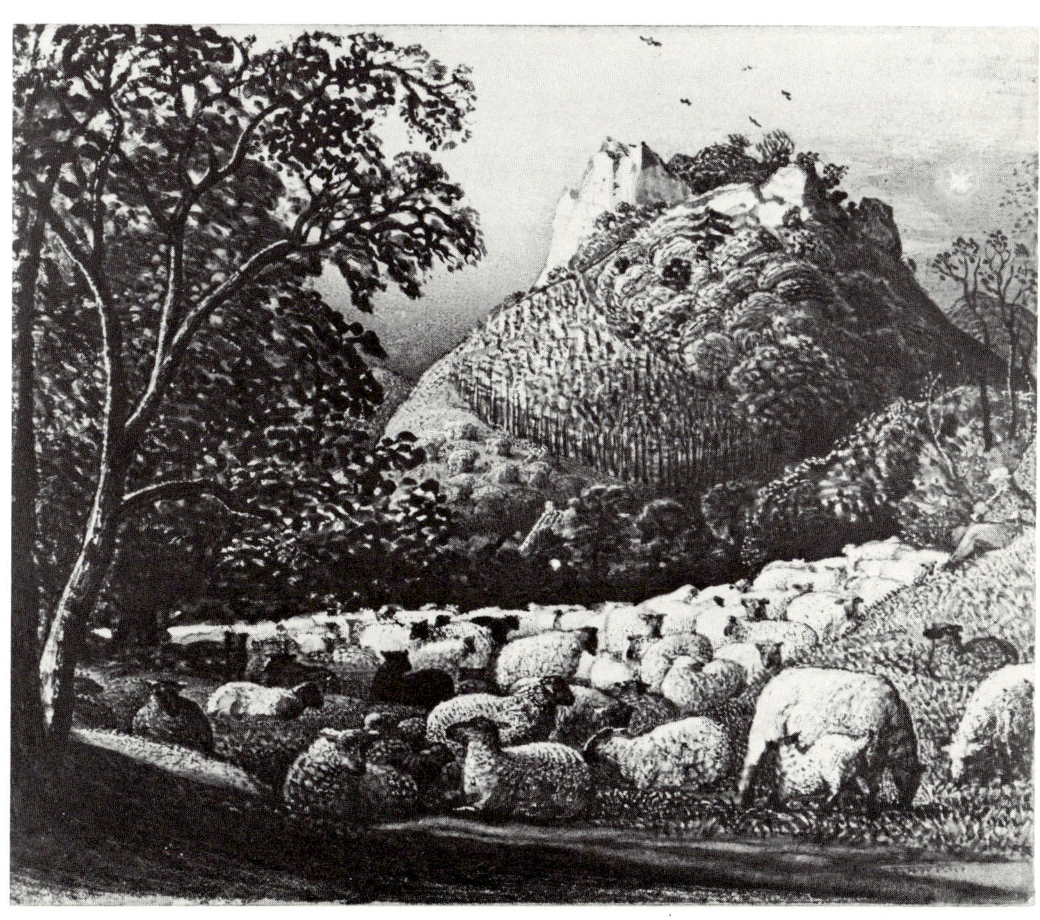

76 *The Flock and the Star*, 1831/2 (Ashmolean Museum)

at Shoreham. The idea of a wife must have seemed even more attractive and it is reflected in these drawings by this shift of the moon to the lighted window, Palmer equating wife with home. These drawings are also much more 'finished' than the ones immediately preceeding them. Having, as it were, used up the energies of his sexual naggings he is able to work in quiet concentration upon the sheep in *The Flock and the Star* and *The Folded Flock* and the stooks of corn in *Cornfield and Shoreham at Twilight*. But in *Moonlight, a Landscape with Sheep* the moon again makes her appearance.

Palmer was to do much painting over the next few years even if by the end of 1835 his visionary powers were seriously declining. He was also having more pictures accepted for exhibition – five in the Royal Academy in 1833,

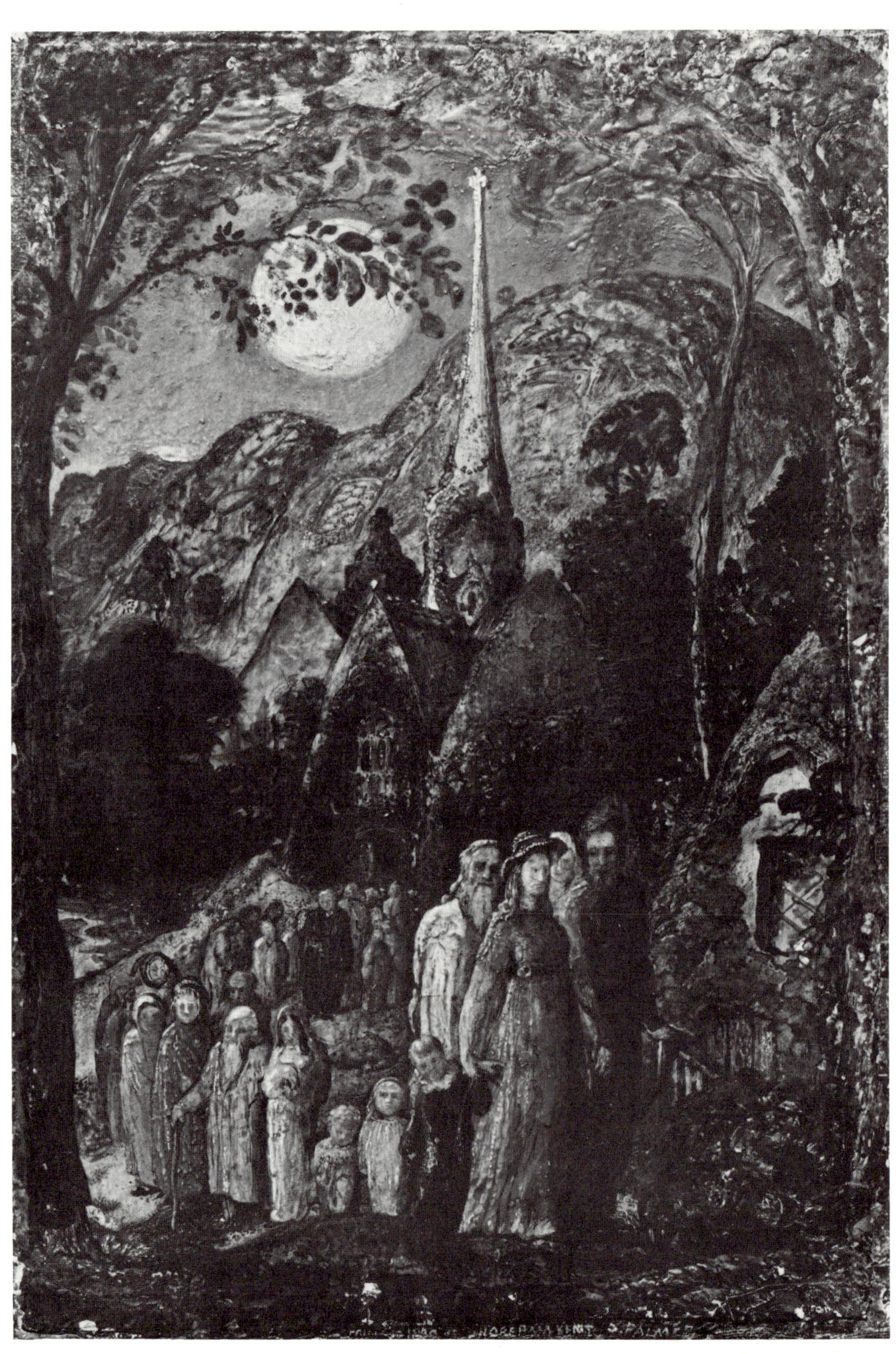

77 *Coming from Evening Church*, 1830 (The Tate Gallery)

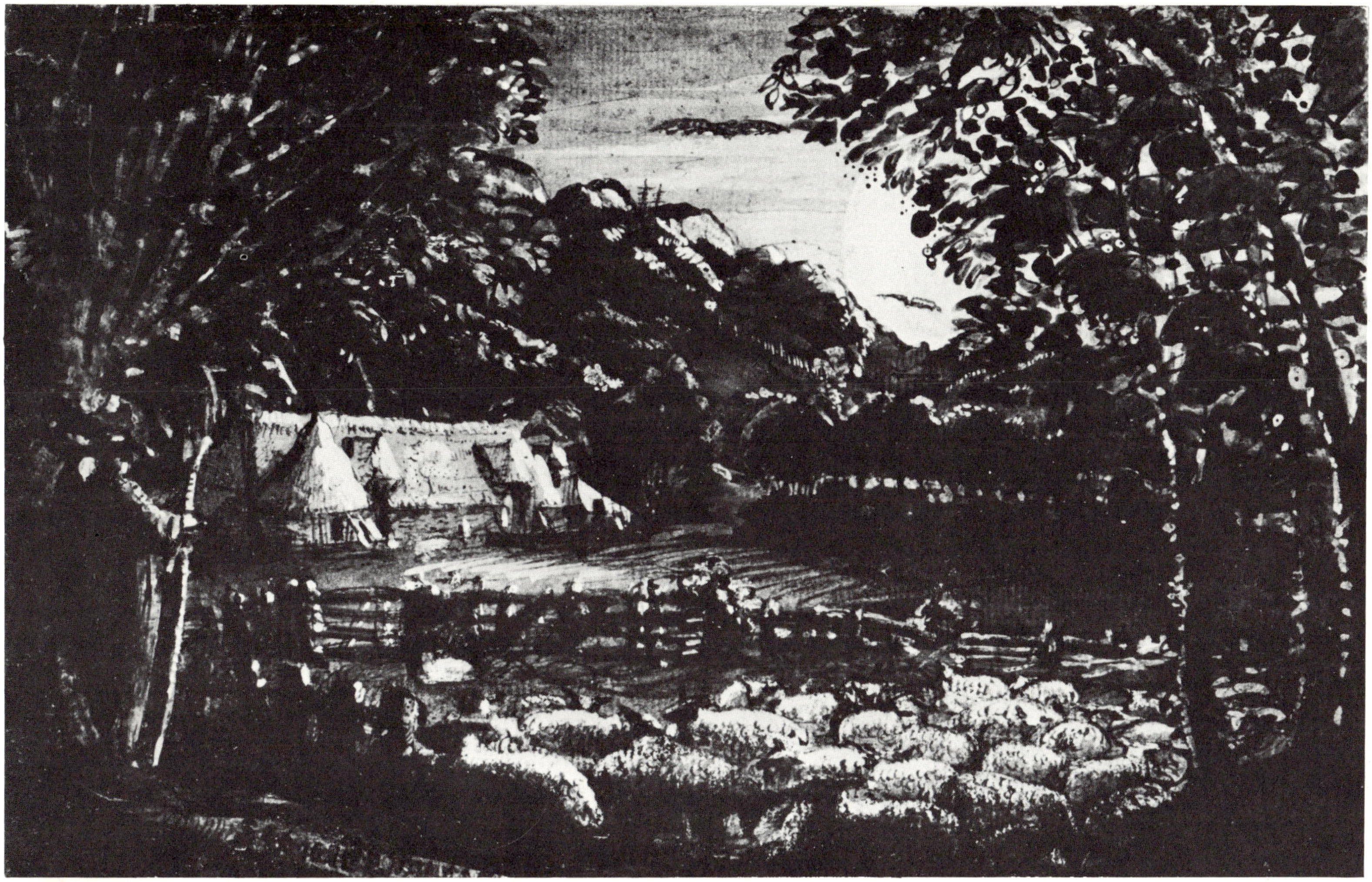

78 *Sepham Barn*, 1831 (Private Collection)

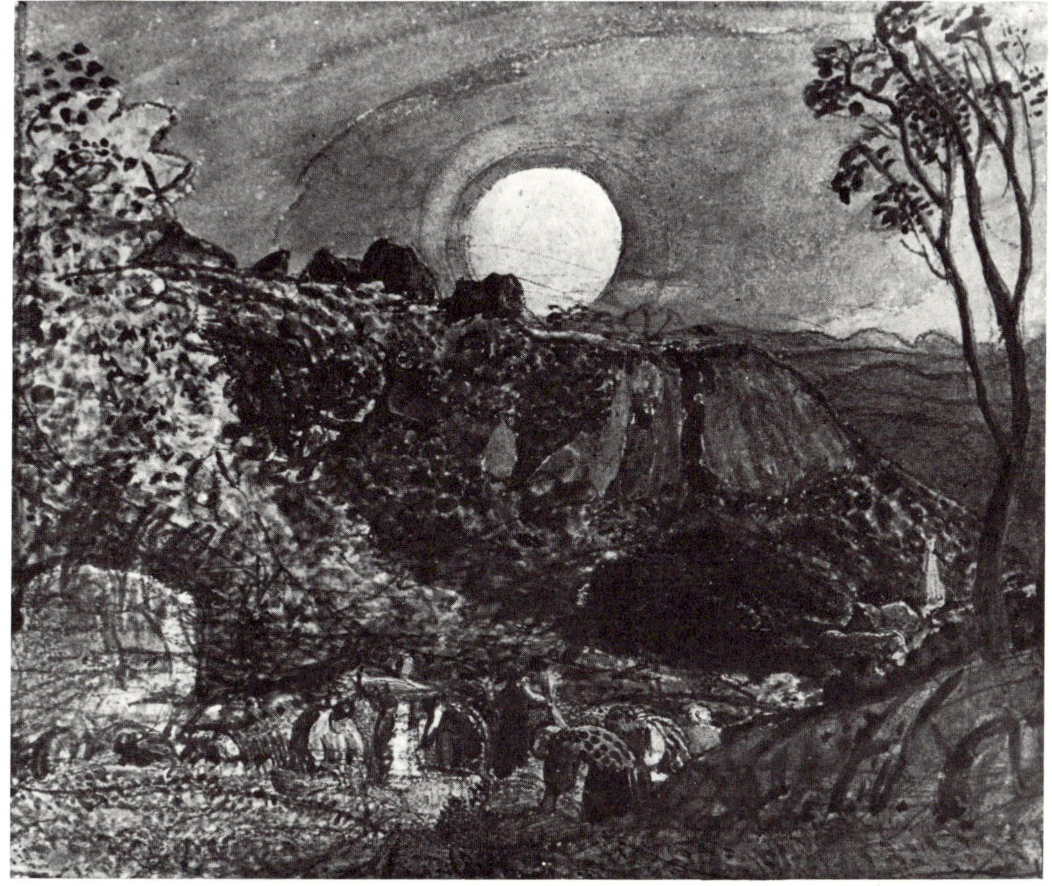

79 *The Harvest Moon*, 1830/31 (Carlisle Museum and Art Gallery)

two in 1835, five in the British Institution in 1834 and four in 1835. Of these only a few, unfortunately remain. By 1832 he had already begun to retire from Shoreham. He had been left another small bequest with which he bought two cottages at Shoreham and also a small house in London, 4 Grove Street, Lissom Grove, the Richmonds, Calvert, Linnell and the Tathams all living quite near, but he did not leave Shoreham altogether and continued to return there occasionally until the autumn of 1834. He was, of course, trying to make some money and to achieve a reputation. A suggestion to Linnell that he might make a living as an engraver had led to his move to Lissom Grove where he was also trying to establish himself as a teacher.

The paintings of this period are difficult to date accurately and it is quite likely he did some of them away from Shoreham relying upon studies he had made when in Kent. A number of them reflect very powerfully his feelings about the changes that were sweeping the country at the time, the series of the 'Bright and White Clouds' being an excellent example. In three of these, drawing for *The Bright Cloud* (*80*), *The Bright Cloud*, and drawing for *The White Cloud* (*81*) can be felt an air of tempestuousness. The trees are no longer moving by their own life force but are being shaken by an outside agency, and over all hangs the thunderous cloud under which the sheep are not merely resting but are huddled in apprehension.

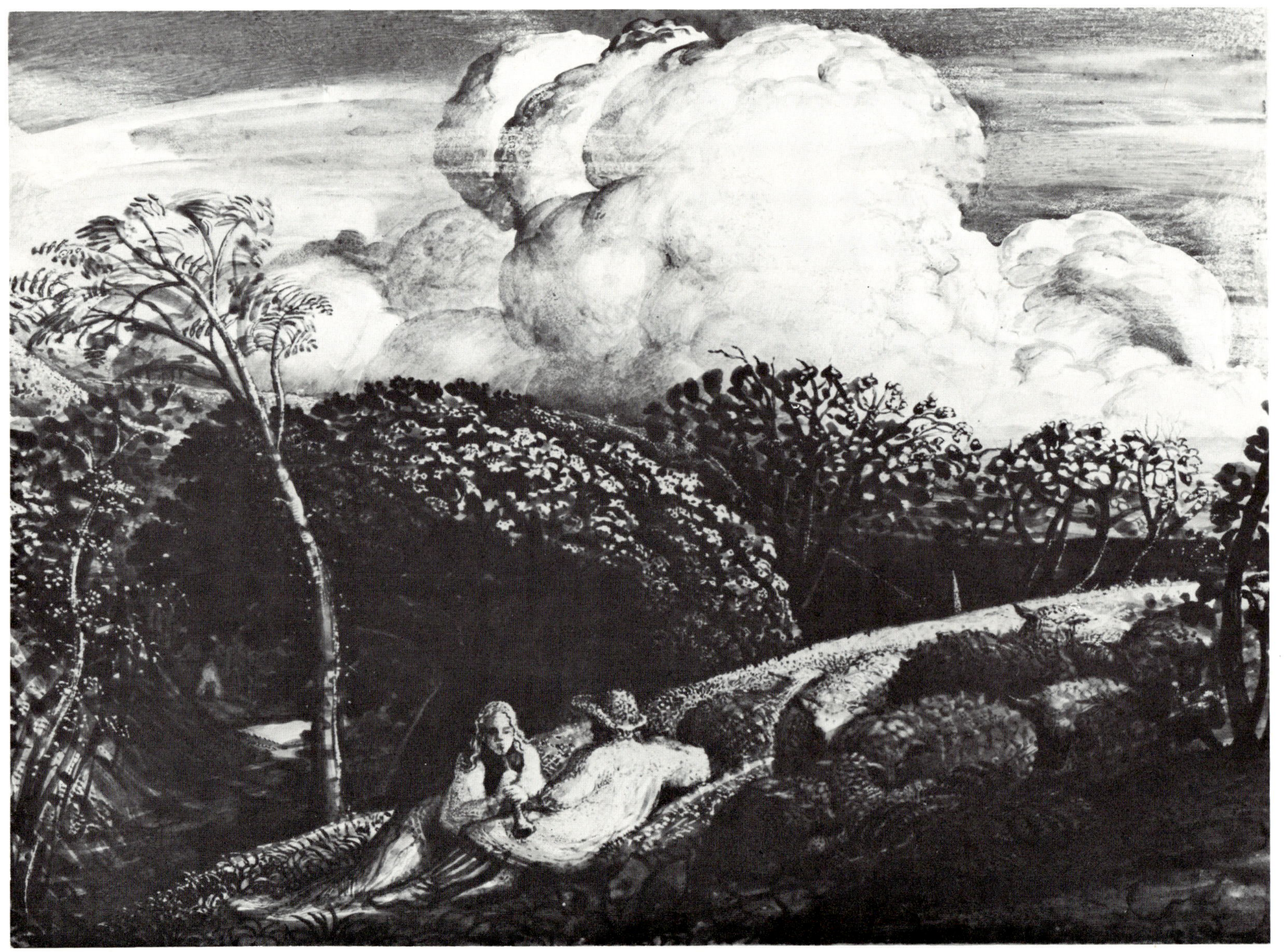

80 Drawing for *The Bright Cloud*, 1831/2 (The Tate Gallery)

81 Drawing for *The White Cloud*, 1831/2
(Ashmolean Museum)

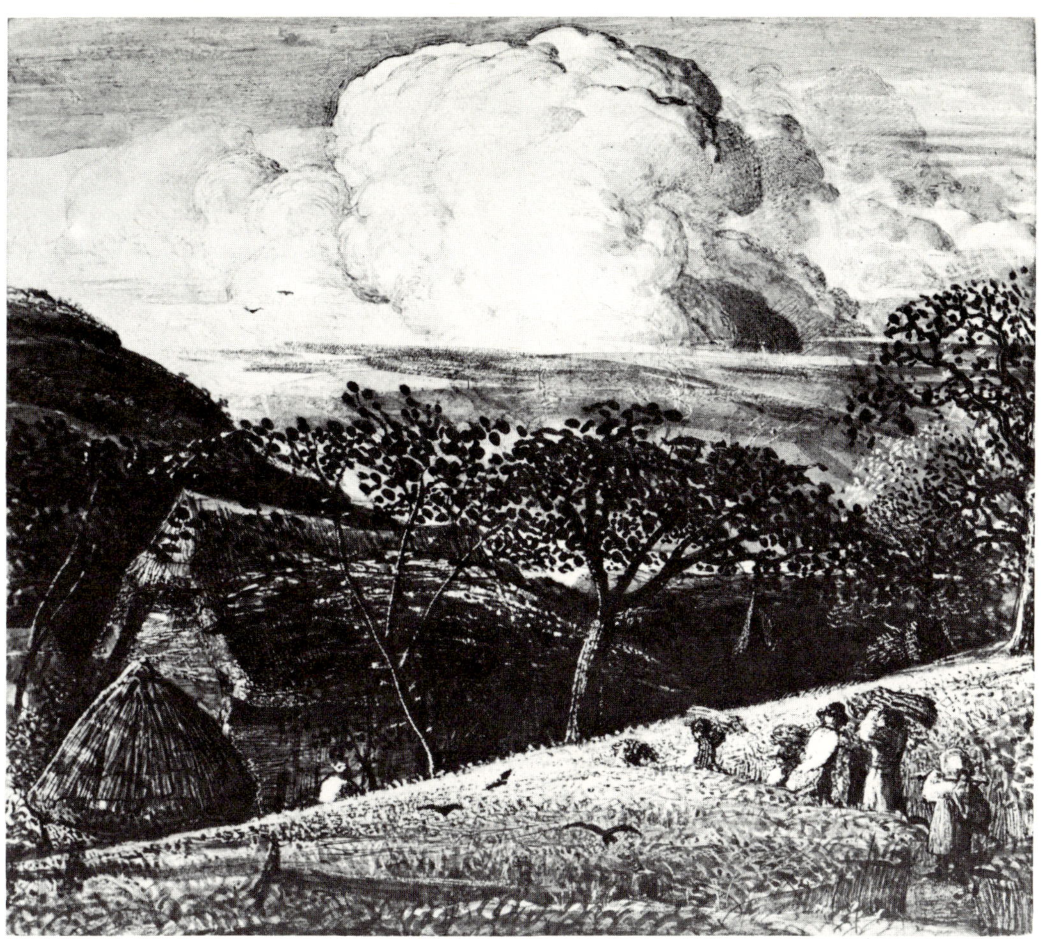

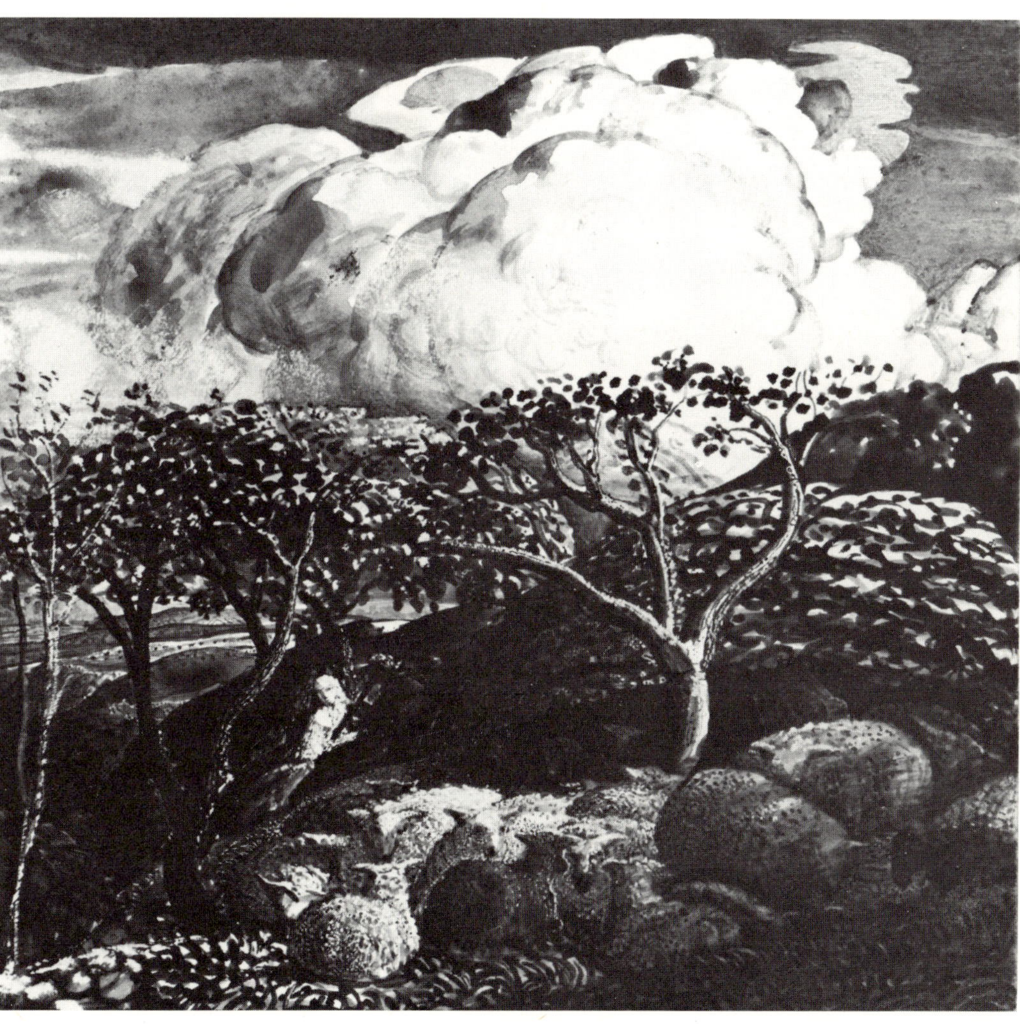

82 Drawing for *The Bright Cloud*, 1831/2
(British Museum)

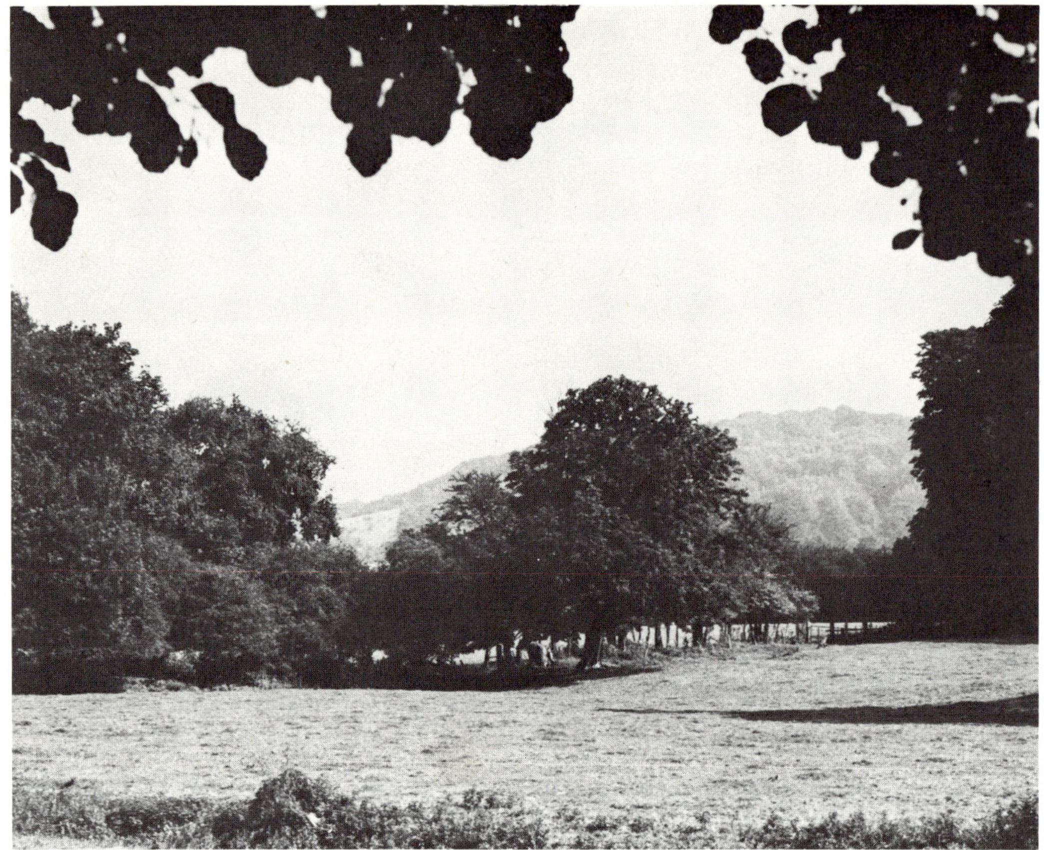

83 Landscape near Shoreham

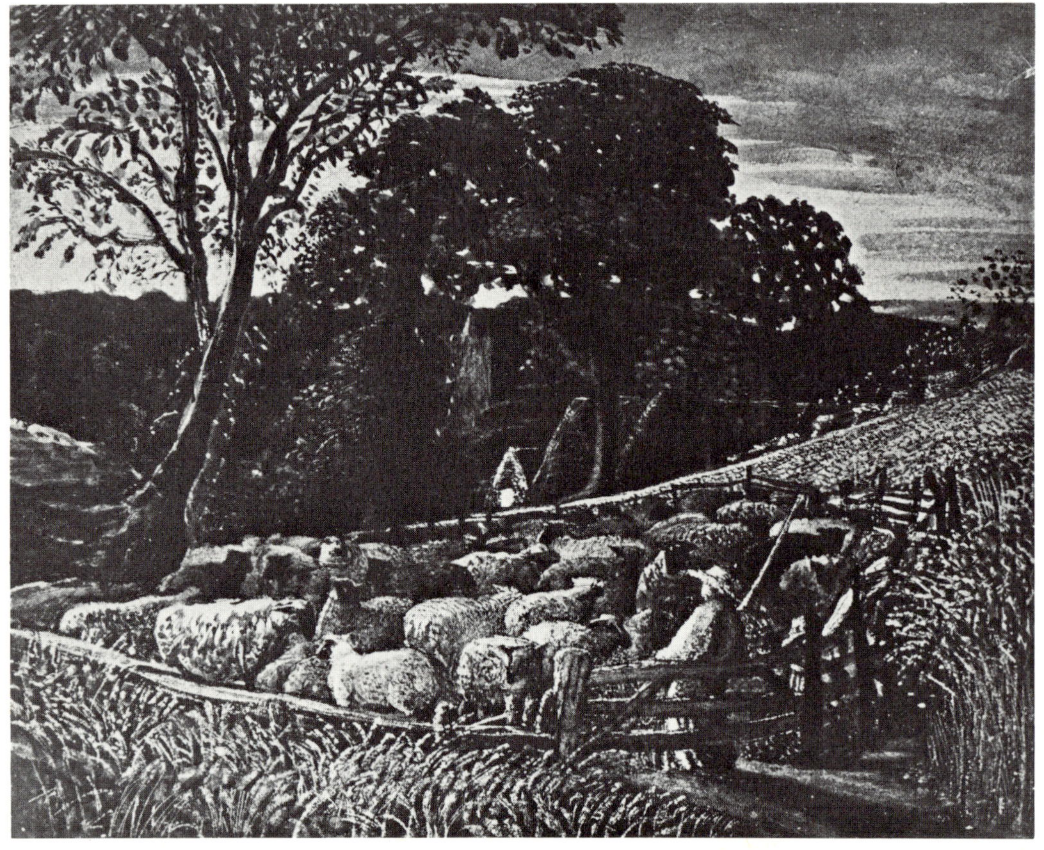

84 *The Folded Flock*, 1831/2 (Private Collection)

85 *Cornfield: Shoreham at Twilight*, 1831/2 (Private Collection)

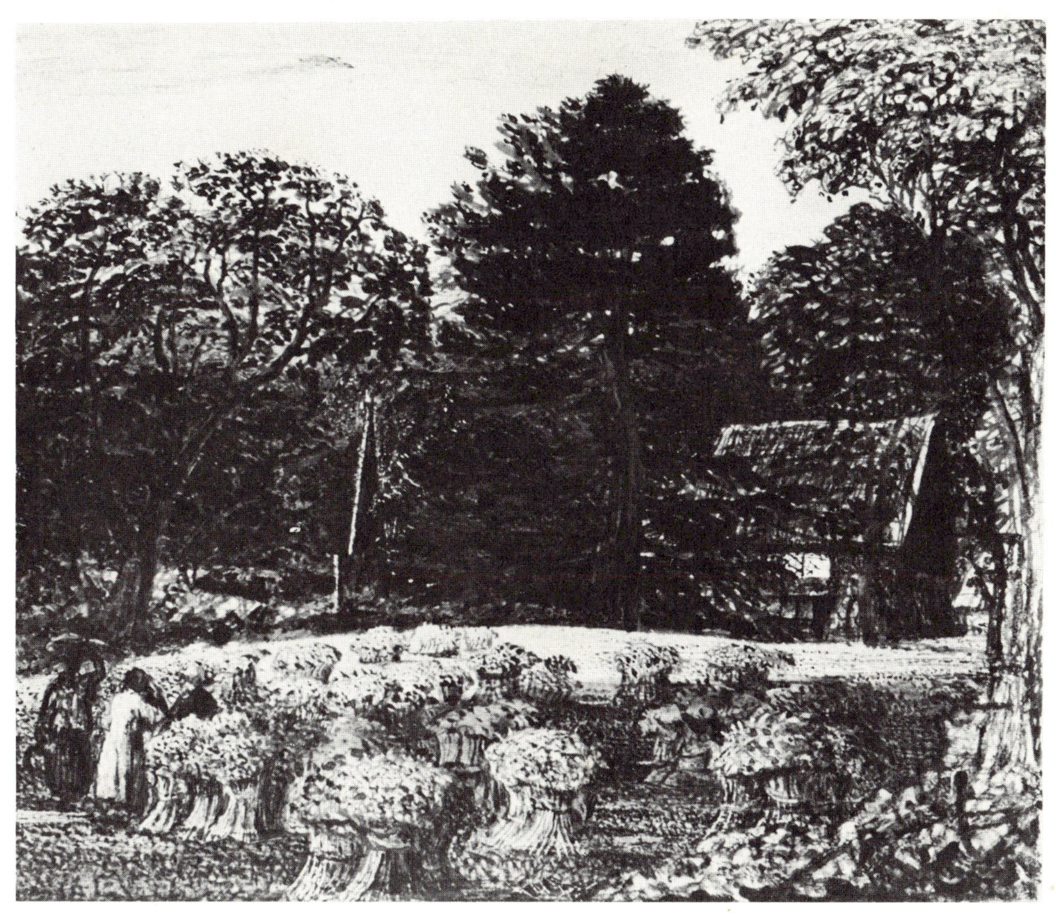

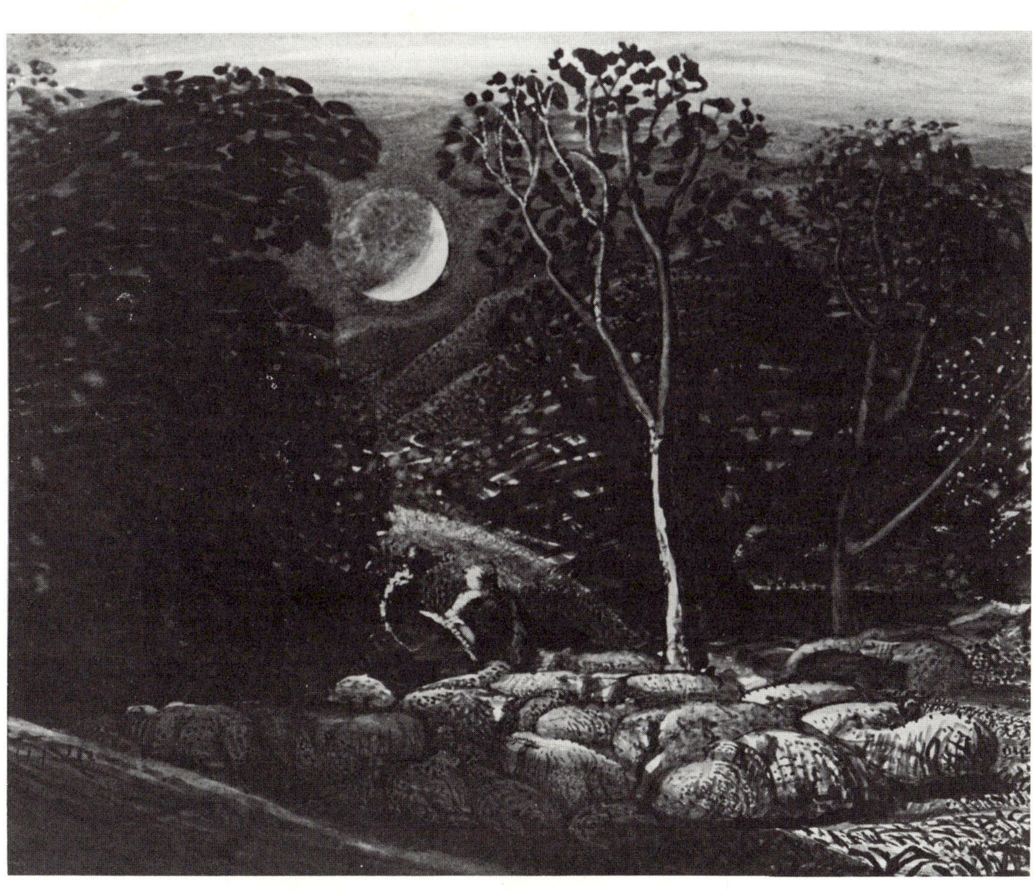

86 *Moonlight: A landscape with Sheep*, 1831/2 (The Tate Gallery)

An interesting assumption might be made here by comparing the 'Bright and White Cloud' series with the storms and lightning which are often used as symbols of desire in Indian miniature painting such as the Garwhal *A Night of Storm* and *A Lady at the Tryst*.[8] It is not impossible that Palmer was again in love when he did these paintings, if not yet with Hannah Linnell, the girl who used to run out ahead of the other children to meet Palmer and Blake when they went visiting on Hampstead Heath and who he was to marry in 1837, possibly with a girl about whom he says nothing in his letters although his destroyed notebooks may very well have held some information on this score. This is mere speculation, but in the light of visual depiction of emotional disturbances and reactions in other works it cannot be ruled out entirely. It is one of Palmer's great strengths that he cannot stand aside in his art but must bring his whole being to bear, producing those profound emotional responses which is the very basis of his art. If Blake had perfect contact with his subconscious which he was able to draw upon at will, Palmer, through the act of creation, could tap his inner emotional life and bring it to expression. It is the difference between the two men, Blake the child of the eighteenth century, the age of reason, Palmer, not just accepting nature and 'improving by receiving into the soul' but passing it 'thro' the intense purifying, separating, transmuting heat of the soul's infabulous alchimy'.

Among the works that he was to do before his vision finally left him are a number of oil and tempera paintings all of which, though lacking fire, are extremely beautiful in their use of light, richness of technique and utter

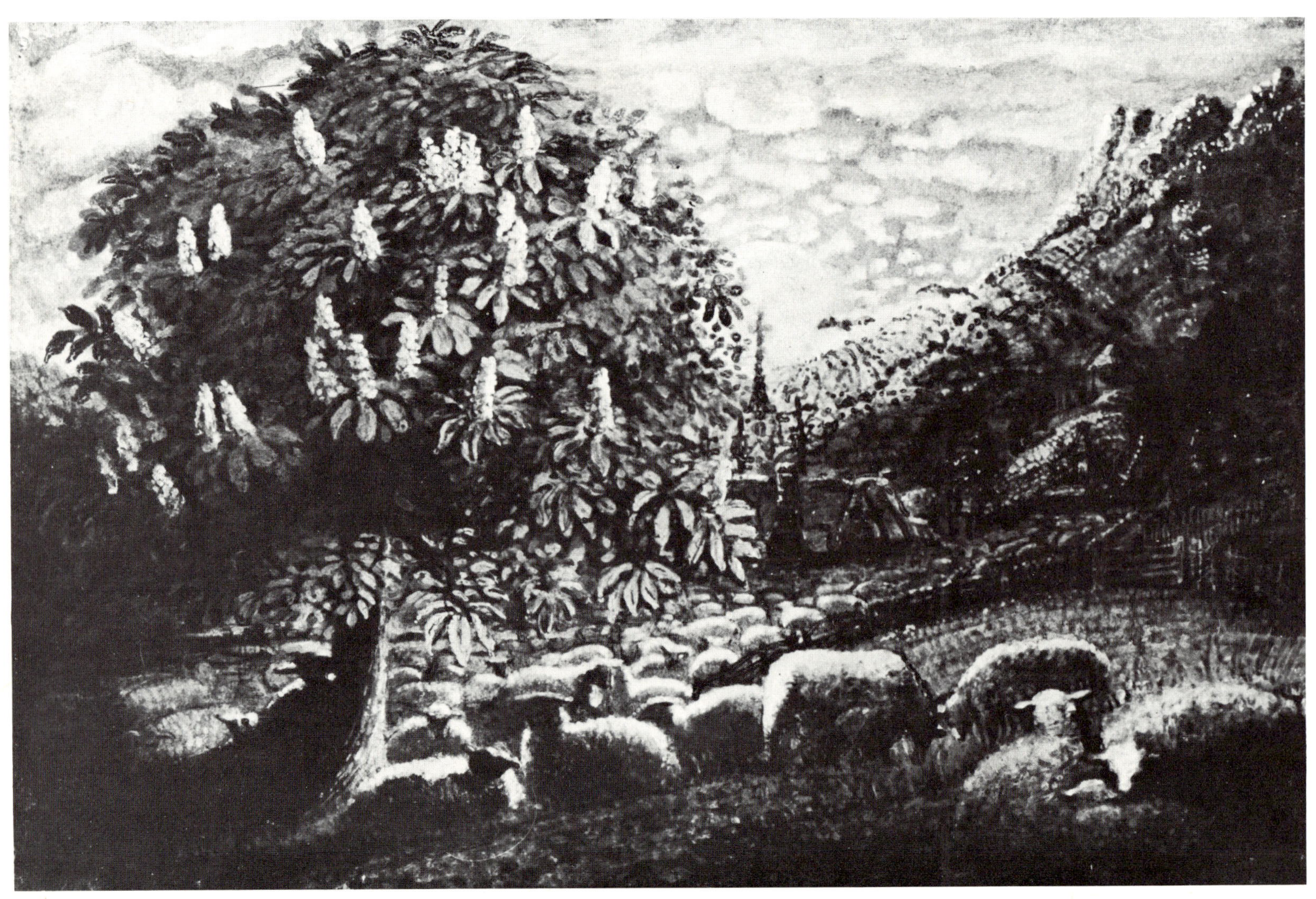

87 *Shoreham at Twilight*, 1831/2 (Private Collection)

serenity. One of the finest is *The Gleaning Field* (50) with its still, almost breathless quality of the English landscape in late summer, closely rivalled by *A Pastoral Scene* (73). This has lost the intimate quality of *The Gleaning Field* and has begun to broaden out into a majestic view suggestive of a grand manner, a feature often to be found in his later work. But there is a passage in the cornfield which in its interpretation of figures in a landscape is as fine a piece of painting to be seen in any of his work. The *Cornfield Bordered by Trees* (90) although clumsier in many respects, still contains some aspects of his Shoreham paintings in the wild trees and the animals being driven between the standing corn. Two more paintings *Scene at Underriver* and *The Bright Cloud* are closely related in composition, having equestrian figures riding from left to right between fields of standing corn, and in extremely rich texture and colour. Particularly the *Scene at Underriver* where almost the whole surface of the panel is covered with bejewelled vegetation.

One or two monochrome works also exist dating from 1833/4, one of which *Barn at Shoreham* (89) has certain curious features. It has not previously had a date ascribed to it and at first sight it would appear to belong to the same year, 1828, as *Lane and Shed, Shoreham* (35). The subjects being very similar and

88 *Young Man Yoking an Ox*, 1831/2 (Ashmolean Museum)

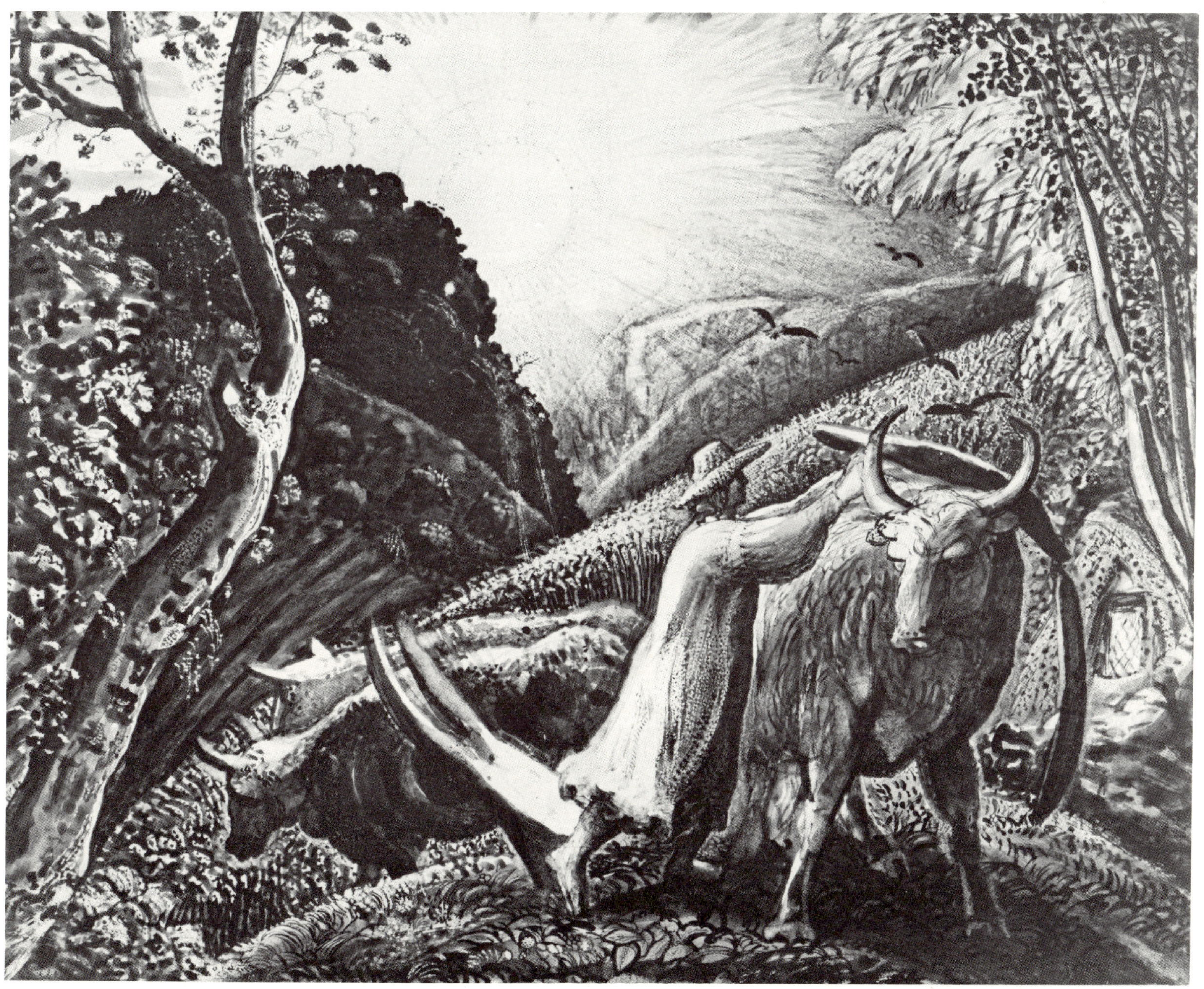

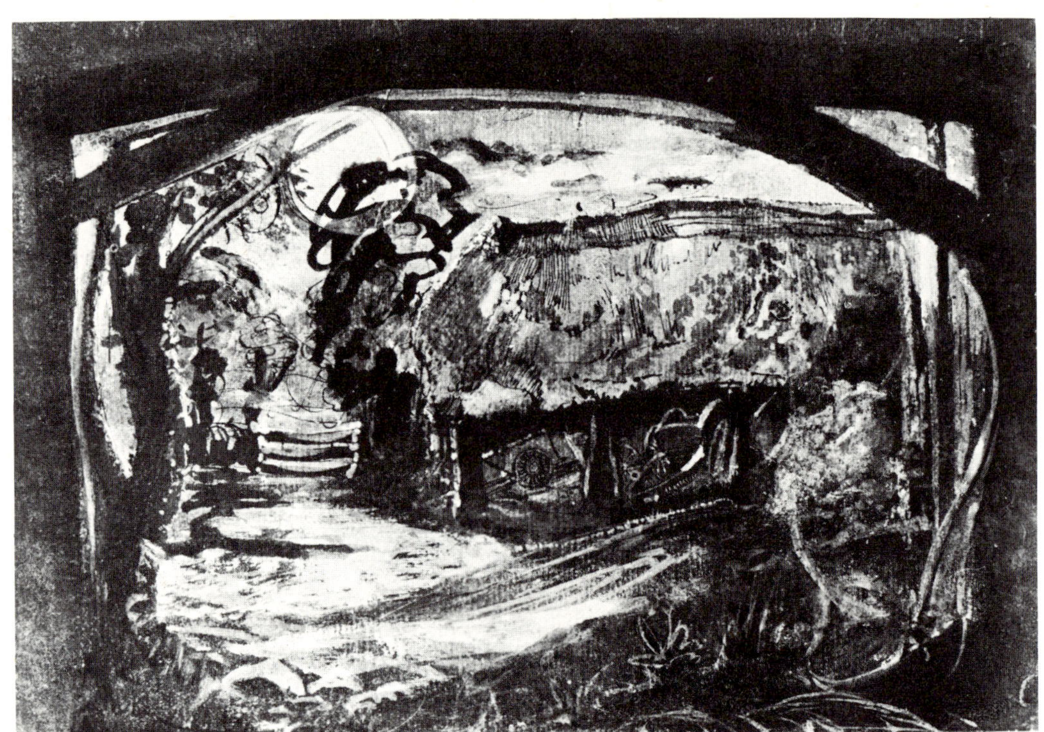

89 *Barn at Shoreham*, 1833/4 (Private Collection)

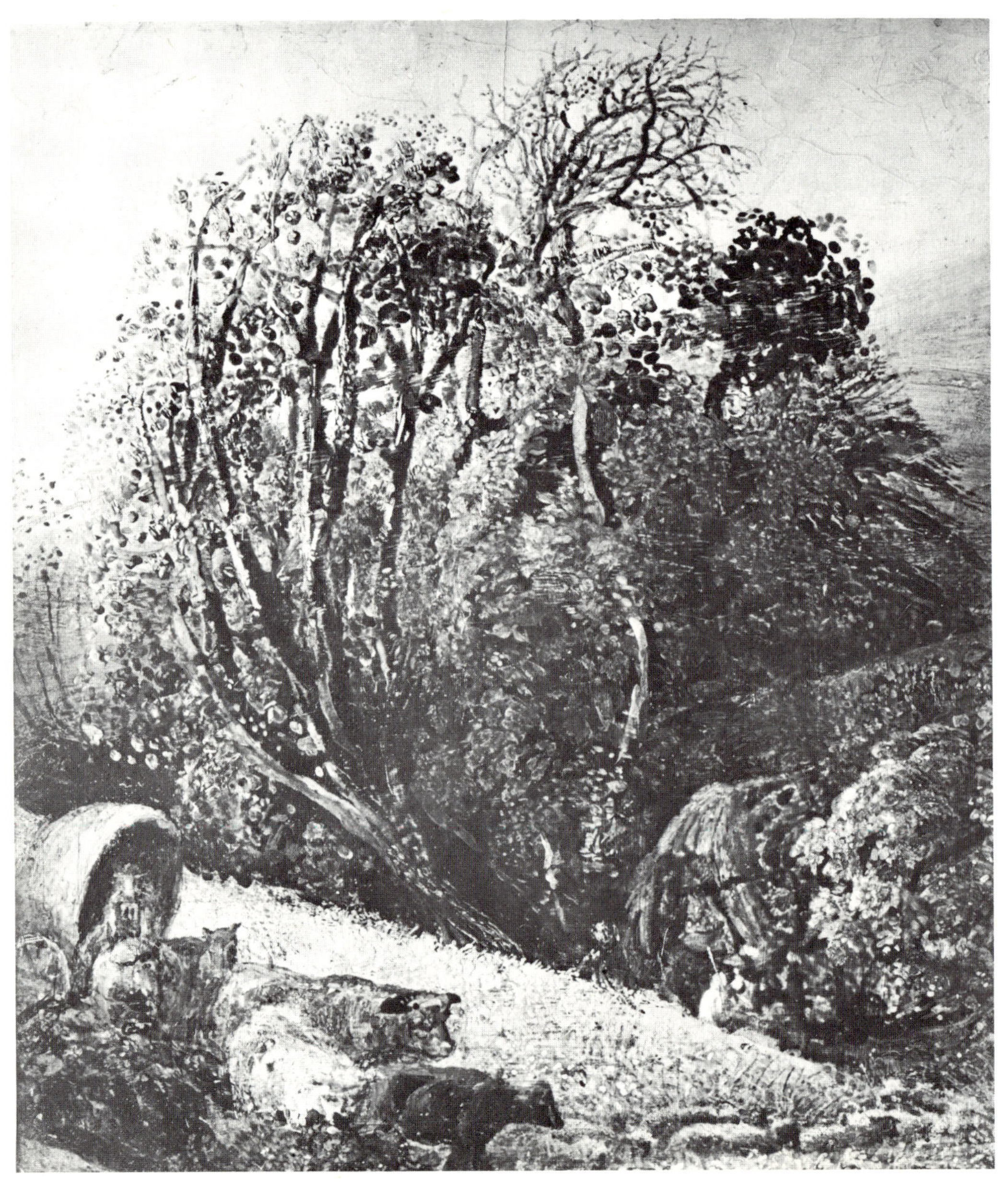

90 *A Cornfield Bordered by Trees*, 1833/4 (Ashmolean Museum)

the medium, sepia mixed with gum, one he used in his earlier work. In other respects it is related to a much later painting, *The Shearers* (*91*) of 1833/4. It is framed in the same manner by the large doorway of a barn with, on the left, a tree of similar form while on the right appear both the basket and the scythe in the same relative positions as in *The Shearers* but with the handle of the scythe reversed. If a closer look at *The Shearers* is made it will be noticed that the handle of the fork behind the basket corresponds to the shape and position of the scythe handle in *Barn at Shoreham*. It is as if a tracing had been made of parts of one painting and added, with mistakes, to another.

Palmer had probably made his first journey to Devon in about 1832–3. In 1833 he had a painting, *Scene from Lee, North Devon*, hung in the Academy and *A Pastoral Scene* of 1835 has qualities of the Devonshire landscape in the coomb on the left and the distant view of the sea. According to his son the journey he made was prompted by his father seeing a print of Combe Martin bay in a shop window and, he goes on to say, 'stirred up by that, he went westwards till he found in the "heaped up richness" of the loveliest of counties nearly all he desired in landscape.' But perhaps he was also beginning to find the close proximity of Linnell already irksome for there is a freedom of spirit reflected in the drawings and water-colours that he made on his journeyings, particularly in *At Score near Ilfracombe* (*94*), *Culbone, Somerset* (*92*), and *View at Linton, Devon* that suggests a new found happiness. *Culbone* and *View at Linton* have much in common, being landscapes with steep-sided vales leading down to richly wooded dells with, in the former, a track disappearing into the lush vegetation. They are remarkable for their resemblance to female forms. The smooth belly of the land above dips sharply over a shadowy pubic mound textured and patterned with trees and shrubs while, on either side spring the thighs of the valley. Symbolically, and in technique, they are closely related to his later Shoreham works and are also perhaps the last things he did that retain any of the visionary qualities of his earlier years. On viewing these water-colours it is not surprising that he had such an affection for this landscape, he must have felt that he had found new pastures, in which, from this fresh stimulus, his visionary powers would take breadth and lead him on to even greater excess than before.

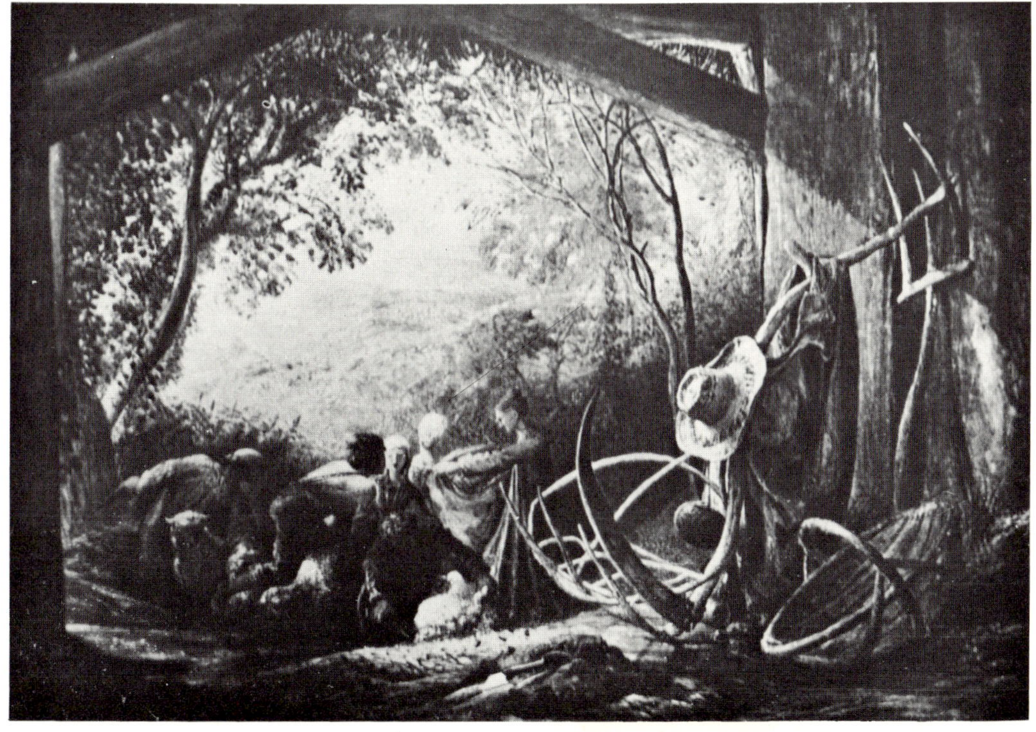

91 *The Shearers*, 1833/4 (Private Collection)

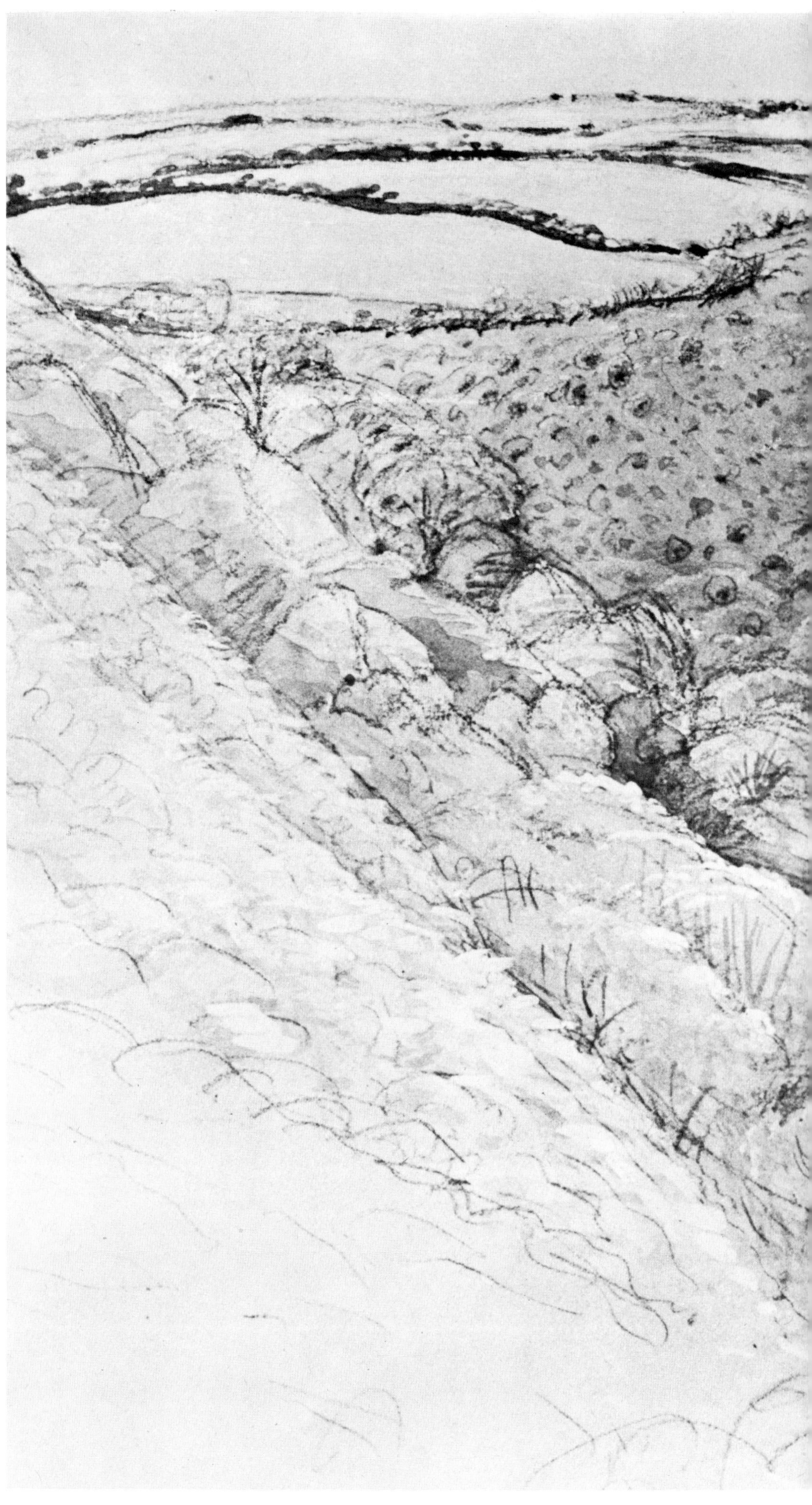

92 *Culbone, Somerset*, 1832/3 (formerly Melbourne Art Gallery)

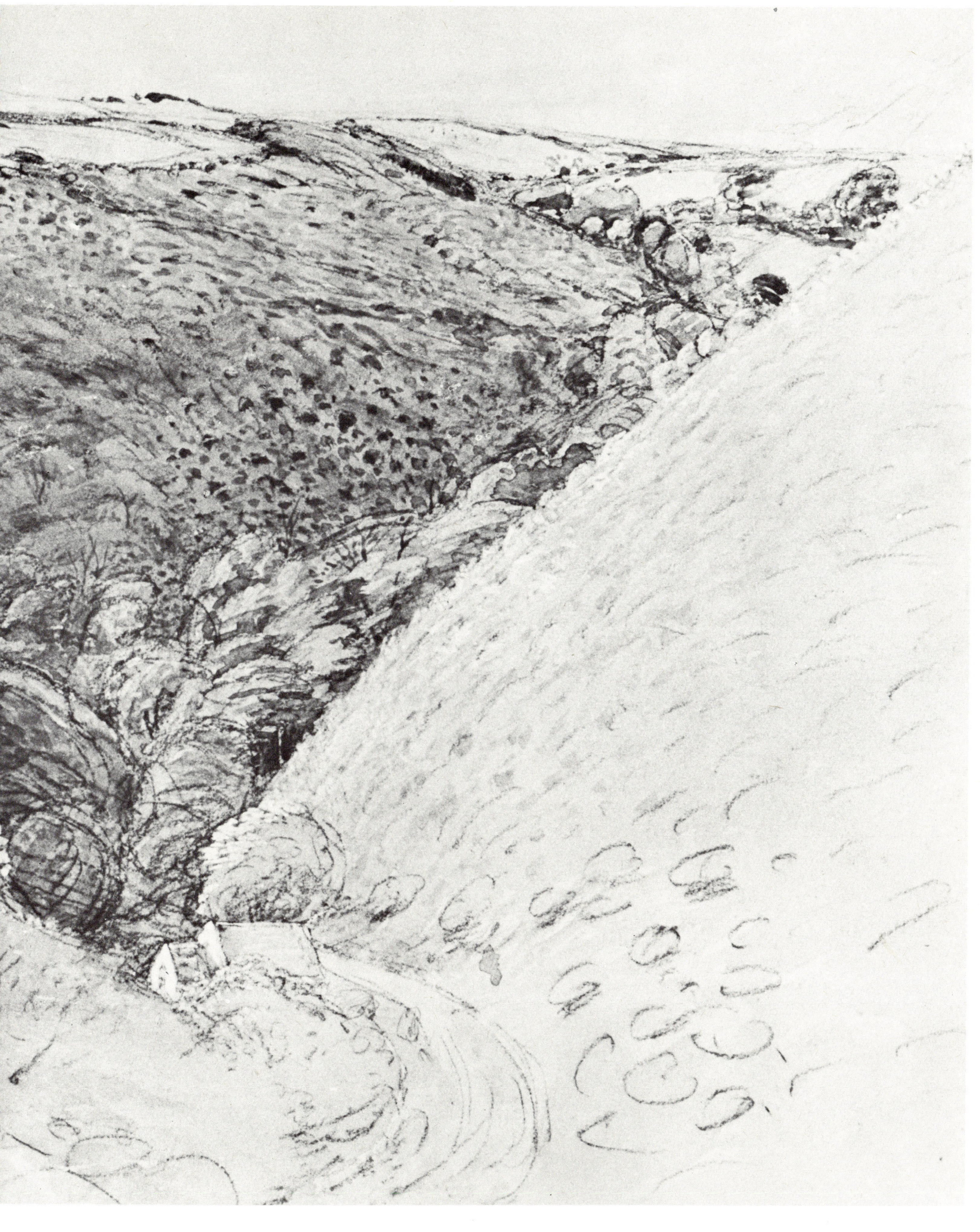

Unfortunately it was not to be. On his next excursion, by steamer this time to North Wales with Henry Walter in 1835, the change in his style becomes obvious. Beautiful in technique and exquisite in their draughtsmanship though such works as *Tintern Abbey* (*99*), *Study of Trees*, (*96*), and *Cottage at Tintern* no doubt are, they lack the intensity and intimacy that characterizes his work of the visionary years and, because they are without selection they have lost all symbolic content, becoming merely charming topographical records. It is interesting in this context to compare the watercolour *Near the Travellers' Rest Inn, Dolgelly* (*98*) done in Wales with the Devon and Somerset subjects for although there is a similarity in handling the true relationship is with the Tintern Abbey works; it is an excellent example of an intermediary work exhibiting the change in his art actually taking place.

At Tintern he was stranded with insufficient money to return to London so he wrote to George Richmond[9]: 'Tintern Very Deep Twilight. Wednesday August 19th, 1835.

The address for letter is to us at Mr. William Hiscock's – Black Lion, Tintern Abbey, Monmouthshire.

My Dear Sir,
Our Ossian Sublimities are ended – and with a little more of McPherson's mist and vapour we should have had much more successful sketching – but unfortunately when we were near Snowdon we had white light days on which we could count the stubbs and stones some miles off – we had just a glimpse or two one day through the chasms of stormy cloud which was sublime – however we have this evening got into a nook for which I would give all the Welch mountains grand as they are and if you and Mrs. Richmond could but spare a week you might see Tintern and be back again. The Bristol Stages start daily, the fare I believe is low and there is a steam boat

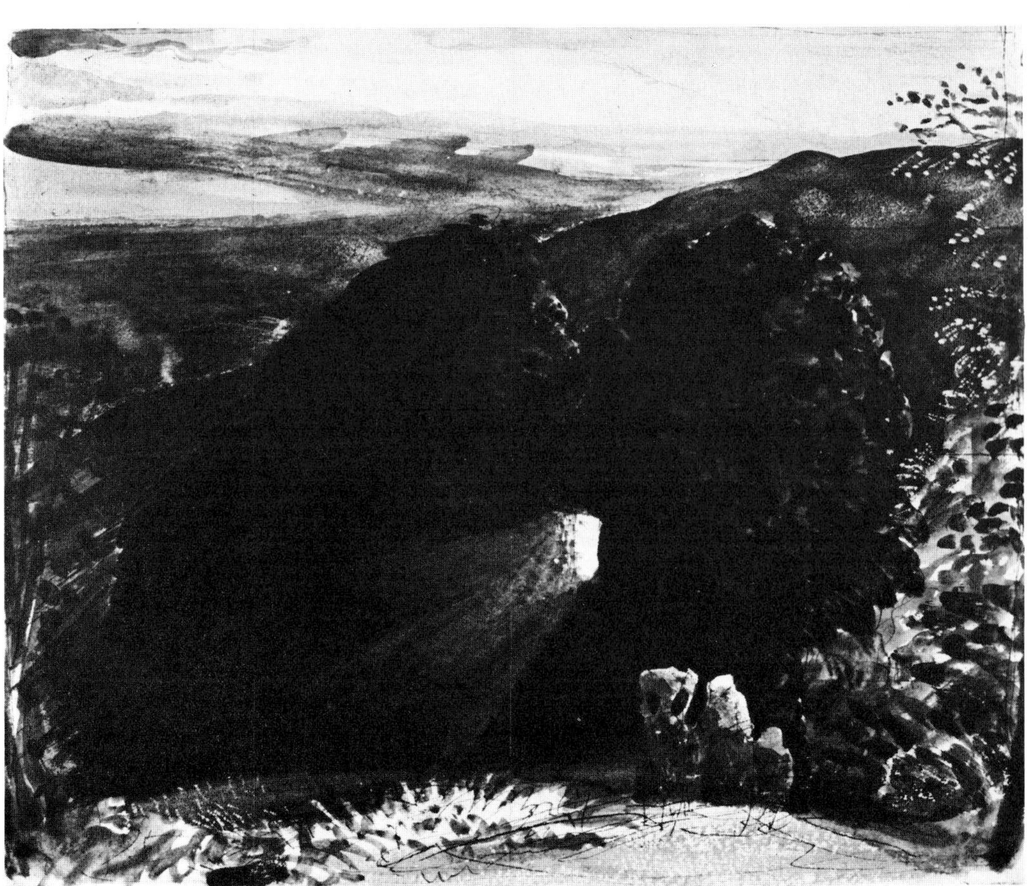

93 Drawing for *Landscape Twilight*, 1833/4 (Victoria and Albert Museum)

daily thence (only three hours' passage) to Chepstow within 6 miles I think of the Abbey – and such an Abbey! the lightest Gothic – trellised with ivy and rising from a wilderness of orchards – and set like a gem amongst the folding of woody hills – hard by I saw a man this evening literally 'sitting under his own fig tree' whose broad leaves mixed with holyoaks and other rustic garden flowers embower'd his porch. Do pray come – we have a lodging with very nice people under the walls and three centuries ago might have been lulled with Gregorian Vespers and waked by the Complin to sleep again more sweetly – but the murderer of More & Fisher has reduced it to the silence of a Friend's meeting house. Mr. Walter was shown the inside and says it is superb. After my pastoral has had a month's stretching into epic I feel here a most grateful relaxation and am become once more a pure quaint crinkle-crankle Goth – If you are a Goth come hither, if your're a pure Greek take a cab and make a sketch of St Paul's Covent Garden before Breakfast. Addison speaks of the Cathedral of Sienna (one of the richest in the world) as the work of barbarians – clever savages almost – what a 'Spectator' – he could not bear too lofty and pointed a style – pity he died before the œra of Doric watchhouses, Ionic turnpike gates and Corinthian ginshops! – his taste outran his age – ours hobbles after –

Thursday Even. Poetic vapours have subsided and the sad realities of life blot the field of vision – the burthen of the theme is a heavy one. I have not

94 *At Score near Ilfracombe*, 1832/3 (Victoria and Albert Museum)

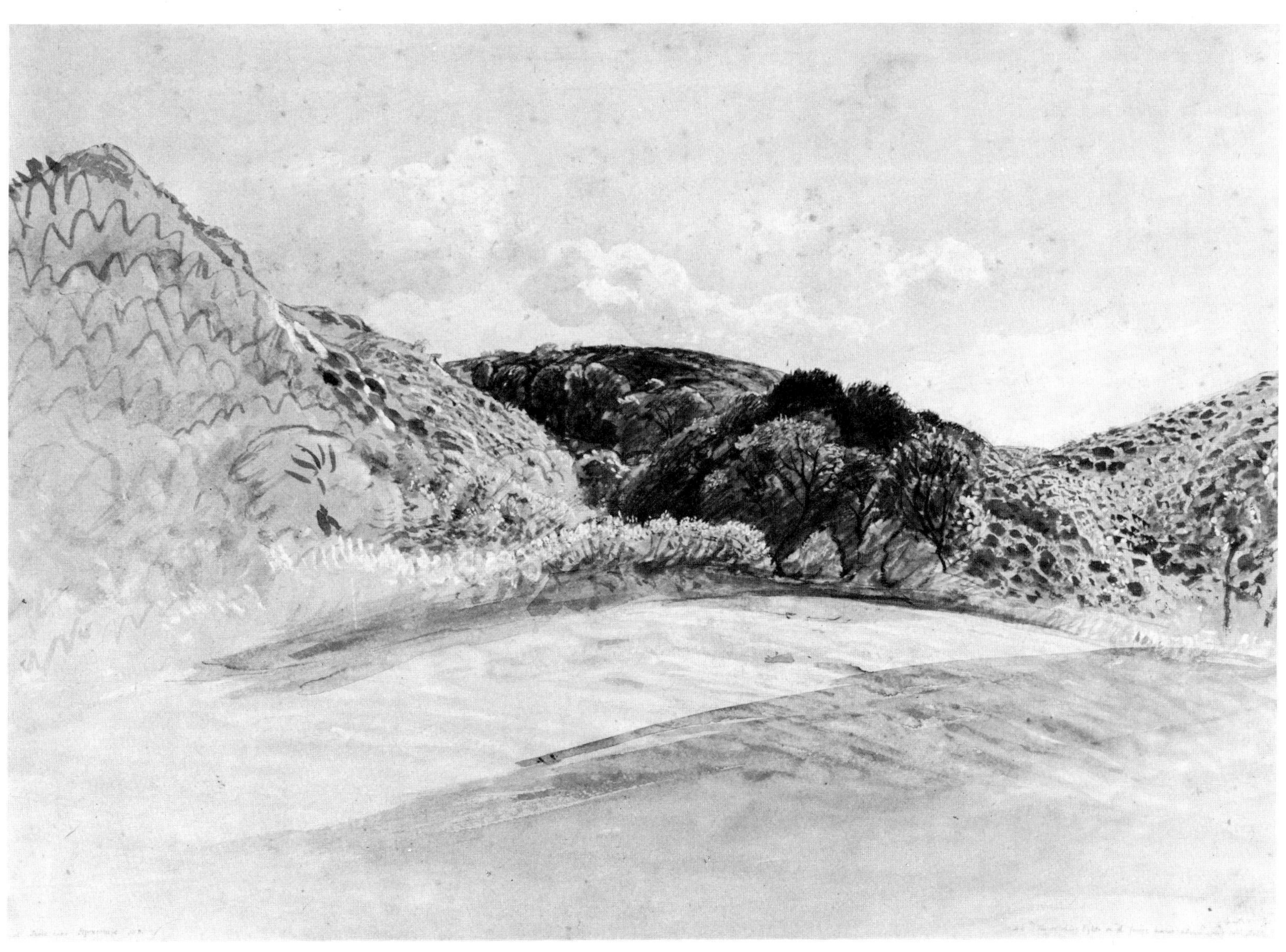

cash enough to carry me to London – O miserable poverty! how it wipes off the bloom from everything around me. Had I conceived how much it would cost I would as soon have started for the United States as Wales – but I have worked hard – seen grand novelties and enlarged the materials of imagination – if I could but sell a picture or clean another Opie or two – but I am all in the dumps 'shut up and cannot come forth' and feel as if I alone of all mankind were fated to get no bread by the sweat of my brow – 'to toil in the fire for very vanity' – If you've a mangy cat to drown, christen it 'Palmer' – If you could oblige me by the farther loan of three pounds my Father will repay you I dare say if you can call at Grove St – but I shall very soon be in town myself only – I want enough both to bring me home and enable me to stay a little longer in case I should find subjects which it would be short-sighted policy not to secure – but I hope not to spend so much – if the Movement Party want a professor of drawing in the Marylebone Charity Schools pray canvas for me. Things are come to a crisis now and I must begin to earn money immediately or get embarrassed – horrid prospect – the anxieties of debt on the back of the perturbations of aspiring studies. The refuge I know is in Faith and Prayer – but is daily bread promised to those who over-spend their income – which I am afraid is now my case – however I was deceived by the strange mistatements about cheap living in Wales – otherwise my muse should have donkeyfied upon thistles from Husky Hampstead this summer – with a log at her leg. Well! I must come to London sell my pianoforte and all my nice old books – and paint the sun moon and seven stars upon a signboard I suppose – would I could get it to do! I find I am writing strange stuff and boring you with my own selfish troubles so I'll have done. If you can favour me with the three points would you have the farther kindness to send it as soon as possible and with a very full and legible direction on the letter – what if it should miscarry! I must stay at Tintern and go to plough – could you send by return of post? The

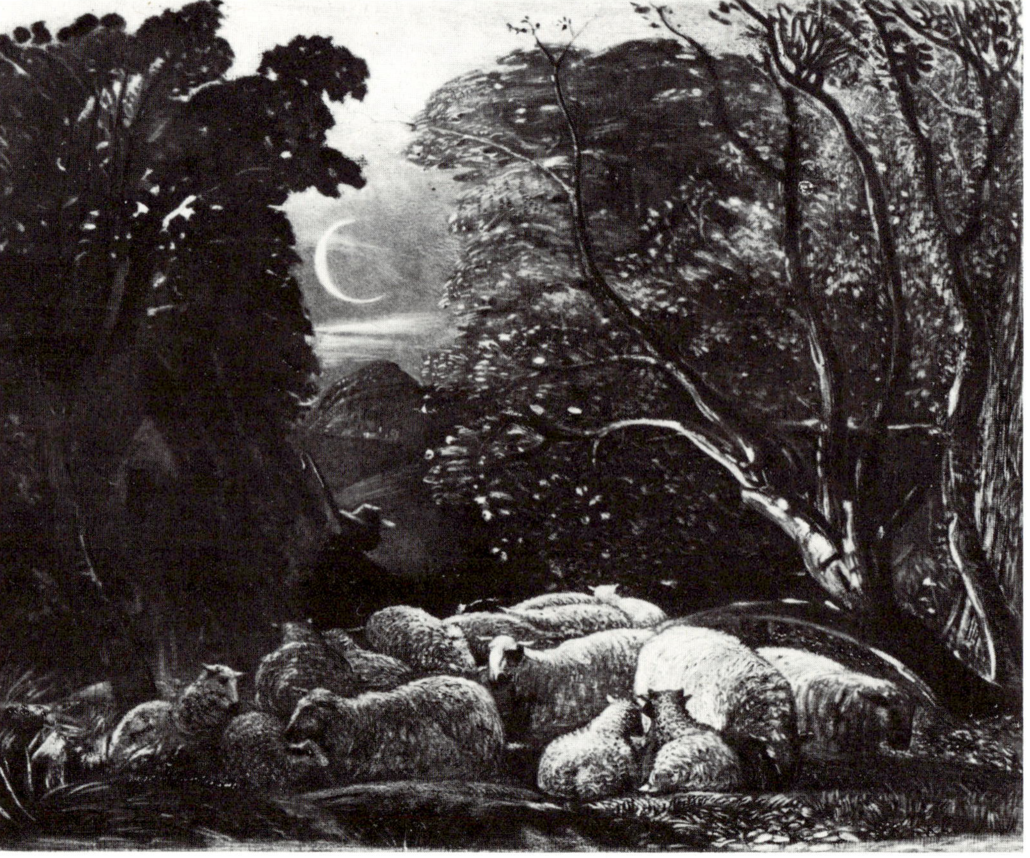

95 Welby Sherman after Palmer, *The Sleeping Shepherd*, 1834 (The Tate Gallery)

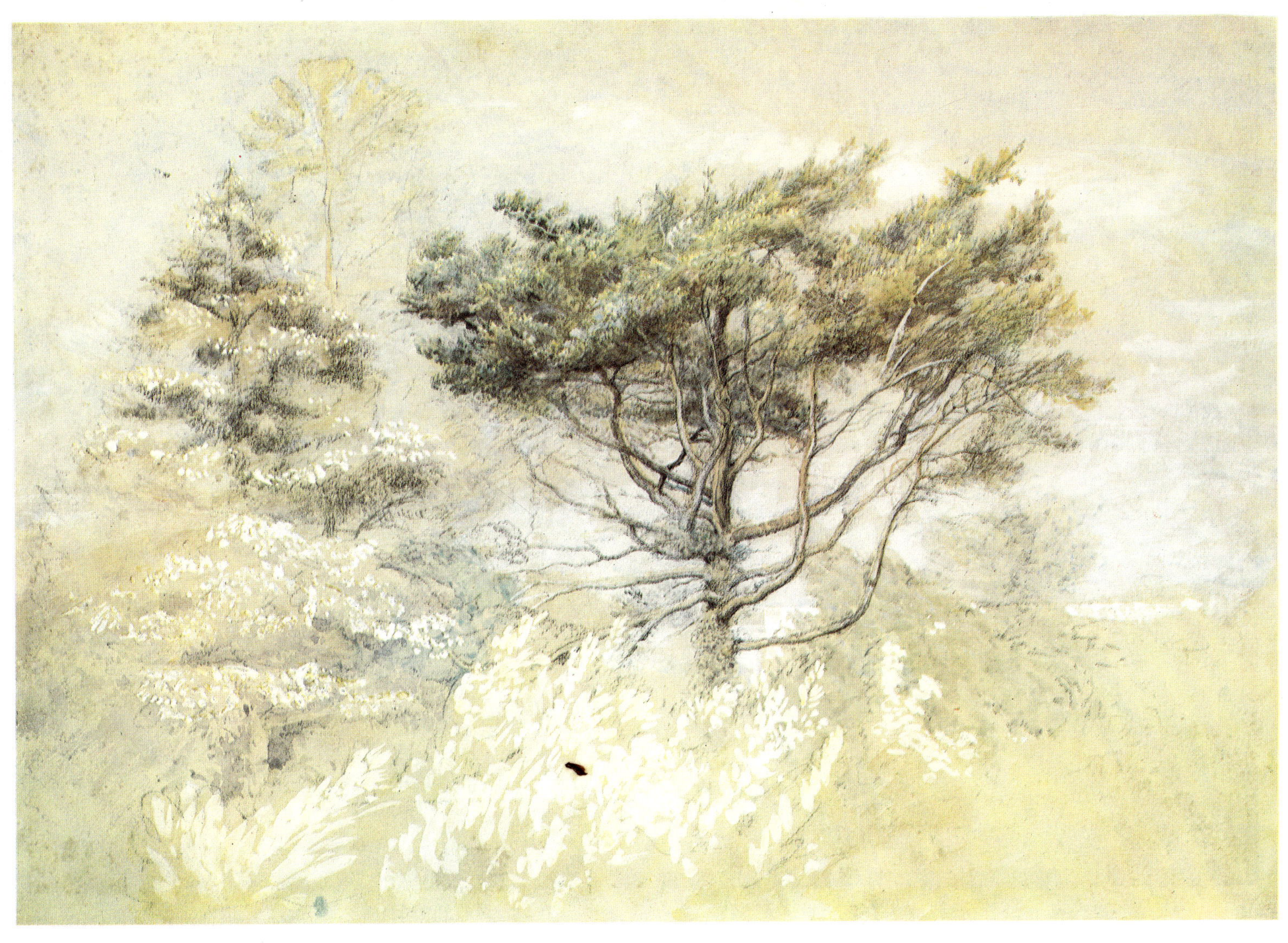

96 *Study of Trees*, 1835? (Ashmolean Museum)

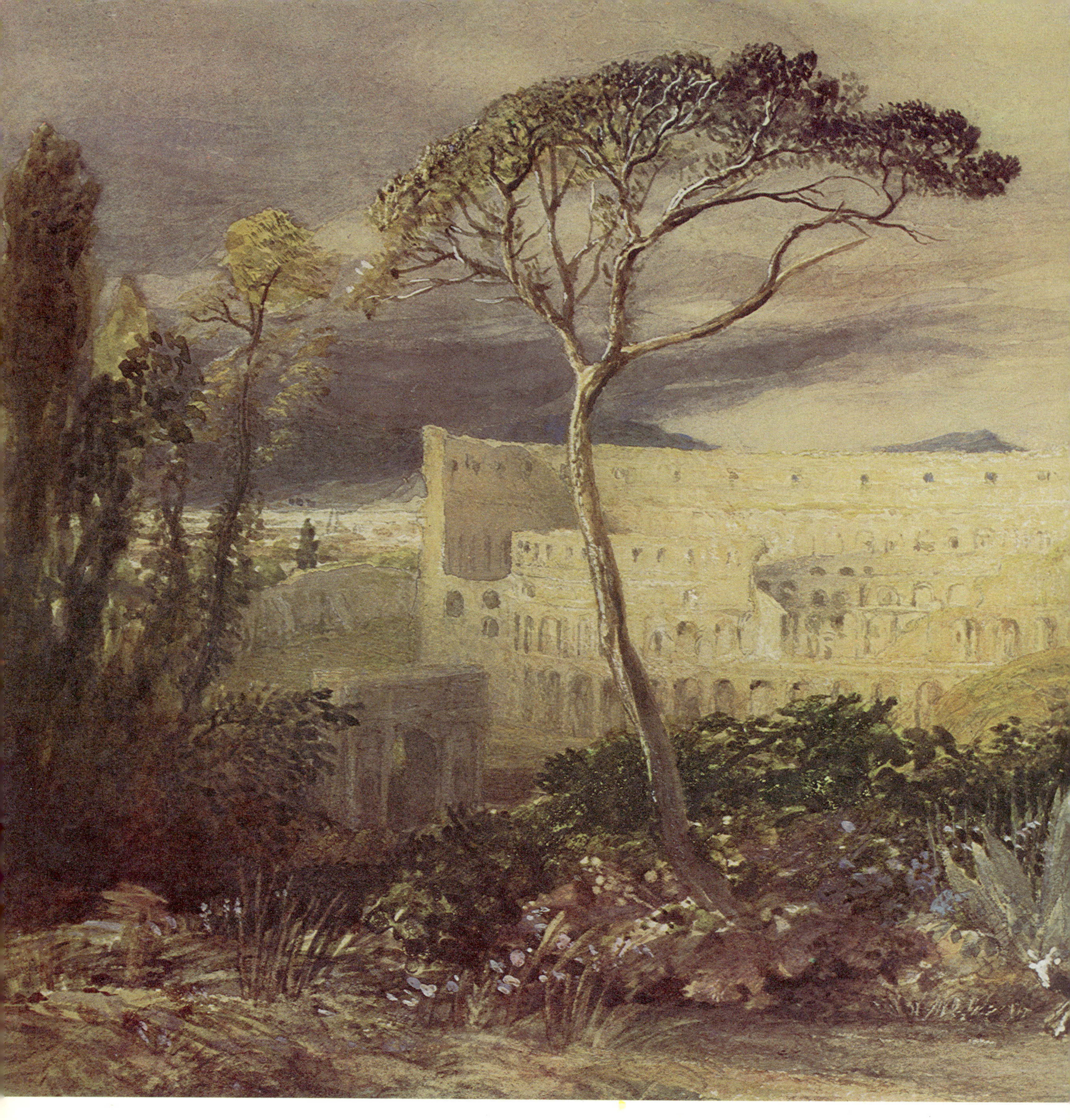

97 *The Colosseum and Alban Mount*, 1840?
(Ashmolean Museum)

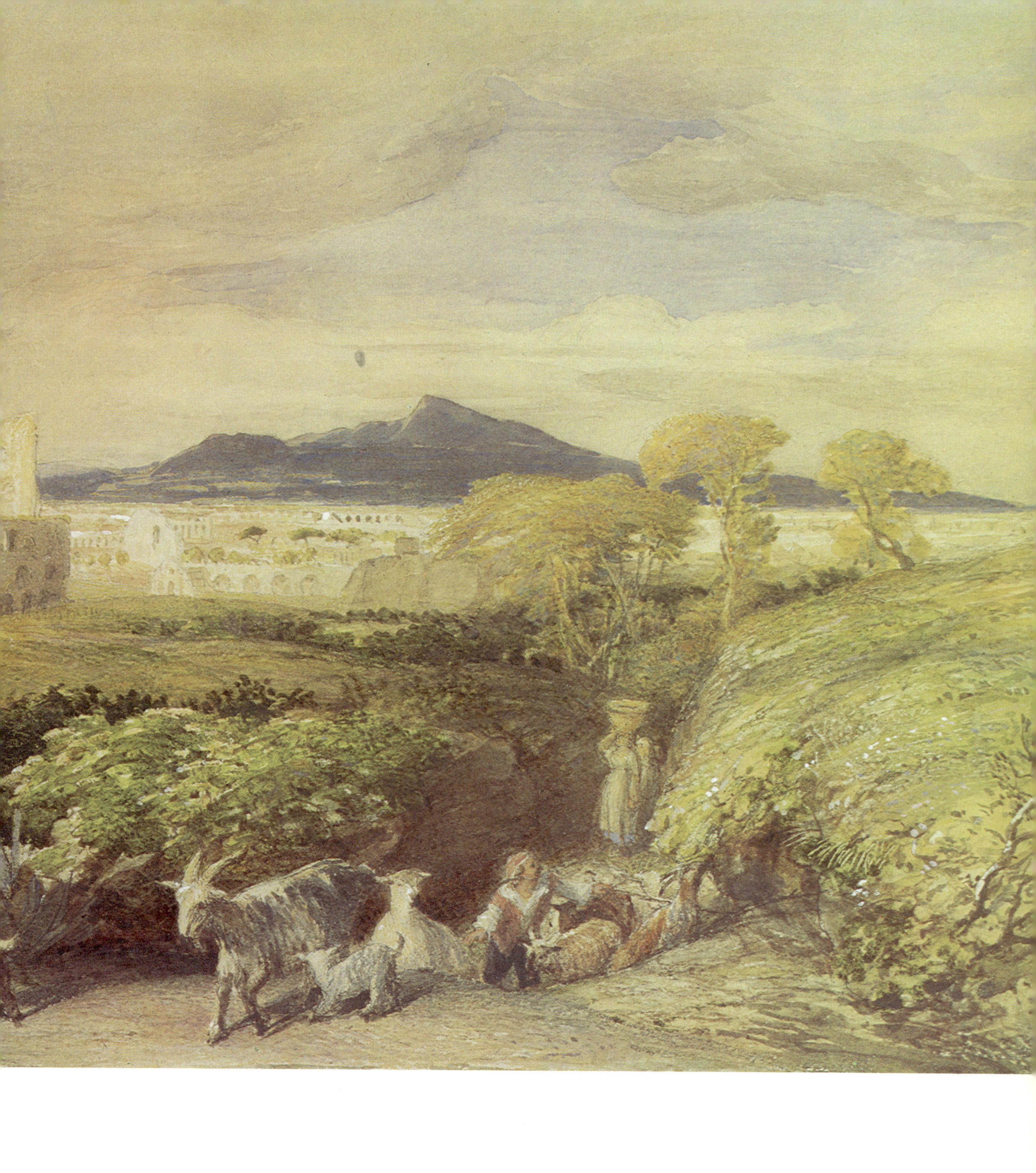

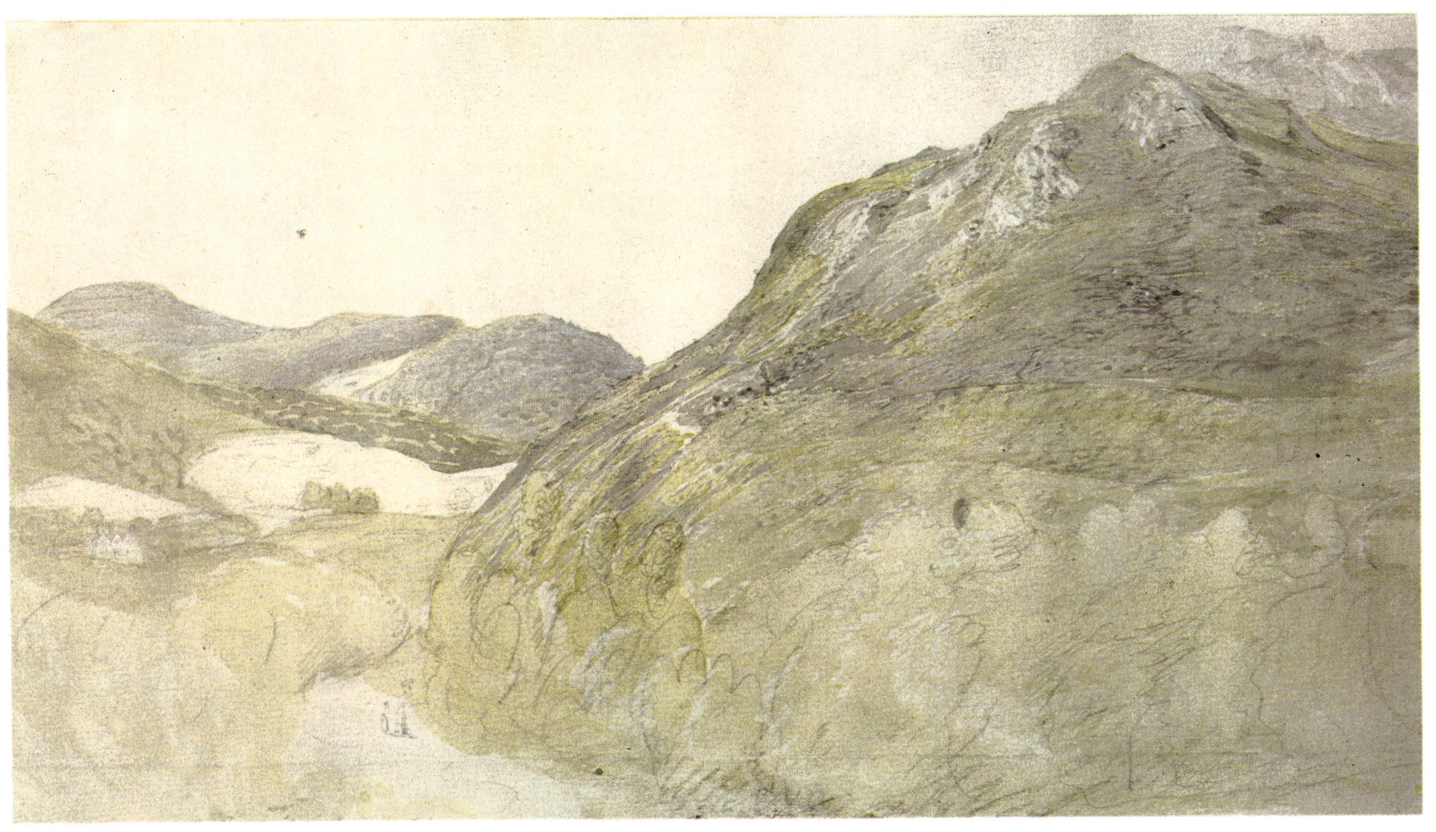

98 *Near the Traveller's Rest Inn, Dolgelly*, 1835 (Victoria and Albert Museum)

99 *Tintern Abbey*, 1835 (Victoria and Albert Museum)

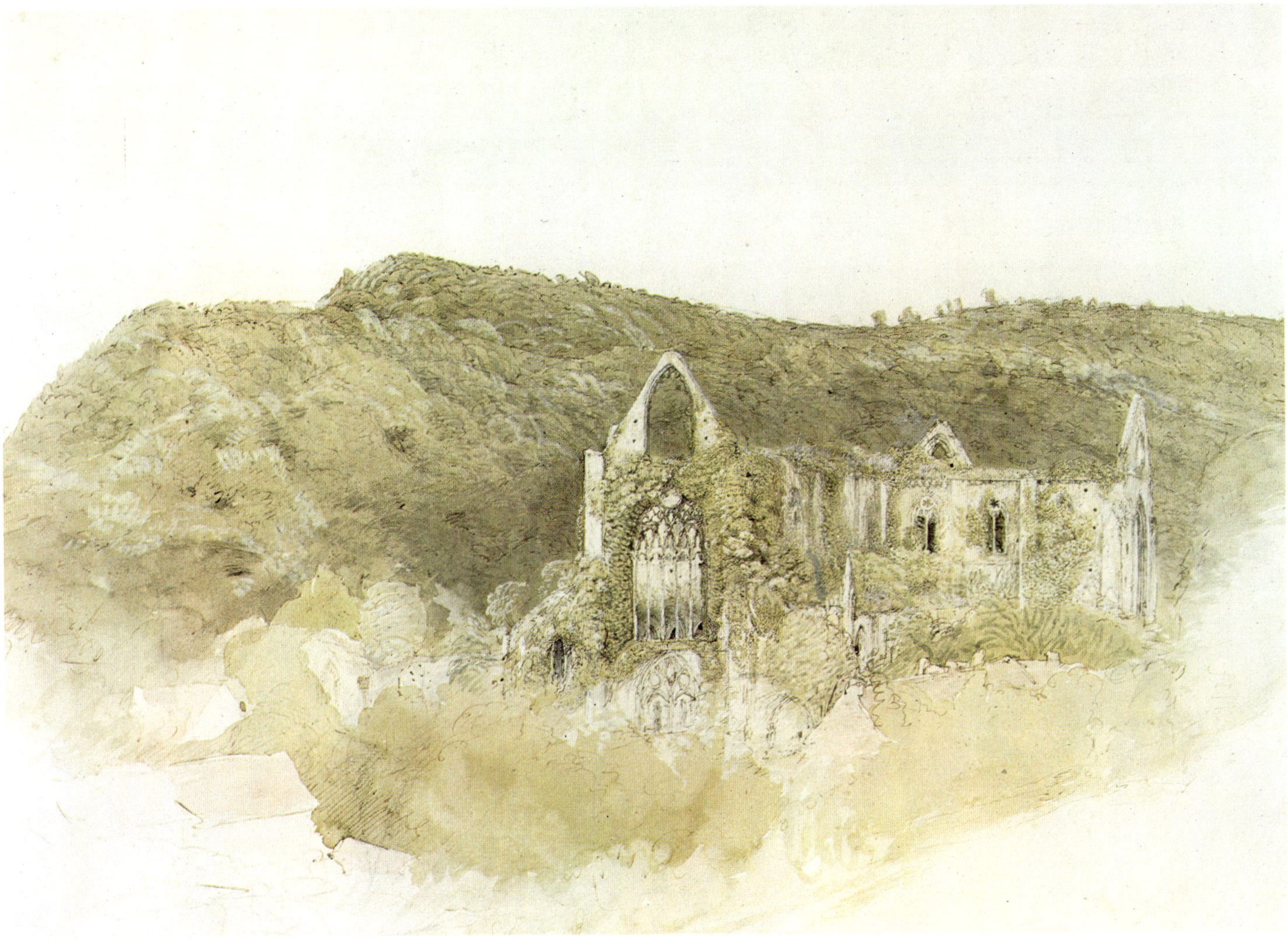

candle is going out as did the light of my mind some hours ago so I must wish you miserably good night.

Mr. Walter desires me to give his love and say that he wishes to return directly but not having the means would be obliged if you would make it up to a Five Pound Note – I will pay the postage of this when I see you –

With kindest love to Mrs. Richmond and such old friends as you may happen to see I remain

My Dear Sir
Your affectionate friend
Samuel Palmer'

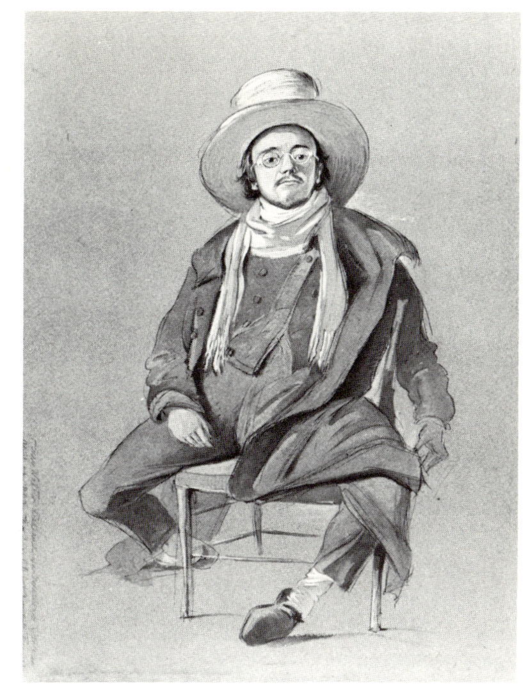

100 Henry Walter, *Samuel Palmer*, *c.*1835 (British Museum)

It was probably at this time that Walter drew the portrait of Palmer (*100*) in his broad-brimmed hat which is worth comparing to Palmer's self-portrait done seven years earlier (*55*).

Although he does not seem to have had any great liking for Wales, A. H. Palmer remarks 'He even went so far as to place his "Habitable lattitudes" south of the railings of Hyde Park, and their kernel in Devonshire', he made another journey there in 1836, this time with Edward Calvert as companion. During his wanderings in Wales he met with two other tourists, Crabb Robinson and his friend, the portrait painter, Masquerier. Robinson describes their meeting in a notebook in which he recorded his Welsh journey. 'This is one of the best days of my journey and reminded me of my travelling in early times – I arose and was on my way at ½ p 7 and at 9 had reached the small house at Dol y Melynllyn where is one of the three famous cataracts of this vicinity – Telling the landlord that I had heard of this house from a painter whose person I described, he said – he is now in the house, would you like to breakfast with him – I at once acceded and this led to one of the most agreeable incidents or rather the most agreeable incident of the journey – M(asquerier) had fallen in with this pedestrian tourist,

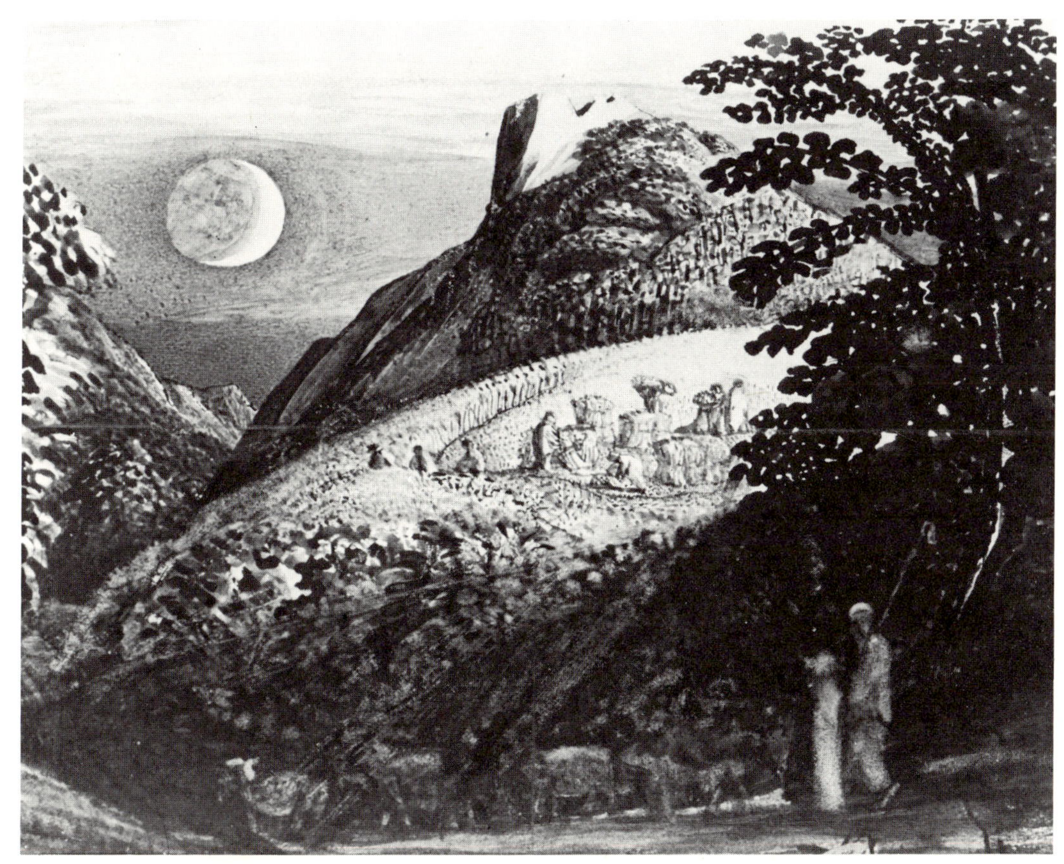

101 *The Harvest Moon*, 1835 (The Tate Gallery)

making sketches and had conceived a low opinion of him as an artist – I was pleased with his appearance on our return from Llanberis, and had alighted from the car, to give M: an opportunity of inviting him to ride the last two miles – For this good nature on my part I have been rewarded – After our breakfast the yet unknown artist, whose eye of deep feeling and very capacious forehead had inspired me to predilections for him, prepared to set out to one of the waterfalls I had come to see, I Proposed to accompany him and so an acquaintance was formed. He incidentally spoke of Blake as the greatest genius in art of modern times tho' little known – This made me more interested in him – I spoke at length of Blake and my acquaintance with him, and soon satisfied him, that in calling B insane I was not repeating the commonplace declamation against him. He at length yielded to my statement – Tho' he at first tried to maintain that in asserting the actuality of spirits he was but giving personality to ideas as Plat had done before. On my mentioning my name he said he had heard of me both from Blake and his wife – I found too that he had been to see Mr. Aders pictures and had heard of Gotzenberger.

'I enquired whether Linnel is not a man of worldly wisdom – He understood the insinuation and said, only defensively, and he represented Linnell's conduct as having been very generous towards Blake. This is contrary to my impression concerning L: Palmer, for so he named himself, is also acquainted with Daniell who he says did him a service in showing some of his sketches to Mr. Boddington who bought them – I was so much pleased with Mr. P: that

102 *Study of Trees, Clovelly Park, c.*1835 (Ashmolean Museum)

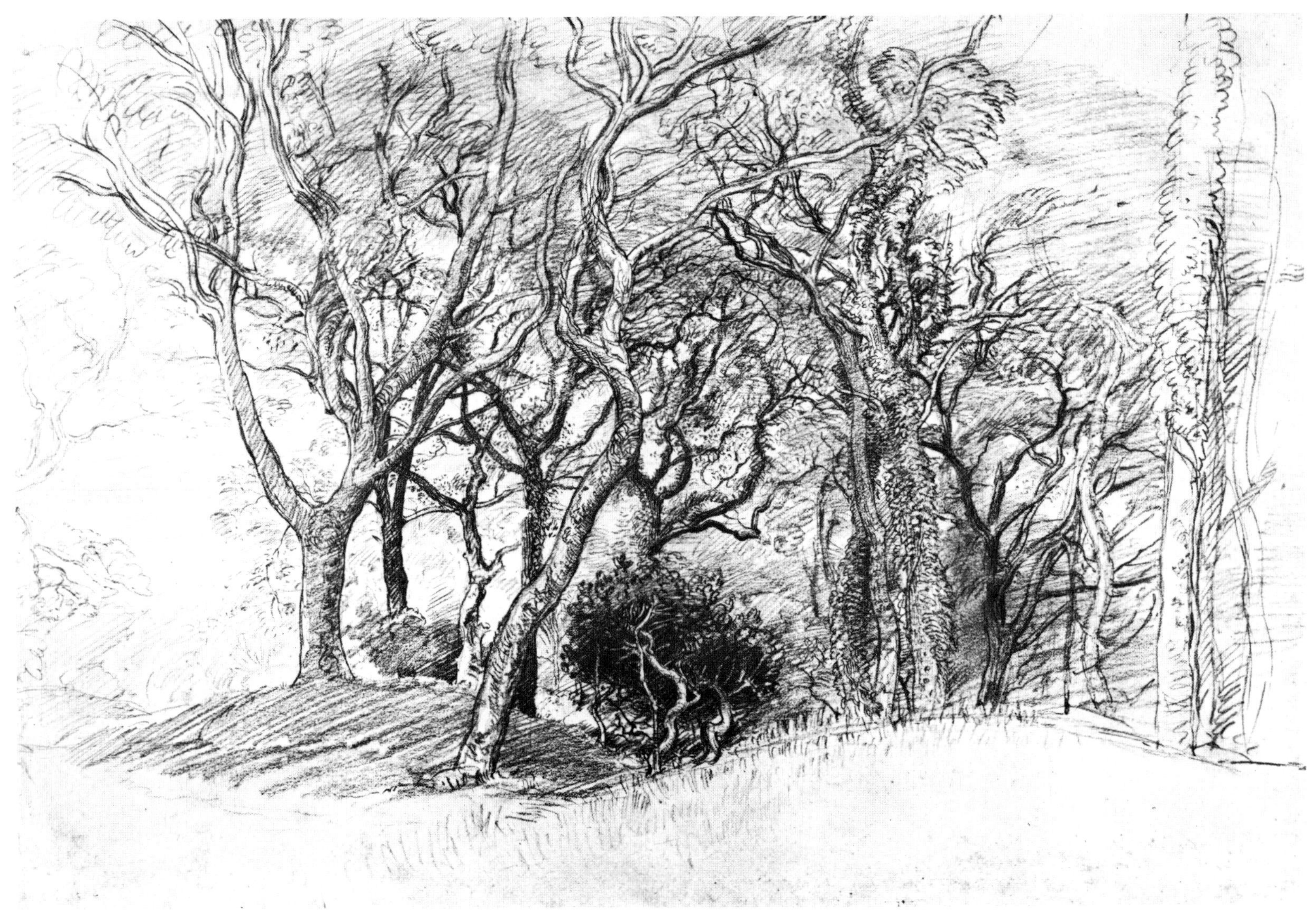

I mean to buy of him a sketch of Pistl y Cayne to which we went by the road on the left bank of the Maw which we crossed by the white footbridge I crossed the day before. It was a new way even to P: and we therefore entangled ourselves in a forest, but the mountain torrent afforded us great pleasure. In less than two hours we came to the waterfall Rhaiadyr y Mawddack which is a double and very fine one especially on the South Side on which we were – Above the fall is a bridge – We crossed it and after looking at the fall on this side we came to the spout of the Cayne, a single lofty and most elegant fall which I left Mr. P: to take a sketch of, which I mean hereafter to buy. He has promised to call on me. I left him at one.' Palmer called on Crabb Robinson in November of the same year and Robinson bought *A Waterfall with a distant view of Snowdon* for 10 guineas. Crabb Robinson liked Palmer although he was disturbed by some of his views. 'He is so much behind on moral subjects as to disapprove of the repeal of the Corporation and Test Act! He believes in witchcraft', he writes in amazement. Nevertheless they spent much time together, Palmer paying visits in the evenings and it must have been an encouragement for him to sell some of his work.

103 *The Waterfalls, Pistil Mawddach, North Wales*, 1835/6 (The Tate Gallery)

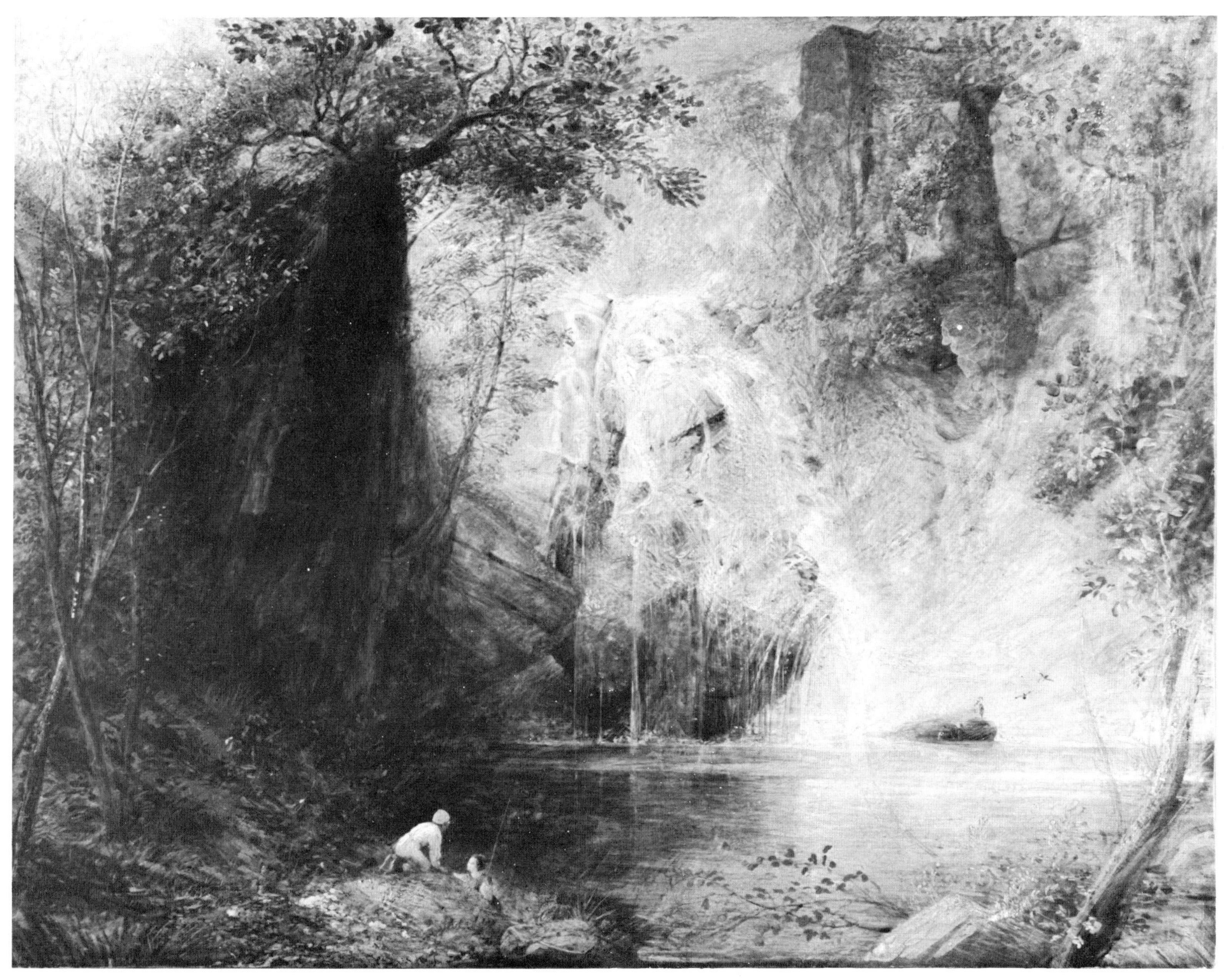

THE LATER YEARS

1837–1881

In 1837 Palmer's life was to change once more. In January, his old nurse died, 'My dear Nurse and most faithful servant and friend, Mary Ward, died at 5 minutes to five o'clock 18th January 1837, the same day of the same month on which my Mother died, confined to her bed 11 days.' Without feminine companionship Palmer was lost and it is reasonable to make the assumption that the death of his nurse was in part at least responsible for his marriage to Hannah, oldest daughter of John Linnell, in the autumn of 1837. Linnell insisted that 'his daughter should never be married in church' and Palmer wrote, '1837 SP was married at the Court House, Marylebone; he a churchman!' But he was able to escape from the physical presence of his father-in-law for a time at the beginning of his married life. George Richmond proposed that the newlyweds should accompany his wife and himself to Italy, where he was going to study, and offered Palmer enough money which, together with his own small savings, would give him a start. Palmer readily accepted.

At first it was a success, Hannah was glad to get away from the drudgery of housekeeping for her father and the ministerings of her mother and Palmer was off at last to see Italy which he had longed to do for years but as a honeymoon it quickly became a disaster. Four weeks after leaving England they arrived in Rome, that 'wilderness of wonders' as he called it. 'A letter he wrote to Mr. Richmond in September 1828, shows that even then he was keenly sensitive to the associations in the midst of which he now found himself, and in after years he wrote, "Rome is a thing by itself which, once seen, leaves the memory no more. A City of Art which one had dreamed of before, and can scarce believe that one has really seen." But the time of dreams and reveries was gone by, and though, in his short autobiography, my father speaks lightly of this Italian sojourn as his 'wedding trip', never have those words been so singularly applied. He and his young wife set themselves tasks whose difficulty and laboriousness might have daunted the strongest and most accomplished veteran. Every hour seems to have had a labour of its own; and almost every form of pleasure-taking was made impossible by a penurious economy. Enthusiasm for the associations and admiration of the beauty of what they set themselves to paint carried them through; but the girl, so fresh from her mother's nervous guardianship, broke down at last from the sheer hard, unhealthy, drudgery of working early and late at copies from the Old Masters, including the Stanze of Raphael, and the frescoes of the Sistine Chapel.'

104 John Linnell, *Self Portrait* (National Portrait Gallery)

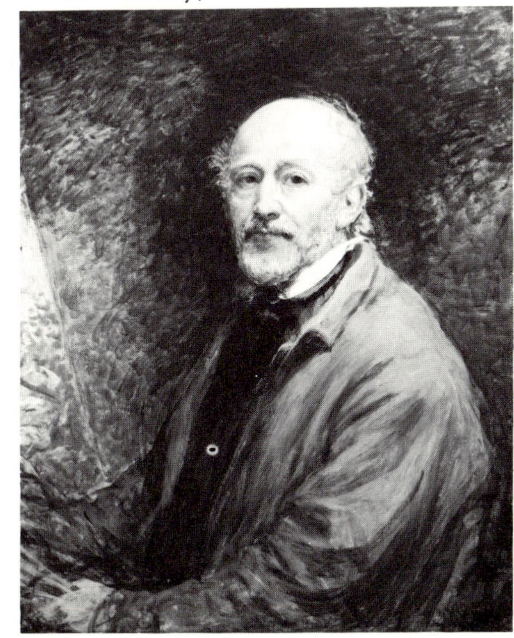

They stayed in Italy for two years and although Richmond lent them money, every penny had to be counted. At one time in Rome in winter they

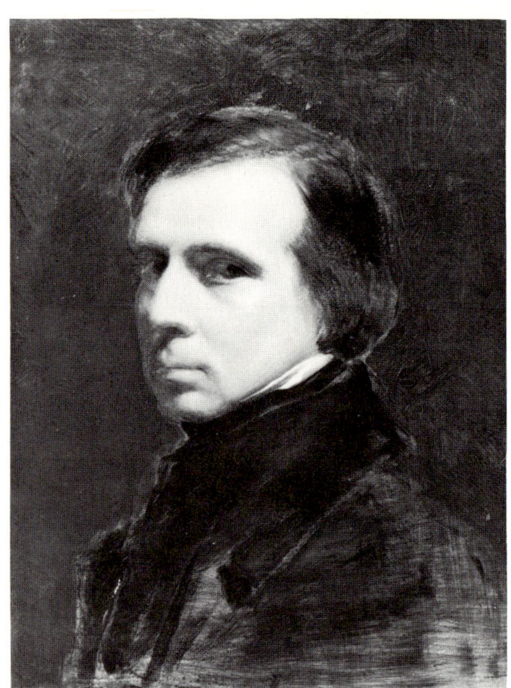
105 George Richmond, *Self Portrait* (National Portrait Gallery)

lived in a room without a fireplace. Afterwards he told Edward Calvert 'The weather was for months very rainy, and so cold that I wore a waistcoat lined with flannel, and Mrs Palmer wrapped up like a Mummy.'[10]

Because of his poverty he was unable to attract patrons for which he would have had to lead a social life requiring good clothes and a certain social ease. Palmer had never given much consideration to his appearance and was now so shabby that he was stared at in the street and his conversation was far too unconventional for a Roman salon – the result, no commissions. Richmond, on the other hand, was in his element to the extent that he was able to return to England with considerably more money than he had originally taken with him.

In the spring the Palmers went to Naples, suffering the fleas and what Palmer called 'a pestiferous little den with only a thin roof between us and the sun in a bed not large enough for one person, with a window opening inwards to the shaft or funnel of the house, ventilated only by blasts from drains and kitchens'. Then on to Pompeii for a month, living among the ruins in a room with an unglazed window while Vesuvius erupted above and 'the makeshift door shook and the watchdogs bayed'; in the evenings they read Bulwer Lytton's *The Last Days of Pompeii.*

At the end of the summer they returned to Rome. Linnell was becoming impatient with their protracted 'wedding trip' as Palmer called it, and in one of the many letters to his daughter – he wrote once a fortnight – he writes, 'July 30, 1839. (To Hannah) . . . The completing a tour like yours is something like completing a picture. It may be spoiled by dwelling too long upon it, and should be ended suddenly; for going on proceeds often from the habit of going on, rather than a clear perception of advantage. To know when to leave off is a great art in everything. If you can make your escape now, do not lose the opportunity, but come over the first bridge that presents itself to your notice. I wait, however, in despair of being able to influence the Governor, whose immoveable walk-through-rivers disposition, which he inherits from his no-thoroughfare-path-papa, I too well remember. I ought, however, to say what I can to cheer him up in his troubles, though I only say these things about rivers to help him over the bridge if I can; but he is such a neck-or-nothing man . . . The whole machine of our family goes on pretty well, but I feel as if I were in a treadmill sometimes, obliged to go faster than I wish, and that if I did not keep step, I should be in danger of breaking my shins, or something worse.'

Palmer was disinclined to return immediately and proposed to Linnell that they should visit Florence where Hannah could make more copies of the Old Masters – Linnell was paying his daughter six shillings and ninepence each for these – but in the event permission to work in the galleries was so delayed that they abandoned the project and started homeward arriving in England in November. His son records that 'It was with tears in his eyes that my father turned for the last glimpse of the land where he said he left his heart . . . He also wrote "Hail Railroads! Hail!" – a prophetic lament for the England he had loved.'[11]

The tour of Italy had been a disaster, they had made no money and they had had to work incessantly in the hope of collecting enough to sell on their return to settle their debts. Hannah had become ill trying to fulfil her father's commission and Palmer had fallen under the spell of Italian art thereby wiping away every vestige of his earlier poetic genius. The effect of his Italian journey can be seen in *A Dream in the Apennine* (*134*), *The Colosseum and Alban Mount* (*97*), *View from the Villa d'Este at Tivoli* (*107*), and *Florence* (*106*), all fine examples of his craftsmanship but no more. Even more unfortunate was that he was never able to shake off the influence, carrying it with him in the composition of the *Dream*, into *A Mountain Stream and an Ancient Fortress* (*132*) of 1879, and the cypresses and grandiose views in the etchings he was to make later. His Italian tour was but one factor, if the deciding one, in the decline of his visionary powers which in fact started as far back as 1831. Going to Italy was in the nature of a search for a spiritual support, a hope of rejuvenation, the substitute for Blake which Linnell had failed to become. Ideal art also failed him for all his admiration of Claude. He once wrote 'Ordinary landscapes remind us of what we see in the country; Claude's of what we read in the greatest poets and of their perception of the country.' He probably knew subconsciously but was unable to admit to it that it was but another means, as were his marriage and his treks to Wales, to find a salvation. He had contemplated visiting the Lake District, before embarking for Italy, to search for waterfalls which even at this late stage would indicate that he was led by his intuition in the right direction but without the means for expression.

It would have taken an artist of rare perception, physical stamina and an even rarer quality of genius to have developed the work he had done in the mid 1820s. By the time he returned from Italy he was thirty-four and the sexual drive which he had sublimated through his art had lost the urgency it had had fourteen years before. He was now married so that he no longer needed to channel his sexual impulses. In addition he felt it necessary to earn some money, there had been an almost total lack of support for his Shoreham work, and he did not know consciously what the real basis of his

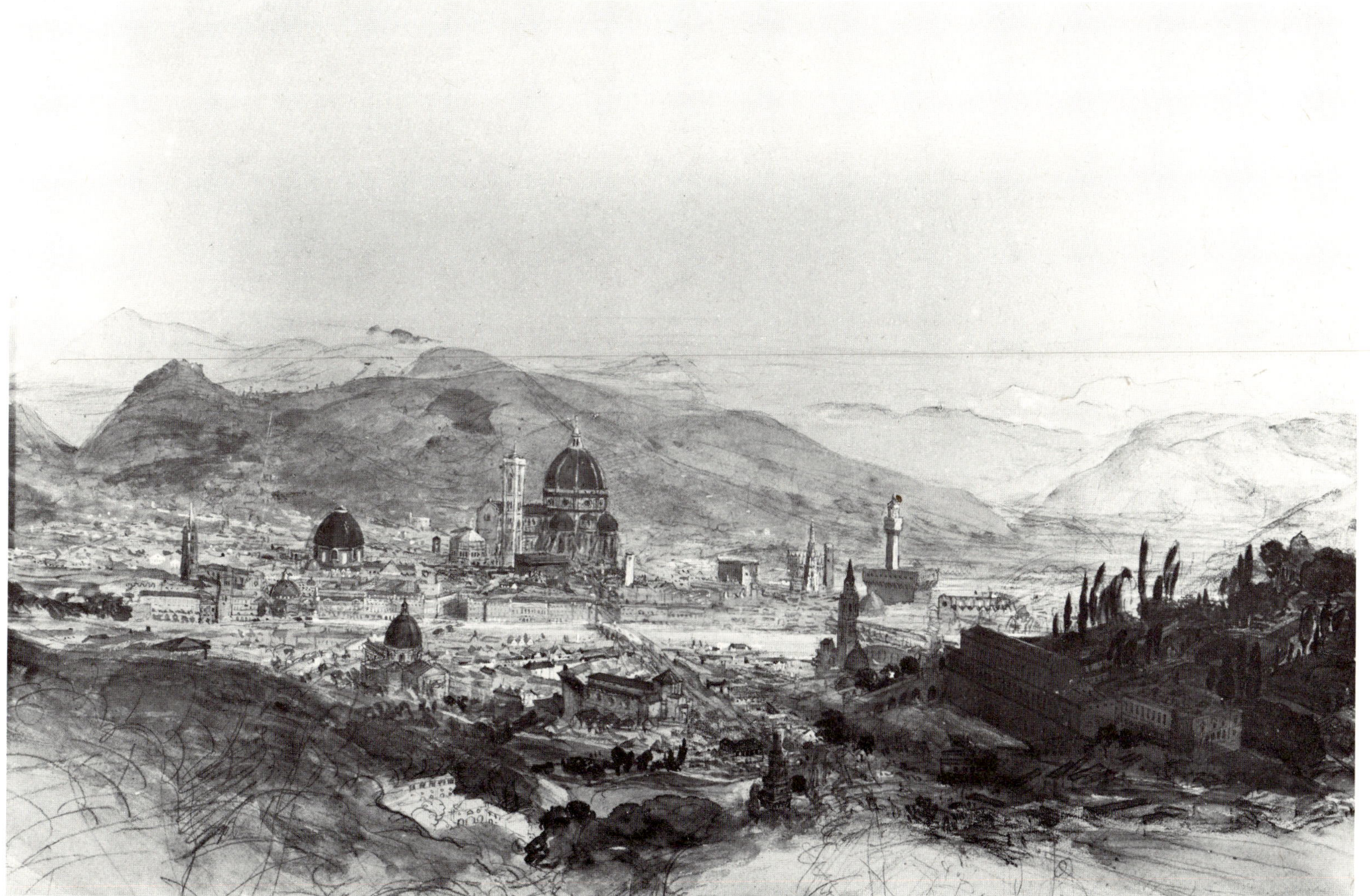

106 *Florence*, 1838 (Victoria and Albert Museum)

art was. He knew instinctively he could not stand still at the point of development he had reached in 1830 and reiterate endlessly upon these elements, his work would have ended as stale and vacuous as any of the 'Moderns with their effects' but, even had he known what was to be done, the problem of how was another question and he had no precedent not even in Blake.

For the time being the Palmers' financial difficulties were in abeyance. Linnell's engravings of Michel Angelo's paintings in the Sistine Chapel, which they had taken with them and coloured from the originals, sold for good prices as did Hannah's copies of the Old Masters, but this source of income was soon exhausted and Palmer had to face the problem of making a living, a task for which he was singularly unsuited. It had been his intention to return to his Shoreham studies and, from the benefit of his Italian experiences, make them into oil paintings. But whether the two years of almost unremitted water-colour practice had, for the time being, made oils difficult or uncongenial, or whether there were additional discouraging personal influences, the oil pictures of this time were weak and timid to a degree surprising to those who are familiar with the crisp touch, glowing colour, and bold impasto of the best Shoreham panels. The composition might be graceful, the light and shade well studied, but the love of higher qualities than these, the 'double vision' so peculiarly evident in those works appeared no longer.

Palmer maintained that had he had encouragement or advice at this time he might have succeeded with this venture into a new dimension with oils. But given his emotional development at this stage of his life this seems unlikely. Matters were not prospering in other directions, in a notebook of 1840 he writes, 'Supposing lessons stop, and nothing more is earned – avoid snuff, two candles, sugar in tea, waste of butter and soap . . . But it is more difficult at present to get than to save. Query. Go into the country for one month to make little drawings for sale? Two candles a night are not a remarkably liberal allowance for a hard-working artist and his wife, but he is prepared to go back to the still narrower rations of the "Epic Poet".' From this it appears that he had at least found some teaching and from a later remark by his son in *Life and Letters* we find that in 1841 he was staying with a Lady Stephens in Dorset, teaching and painting pictures, such as the *View of Lulworth Cove*, which, however, he was unable to sell.

From an 1842 memoranda we have a picture of the ebb to which his fortunes had fallen. 'Our professional experience, 1842. February 3, I went to the British Gallery, and found both my pictures and one of Anny's rejected. March. Mr. Ruskin and others were shown our drawings. Mr. Nasmyth was to name me as a teacher to Admiral Otway. I offered Miss B——, Addison Road, to teach one pupil for 10s. per annum. (This was a school) Went to British Artists, and found one picture hung near the ceiling, another rejected, and Anny's Job rejected. Mine were the same pictures I sent to the B: Gallery, for the new frames for which I had paid £5 8s.' His oldest son was born on the 27th of January, 1842, whom he named Thomas More after the Chancellor whose portrait had hung at Shoreham to 'frown away vice and levity and infidelity', and from August until October the family moved to Thatcham in Berkshire. A. H. Palmer records that he painted two water-colours during his visit which were exhibited in the Gallery of the Old Society.

By now he was beginning to relinquish the idea of painting in oils and, although he was not to abandon oils completely, he was practising more and more in water-colours and in 1843 he was made an Associate of the Royal

Society of painters in Water Colour. His son remarks, 'As my father was one of those who are liable to be depressed by failure and exhilerated by success far more than is usual, it is probable that Napoleon after Austerlitz was less elated than he, when the Secretary's letter arrived.' One of his drawings *Evening, the Ruins of a Walled City* sold for £30 which was a considerable sum of money for him at that time. In September of the same year he again set out for Wales, the manner of his going and equipage for these expeditions are well described in *Life and Letters*: 'The sketching expeditions were not made in at all a luxurious manner. The apparatus carried was as simple as it was complete. A deal case or a portfolio slung round the shoulders with a strap held a good supply of paper, together with two large but very light wooden palettes coated with home-made white enamel and set with thick clots of colour so prepared as to be readily moved by the brush or the finger. A light hand-basket held a change or two of linen, reserve colours, an old campstool which had seen service in Italy and, when necessary, the lunch or dinner. The coat was an accumulation of pockets in which were stowed away the all-important snuff-box, knives, chalks, charcoal, coloured crayons, and sketchbooks, besides a pair of large, round, neutral-tint spectacles made for near sight. These were carried specially for sunsets and the brightest effects on water; and, together with a small diminishing mirror, completed the equipment. The minimum of the plainest clothes and boots heavily nailed furthered the sketcher's object, which was to travel on unfrequented tracks or mountain paths, in any company or none, and utterly unfettered. A good constitution and the training of his youth made him indifferent to

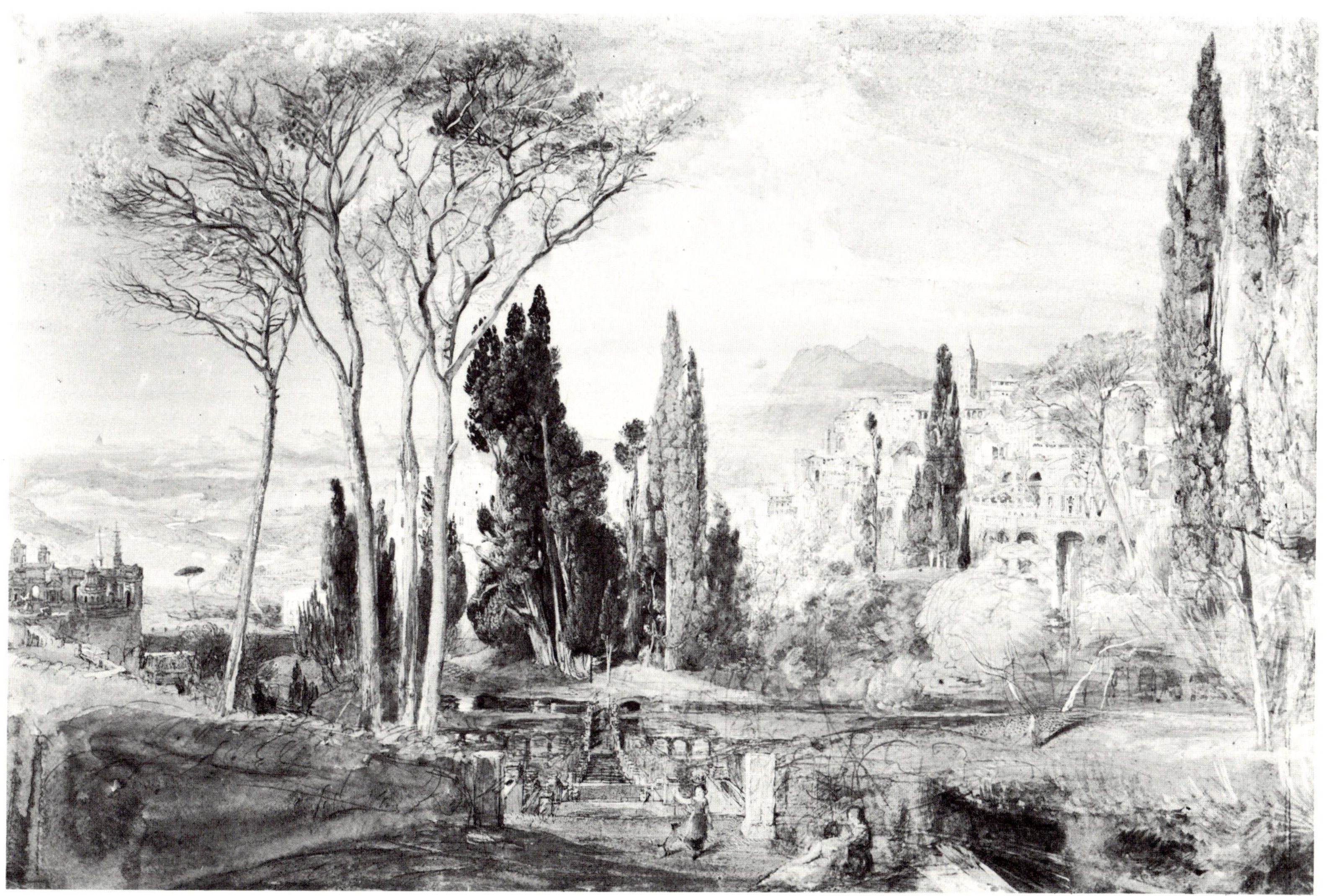

107 *View from the Villa d'Este at Tivoli*, 1839 (Ashmolean Museum)

rough quarters and rough diet. He writes, "In exploring wild country I have been for a fortnight together uncertain each day whether I shall get a bed under cover at night; and about midsummer I have repeatedly been walking all night to watch the mystic phenomena of the silent hours." He seemed as much at home in clambering down a Welsh mountain towards dusk after a hard day's work, guided only by the roar of a neighbouring torrent, as in joining the evening gossip in the chimney-corner of a village inn, after explaining to some who took him for a travelling pedlar that he had nothing to show. He tells how he read a seven-volume edition of Sir Charles Grandison for the second time while weather-bound in a wild district of Wales; how he foregathered with Crabb Robinson whom he met on one of these occasions; or how he lay in bed while his drenched clothes were being dried for him at a kitchen fire of the inn where he had taken shelter.'

Palmer also recorded his sketching methods in his own system of shorthand in one of his notebooks: 'Very transitory effects, e.g. sunsets. These are generally quite lost through trying to do too much. Long before a palette can be taken out of the portfolio, the cloud has passed off the mountain, or the golden gleam has become dingy shade. Therefore a scratch with pencil in the sketch-book is the first thing – writing what there is no time to draw. Then get out the crayons; and with the scene before you, and the remembrance fresh, try to make something like it. If this comes like, it is enough; if not, keep it with water-colour. It is best done small – half or a quarter size of your portfolio paper (probably $\frac{1}{4}$ Imperial) is enough. Then make a separate, careful outline of the scene, going on if you have time, and adding the local colour etc.

'It is surprising how few sketches of transitory effects painters bring home which, after a lapse of time, reproduce the effects to their memory. Perhaps because they do not confine themselves to the characteristics of the effect – that very something which made them get out their paper; perhaps because they go on with it after the effect goes off, trying to get in some detail, instead of taking another piece of paper. I can paint better from my pencil memoranda of effects than from any other. If an effect be very fine, I think we should, beside what I have recommended, make a little coloured sketch of it immediately on going home.

'Effects, less transitory, of sunshine on beautiful matter. Little, careful sketches about $\frac{1}{4}$ of the portfolio size, in water-colours on white paper. How many beautiful recollections might be brought home from a fine country, if we would but limit our attempts to the measure of our time and means, and try, at all events, to secure the characteristic features and hues, instead of making ambitious attempts where time and opportunity are small.'

In 1844 his second child, Mary Elizabeth, was born and in the autumn they all went to Guildford where, to judge by the notes he made, he was in far more cheerful spirits than had prevailed since his return from Italy. He begins by making a careful and poetic analysis of the light: 'Guildford 1844. The lights in nature are more distinct from the shadows (however modified by reflection) than in pictures. The shadows are very deep relatively to the lights, yet seem clear and full of reflected light. This quality is worth a most serious effort. It is much seen in shady lanes. The want of it gives a dismal, indoor look to the picture. Cast shadows across lanes &c, are not hard, or cut out, or all of a depth – some very dark and sharp winding up to the emphasis against the brilliant light. With these are intermixed tender, transparent shadows, and half-shadows, in every variety of intermixture and gradation. But the first thing that struck me on coming here was the POSITIVENESS, INTENSE BRIGHTNESS, and WARMTH of the

LIGHTS; and that the SHADOWS are full of REFLECTED LIGHT, though very deep.'

He then goes on to suggest the means to be employed to capture these qualities: 'The shapes of the focal lights and touches must be thoroughly understood and drawn to give any chance of imitating the vivid splendour of nature's lights. The shadows in nature are very deep compared with the wonderful light; and themselves, nevertheless, are clear, beautiful, and clean in colour, and full of reflected light, warm or cool. The smiting of the light upon the shade is accompanied by its opposite, viz. endless play and gradation. Nature seemed WARMER than ever, but with a perpetual interplay of greys.

'Some of the conditions of the glitter in sunshine IMPORTANT: Holes of dark. Cast shadows; as well as the incessant play of the common shadows.

'To a black or dark animal and a white one, all the landscape – excepting stubble fields and suchlike – will be a MIDDLE TINT.

'Glitter of a white or very light object will be helped by its SQUARENESS of shapes, GENUINE MIDDLE TINT of its BACKGROUND, a mass of something relieving dark near it, and the play of CAST SHADOWS and HOLES of dark, which are the enrichment of nature's breadth. These, I think, govern and mass the varieties of colour in banks of wood &c., and make smooth, enamelly hills precious'.

These and many like observations appear to have been condensed, and the result entered as follows on a slip of cardboard: '1844. WHITE in FULL

108 *Farmyard near Princes Risborough*, 1848 (Ashmolean Museum)

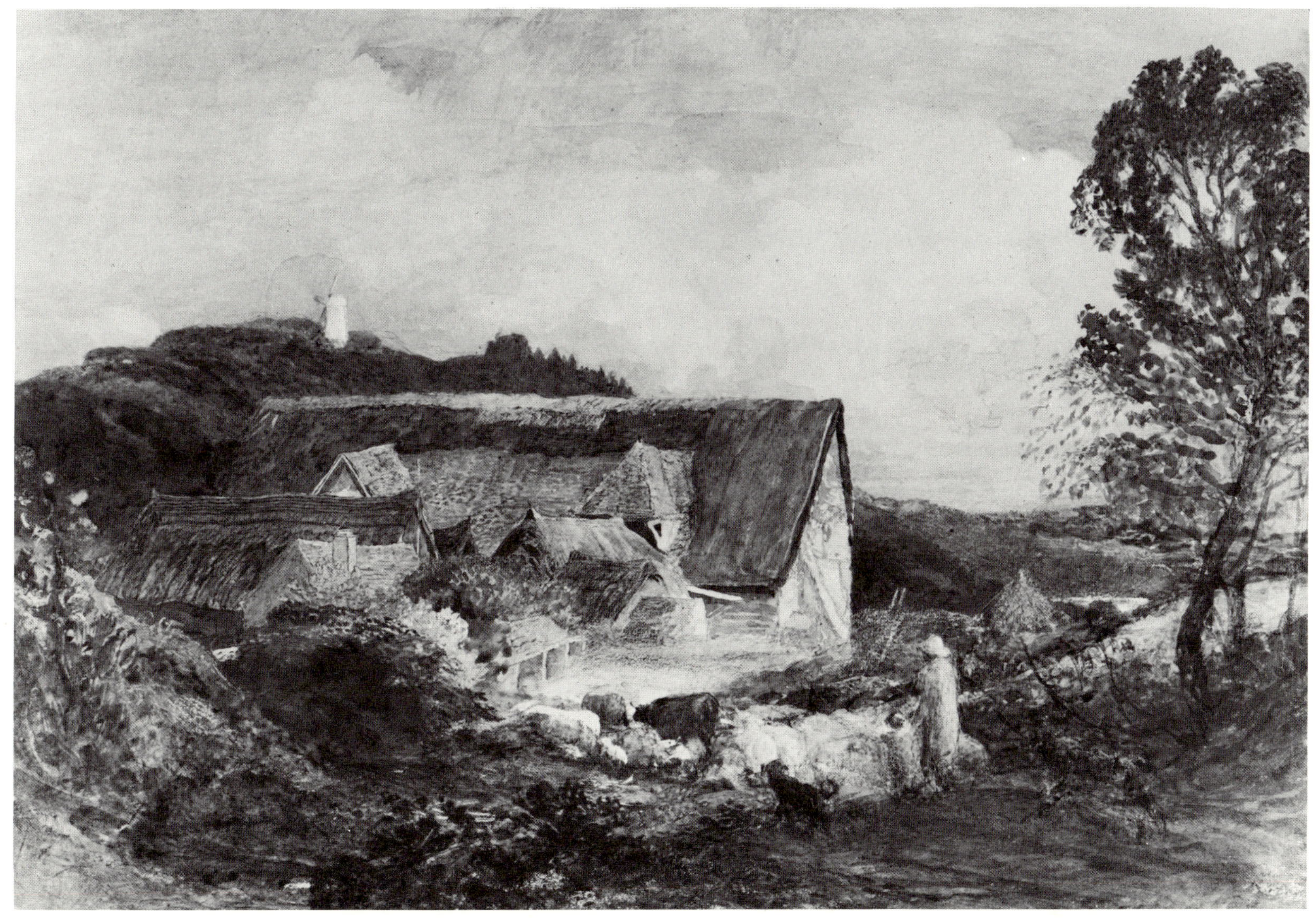

POWER from the first. Remember blazing days wherein it makes middle-tint colours in sunshine seem dark, AND GRAYS COOLER THAN WHITE. WHITE NOT TONED WITH ORANGE, but in juxtaposition with the PRIMITIVES.
DEADLY DARK BROWNS LAID ON AT ONCE.
FLASHES of LIGHT, or BLOW of DARK.
To get vast space, what a world of power does aerial perspective open! From the dock-leaf at our feet, far, far away to the isles of the ocean. And thence – far thence, into the abyss of boundless light. O! what heavenly grays does this suggest!' After Guildford he went to Wales for another three weeks collecting material for paintings but in spite of all this hard work 1844 was financially his most unsuccessful year since 1839 and it was only through his teaching that he was able to remain solvent.

The family went to Margate in 1845 and Palmer spent a good deal of his time with them but later visited Princes Risborough in Buckinghamshire where he painted the water-colour *Farmyard near Princes Risborough* (*108*), a beautifully-drawn work if unexciting in colour and still showing traces on the roofs of the barns of the lessons he had learned from the thatched barns of Shoreham. Palmer seems to have been taken with Princes Risborough for he returned there in 1848 and painted another view of the same farmyard (*112*) with the same care and skill he had expended before. But it is in the first painting and in notes he made about this time that we have a picture of how far behind him now were the visionary years. He writes 'Claude brought together things in which all men delight. Majestic trees, sunny skies, rivers with gentle falls, venerable ruins and extensive distances. His ground was soft for pasture or repose. The accident which most quickens such beauty, is LIGHT.

'2nd. SUBJECTS in which ELEMENTS, or their combinations or secondaries, are the principal matters, as such in which are expressed DEW; SHOWERS or MOISTURE; THE DEEP-TONES, FERTILIZING RAIN-CLOUD; DROUGHT, with its refuge of deep, hollow shade, and a cold spring; the BROOK; THE GUSHING SPRING, or FOUNTAIN; AERIAL DISTANCE.

'3rd. LIGHT either produced by its great enforcer cast shadow, or by great halved opposites, as when the sun is in the picture.

'4th. DARKNESS, with its focus of coruscating light, and a moon or lanthorn. The precious and latent springs of poetry are to be found here.

'FIGURES, which in landscape are an adjunct, should if possible be in ACTION, and TELL a STORY.

'PRUDENTIALLY it is important (1) to ATTRACT the EYE. These attract the eye – BROAD EFFECT; STRONG CONTRASTS, as warm and cool, bright light and deep shade; VIVACITY; SPARKLE; FRESHNESS; EMPTY and FULL.
(2) TO FIX THE ATTENTION by FULNESS and INTRICACY;
(3) TO AWAKEN SYMPATHY by doing what WE STRONGLY LOVE.
(4) TO DELIGHT by close IMITATION, at least on the points which first meet the eye, and by EXECUTION.'

The trouble has always been that men do not know, any more than Palmer knew at this time, in what they delight. And in spite of all the work, the attempts to delight men – perhaps because of it – he was able to earn only the barest income from his paintings. A set of four illustrations for the first edition of a Dickens' *Pictures from Italy* paid him £21 in 1845 and for the years 1843 to 1853 the total of his earnings by his paintings amounted to £45. But for his teaching he could not have survived.

On December the 15th 1847 Mary Elizabeth, his daughter, died. Edward Calvert did what he could to comfort the parents, spending every evening with them but Palmer's grief was intense. His son records, 'What he felt was an intense, ceaseless, and insufferable torture to which, but for that one hope of ultimate reunion which forms so strong and beautiful a feature of Christianity, death would have been far preferable. His grief was also the harder to bear by means of his almost childish inability to restrain it. He had to go about his work and to keep his teaching engagements with eyes bleared and a voice often choked by sorrow'. By the spring of 1848 the associations with his daughter of the house in Grove Street became overpowering and the family moved to 1a Victoria Road, Kensington. By all accounts Lissom Grove had become a noisome place and the move may also have been expedient in other respects. Kensington helped to ameliorate Palmer's loss, he found himself in the midst of an artistic circle where he made a number of friends and the proximity of the Gardens formed a better apology for the country than Grove Street had done.

In the summer he wavered between going to Yorkshire or the South West but his old prejudices against the North prevailed and he spent most of July in Cornwall where he amassed a large number of pencil, chalk and watercolour sketches, including a series of sunsets, painted each day for three weeks from the same location foreshadowing Monet. He afterwards remarked that they were of great value to him and possibly the result of these

109 *At Redhill*, 1848 (Ashmolean Museum)

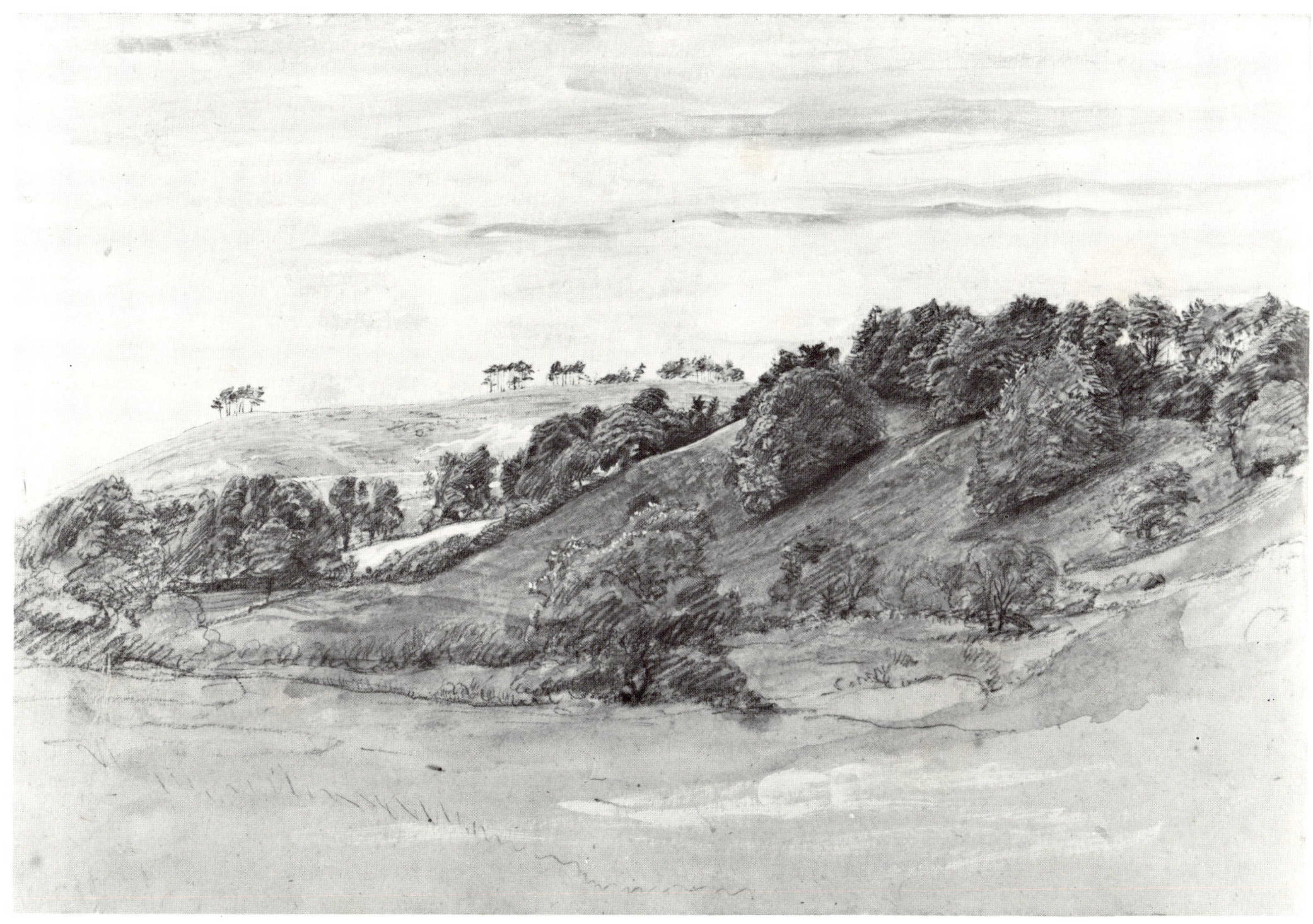

studies can be seen in such works as *The Shadowy Stream* (*135*) and *Going to Fold* (*136*).

Nearly two thirds of his income in 1848 was derived from teaching, his drawings and paintings, considering the time and devotion lavished upon them were still selling at absurdly low prices, however, he occasionally received moral support from fellow artists. He writes 'This year I made a great advance in the estimation of artists by my mottled-sky drawing begun at Margate'. This was *The Watermill* (*111*) and the 'Margate Mottle', as he called it, may be seen in *The Shadowy Stream* and *Going to Fold* but is absent in *At Redhill* (*109*) also painted in 1848.

On the 17th of December Palmer's father died and he was again grief stricken, 'How he loved my childhood's soul and MIND – how he laboured to improve them, sitting in the house and walking in the fields!' The following summer he took his family for a visit to Red Hill in Surrey, then a quiet and pleasant neighbourhood. 'Here' wrote his son, 'Mr Linnell now ruled his small dominion of "Redstone Wood" as independently as an eastern chief. Designing his own house, and personally supervising the fitting of almost every block of stone in its strong walls, he had so placed it on the brow of a well-timbered hill sloping towards the west that it served as his observatory for those effects for which he was soon to become celebrated. He had, as it were, fortified a stronghold in the midst of the placid and conventional country society, and there revelled in his art, pored over Greek and Hebrew, ground his corn, baked his bread, brewed his ale, and thundered forth his denunciations of men and opinions that displeased him; being aided and abetted in all that he did by a family to whom, for the most part, every word of his was an irresistible ukase.'

Palmer had now moved once again, this time to 6 Douro Place, also in Kensington, described as a small ugly villa, semi-detached from the piano of an ultra-modern, geranium-growing family next door. So vigorously did the neighbours protest against the weeds allowed to mature in Palmer's garden as lessons for his pupils, that there was no resource but the scythe. 'Farewell soft clusters', he wrote, 'the only pretty things about these premises; ye are to be mowed this evening, and to leave a scraped scrap of respectability!' Since he was earning most of his living as a teacher he had no option but to conform to the Victorian middle class social life upon which he depended, keeping two servants and in other ways trying to maintain a style in which Linnell, now a fashionable and successful painter, considered his daughter should be supported.

The house in Douro Place, in spite of its expense, was too small. There was no proper studio and hardly space to teach his pupils and the kind of teaching Palmer was reduced to was anything but rewarding, except financially. 'In nine cases out of ten', he wrote, 'people don't want real teaching for their daughters but some fine touched up drawings to show in which they do not reflect themselves but their masters'. He was in a vicious circle, the teaching took up much of his time, unless he could continue his painting he would fail to be accepted in the Academy and other societies of the day and therefore would lose his standing as a teacher and cease to attract pupils. Yet he was able to make a tolerable, if irksome, living and Kensington had compensations, at least he was still far enough away from his father-in-law to keep the peace between them. He had made friends locally and it was at this time that he became a member of the Etching Club which stimulated him to an interest in the medium in which he was to achieve some of the best work of his later years. He was still able to escape to Devon, Cornwall and Wales on sketching expeditions. Between 1848 and 1858 he visited Devon

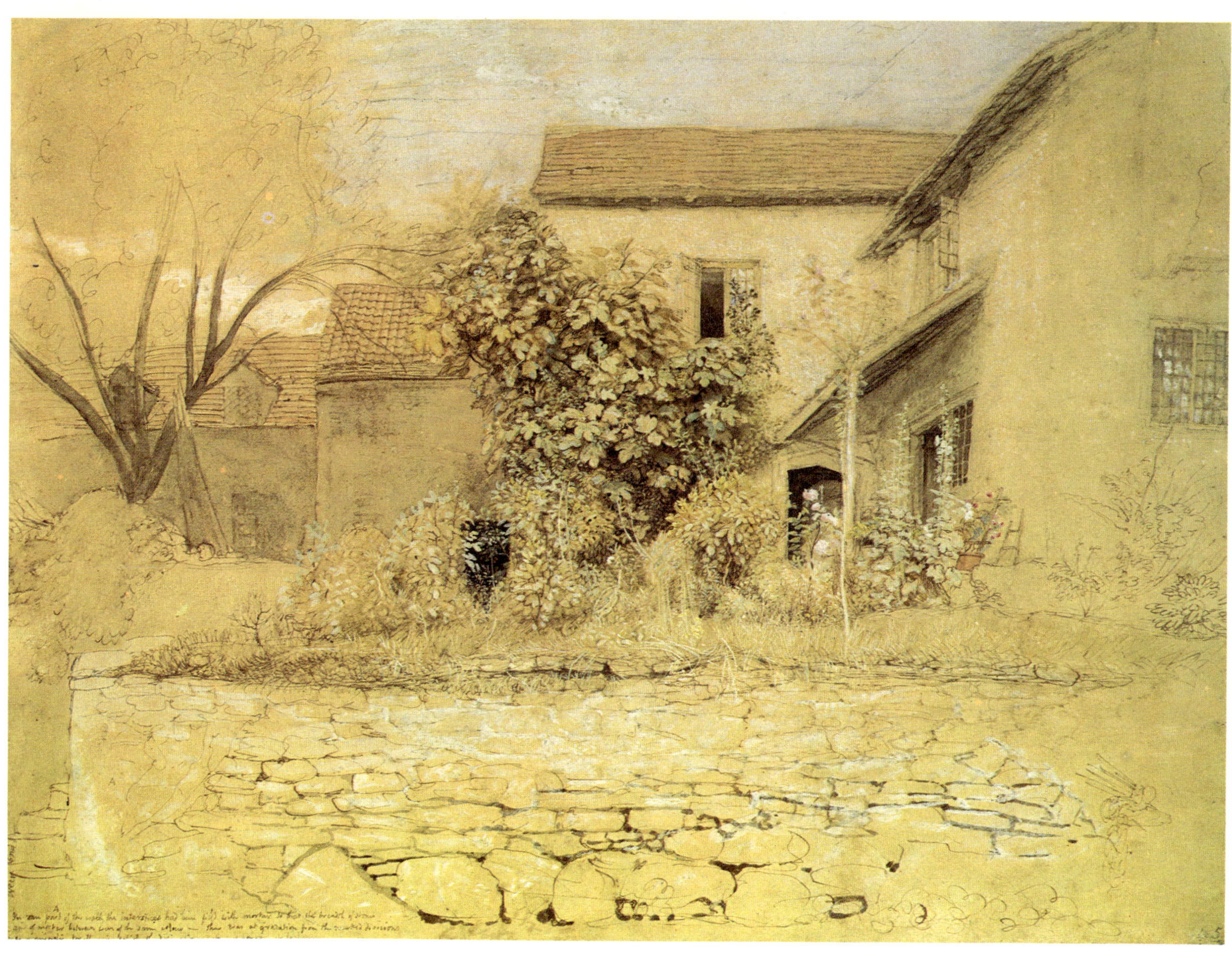

110 *Study of a Garden at Tintern*, 1835 (Ashmolean Museum)

OVERLEAF
111 *The Watermill*, 1848 (Ashmolean Museum)

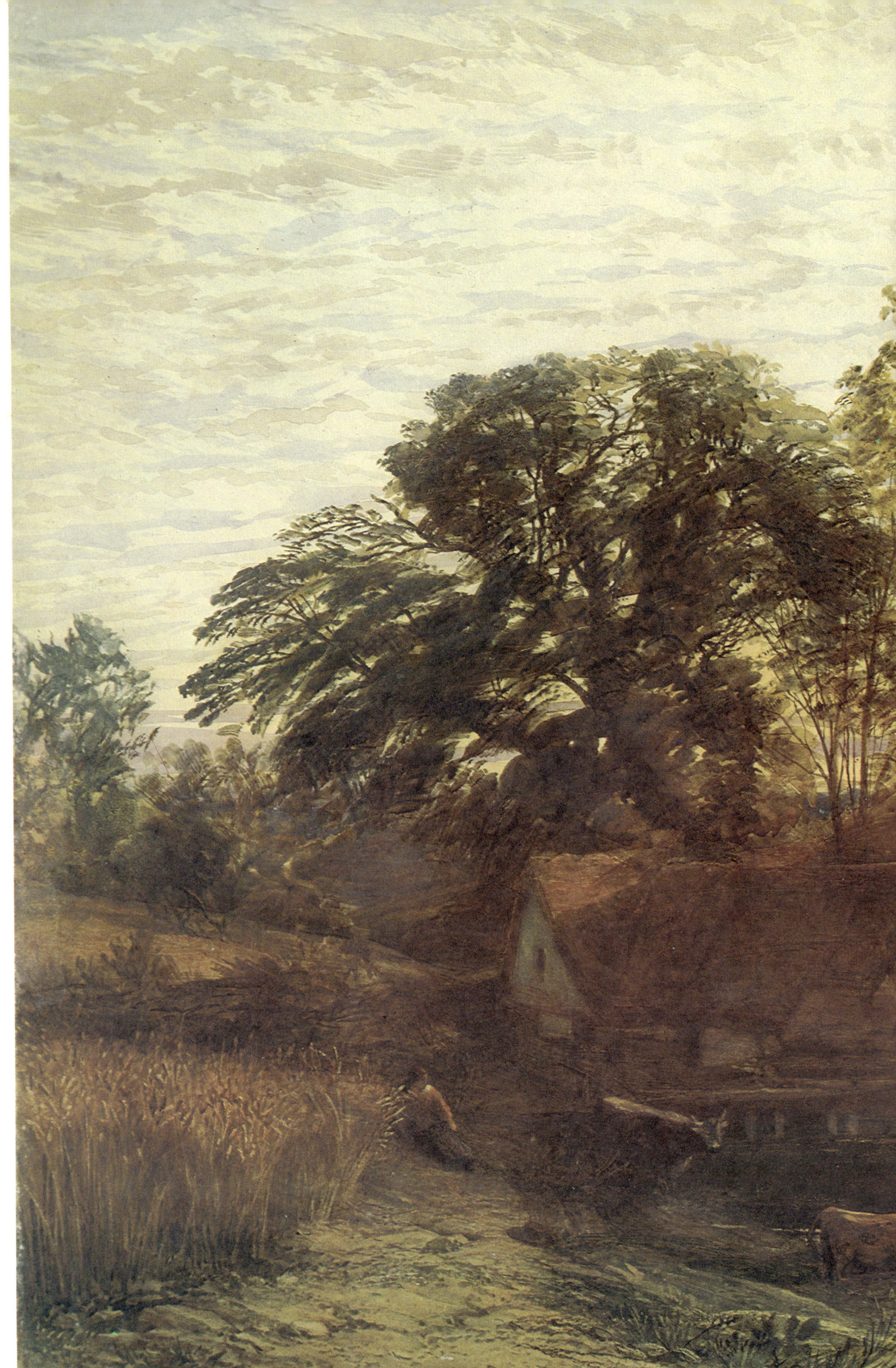

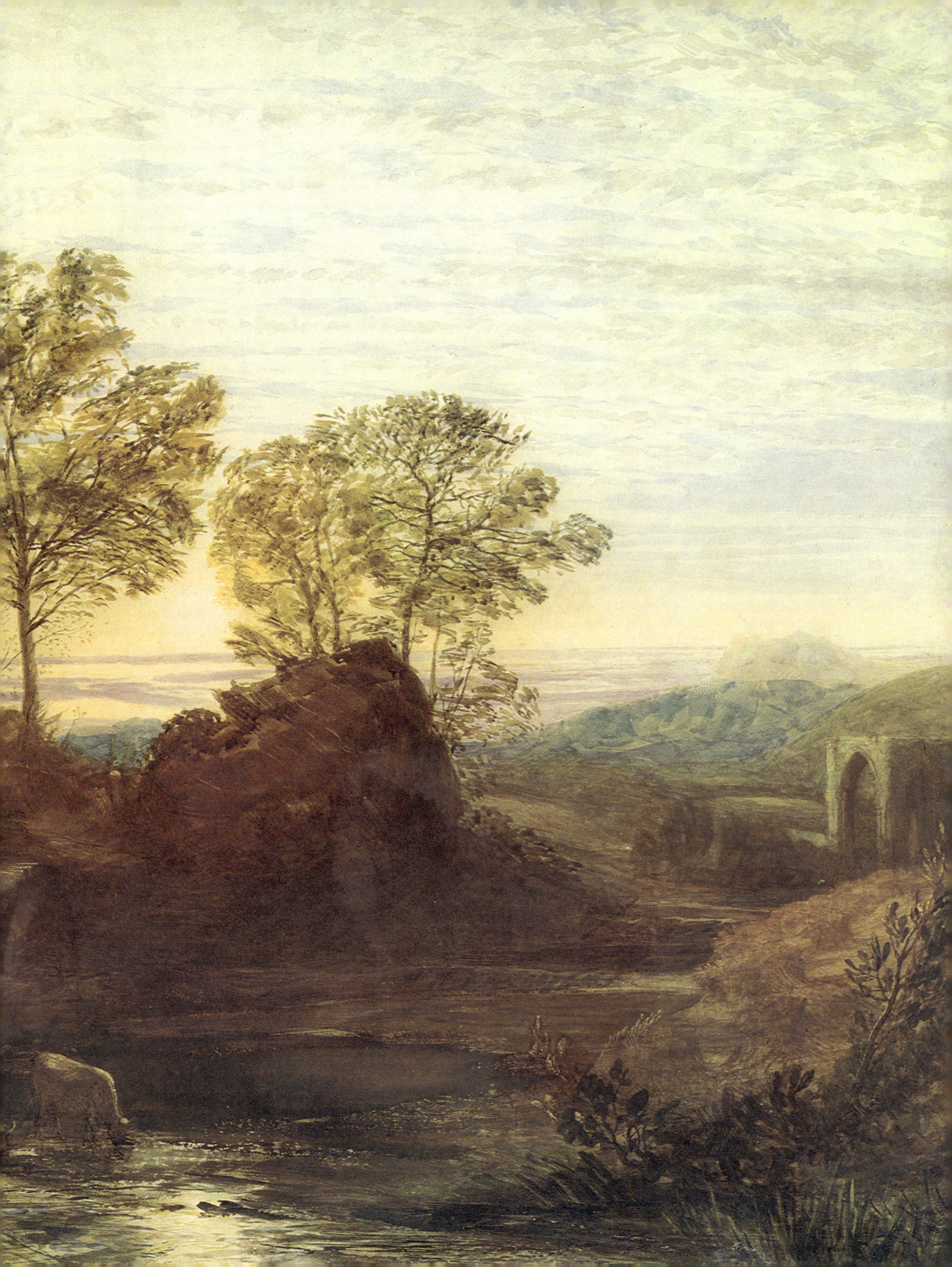

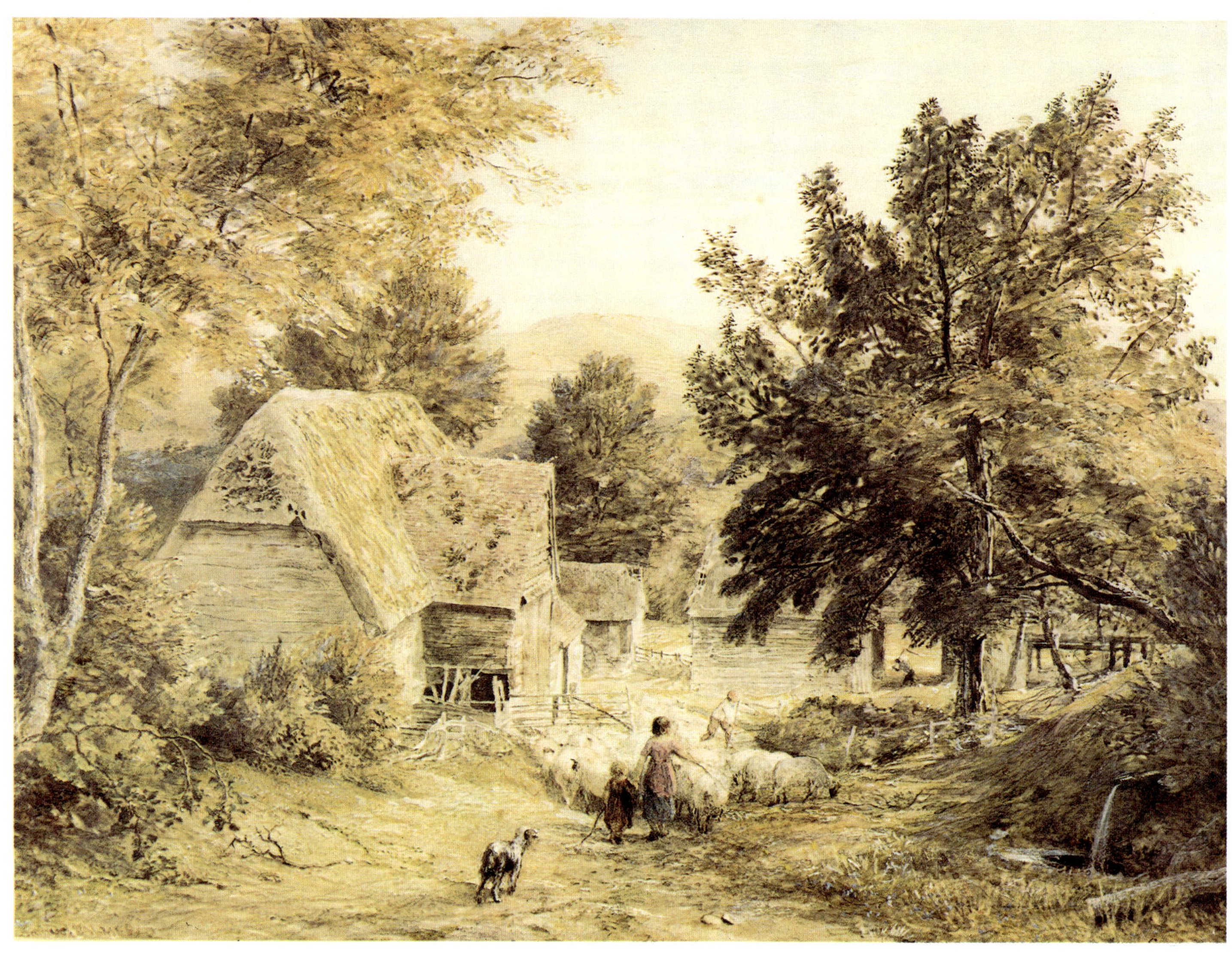

112 *Farmyard near Princes Risborough*, exhib. 1846 (Victoria and Albert Museum)

and Cornwall four times when he probably made the sketches of the Cornish coast (*113*, *114*), very different in their broad generalizations to the studies of minutiæ in 1824. Another work painted on these expeditions was *Tintagel Castle* (*115*), very richly painted with masterly craftsmanship in the study of light on the rock. It well exhibits one of Palmer's recurrent themes, that of the road on the right bordered by a low stone wall, which had first appeared in *A Dream in the Apennine*, and is found as late as 1879 in *Mountain Stream and an Ancient Fortress.*

His equipment was simpler than ever and, of course, he did much walking about. He writes, 'This would be a thing to do very leisurely; no luggage, but one spare shirt. Sketching portfolio with thin plate-paper, and Richard and Wilson's thin brown paper, which would weigh lightly. In pocket, case of pencils and black and white chalk, and light little box for reserve black and white chalk, and the three chromes, and blue and browns for slight indications of local colour on the brown paper. This, on the whole, I find the most rapid method of sketching.' He says elsewhere 'If I am spared to go again into the country I hope to begin a new plan – not sitting down to local

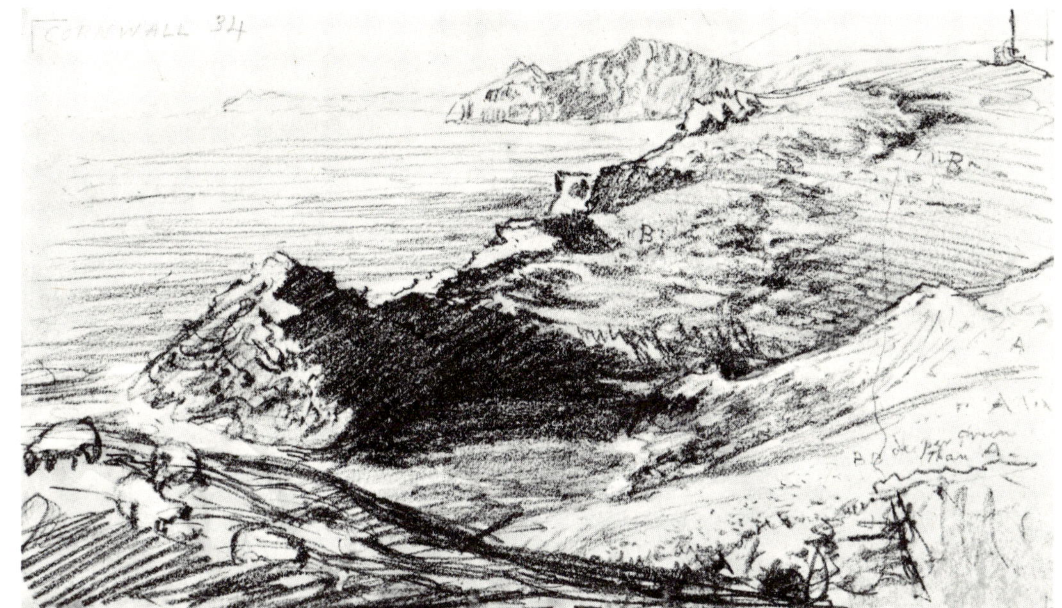

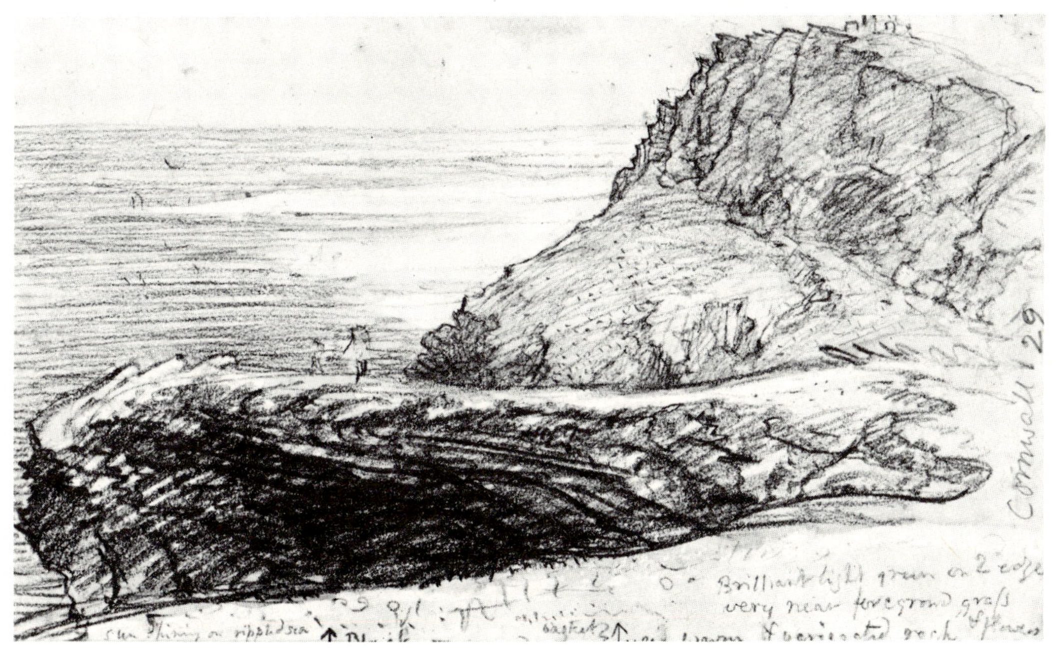

113, 114 Two Sketchbook pages 24 and 34, *Cornish Coast*, between 1848/58 (Victoria and Albert Museum)

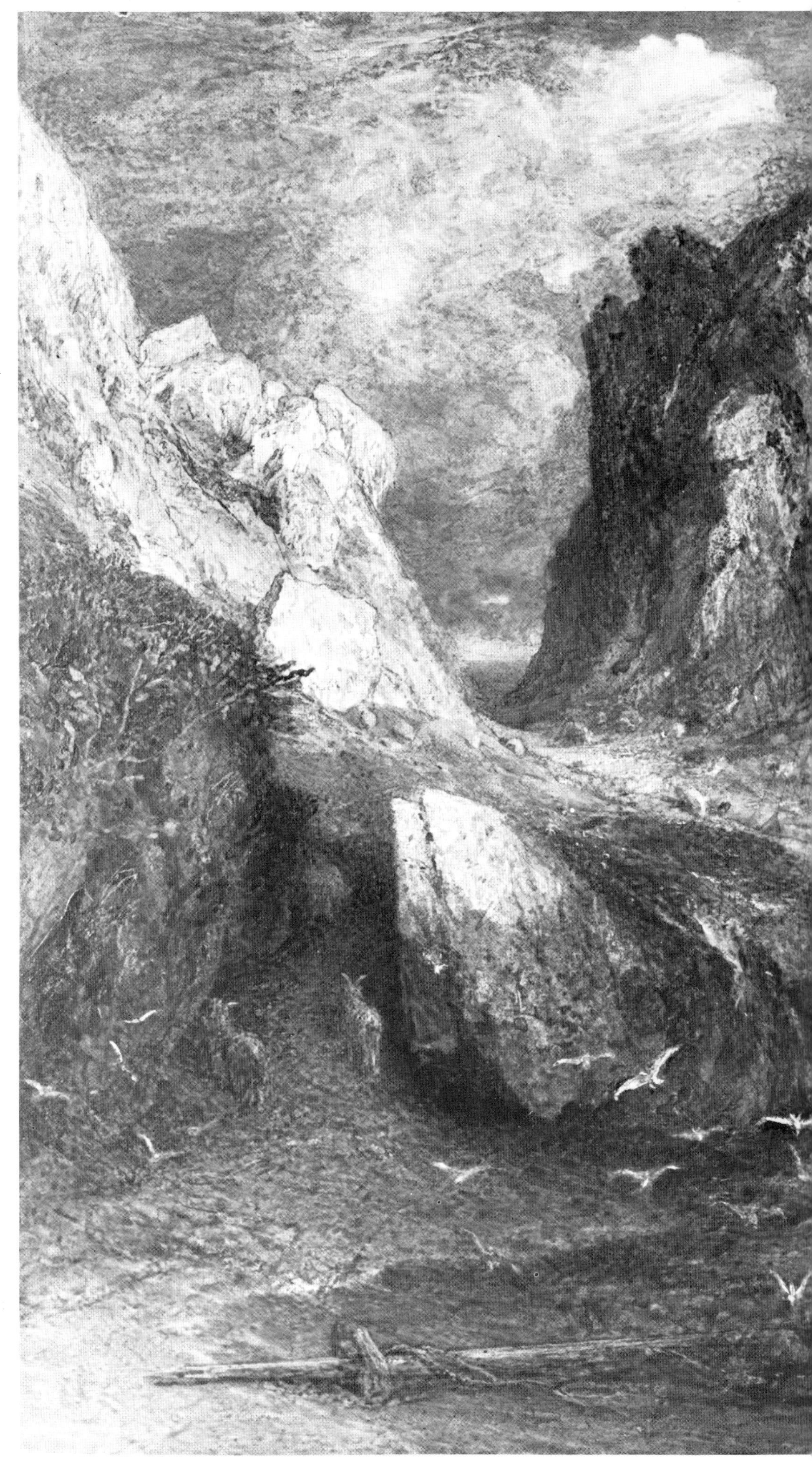

115 *Tintagel Castle, Approaching Rain*, 1848
(Ashmolean Museum)

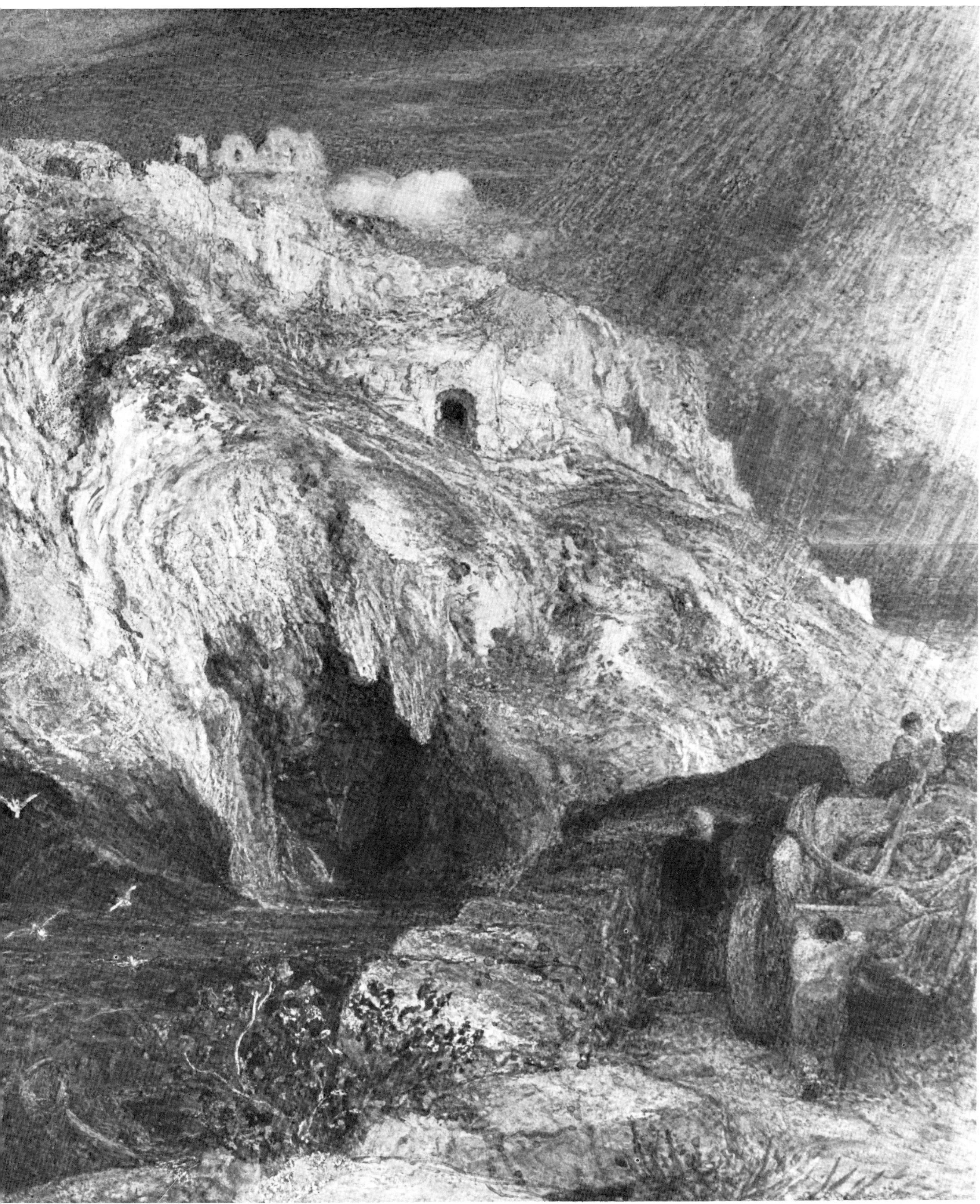

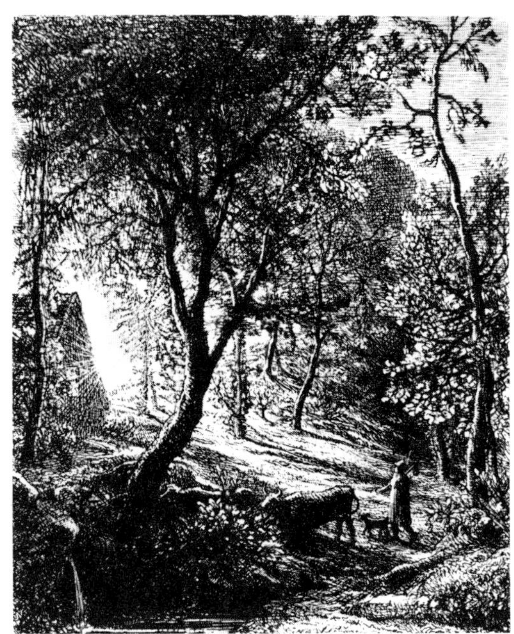

116 *The Herdsman's Cottage* or *Sunset*, 1850 (Victoria and Albert Museum)

matter, but WALKING and WATCHING,' and again, 'I coasted round as far as Ilfracombe – waterfall into the sea – then back, and landed at Combe Martin, walking home to Berrynarbour.'

In London he was now lonelier than ever. His wife spent more and more time at her parents' home and he wrote to Hannah in 1858 'It will require such undivided attention to maintain and, DV., improve in the step which I have for the last two or three years, by the kind providence of God, made in public estimation, that for the future, when I settle down to my exhibition work it will not do for you to be absent.'[12] He was also suffering more from the attacks of asthma to which he had been subject since his return from Italy, writing in 1859 to Hannah from Hastings he noted 'I feel a strange relief since the squally, strange change in the atmosphere. Before the two thunderous days, it was what I call gasping weather . . . I DREAD the DUST of town, which withers me whenever I get out'. Not only was he unwell himself but his son, More, was beginning to show signs of strain and by the spring of 1861 he was in need of complete rest. More was nineteen, very intelligent – he was next to head boy at school – and had always been full of energy, which Palmer had stimulated by every means in his power, but now he complained of exhaustion and lassitude. Palmer moved his family to a farmhouse, 'High Ashes', up in the Surrey hills with extensive views of the countryside. A number of Palmer's letters attest to his own ill health at this time, but on visits to 'High Ashes' he filled sketch-book after sketch-book with studies of the pastoral landscape.

On returning to Kensington himself he wrote to a friend in April 1861, 'You will be pleased to hear that poor More is really better. They are all crammed into a little farm house just on the top of Leith Hill, the summit of which is 900 feet above the sea-level! More just crawls about and vegetates, and has taken my violin – is perhaps at this moment frightening the pigs with his first scrapings. Of course he can get no teacher there, but then he pegs very earnestly into anything he undertakes. He says he is living discreetly "a la cabbage", and he is going to press and preserve flowers.

'He has taken a huge chest of Latin and Greek books down (I forget how much they cost by railway), to attach by and bye, if it pleases the Divine Disposer to restore him.'

More, Palmer's favourite son with whom he had always been very close, gradually became worse and they got him a donkey chaise so that twice a day he was able to ride propped up with pillows, his mother walking beside him in the shade of the pines. Although on July the 2nd More himself wrote to a friend that he believed the crisis was passed, nine days later he was dead. His brother wrote, 'That awful cry that rang out of old over all the land of Egypt never echoed more mournfully than at "High Ashes" farm. It was very gently that they prepared the father for the news that his first-born was dead; but he rushed from the house in bewildered agony and never re-entered it. One of the doctors, seeing his critical condition, drove him in his carriage to the house of his brother-in-law, Mr. James Linnell, at Red Hill, and he saw Abinger no more from that day.

'The mother followed her son for the last time through the shadows of the pines, and laid him beneath the yew-tree in Abinger Churchyard, near the ancient woods known by the familiar name of Evelyn. Not long before he had sketched the very spot where he was buried, while he was on a walking tour with a school-fellow, little thinking how soon he would repose in that quiet place.'

It was to Edward Calvert that Palmer turned to once again in his sorrow, as he had when his daughter died. 'As you are the first of my friends whom I set down to make partaker of my sorrow, I will not wait for black-edged paper, which is sent for. You I take first, for you were first with kindness when dear little Mary was called away, and your kind, kind heart will be wrung to hear that at our lodging at "High Ashes", near Dorking, on Leith Hill, my darling Thomas More left us at a quarter to six. It was effusion of blood on the brain.' Palmer suffered a secret remorse for many years after the death of his son, secret, for he never acknowledged it. He denied that he had been instrumental in his son's death by over-encouraging him to work but, subconsciously he must have realized that he had been unwise in taxing his son, willing and precocious as he was, but physically frail.

He now had to urge himself to work in his sorrow. 'If it be the Divine will that I live on after this calamity I must try to do my DUTY – my duty towards God and my duty towards my neighbour. My wife and child are my nearest neighbours. I must use my calling for their support. How can I make works which will cheer others when quite cheerless myself?' The result of this attempt to bury his grief in a sense of duty was that no less than five pictures were to appear in the Summer Exhibition of 1862.

The house in Kensington had, of course, to be given up as had the one in Lissom Grove after the death of Mary. At first the family took lodgings on Red Hill Common and then in September 1861 a cottage was found at Reigate. The place was so damp however that Hannah was crippled with rheumatism and she retreated again to her father's house at Red Hill. After spending a miserable winter in the cottage Palmer began again to search for another house, exploring Surrey for somewhere within reach of London, for he felt that if all else failed, he could once more resort to teaching for his livelihood. Eventually he came back to Red Hill settling in 'Furze Hill House'

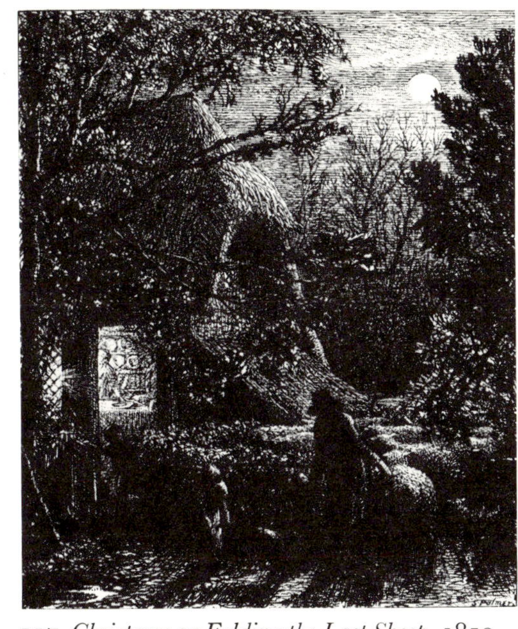

117 *Christmas* or *Folding the Last Sheep*, 1850 (Victoria and Albert Museum)

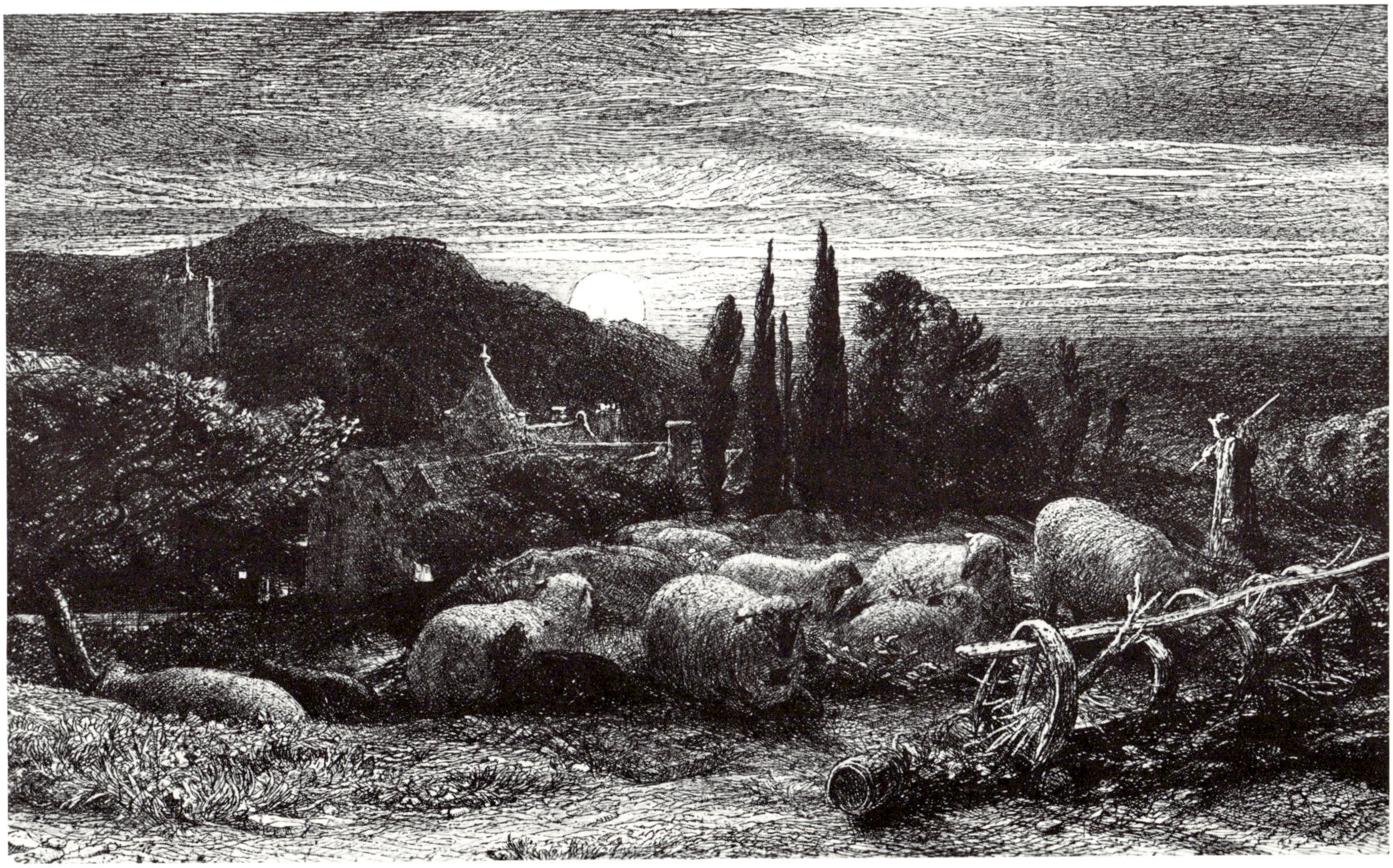

118 *The Rising Moon* or *An English Pastoral*, 1857 (Victoria and Albert Museum)

near Reigate. It was what the house agents called a 'Gothic Villa', pretentious, inconvenient and suffering from the worst aspects of the 'Genteel' that Palmer loathed, so he sarcastically gave grand names to its appointments, calling the drawing room 'The Saloon', one bedroom 'The Boudoir' and another which was damp 'Bronchitis Bower', but the worst disadvantage was its proximity to John Linnell's house 'Redstone Wood'. A. H. Palmer observed, 'Of all the blunders of my father's career, none was greater, so far as he himself was concerned, than the choice of a new house so close to the famous despot'. There was now an open hostility on Linnell's part towards Palmer and he was to suffer much from his father-in-law's overbearing personality. Nor did any of Linnell's family understand him as can be seen from the notes written by Linnell's son, intended for a life of his father, where Palmer is described as 'Having a mind too fanciful and wild; extravagant; not controlled sufficiently by reality and sober truth', as 'indulging in a fanciful sentiment', and of 'living in an atmosphere of sentiment, imagination and feeling not always in touch with truth and real fact'. A. H. Palmer remarks upon this 'It did not occur to the writer that, in condemning Blake's disciple, he also condemned Blake himself'.[13]

It is incredible that Palmer's spirit survived the onslaught but, due to his innate sense of humour and his devotion to his work, survive he did, to produce the best work of his later years. 'Furze Hill House' had at least one advantage over Kensington, it had a garden, and he was far enough away from neighbours to cultivate his weeds without protest. He wrote to a Miss Redgrave – a very favourite correspondent of his – 'I will have my

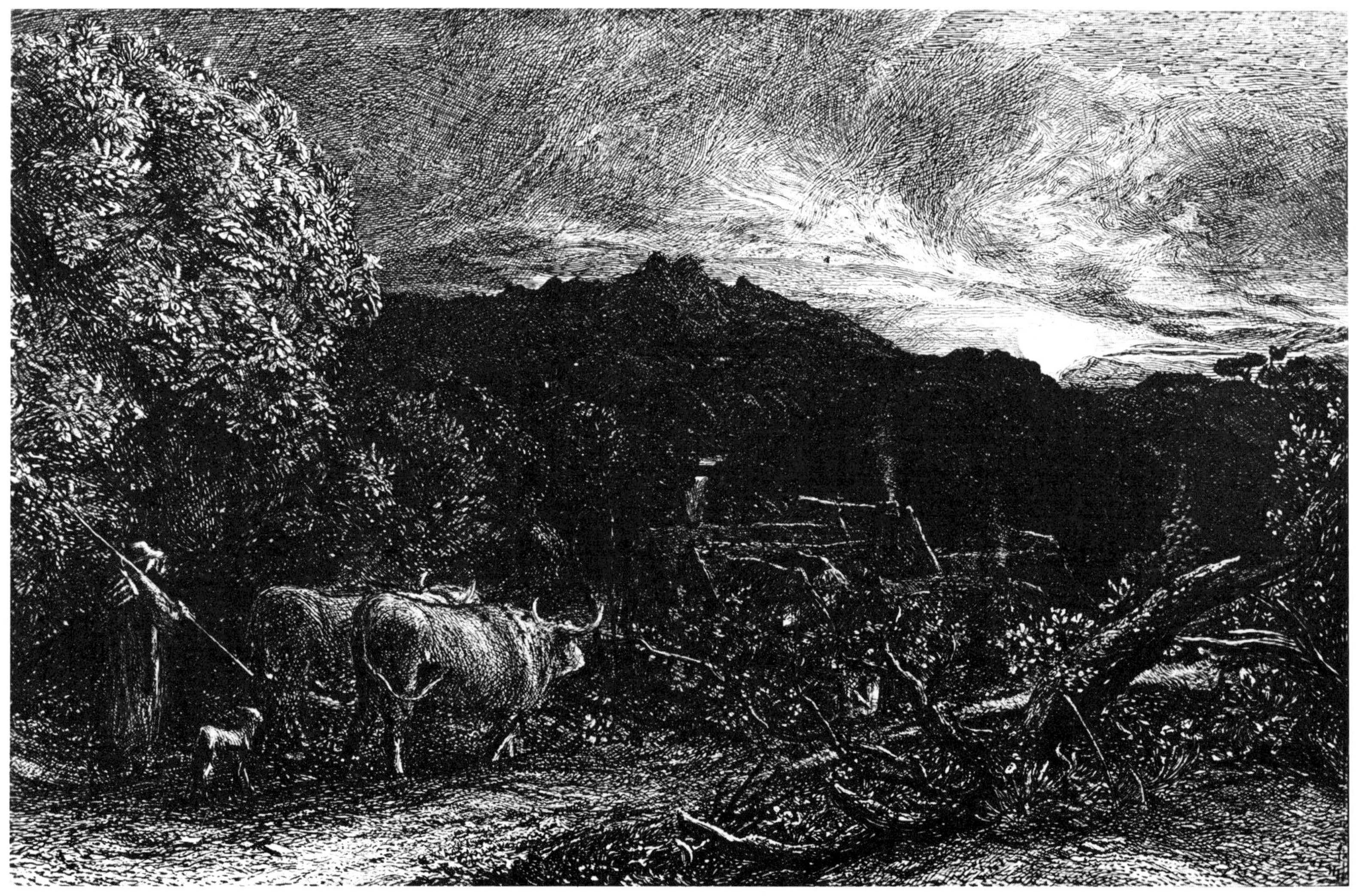

119 *The Weary Ploughman* or *The Herdsman* or *Tardus Bubulcus*, begun 1858 (Victoria and Albert Museum)

weeds though. The white convulvuli are commencing their tortuosities and Herbert has made a bench for the arbour. Miss Mary (a new housemaid) commenced weeding the other day, and pulled up both my hairbell roots, that I have been coaxing for three years into the garden.' Whenever this occurred he would replace them or, if irretrievable, introduce more plants from the surrounding countryside.

With the help of his son he also raised a small mound, 'The Spectacular Mound' as they called it, upon which they could stand and see over the palings to the surrounding landscape and they cut lanes in the undergrowth leading to 'Sylvan arbours' where they could also get a 'peep of the distant country'. 'All we did was accomplished clumsily and with labour; moreover the soil was so barren, our supply of water often so inestimably precious (for we depended entirely on the rain) that everything was against us. I do not think I have ever seen my father do anything with greater care and pleasure than, in the dry summer weather, the doling out of a little water to his favourite "weeds".'

And there were his trips to London which are so excellently described by his son. 'For days, perhaps weeks, beforehand a list of things to be seen, done, and got, was carefully compiled upon a leaf of a small sketch-book, and the route was systematically planned out, so as to economize time to the utmost. On the eventful morning the broadcloth coat with long, flowing skirt was brought forth, and the white cravat was adjusted with unusual care. One or more sets of underclothing was donned, according to the time of year, and sometimes indeed a second pair of trousers in severe weather.

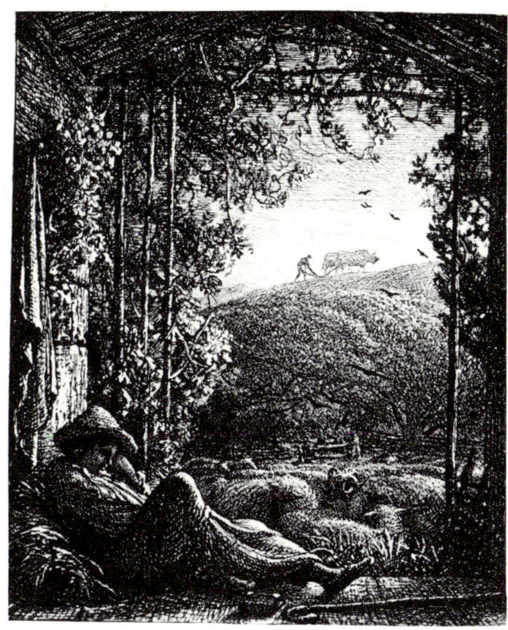

120 *The Sleeping Shepherd: Early Morning*, 1857 (Victoria and Albert Museum)

121 *The Early Ploughman* or *The Morning Spread upon the Mountains*, begun before 1861 (Victoria and Albert Museum)

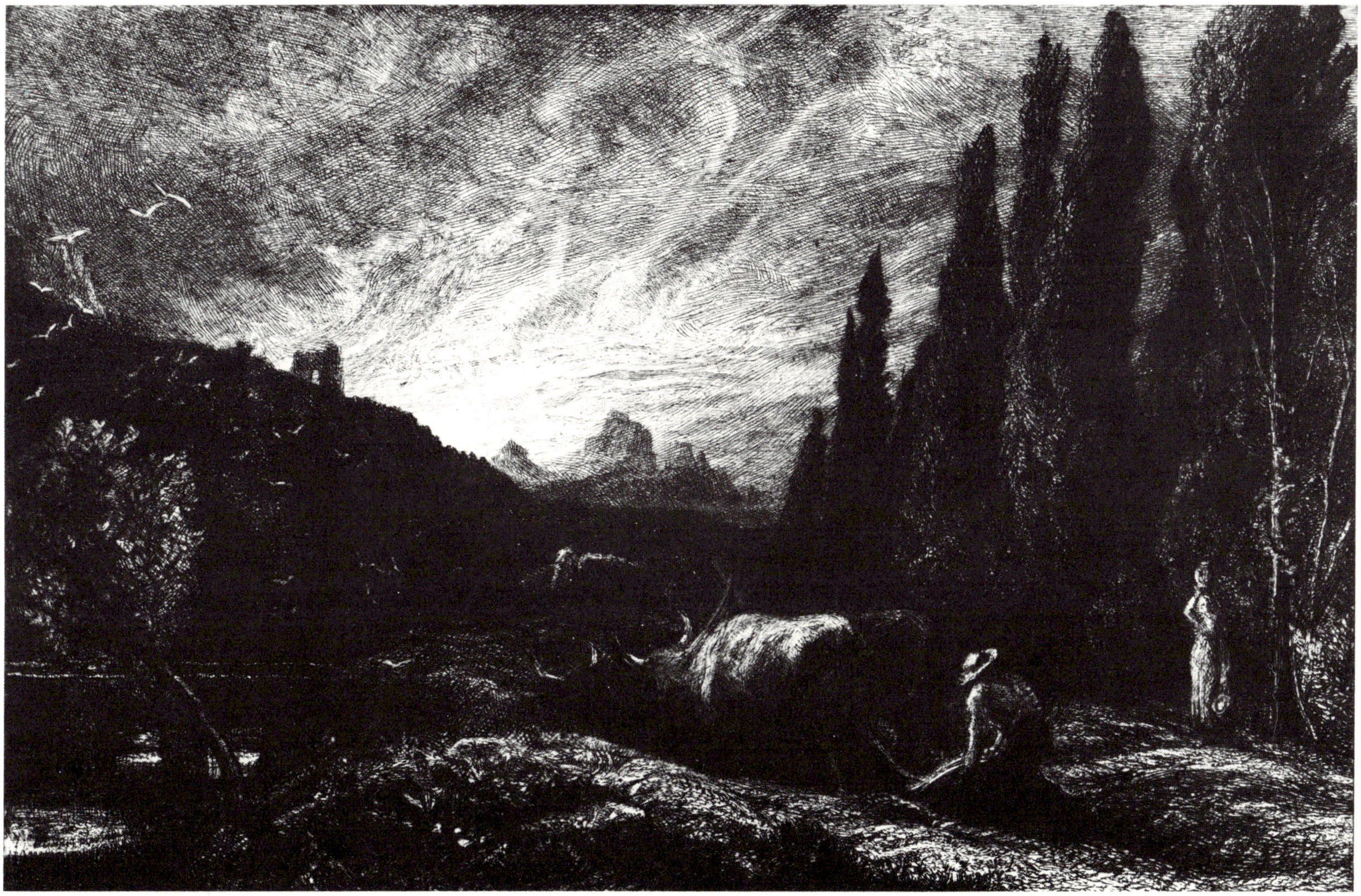

The silver spectacles were reluctantly laid aside for those of thin steel, and a mighty silk hat was disinterred from a box where it dwelt secure for months together. What a hat it was! But for his limbs my father would have been a big man and I verily believe that hat (though it fitted him) was the biggest that could be bought. The label on the bandbox had been directed by the hatter to "The Rev. S Palmer" and there was certainly a sort of very venerable curl about the brim.

'Arriving at the station in a flutter of excitement, and not less than half an hour or so too early, we patrolled together, my father quite unconscious of the attention that his peculiar dress attracted, or if sometimes made conscious, not in the least put out. Once fairly in London he devoted himself to showing me everything of interest that lay in our route, and it was astonishing how much he knew of the history and the associations of every nook and corner of older London. Regardless of staring, laughter, or jostling, he would stop dead in the middle of the pavement, or in a most conspicuous place, to point out to me some classic spire or memorable house, or the ancient haunt of one of his heroes. On one occasion he stopped thus, when he was walking with a young friend, before a milliner's shop and began, with some vehemence of action, to declaiming his high, tenor voice against the "Jezebel Tops" within. A few passers-by, scenting any eccentricity in the usual unerring way, also stopped; and my father happening to turn, found his companion fled, and himself the nucleus of a growing crowd.

'I remember particularly, the courtesy of his manner to all with whom our travels brought us into contact, without any distinction of class, of any

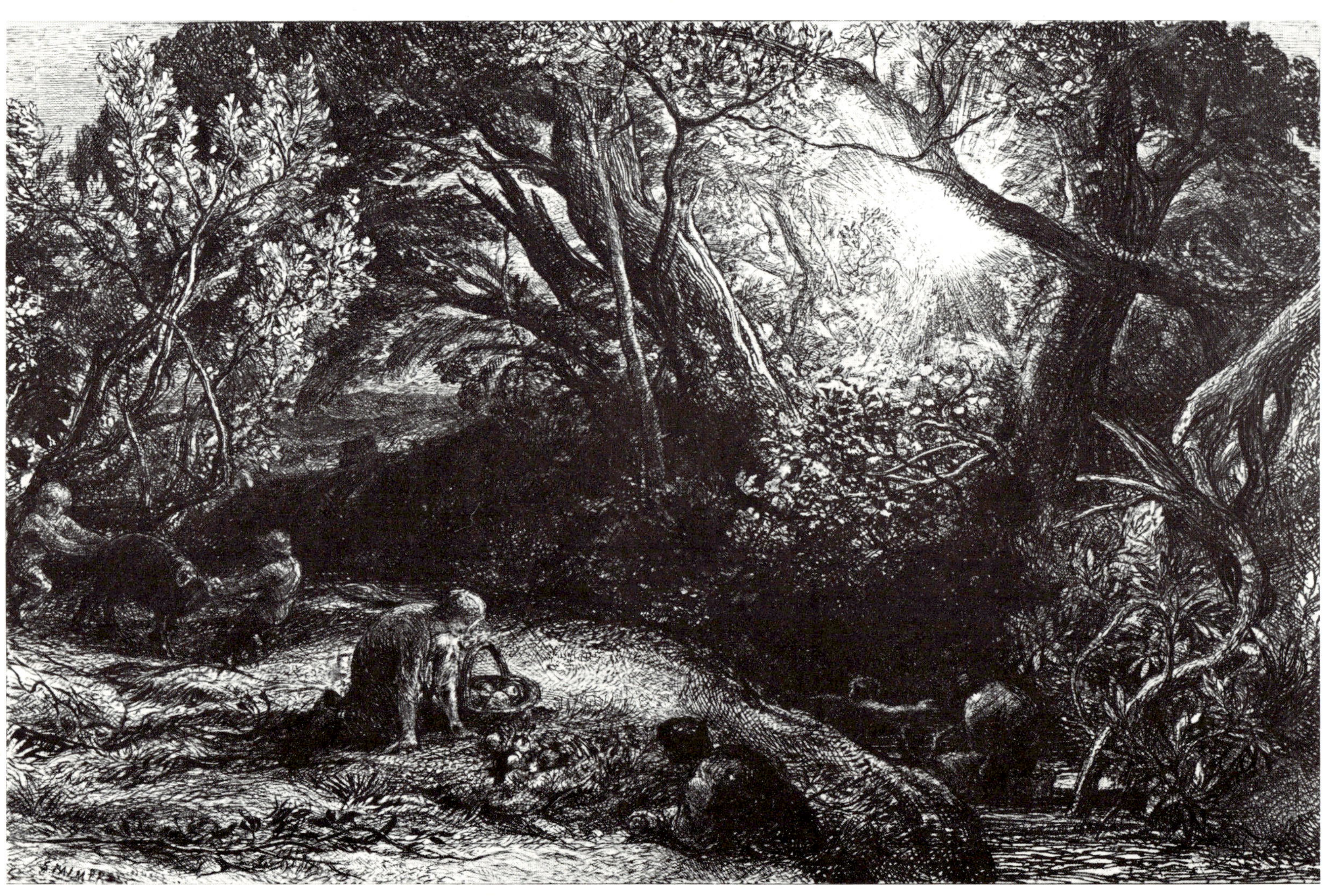

122 *The Morning of Life*, 1860/1 (Victoria and Albert Museum)

nicely-gauged discrimination of relative wealth. In the pursuit of the chief object of the day he was tenacious and patient as a bloodhound; and so, when we returned home in the evening, and dragged our weary legs up the steep homeward hills, we were able to reflect that not one single minute had been wasted.'

One of the rooms at 'Furze Hill' he converted into what he called his study being in effect a studio and workshop combined to which he repaired every morning and again of an evening, working into the small hours. Here he would receive only very special friends, even Hannah was never seen to

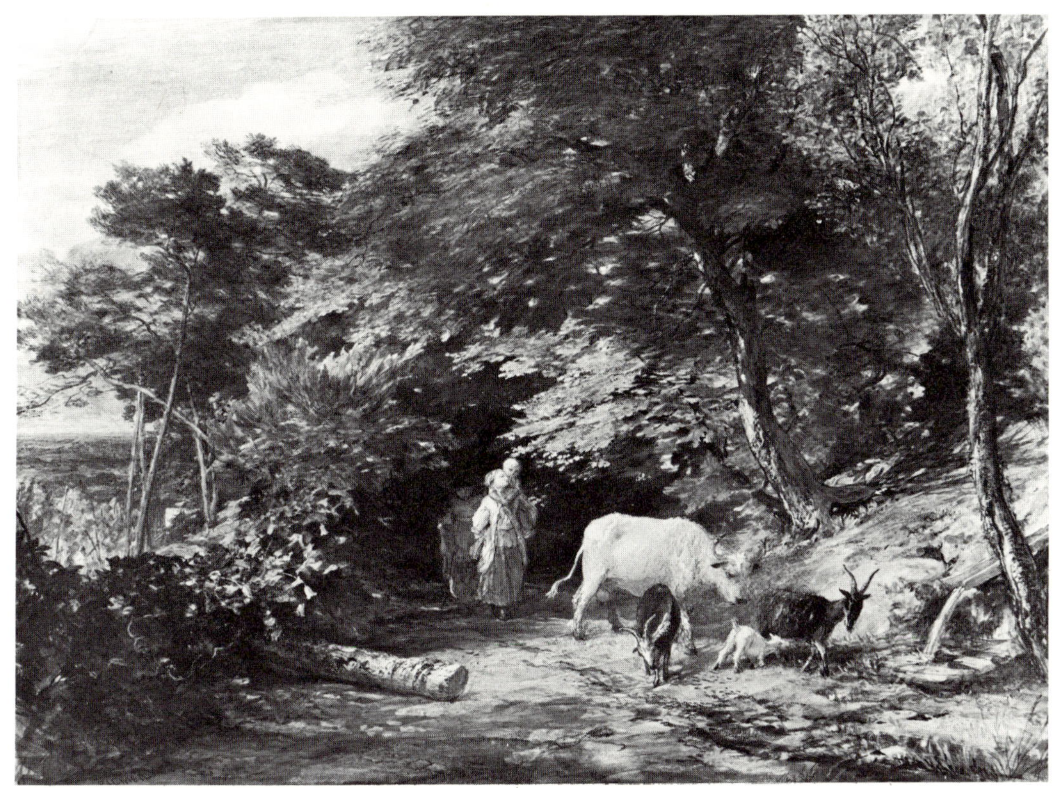

123 *The Wooded Lane*, after 1861 (Ashmolean Museum)

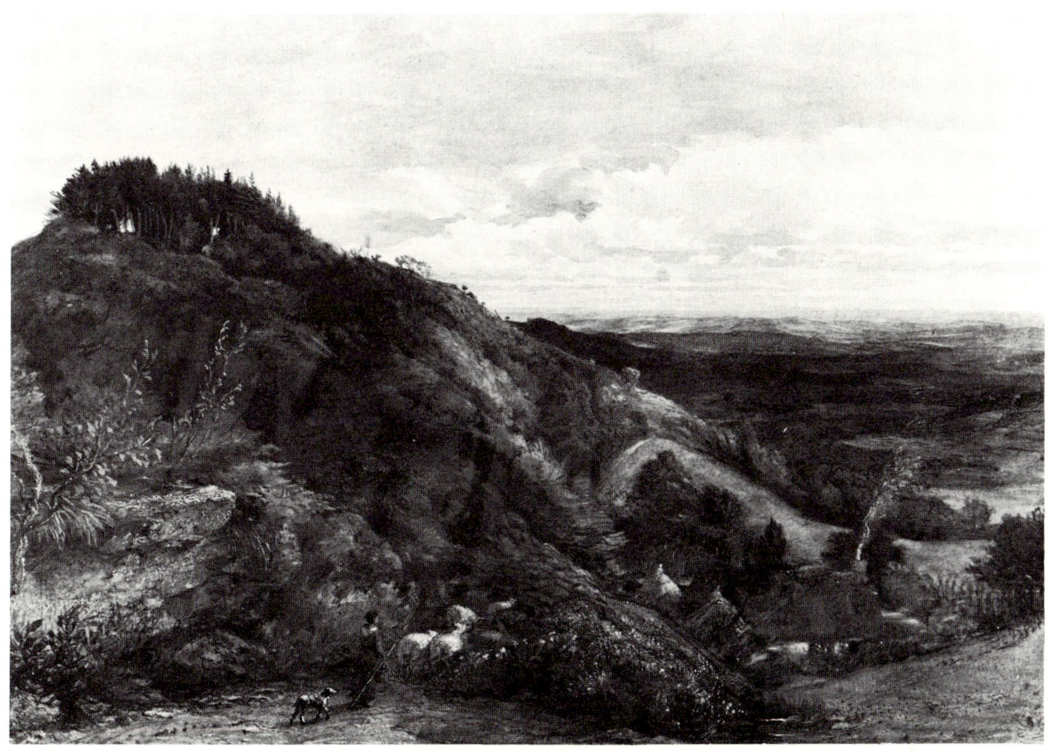

124 *Landscape with Woman driving Sheep*, after 1861 (Victoria and Albert Museum)

enter. 'The study had a very pronounced sentiment of snugness about it; being neither too orderly, nor too empty, nor too large. A bow window of western aspect looked out upon Leith Hill, and the curtained shelves which lined the opposite wall bore a heavy load of plaster casts from antique gems and busts, wax models of the figures of designs which were in progress, many colours, and very many books. Here lay one of the beautiful smock frocks once worn by so many of the peasantry, there a relic of Mary Ward – her battered tin ear-trumpet; and there again, unstrung and silent, the old violin, once eloquent with many an ancient air on the banks of the Darent. Some much larger shelves on one side of the room held, in classified portfolios, the innumerable sketches of all sizes, all degrees of finish, and in all materials; a long life's selection from much of the choicest scenery in England. Five or six box-portfolios beneath contained the more elaborate studies, British and Italian.

'Next to the sketches, a chest of drawers bore upon it a home-made cupboard. This contained a set of well-used etching-tools with other etching materials, and a few miniature antique busts in wooden cases or calico bags. This was the favourite corner of the room, and great was my father's rejoicing when, one day, the "Etching Cupboard" was evolved from an old packing-case. Not the least important item among the contents of the drawers was a tiny box labelled "BRIGHTS". In this there dwelt, protected from all contamination, and each in a white paper jacket neatly fitted over the upper part of it, certain cakes of the colours with which my father worked on the brightest passages in his drawings. As he sometimes attempted "a focus" which was "a well-head of dazzling light", and often the very sun himself, such care was well repaid.

'Finally, there was one rarely-opened drawer holding a few relics of his dead children, at which my father dared not look, though perhaps he liked to have them near him.

'Upon the plain, deal easel some disjointed words were chalked, each being a clue to some truth or maxim which he wished to keep before his mind. For instance, the single word "PARSLEY" was the most conspicuous, and referred to an anecdote in Mr. Hamerton's *Intellectual Life*, thus related:–

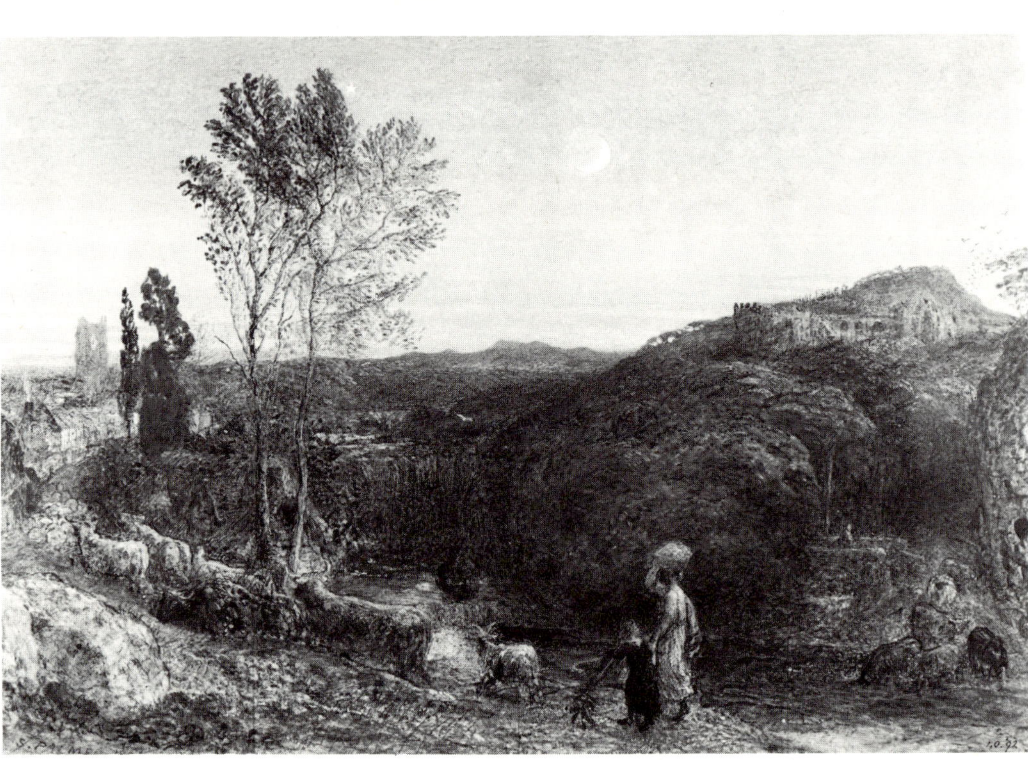

125 *Going Home at Curfew Time*, 1864 (Victoria and Albert Museum)

"I happened one day to converse with an excellent French cook about the delicate art which he professed . . . Among the dishes for which my friend had a deserved reputation, was a certain gateau de foie which had a very exquisite flavour. The principal ingredient, not in quantity but in power, was the liver of a fowl; but there were several other ingredients also, and amongst these a leaf or two of parsley. He told me that the influence of the parsley was a good illustration of his theory about his art. If the parsley were omitted, the flavour he aimed at was not produced at all; but on the other hand, if the quantity of parsley was the least excessive, then the gateau, instead of being a delicacy for gourmets, became an uneatable mess."

'Next to the easel stood the painting-table, which on examination, revealed itself as an old wooden washstand! Now, it creaked under an unwonted load, consisting of a large rack full of china palettes; under brush-cases, mugs, saucers and gallipots; most of them containing the rich succulent masses of colour my father delighted to use, mixed with the last of a long series of vehicles invented successively, since the days of the notable "egg-mixture".

'Many of these materials were, like the furniture, very different from those usually found in the water-colour painter's studio. Some of the brushes seemed large enough for fresco, though the series included the tiniest sables. Throughout the room, till you came to the last of the rough and heavily-laden bookshelves and a decreped arm-chair, there was nothing that was

126 *The Lonely Tower*, 1879 (Victoria and Albert Museum)

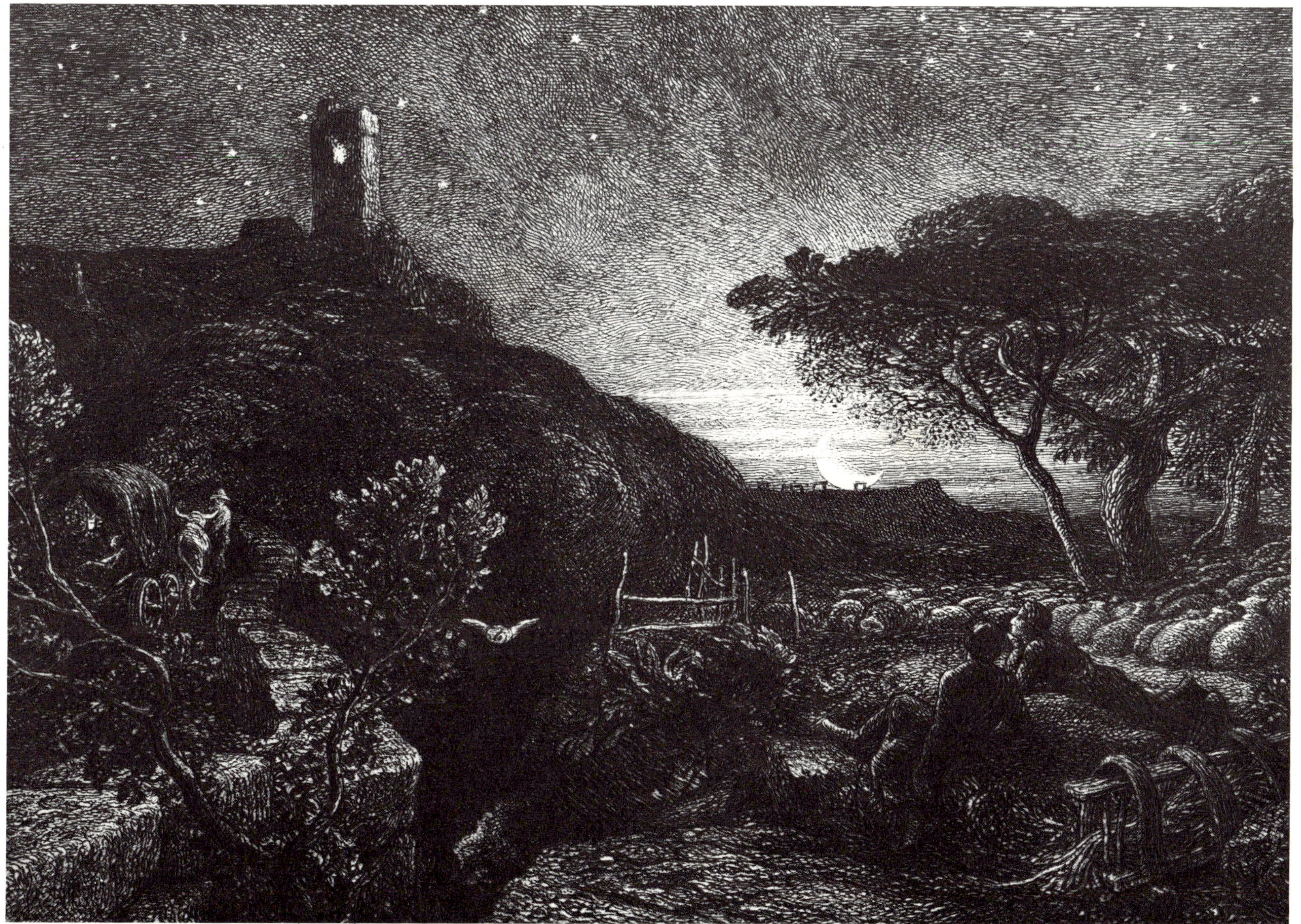

costly or conventional, or even what would be called by many, "respectable"; and there was little that did not bear evidence of our clumsy tinkering.'

Palmer's circumstances were now improving so far as money was concerned. Thanks to the boom in art in Victorian England he was able to command much higher prices and he also fulfilled a number of commissions. In 1863 at an exhibition of the Royal Water Colour Society, one of his drawings was sold to a Mr. L. A. Valpy who became his one and only patron. Valpy was a shrewd business-like lawyer with a 'caution worthy of a veteran merchant' who shortly after purchasing Palmer's picture asked to be shown any other work he had in hand which 'specially effected his inner sympathies'. Palmer, who was contemplating at this time a series of designs 'to realize after a sort the images of Milton', replied 'Only three days have passed since I did begin the meditation of a subject which, for 20 years, has affected my sympathies with seven fold inwardness.'

Valpy thereupon asked Palmer if he would make a set of drawings illustrating Milton's minor poems and, in April 1865, after some discussion, this was agreed upon. Much correspondence ensued with Valpy expressing his own ideas as to how the designs should be done which resulted in a deal of disagreement but in the end he wisely let Palmer have his own way. Many of the original sketches were done very quickly, Palmer's ideas coming to him 'unawares', but the completion of the drawings into finished works took a further sixteen years, Palmer taking infinite pains and constantly re-working them, as we can see from the letter he wrote in reply to Valpy who had asked for a reduction in price. 'In the same time, I could have made thrice the number of telling and effective drawings of the same size, but I considered your taste and feeling so much above the ordinary standard that in order fully to satisfy them, I have lavished time without limit or measure even after I myself considered the works complete!'

One of the many studies that he did, *The Waters Murmuring* (*127*), comes as near to the Shoreham works as he was ever to approach but, although there is evidence of a great deal of energy having been expended, it is without the essential fire and intensity that was so natural an extension of himself forty

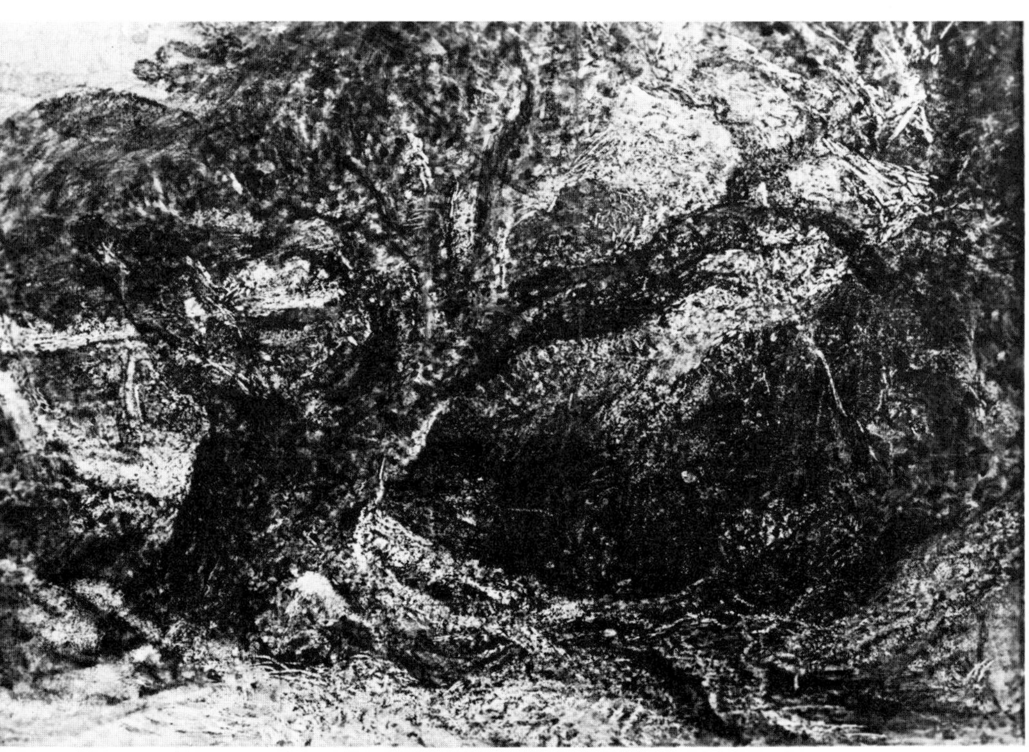

127 *The Waters Murmuring*, 1879 (Victoria and Albert Museum)

years earlier. This lack stems from the manner in which it is painted. Where before he was able to handle masses of light and shade almost with one application of the brush, now it is broken down into hesitant and repetitive applications of the medium and many second thoughts have taken place in the scratched areas where once this technique had been used only as heightening or for its own intrinsic qualities. Undoubtedly the Milton series contains some of the finest work he was to do in his later years, the studies in particular, which in their looseness of handling lends a simplicity and breadth that cannot be found in such works as *Mountain Stream and the Ancient Fortress* and *The Western Shore* (*128*), for all the care and experience that has gone into the application of the water-colour.

About this time Palmer acquired his own etching press and had his son taught the technique of printing by Frederick Goulding. Goulding was one of the finest copper-plate printers of his day and Palmer did well to engage him, for nothing can mar an etching so surely as bad printing, the technique being almost as great an art as the making of the plate. Palmer's etchings are indeed great works of craftsmanship and it says much for his son that he was able to produce such fine prints from his father's plates, for none of them would be an easy proposition. It would have been very easy to ruin his father's intentions had he not been able to work both with skill and understanding. Palmer had made etchings as long ago as 1850, examples of which are *The Herdsman's Cottage* (*116*) and *Christmas* (*117*) but these do not have the completeness or power of the ones he was to begin in 1858–60, completing some of the plates only many years later. These early attempts are rather in the nature of trials in the craft through which his draughtsmanship carried him. In 1857 he began to handle those characteristic luminous masses of dark which are to be the hallmark of much of the work done in this medium. These masses, it should be emphasised are not there entirely for their own sake, they also act as a means to intensify the dramatic lighting of a setting sun or rising moon. It is into these dark luminosities, however, that Palmer nevertheless poured his energies.

Considering that etching is basically a medium in which line is all important, where every mass has to be built up with the painstaking multiple application of such lines, it is curious that Palmer did not resort to

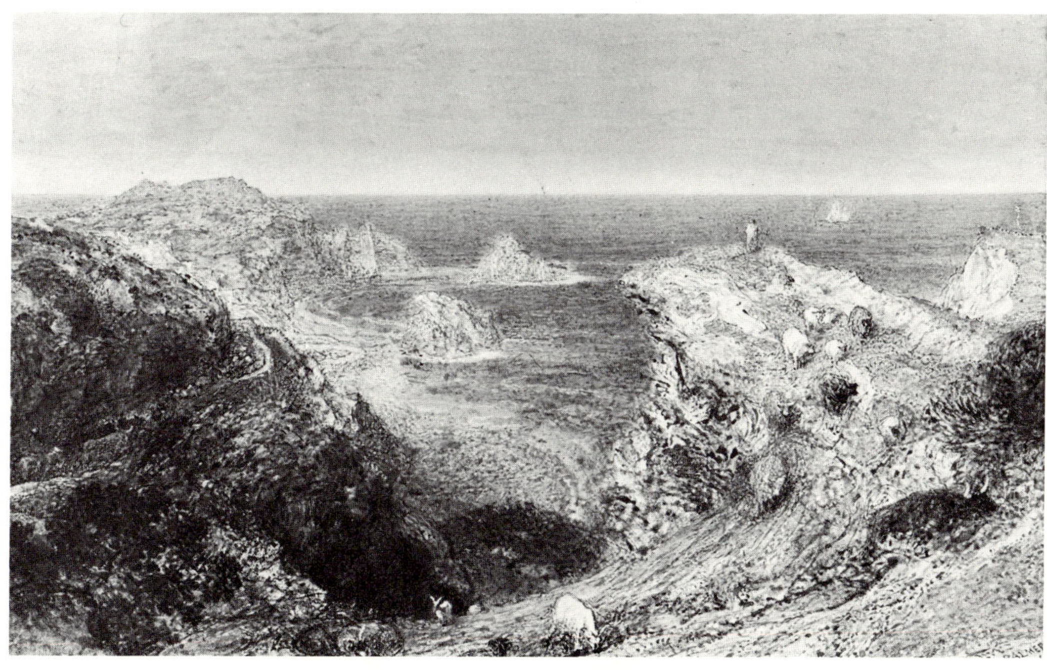

128 *The Western Shore*, 1879 (Victoria and Albert Museum)

aquatint where broad masses can be applied as with a brush stroke and without the necessary niggling with burnisher and scraper that mezzotint requires. Perhaps he had no knowledge of aquatint but this seems unlikely since he had contact with Frederick Goulding who would almost certainly have been acquainted with all the intaglio processes. However, it is interesting to speculate whether he would have been able to rid himself, in the use of a broader medium, of the Italianate mountains and trees that appear in *The Bellman* (*131*), *The Weary Ploughman* (*119*), *Opening the Fold* (*130*), and *The Early Ploughman* (*121*): or whether he would have given us as succinct a statement of the trees in *The Morning of Life* (*122*) as there is in *Evening; a Church Among Trees*. Perhaps he would have had to reject the medium in any case for he had now gone too far along the road of Victorian art with its insistence on the incongruities of verisimilitude and 'effects' to return even had he been physically capable, to the prompting of his youth.

The thought, however, of what he might have produced had he attempted etching in 1828 cannot but give rise to splendid visual imaginings, especially if we compare the study of *The Bellman* (*129*), with its simplified shapes, to the etching and imagine what the youth of twenty-three would have created with the same subject. For all the elements are here, it is the forms and their juxtaposition that are wrong losing as a consequence their meaning and, without the intimate associations that occur in works such as *A Hilly Scene*,

129 Study for *The Bellman*, 1879 (Victoria and Albert Museum)

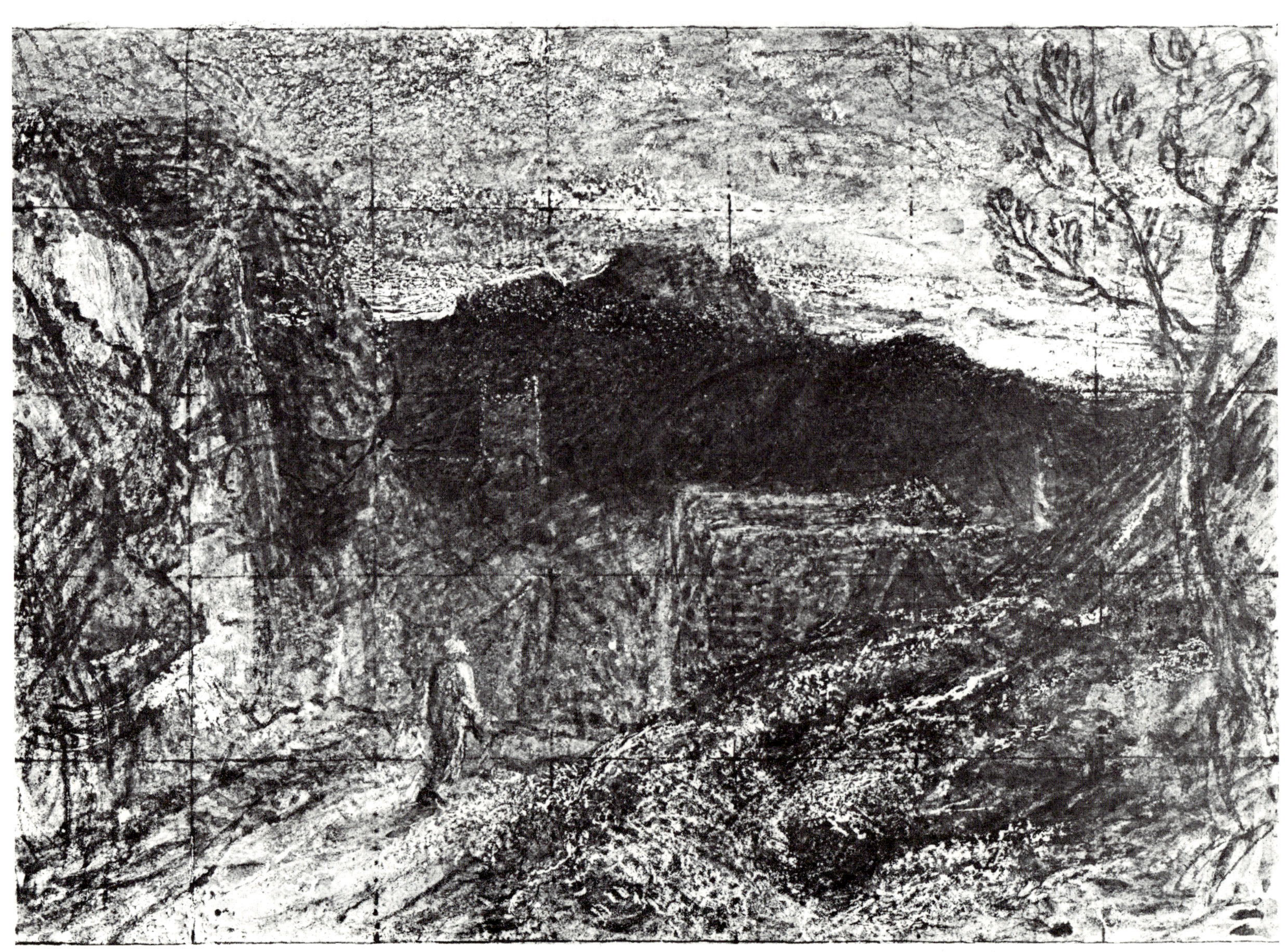

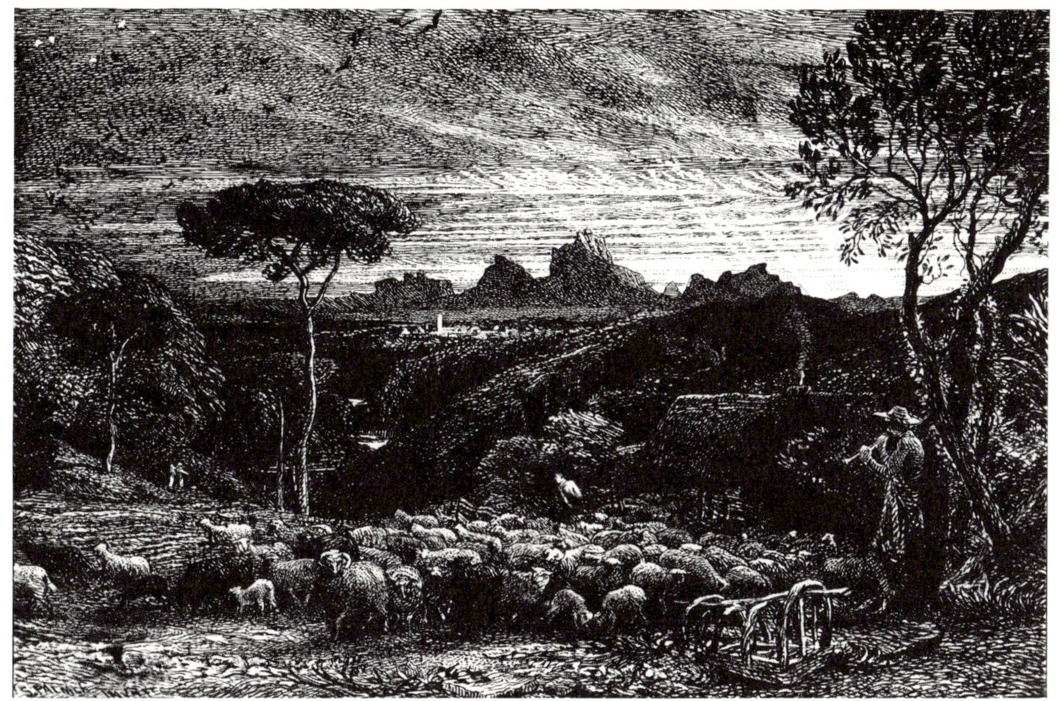

130 *Opening the Fold* or *Early Morning*, 1880 (Victoria and Albert Museum)

131 *The Bellman*, completed 1879 (Victoria and Albert Museum)

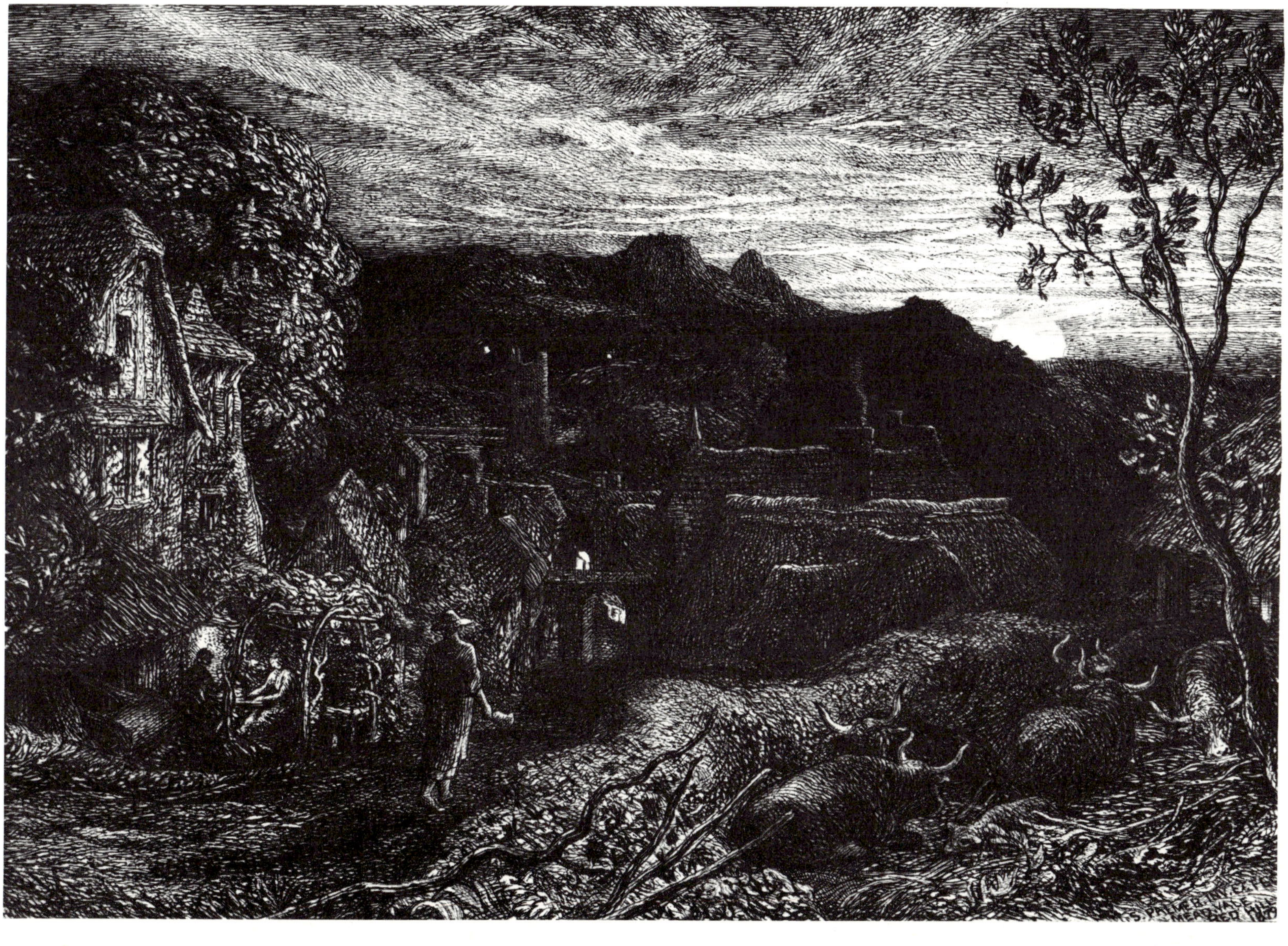

remaining purely a skilful assembly of parts. It is significant that the church in *The Bellman* no longer has a spire.

Palmer's last project was a series of etchings to the *Eclogues* of Virgil and although he produced many water-colours and drawings for the subject, only one plate *Opening the Fold* was finished by the time of his peaceful death in 1881. Many of the water-colours of these last months of his life have a lot in common; small size, very rich colour and featuring sunsets, possibly from the Cornish studies. The design for Virgil's sixth *Eclogue* is typical of several, appearing in three versions, two in water-colour, *Going to Fold* being one, almost identical and one in sepia and pencil. Repetition is not uncommon in Palmer's work at this time as in *The Shining River* (*138*) and *The Winding Stream* (*137*). It is unlikely that he was trying to perfect the composition or improve certain qualities in other ways, probably the truth is that the landscapes were merely vehicles for the glowing sunsets, the opportunity to use the delicate touches of madder upon the backs of the sheep and cattle and the 'Margate Mottle' as in the skies of *Church by a Mill* and *The Shadowy Stream*. In the beautifully-drawn study for the ninth *Eclogue* (*139*) – almost echoing in style the studies he did for Linnell at Shoreham – the descending sun is again a prominent feature. At the last Palmer was to hear his inner voice as he had at Shoreham and again, without conscious knowledge, create the only meaningful symbol of his last years.

The last fifteen years or so of Palmer's life were spent quietly, although with great energy, working on his etchings and the designs for Milton and Virgil. He was now no longer able to make sketching trips to Devon and Cornwall and, as he grew older, he even had to give up his excursions to London and his evening visits to old friends in Reigate. But he was not lonely as many of his friends still paid him frequent visits, his cousin John Giles, for instance, who had spent Christmas with him for over fifty years. From the moment of Giles' arrival, they would retreat to the study, safe from interruption, Palmer would open his Shoreham portfolio and they would discuss the works and re-live those years of happiness. Giles' admira-

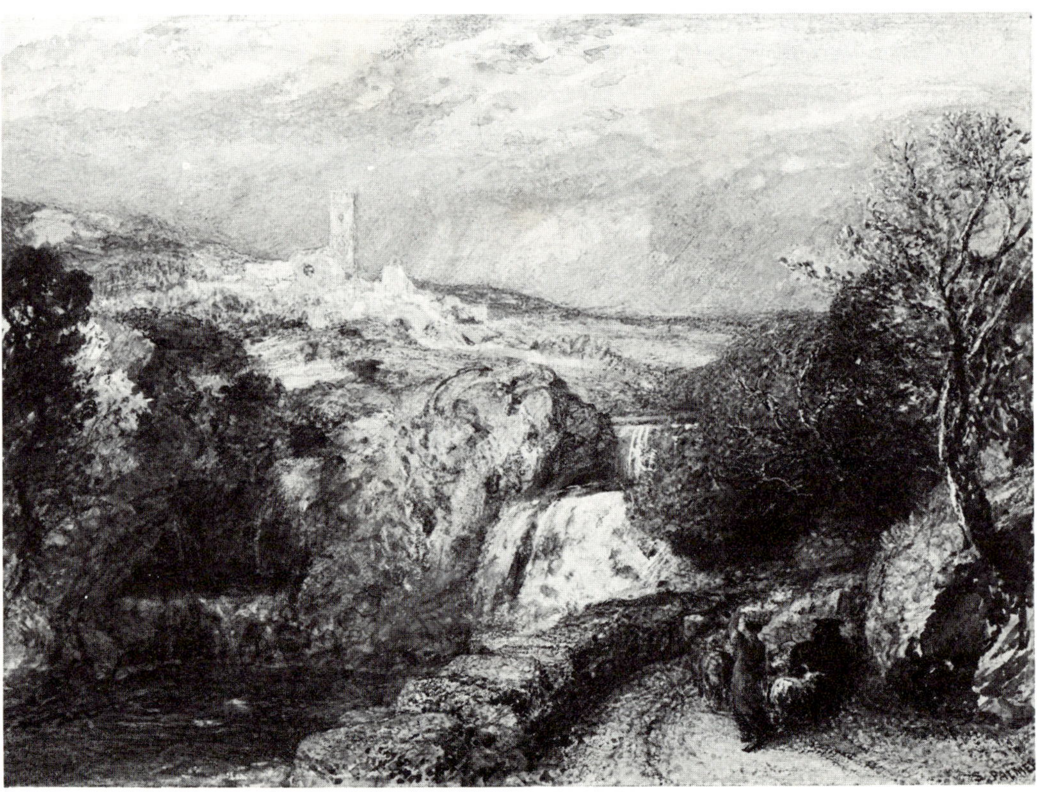

132 *A Mountain Stream and an Ancient Fortress*, 1879 (Victoria and Albert Museum)

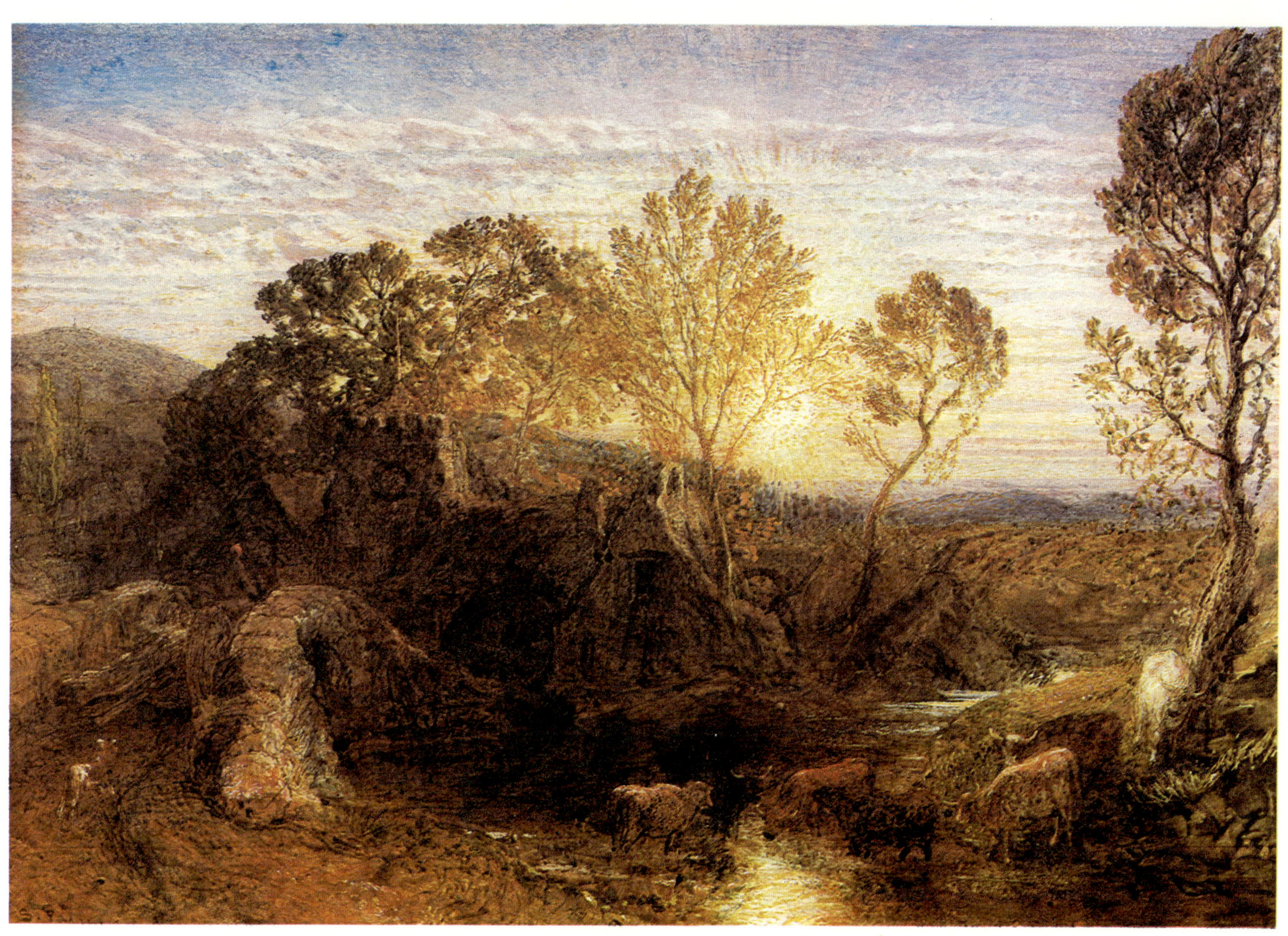

133 *Church by a Mill*, 1879/80 (Private Collection)

OVERLEAF
134 *A Dream in the Apennine*, exhib. 1864 (The Tate Gallery)

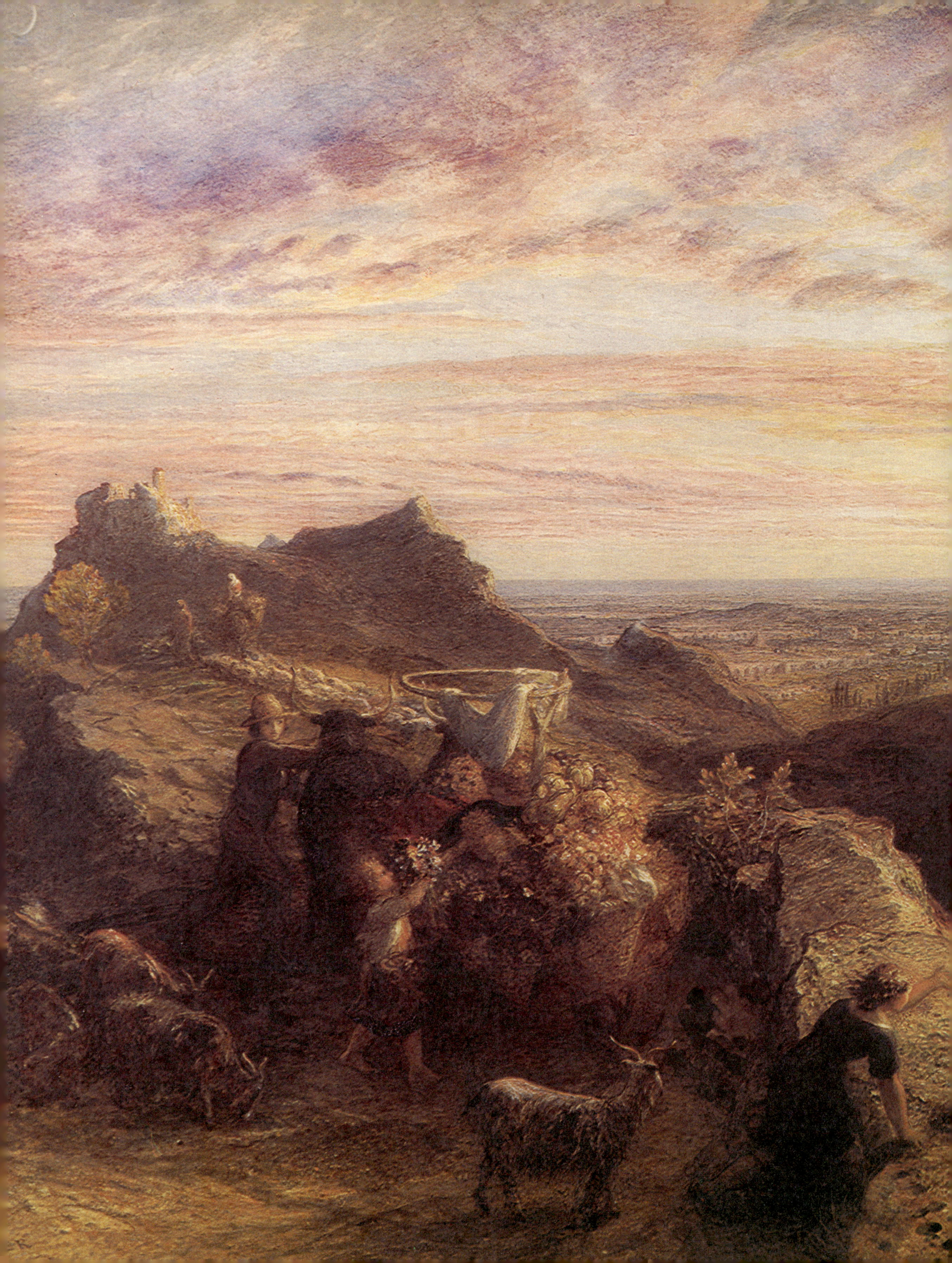

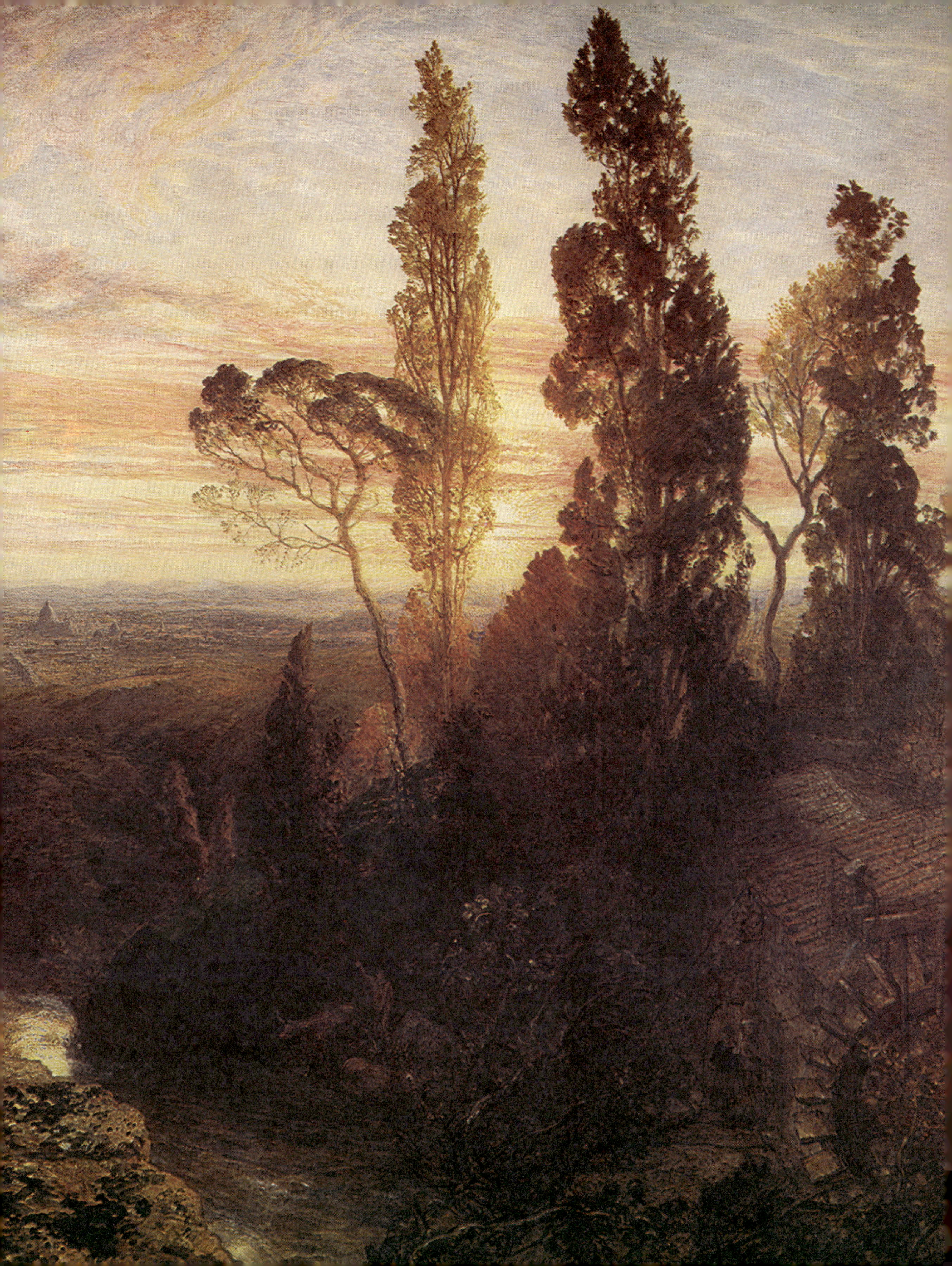

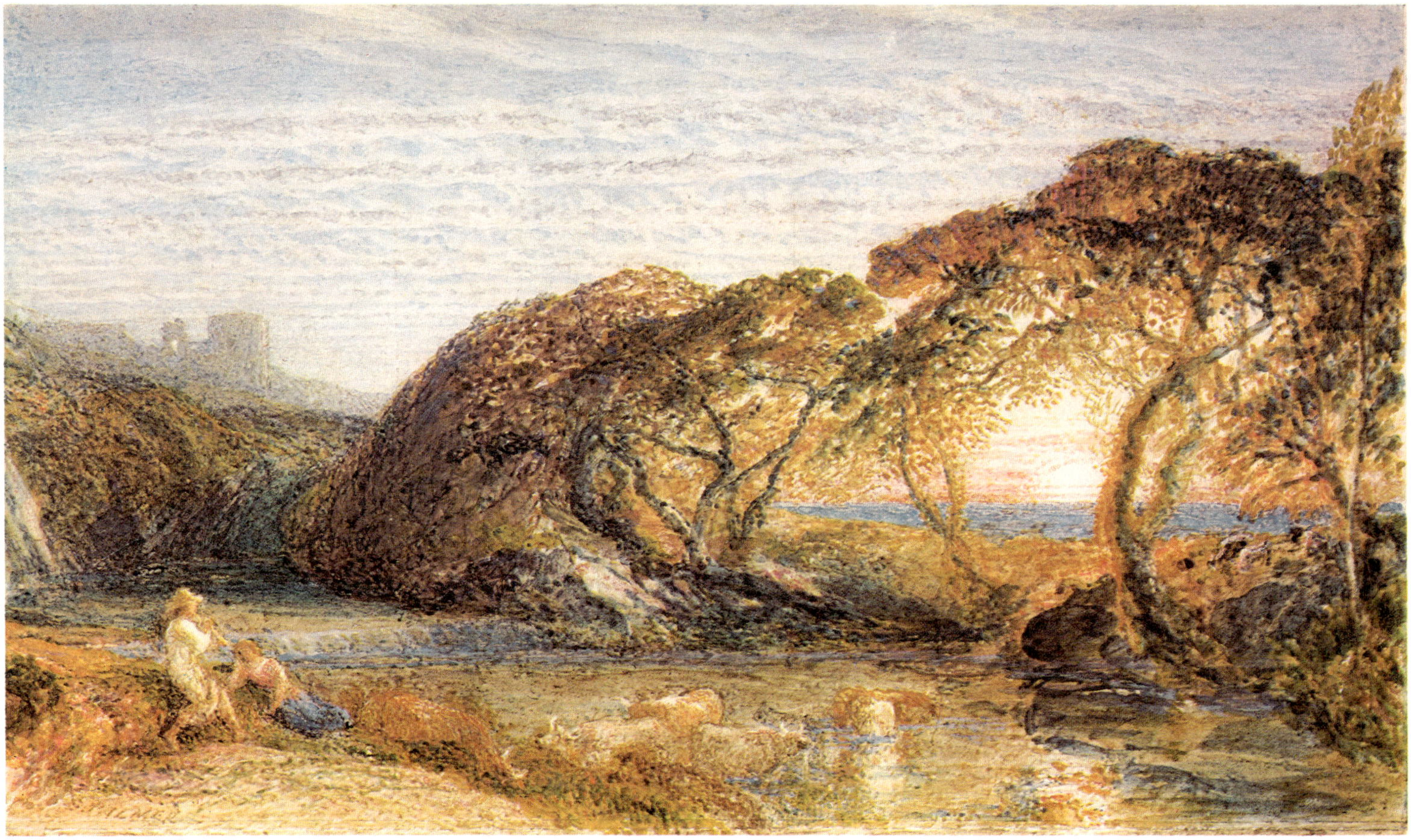

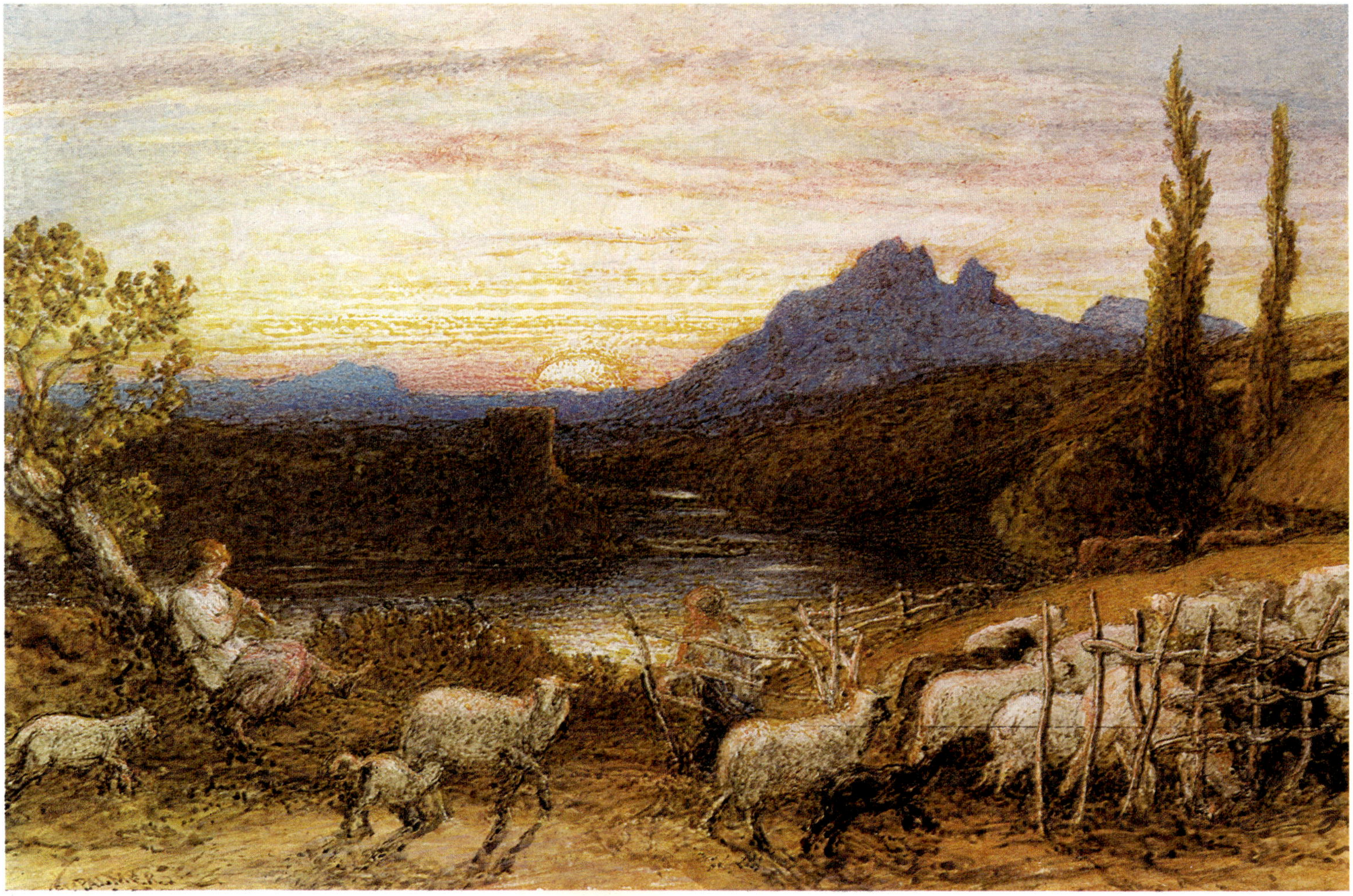

tion for the Shoreham drawings and paintings had steadily increased over the years and by degrees he bought a number of the finest works. After each sale, Palmer would resort to 'touchings up' which necessitated the opening of the old oil colour box and no doubt he was 'refreshed by the well-remembered smell of copal and spike lavender, though it reminded him of disappointed hopes.'

Palmer's mental faculties continued unimpaired and in the evenings, when exhausted by the strain of designing, he turned for light amusement to practising mathematics, afterwards reading until bedtime, which for him was in the early hours of the morning. Old age had crept up on him by degrees and his physical decline was gradual, he was fortunate in not suffering from any of the more distressing ailments of advancing years. In May, 1881, he became severely ill, presumably with an asthmatic complaint, but even then, only six days before his death, he was cheerfully discussing with his son ideas for the Virgil project. He was buried in Reigate churchyard and his son reports that a skylark sang above them during the service and, as the last words died away, dropped silently into the grass.

In Palmer we have a picture of an artist who, rich in the will to create,

OPPOSITE
135 *The Shadowy Stream*, 1880 (Victoria and Albert Museum)

136 *Going to Fold*, 1879 (Victoria and Albert Museum)

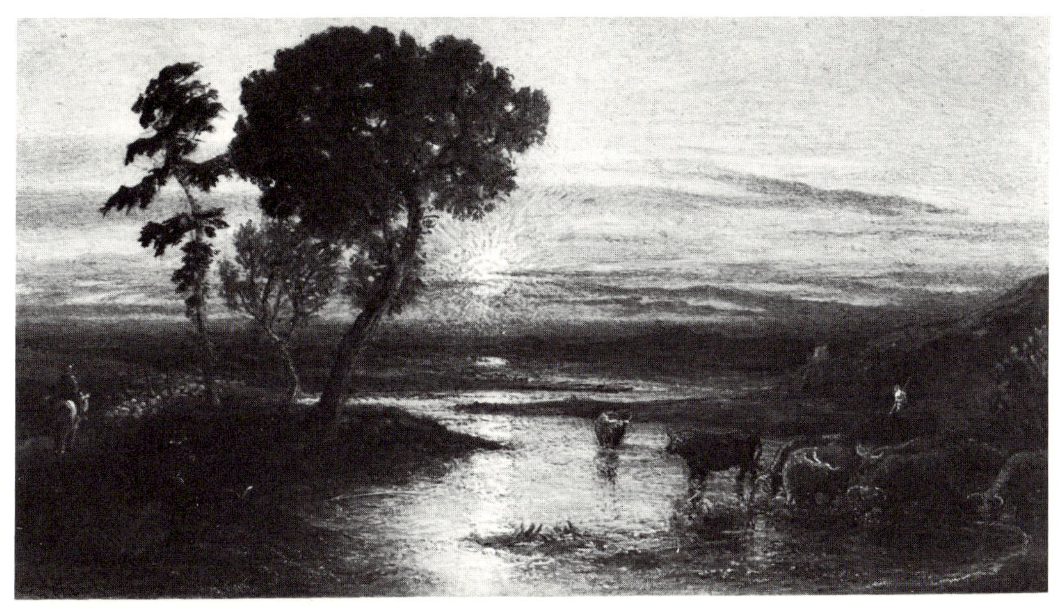

137 *The Winding Stream*, 1880 (Victoria and Albert Museum)

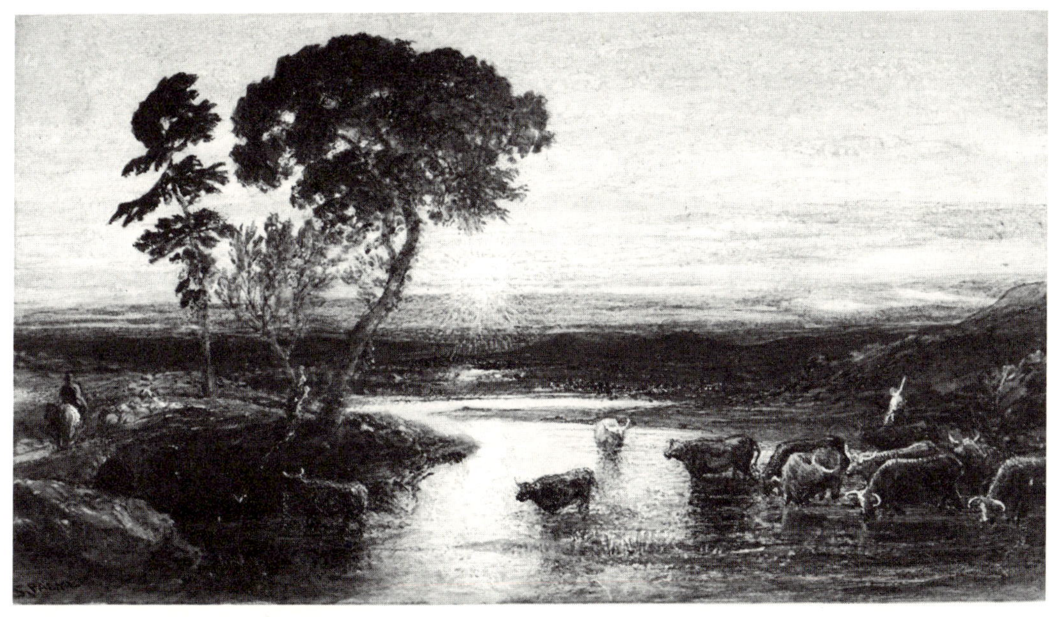

138 *The Shining River*, 1880 (Victoria and Albert Museum)

tragically bereaved of two of his children, harried by life in the person of his father-in-law, to an extent we can only guess at, and by the neglect he suffered from the public, never stopped his activities to ask what or why he was creating but continued in the blind faith that man at his best can do no other. His soul may be described not only as simple, but as symmetrical; and as he himself once said 'a symmetrical soul is a thing very beautiful and very rare'.

The sunsets of Palmer's last works can be seen in the later paintings of another artist, Paul Nash, whose insight into and love for landscape had much in common with Palmer to whom he is also linked by the common denominator of Blake. But it was not until a hundred years after Palmer's 1825 sepia works that another artist appeared who picked up the threads of Palmer's art. In 1925, inspired by Palmer's etchings, Graham Sutherland visited Shoreham. Here he produced a series of etchings, comparable to Palmer's more in their richness of needling and accuracy of observation than in the objects portrayed, which arrived at the very essence of Palmer's art in their revaluation of natural phenomena. This revaluation and its meaning for us is further developed in Sutherland's *Pastoral* of 1930 and the *Green Tree Form* of 1940 and his statements were further refined when, like Palmer, he visited Wales but with eyes sharpened by the devastation of the Second World War. The climax of Sutherland's art, *Entrance to a Lane*, is the apotheosis in twentieth-century terms and for twentieth-century man, of what Palmer had to say. But it is doubtful whether we, any more than the Victorians had been, are prepared to listen.

The spirit of Palmer can again be seen in the slight but pleasing work of a number of young English artists who, isolated from continental influences during the Second World War and influenced by Sutherland, turned to their native romantic foundations. John Minton's *Sunflowers* (*142*) and Keith Vaughan's *Valley Landscape* (*143*), both painted in 1945, reflect Palmer's twilight shapes and Sutherland's mixed media. But sadly, much of the work at this time is merely an iteration of a style in vogue rather than an examination of fundamental realities. A foray into Palmer's world was made by Alan Reynolds at the start of his career and something of Palmer may be

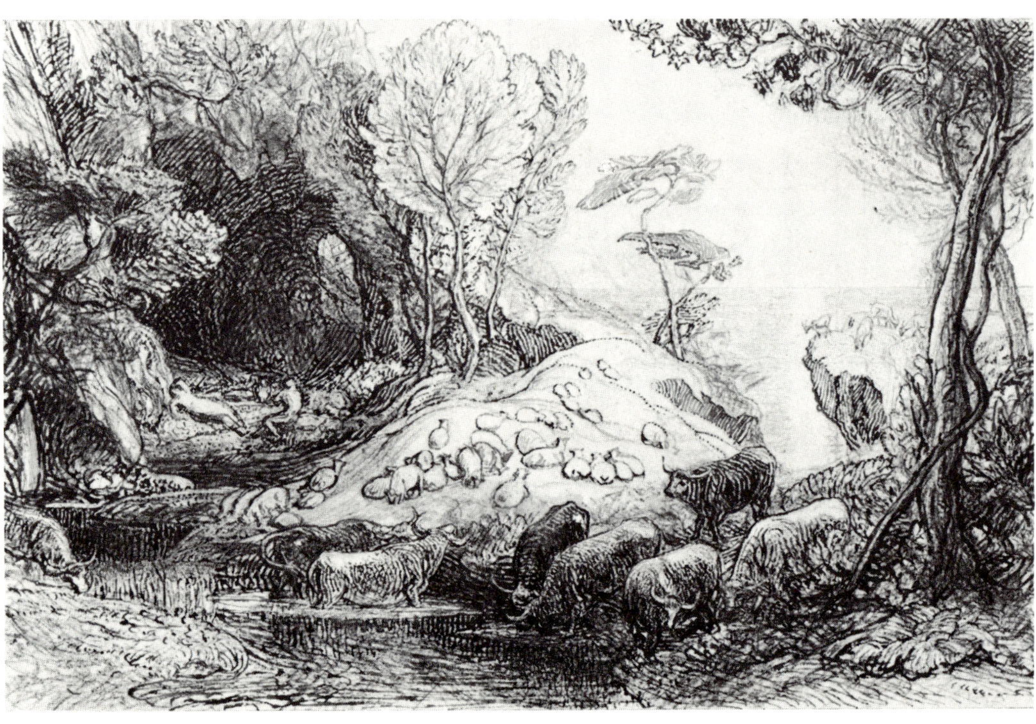

139 Drawing for the *Ninth Eclogue* of Virgil, 1880 (National Gallery of Canada)

140 Graham Sutherland, *Pecken Wood*, 1925
(The Tate Gallery)

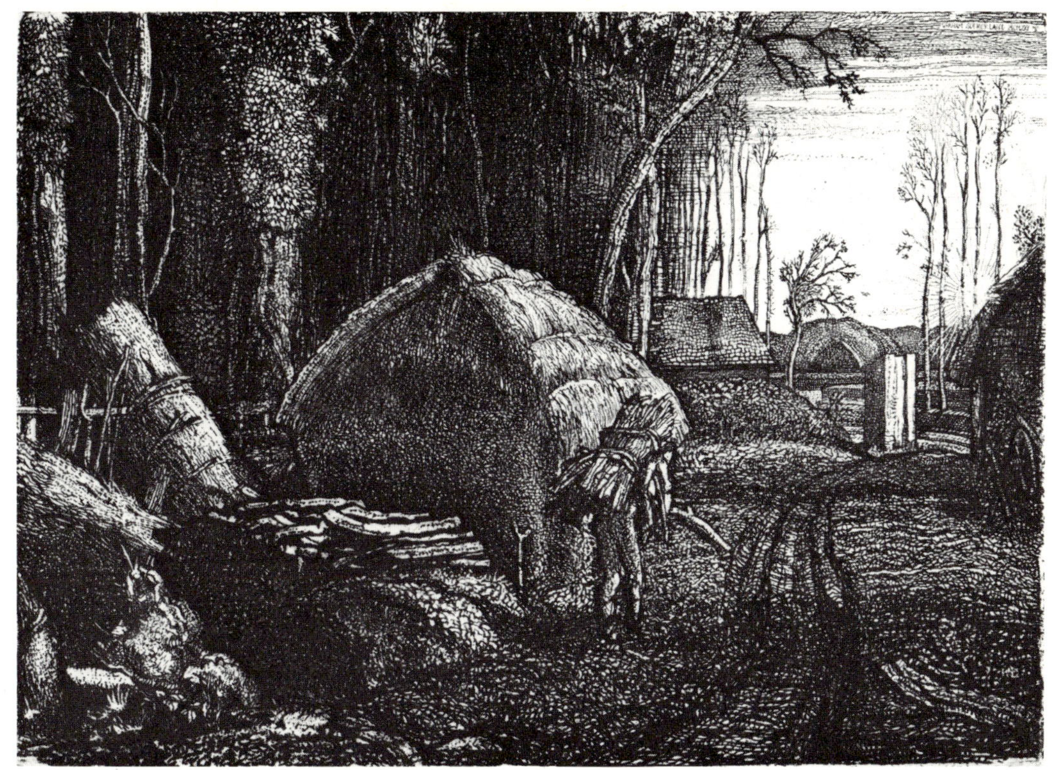

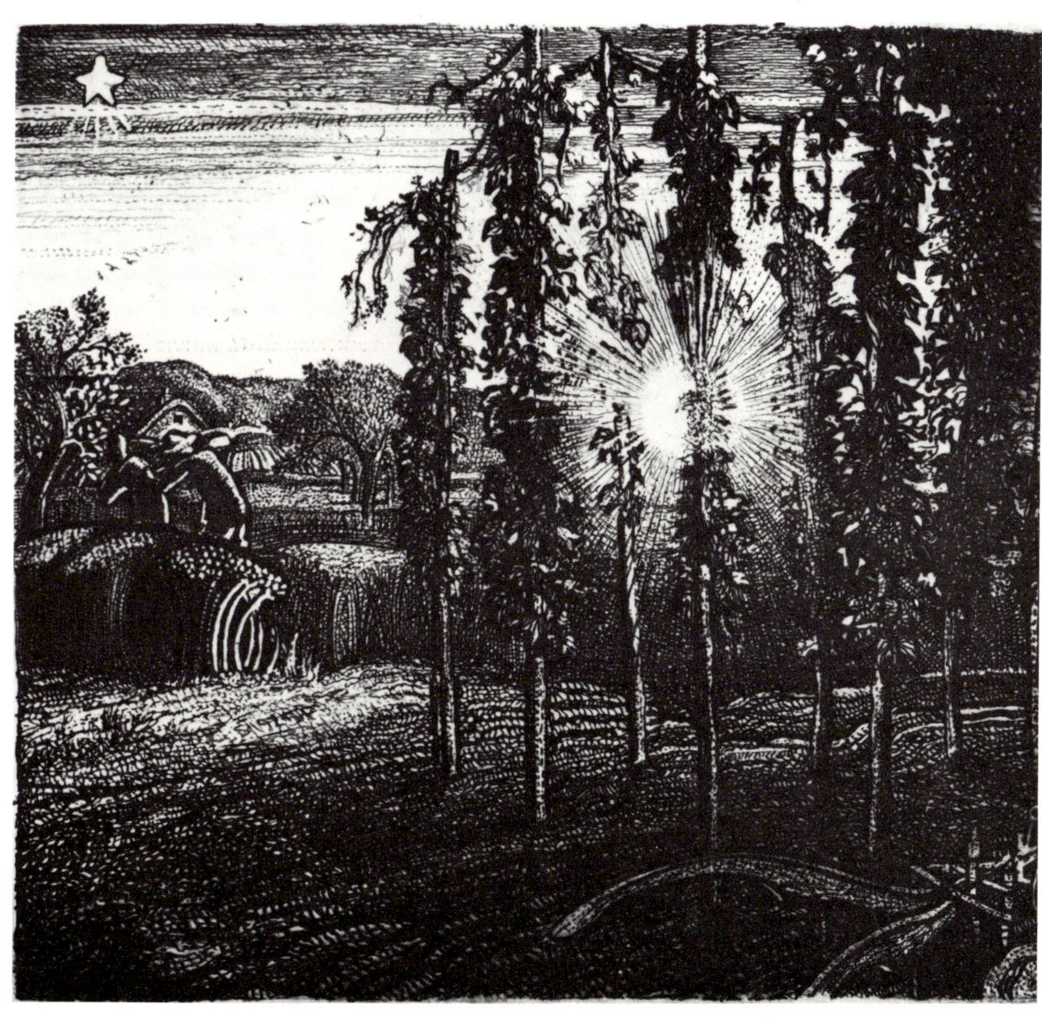

141 Graham Sutherland, *Cray Fields*, 1925
(The Tate Gallery)

felt in Reynold's *Keeper of the Dark Copse* (*144*). But this already contains within it the seeds of its destruction in the abstraction of the ground plane and the figure in its contrived and totally unconvincing guise as a 'Presence' which have little relevance to the fine invention in the forms of some of the trees. Perhaps if these artists had been able to withstand the onslaught of Picasso, Matisse and Braque unleashed upon them after the Second World War they might have gone on to develop where Sutherland had begun to decline. An art such as Palmer's requires more than the initial revelation that forms in themselves are meaningless, it requires a capacity to divine their meaning and its relevance to man.

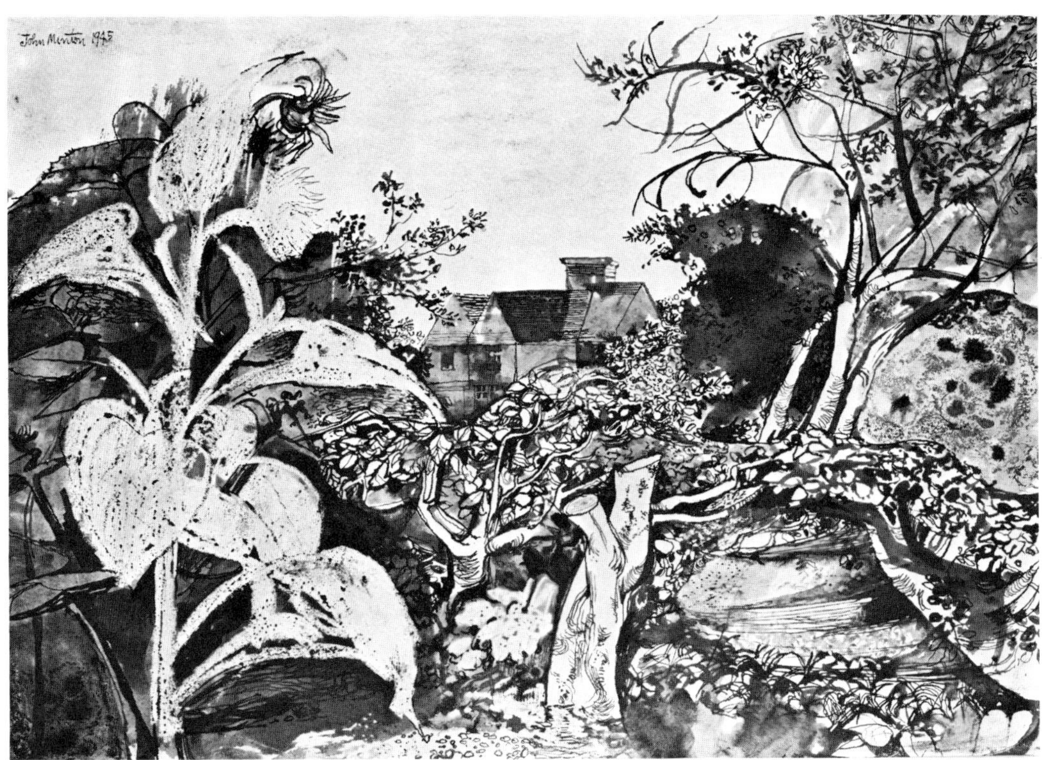

142 John Minton, *Sunflowers*, 1945 (Victoria and Albert Museum)

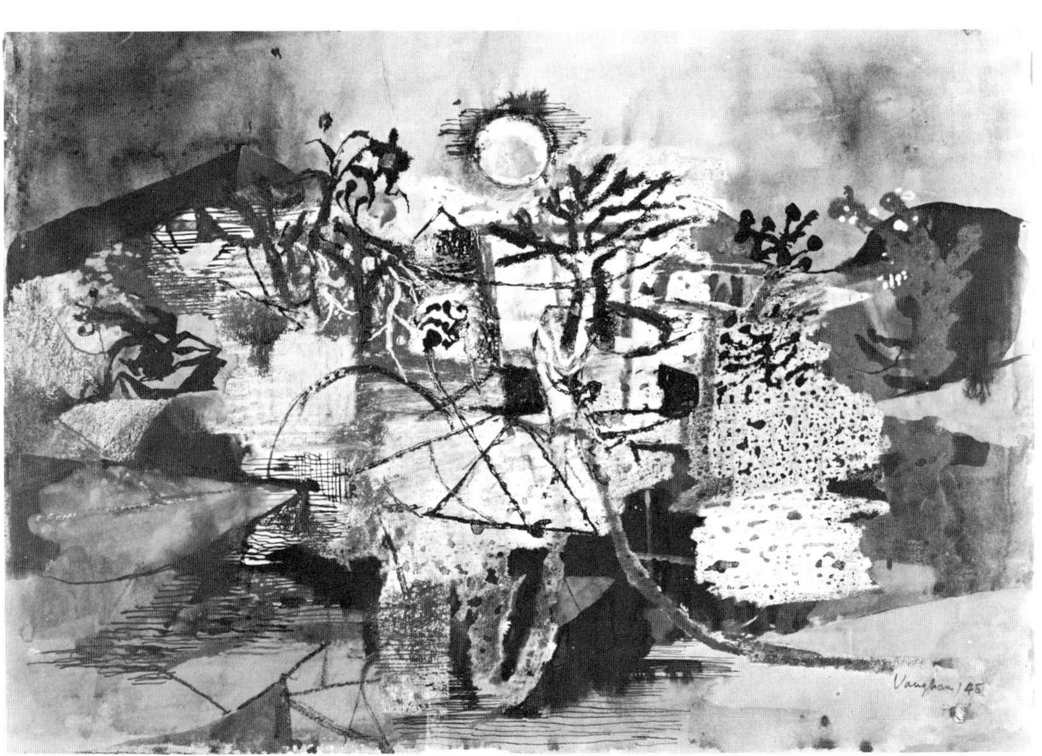

143 Keith Vaughan, *Valley Landscape*, 1945 (Victoria and Albert Museum)

For ten 'visionary' years, Palmer was that rare occurrence in English art history – an English landscape painter. That is, a painter essentially unaffected by influences generated outside England and one whose work was inspired by the unique qualities of English landscape. Constable and Turner have been described as the most English of painters, but Constable's countryside, East Anglia, like his art, owes more to the Low Countries than the English tradition. Turner never recovered from his visit to Italy. His storms are Alpine storms, not the comparatively homely depressions visited on the English countryside and his vast canvases of even vaster landscapes reflect an altogether 'nobler' vision of the world at odds with the essentially intimate quality of the English countryside.

Palmer's countryside was that part of England 'South of the railings of Hyde Park' that has no parallel elsewhere. A quiet, close landscape of tiny fields, hedges, winding lanes, thatched cottages, and mixed farms that long typified, and for many still does, rural England. Such continental artists as Dürer, Breughel, and Bosch whose forms were absorbed and transmuted by Palmer significantly drew on the same Gothic vision that had been common to all northern Europe, the tradition that had inspired those distant forebears of Palmer, the anonymous sculptors and artists of the English Romanesque.

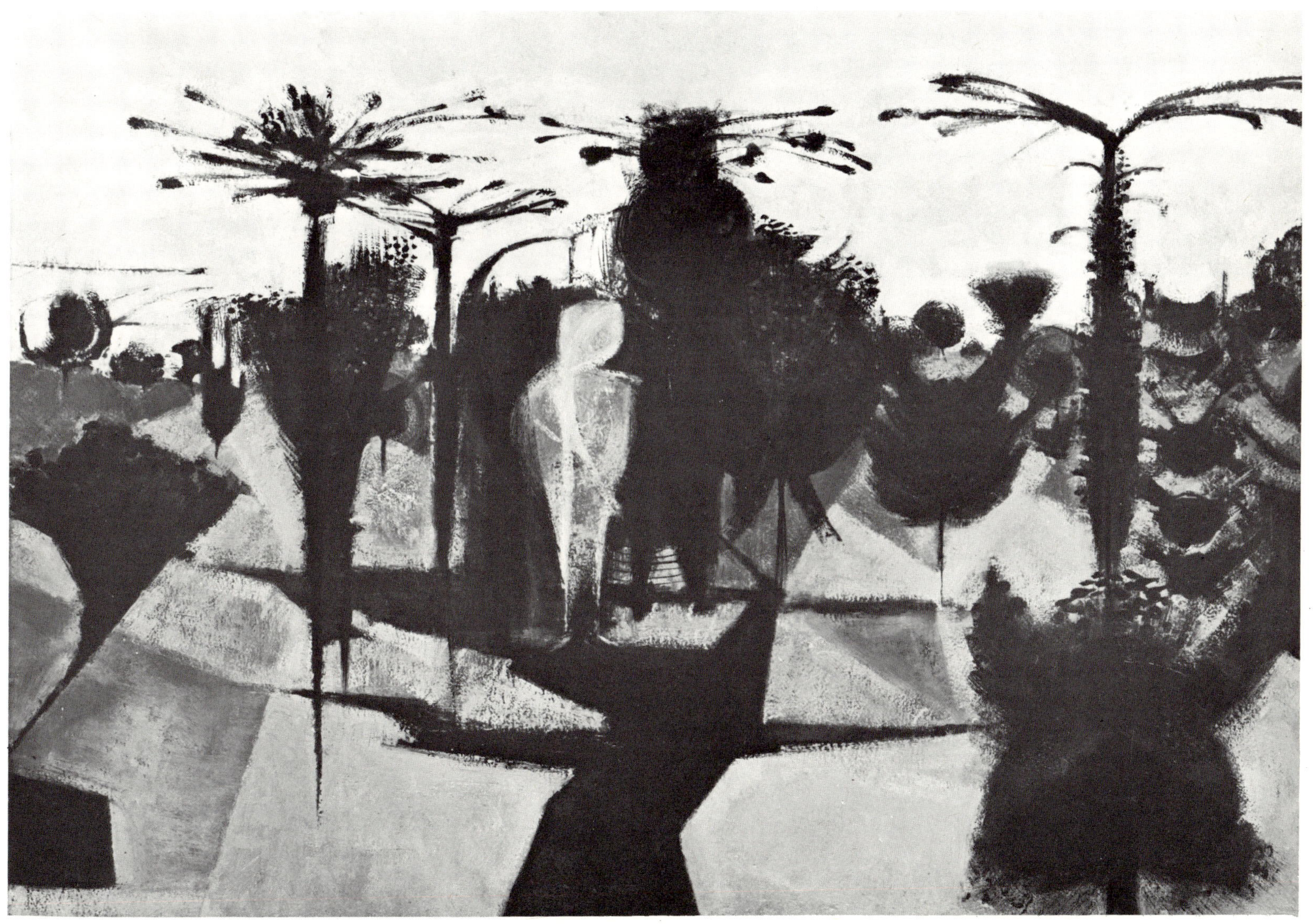

144 Alan Reynolds, *Keeper of the Dark Copse*, 1951/2 (The Tate Gallery)

CHECK-LIST

This check-list is an attempt at a preliminary catalogue of Samuel Palmer's work. Much of this was destroyed by his son in 1910, over the years more has been lost or survives untraced and unrecognized. Not least amongst a cataloguer's problems is that of the titles of many of Palmer's pictures which often vary according to the source that is consulted so that it is difficult to establish whether the same or different pictures are under discussion. This check-list is, therefore, divided into two sections, A and B. In SECTION A are listed those works whose whereabouts are definitely known. In SECTION B works known to have existed when, for example, the Victoria and Albert Museum Exhibition was held in 1926; those which have been described or listed by authorities like Geoffrey Grigson; and those which have gone through the sale rooms and dealers and which, presumably, are now in private or public collections but have not been catalogued or traced. The existence of a date does not necessarily guarantee that the particular work is still extant, conversely the absence of a date does not imply that the work is no longer in existence.

All measurements are in inches: abbreviations used are G, reproduced or listed in Geoffrey Grigson, *Samuel Palmer – The Visionary Years*; L, a reproduction in the very full records of the Leger Galleries, London; V, reproduced or listed in *Drawings, Etchings and Woodcuts by Samuel Palmer and other Disciples of William Blake*, catalogue of a Victoria and Albert Museum Exhibition, 1926.

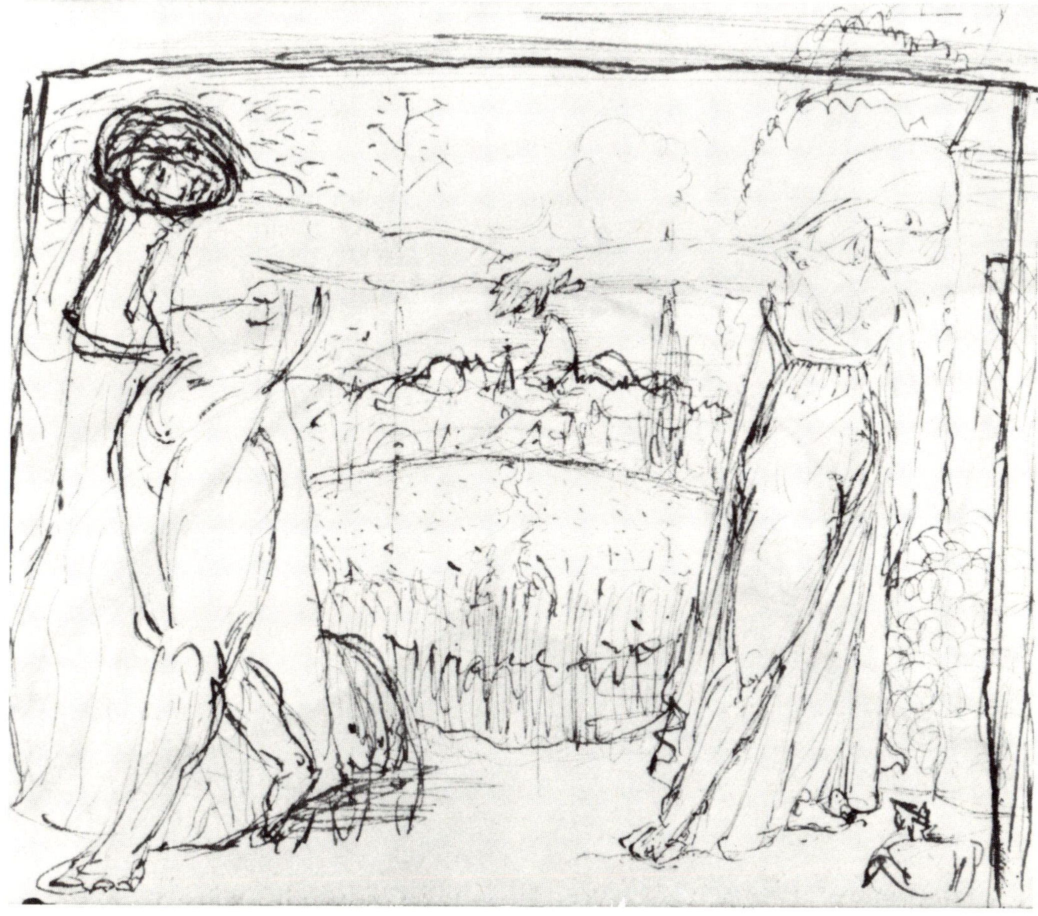

145 Page 133, Sketchbook, 1824 (British Museum)

SECTION A

Pollard Willow, Tottenham Marshes, *c.*1819
Pencil, $7\frac{5}{8} \times 4\frac{7}{16}$. Private Collection

Potato Shed, Tottenham Marshes, *c.*1819
Pencil, $4\frac{7}{16} \times 7\frac{5}{16}$. Private Collection

Sketchbook, 1819
40 pages, $7\frac{1}{4} \times 4\frac{1}{2}$. British Museum

Evening, 1821
Pen and bistre, $7\frac{1}{2} \times 10\frac{1}{2}$. Victoria and Albert Museum

Studies of Cottage Scenery, 1821
Two on one sheet, each $2\frac{3}{8} \times 4$. Private Collection

Old Cottage and Elms, *c.*1821
Sepia, $2\frac{3}{4} \times 4\frac{5}{8}$. Victoria and Albert Museum

Study of Old Buildings, 1821
Pen and sepia wash, $7\frac{1}{2} \times 10$. Collection Mr. and Mrs. Paul Mellon

Sussex: Storm Approaching, 1821
Water-colour, $8\frac{5}{16} \times 12\frac{1}{2}$. Collection Mr. and Mrs. Paul Mellon

A Study from Nature, Storm Approaching, 1821
Pen and sepia wash, $7\frac{3}{4} \times 10\frac{3}{4}$. Private Collection

Sketchbook, 1824 (*Plates 4–10, 15–22, 24, 145*)
91 pages, $4\frac{5}{8} \times 7\frac{1}{2}$. 86 in the British Museum, 5 in the Victoria and Albert Museum

The Repose of the Holy Family, *c.*1824/5 (*Plate 11*)
Oil and tempera, $12\frac{3}{4} \times 15\frac{1}{2}$. Ashmolean Museum

Study of a Hand holding a knobbed stick, 1825 (*Plate 25*)
Pen and chalk, $4 \times 2\frac{3}{4}$. Victoria and Albert Museum

Sketchbook page, *c.*1825
Pen and pencil, $7\frac{1}{8} \times 4\frac{9}{16}$. Collection Mr. and Mrs. Paul Mellon

A Rustic Scene, 1825 (*Plate 34*)
Sepia mixed with gum, $6\frac{7}{16} \times 9\frac{3}{16}$. Ashmolean Museum

Valley with a Bright Cloud, 1825 (*Plate 27*)
Sepia mixed with gum, $7\frac{1}{8} \times 10\frac{15}{16}$. Ashmolean Museum

Early Morning, 1825 (*Plate 26*)
Sepia mixed with gum, $7\frac{7}{16} \times 9\frac{3}{16}$. Ashmolean Museum

Late Twilight, 1825 (*Plate 29*)
Sepia mixed with gum, $7\frac{1}{16} \times 9\frac{1}{8}$. Ashmolean Museum

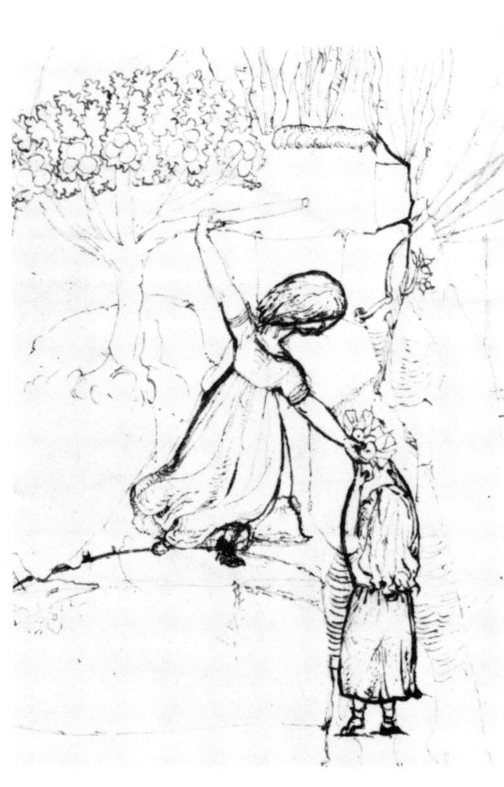

The Skirts of a Wood, 1825 (*Plate 14*)
Sepia mixed with gum, $6\frac{13}{16} \times 10\frac{11}{16}$. Ashmolean Museum

The Valley thick with Corn, 1825 (*Plate 13*)
Sepia mixed with gum, $7\frac{1}{8} \times 10\frac{7}{8}$. Ashmolean Museum

Ruins on a River Bank, 1825/6
Pen and sepia, $11\frac{1}{8} \times 7$. Private Collection

The Haunted Stream, *c.*1826
Sepia, $3\frac{5}{8} \times 4\frac{3}{4}$. Private Collection

A Shepherd and his Flock under the Moon and Stars, *c.*1826
Sepia and chinese white, $4\frac{1}{4} \times 5\frac{1}{8}$. Collection Mr. and Mrs. Paul Mellon

Landscape: A Girl Standing, *c.*1826 (*Plate 30*)
Sepia, $4\frac{1}{2} \times 5\frac{1}{4}$. The Tate Gallery

Harvest under a Crescent Moon, *c.*1826 (*see title page*)
Wood engraving, $1\frac{1}{16} \times 3\frac{1}{32} \times 1\frac{1}{32}$. Ashmolean Museum

Windmill and Cornfield, *c.*1826
Sepia, $2\frac{21}{32} \times 4\frac{1}{8}$. Private Collection

Cornfield, Windmill and Spire, 1826/7 (*Plate 31*)
Sepia, $2\frac{3}{8} \times 3\frac{1}{2}$. Private Collection

A Hilly Scene, *c.*1826 (*Plate 28*)
Water-colour, pen and tempera, $8\frac{1}{16} \times 5\frac{9}{32}$. The Tate Gallery

Moonlight: The Winding River, *c.*1827 (*Plate 40*)
Sepia, $10\frac{1}{2} \times 7\frac{3}{16}$. Collection Mr. and Mrs. Paul Mellon

A Cottage among Trees: Shoreham, *c.*1827
Pen and sepia, $10\frac{1}{8} \times 7$. Collection Mr. and Mrs. Paul Mellon

Dark Trees by a Pool, 1826/7
Sepia, $4\frac{1}{8} \times 2\frac{5}{8}$. Private Collection

Shoreham: Moonlight, 1827
Sepia, $10 \times 11\frac{7}{8}$. Private Collection (*Plate 41*)

George Richmond engraving *The Shepherd* 1827
Pen, $5\frac{1}{16} \times 4\frac{9}{16}$. Private Collection

Landscape with Figure embracing a Tree, 1827? (*Plate 42*)
Pencil and wash. $4\frac{3}{4} \times 6\frac{3}{4}$. Private Collection

Self Portrait of the Artist with Aureole, 1826/7
Oil on panel, $13\frac{1}{2} \times 9\frac{1}{4}$. Private Collection

Stream with Overhanging Trees, *c.*1826/7
Sepia wash and pen, $9\frac{3}{4} \times 7\frac{1}{2}$. Private Collection

Self Portrait, 1828 (*Plate 55*)
Black and white chalk, $11\frac{5}{8} \times 9\frac{11}{16}$. Ashmolean Museum

Meditation upon the Wonderful Providence of God, *c.*1827/8 (*Plate 43*)
Sepia mixed with gum, $7\frac{3}{16} \times 10\frac{3}{4}$. Private Collection

Oak Tree and Beech, Lullingstone Park, 1828 (*Plate 45*)
Pen, ink, water-colour and gouache, $11\frac{3}{8} \times 18\frac{1}{2}$. Private Collection

Ancient Trees in Lullingstone Park, 1828 (*Plate 44*)
Pencil, 10×14. Collection Lord Clark

Oak Trees in Lullingstone Park, 1828 (*Plate 46*)
Pen, ink, water-colour and gouache, $11\frac{5}{8} \times 18\frac{1}{2}$. National Gallery of Canada

Lane and Shed, Shoreham, 1828 (*Plate 35*)
Pen, ink, water-colour and gouache, $10\frac{15}{16} \times 17\frac{9}{16}$. Victoria and Albert Museum

A Timbered Cottage, 1828
Pen, ink and water-colour, $14 \times 17\frac{3}{8}$. Private Collection

A Barn in a Valley, 1828 (*Plate 58*)
Pen and brush with bistre, indian ink and gouache over pencil, $11\frac{1}{8} \times 17\frac{3}{8}$. Ashmolean Museum

The Bridge at Shoreham, *c.*1828
Water-colour, pen and pencil, $8\frac{11}{16} \times 10\frac{11}{16}$. Private Collection

Cottage among Trees, *c.*1828
Pen and wash, $11 \times 7\frac{1}{2}$. Private Collection

Ruth Returned from Gleaning, 1828/9 (*Plate 57*)
Chalk and wash, $11\frac{9}{16} \times 11\frac{1}{2}$. Victoria and Albert Museum

Barn with a Mossy Roof, 1828/9 (*Plate 53*)
Water-colour and pen, $10\frac{15}{16} \times 14\frac{3}{4}$. Private Collection

A Cow Lodge with a Mossy Roof, 1828/9 (*Plate 36*)
Water-colour, gouache and pen, $10\frac{1}{16} \times 14\frac{5}{16}$. Collection Mr. and Mrs. Paul Mellon

The Primitive Cottage, 1828/9 (*Plate 59*)
Pen and wash, $8\frac{7}{8} \times 10\frac{7}{8}$. Victoria and Albert Museum

Christ outside Jerusalem, 1828/9?
Oil on canvas, 41×30. Private Collection

An Ancient Barn, *c.*1829
Pen and wash, $6 \times 10\frac{13}{16}$. Private Collection

Old Barn, *c.*1829
Pen and wash, $8 \times 10\frac{7}{8}$. Private Collection

Cornfield, *c.*1829
Pen and wash, $7\frac{13}{16} \times 13\frac{1}{4}$. Collection Mr. and Mrs. Paul Mellon

Landscape at Shoreham, 1829 (*Plate 61*)
Pen and wash over pencil, $8 \times 12\frac{3}{4}$. Courtauld Institute, Witt Drawings Collection

A Wooded Hillside at Underriver near Sevenoaks, Kent, 1829 (*Plate 64*)
Pen and ink heightened with white. $6 \times 10\frac{3}{4}$ Victoria and Albert Museum

The Primitive Cottage, 1828/9
Pen and sepia wash, $10\frac{3}{4} \times 14\frac{3}{4}$. Private Collection

Pear Tree in a Walled Garden, *c.*1829 (*Plate 54*)
Water-colour, $8\frac{3}{4} \times 11\frac{1}{8}$. Private Collection

A Wooded River Bank, 1829?
Pencil, $8\frac{1}{2} \times 6\frac{3}{8}$. Private Collection

In a Shoreham Garden, *c.*1829 (*Plate 49*)
Water-colour and gouache, $11\frac{1}{16} \times 8\frac{3}{4}$. Victoria and Albert Museum

A Kentish Idyll, 1829/30
Sepia, $3\frac{3}{8} \times 4\frac{3}{16}$. Private Collection

A Shepherd leading his Flock under the Full Moon, *c.*1829/30
Sepia, $5\frac{5}{8} \times 7$. Private Collection

Woman with Full Moon and Deer, 1829/30 (*Plate 66*)
Wash and body colour, $5\frac{5}{16} \times 3\frac{11}{16}$. Victoria and Albert Museum

The Valley of Vision, 1829/30 (*Plate 63*)
Pen and sepia heightened with white, $11\frac{1}{16} \times 17\frac{1}{2}$. Collection Mr. and Mrs. Paul Mellon

Coming from Evening Church, 1830 (*Plate 77*)
Oil and tempera on canvas, $12 \times 7\frac{3}{4}$. The Tate Gallery

A Village Church among Trees, 1830 (*Plate 71*)
Sepia, $7\frac{3}{16} \times 6$. Victoria and Albert Museum

Evening, a Church among Trees, *c.*1830 (*Plate 75*)
Sepia, $6 \times 7\frac{1}{4}$. The Tate Gallery

Cornfield by Moonlight with the Evening Star, *c.*1830
Water-colour, gouache and pen, $7\frac{3}{4} \times 11\frac{3}{4}$. Collection Lord Clark

Shepherds under the Full Moon, *c.*1830 (*Plate 67*)
Indian ink, sepia and body colour, $4\frac{1}{2} \times 5\frac{3}{16}$ Ashmolean Museum

Cornfield and Church by Moonlight, *c.*1830 (*Plate 69*)
Indian ink and wash, $5\frac{7}{8} \times 7\frac{1}{8}$. Private Collection

Yellow Twilight, *c.*1830
Water-colour and pen, $6\frac{1}{2} \times 10\frac{13}{16}$. Private Collection

Study of a Bough loaded with Apples, 1830
Chalk touched with white, $11\frac{1}{2} \times 17\frac{3}{4}$. Fitzwilliam Museum

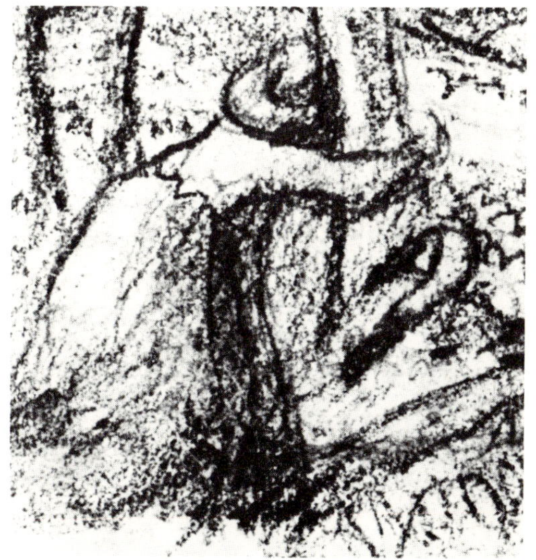

A Country Road leading towards a Church, 1830
Sepia, 7¼ × 5$\frac{5}{16}$. Fitzwilliam Museum

The Magic Apple Tree, 1830 (*Plate 72*)
Water-colour and pen, 13¾ × 10¼. Fitzwilliam Museum

A Church with Bridge and Boat, *c.*1830 (*Plate 70*)
Sepia, 4½ × 3⅜. Ashmolean Museum

The Harvest Moon, 1830/1 (*Plate 79*)
Water-colour, 4⅞ × 5⅞. Carlisle Museum and Art Gallery

A Church with Boat and Sheep, 1831/2.
Sepia, n.a. Private Collection

The Folded Flock or **The Sheepfold,** 1831/2 (*Plate 84*)
Indian ink, 5⅞ × 7$\frac{1}{16}$. Private Collection

Pastoral with Horse Chestnut, 1831/2 (*Plate 74*)
Water-colour, 13 × 10$\frac{5}{16}$. Ashmolean Museum

Old House on the Bank of the Darenth, Shoreham, 1831/2 (*Plate 51*)
Water-colour and pen, 15⅞ × 12$\frac{11}{16}$. Ashmolean Museum

The Flock and the Star, 1831/2 (*Plate 76*)
Indian ink, 5$\frac{13}{16}$ × 7. Ashmolean Museum

Sepham Barn, 1831 (*Plate 78*)
Sepia, 6$\frac{13}{16}$ × 10¼. Private Collection

Young Man Yoking an Ox, 1831/2 (*Plate 88*)
Indian ink, 5$\frac{13}{16}$ × 7. Ashmolean Museum

Shoreham at Twilight, 1831/2 (*Plate 87*)
Sepia and gum heightened with white, 7 × 10⅛. Private Collection

A Thatched Cottage and Church, 1831/2
Sepia, 2⅝ × 4⅛. Collection Mr. and Mrs. Paul Mellon

Shoreham, Kent, 1831/2
Pen and wash, 2$\frac{13}{16}$ × 4¼. Collection Mr. and Mrs. Paul Mellon

Crescent Moon with Sheep, 1831/2
Sepia, 6$\frac{3}{16}$ × 7$\frac{7}{16}$. Private Collection

Moonlight: A Landscape with Sheep, 1831/2 (*Plate 86*)
Sepia, 6 × 7¼. The Tate Gallery

Cornfield: Shoreham at Twilight, 1831/2 (*Plate 85*)
Sepia and indian ink, 5$\frac{11}{16}$ × 6⅜. Private Collection

Bright Cloud and Ploughing, 1831/2
Sepia, 3⅝ × 4¼. Manchester City Art Gallery

Bright Cloud, Shepherd and Windmill, 1831/2
Sepia, 3½ × 4⅜. Private Collection

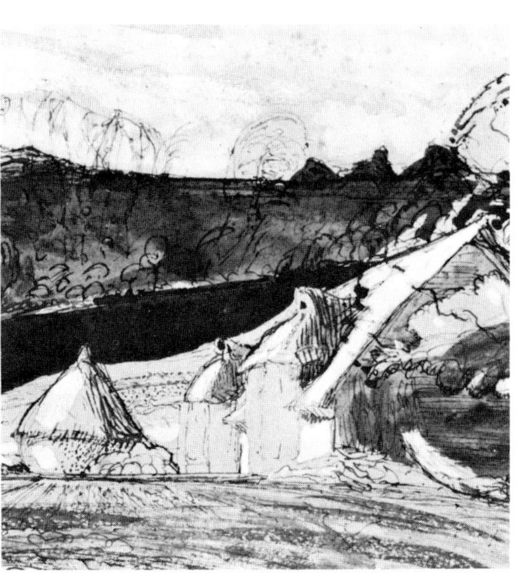

Bright Cloud, 1831/2?
Blue, sepia and yellow wash, 6 × 7⅞. Collection Mr. and Mrs. Paul Mellon

Bright Cloud, Sunshine and Shadow, 1831/2
Sepia, 3$\frac{11}{16}$ × 4$\frac{11}{16}$. Private Collection

Drawing for 'The Bright Cloud', 1831/2 (*Plate 80*)
Indian ink, 10 × 10¾. The Tate Gallery

Drawing for 'The Bright Cloud', 1831/2 (*Plate 82*)
Indian ink, 6 × 6. British Museum

Drawing for 'The White Cloud', 1831/2 (*Plate 81*)
Indian ink, sepia and body colour, 5⅝ × 6$\frac{3}{16}$. Ashmolean Museum

A Man with a Faggot, 1832/3
Sepia, 4 × 3⅜. Manchester City Art Gallery

At Score near Ilfracombe, 1832/3 (*Plate 94*)
Water-colour and pencil, 13½ × 19⅜. Victoria and Albert Museum

Culbone, Somerset, 1832/3 (*Plate 92*)
Pencil and water-colour, 11$\frac{9}{16}$ × 15¼. Formerly Melbourne Art Gallery. Present whereabouts unknown

View at Lynton, Devon, 1832
Pen and brown ink, 7½ × 3⅜. Private Collection

View of River Lyn, Devon, 1832?
Pencil, 7½ × 5. Private Collection

View at Lynmouth, 1832?
Pen and indian ink, 9 × 7½. Private Collection

A Devonshire Cottage, 1832?
Pen and ink, 7½ × 5⅞. Private Collection

The Cottager's Return, *c.*1833
Water-colour and pen, 6¼ × 8⅛. Private Collection

A Cornfield Bordered by Trees, 1833/4 (*Plate 90*)
Oil and tempera, 6$\frac{11}{16}$ × 5$\frac{11}{16}$. Ashmolean Museum

Drawings for 'Landscape Twilight', (Landscape Sketch), 1833/4 (*Plate 93*)
Indian ink wash, 5$\frac{5}{16}$ × 7. Victoria and Albert Museum

Barn at Shoreham, 1833/4 (*Plate 89*)
Sepia and gum heightened with white, 10¼ × 14¾. Private Collection

The Harvest Moon, 1833
Oil (and tempera?), 8¾ × 10¾. Collection Mr. and Mrs. Paul Mellon

The Gleaning Field, 1833 (*Plate 50*)
Oil and tempera, 13 × 18. The Tate Gallery

Scene at Underriver, 1833/4
Oil and tempera, 7 × 10. Private Collection

The Weald of Kent, 1833/4
Water-colour, $7\frac{3}{8} \times 10\frac{11}{16}$. Collection Mr. and Mrs. Paul Mellon

The Timber Wagon, 1833/4
Water-colour, $4\frac{15}{16} \times 6\frac{1}{8}$. Collection Mr. and Mrs. Paul Mellon

Timber Wagon crossing a Stream, 1833/4?
Water-colour and gouache, $4\frac{1}{8} \times 6$. Collection Mr. and Mrs. Paul Mellon

The Golden Valley, 1833/4
Water-colour, $4\frac{15}{16} \times 6\frac{1}{8}$. Private Collection

The White Cloud, 1833/4
Oil and tempera, $8\frac{3}{4} \times 10\frac{1}{2}$. Private Collection

The Bright Cloud, 1834?
Oil and tempera, $9\frac{1}{8} \times 12\frac{1}{2}$. Private Collection

Study for 'The Shearers', 1833/4
Wash and pencil, $14 \times 10\frac{3}{8}$. Private Collection

The Shearers, 1833/4 (*Plate 91*)
Oil and tempera on panel, $20\frac{1}{4} \times 28$. Private Collection

The Sleeping Shepherd, 1833/4
Oil and tempera, $15 \times 20\frac{1}{4}$. Whitworth Art Gallery, Manchester

Landscape Twilight, 1834?
Oil and tempera, $8\frac{1}{2} \times 10\frac{1}{4}$. Private Collection

Evening, 1834
Mezzotint by Welby Sherman after Palmer, $5\frac{7}{8} \times 7\frac{1}{16}$. Victoria and Albert Museum, British Museum and The Tate Gallery

The Young Traveller, 1834
Sepia, $14\frac{1}{4} \times 3\frac{1}{4}$. Private Collection

Study of a Kentish Hop Bin, 1834
Water-colour and pencil, $11\frac{1}{2} \times 12$. Victoria and Albert Museum

Drawing for 'A Pastoral Scene', 1835
Bistre, $7\frac{3}{4} \times 4\frac{17}{32}$. Private Collection

Drawing for 'A Pastoral Scene', 1835
Sepia, $6 \times 7\frac{1}{4}$. The Tate Gallery

A Pastoral Scene, 1835 (*Plate 73*)
Oil and tempera, $10\frac{3}{4} \times 15\frac{1}{2}$. Ashmolean Museum

Study of Trees, Clovelly Park, *c.*1835 (*Plate 102*)
Black chalk, $10\frac{1}{8} \times 14\frac{5}{8}$. Ashmolean Museum

Study of Trees, 1835? (*Plate 96*)
Water-colour and body colour over black chalk, $10\frac{1}{16} \times 14\frac{5}{8}$. Ashmolean Museum

The Harvest Moon, 1835 (*Plate 101*)
Sepia, $6 \times 7\frac{1}{4}$. The Tate Gallery

A View on the North Coast of Devon, 1835
Pencil, coloured wash and body colour, $10 \times 14\frac{1}{4}$. Private Collection

A Rugged Landscape, 1835
Pencil and water-colour, $14\frac{5}{8} \times 18\frac{3}{8}$. Private Collection

The Waterfall at Pistil Mawddach near Dolgelly, 1835?
Water-colour and gouache, $18\frac{1}{2} \times 14\frac{5}{8}$. Private Collection

A View from Rooks Hill, Kent, 1835
Water-colour and gouache, 20×16. Collection Mr. and Mrs. Paul Mellon

Snowdon looking over the Lakes and Inn at Capel Curig, 1835?
Water-colour and body colour, $14\frac{5}{8} \times 18\frac{5}{8}$. Private Collection

Mountains by The Traveller's Rest Inn, Dolgelly, 1835?
Pencil, water-colour and body colour, $11\frac{3}{4} \times 18$.
Collection Mr. and Mrs. Paul Mellon

A Pastoral Scene, 1835
Brush and sepia wash, $3\frac{3}{4} \times 4\frac{3}{8}$. Collection Mr. and Mrs. Paul Mellon

Harlech Castle, 1835
Black chalk, water-colour and gouache, $8\frac{5}{8} \times 11\frac{3}{8}$. Collection Mr. and Mrs. Paul Mellon

Tintern Abbey, 1835
Pencil and body colour, $15\frac{1}{4} \times 9\frac{3}{8}$. Private Collection

Tintern Abbey, 1835 (*Plate 99*)
Water-colour, $9\frac{1}{2} \times 15$. Victoria and Albert Museum

Study of a Garden at Tintern, 1835 (*Plate 110*)
Water-colour and pen, $14\frac{3}{4} \times 18\frac{3}{4}$. Ashmolean Museum

Near The Traveller's Rest Inn, Dolgelly, 1835 (*Plate 98*)
Pencil, water-colour and body colour, $9\frac{3}{4} \times 17\frac{3}{4}$. Victoria and Albert Museum

View of Lynton, Devon, 1835
Pencil and water-colour, $13\frac{1}{4} \times 8\frac{3}{4}$. Private Collection

Underriver Hills, Near Sevenoaks, Kent, *c.*1833/5
Water-colour, $9\frac{1}{2} \times 14$. Collection Mr. and Mrs. Paul Mellon

Mount Siabod from Tyn-y-Coed, near Capel Curig, 1835/6
Pen and water-colour heightened with white, $14\frac{7}{8} \times 18\frac{3}{4}$. Collection Mr. and Mrs. Paul Mellon

The Young Angler, 1836?
Water-colour, $19\frac{5}{16} \times 14\frac{1}{4}$. National Gallery of Canada

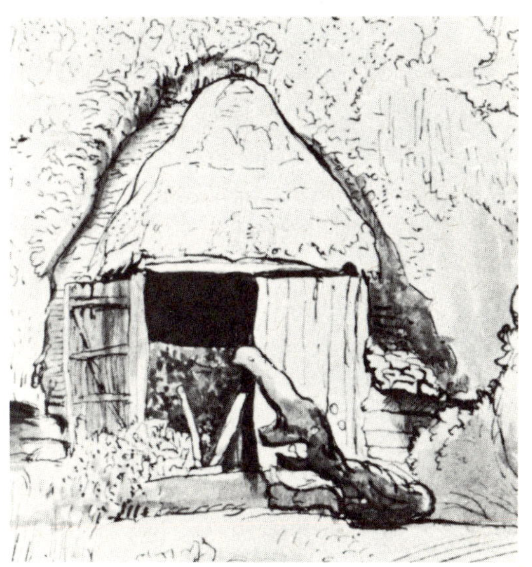

The Waterfalls, Pistil Mawddach, North Wales, 1835/6 (*Plate 103*)
Oil on canvas, 16 × 10$\frac{1}{4}$. The Tate Gallery

Hilly Landscape with Cottages, 1836
Pencil and water-colour, 9$\frac{1}{2}$ × 13$\frac{1}{2}$. Private Collection

The Goatherd, 1836/7
Pen and water-colour, 7$\frac{3}{4}$ × 11. Private Collection

Trefiew Mill on the road from Bettws-y-Coed to Conway, 1836
Water-colour and gouache, 15$\frac{1}{4}$ × 18$\frac{7}{8}$. Private Collection

Pistyll Rhaiadr, North Wales, 1836/7
Water-colour, 7$\frac{1}{2}$ × 9$\frac{11}{16}$. Private Collection

View on the River Machawy, North Wales, 1837
Black chalk and water-colour heightened with white, n.a. Private Collection

The Villa d'Este, 1837
Water-colour, 10$\frac{3}{4}$ × 14$\frac{11}{16}$. Victoria and Albert Museum

Street of the Tombs, Pompeii, 1837
Water-colour, 11$\frac{7}{16}$ × 16$\frac{5}{8}$. Victoria and Albert Museum

Florence, 1838 (*Plate 106*)
Water-colour, 17$\frac{7}{16}$ × 23$\frac{15}{16}$. Victoria and Albert Museum

Modern Rome, 1838
Water-colour, 16 × 22$\frac{1}{2}$. Birmingham City Art Gallery

Vesuvius in Eruption, 1838
Water-colour, 4$\frac{1}{2}$ × 7. Private Collection

The Cypresses at the Villa d'Este, 1838/9
Black chalk, water-colour and gouache, 12$\frac{1}{2}$ × 9. Collection Mr. and Mrs. Paul Mellon

Rome from Santo Spirito, 1838/9?
Black chalk heightened with white, 14 × 23$\frac{1}{4}$. Collection Mr. and Mrs. Paul Mellon

A Pilgrim in Rome, 1838/9
Water-colour, 10$\frac{3}{4}$ × 8. Verso, Study of Man's Legs. Collection Mr. and Mrs. Paul Mellon

Italian Hill Town, 1838/9
Black chalk, water-colour and gouache, 9$\frac{1}{4}$ × 12$\frac{3}{8}$. Collection Mr. and Mrs. Paul Mellon

Civitella di Subiaco, 1838/9
Water-colour and body colour, 11$\frac{1}{2}$ × 16$\frac{3}{4}$. Whitworth Art Gallery, Manchester

View from the Villa d'Este at Tivoli, 1839 (*Plate 107*)
Water-colour and body colour with pen and ink, heightened with gold, 13$\frac{3}{16}$ × 21$\frac{1}{4}$. Ashmolean Museum

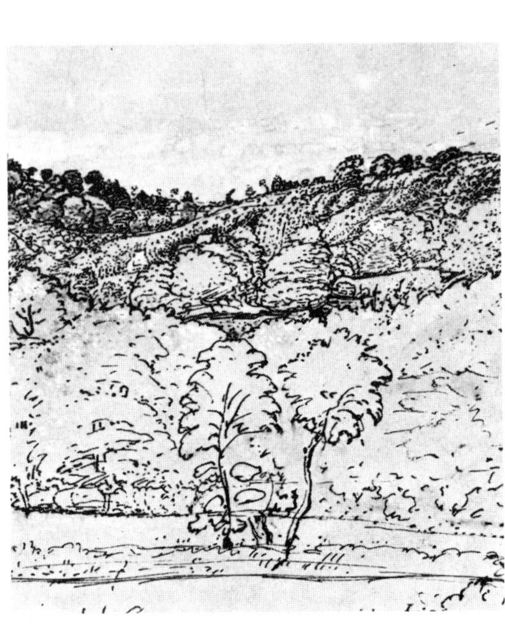

View at Tivoli, 1839
Water-colour, 12 × 16. Philadelphia Museum of Art

Classical Subject, 1840/41
'Narcissus and Echo'? Water-colour, 7$\frac{1}{2}$ × 9$\frac{11}{16}$. Private Collection

The Colosseum and Alban Mount, 1840? (*Plate 97*)
Water-colour and body colour over black chalk, 8 × 15$\frac{11}{16}$. Ashmolean Museum

Lulworth Cove, Dorset, 1841?
Pencil and water-colour, 13$\frac{1}{8}$ × 8$\frac{7}{8}$. Private Collection

Llyn Gwynedd and part of Llyn-y-Ddinas between Capel Curig and Beddgelert, North Wales, 1843
Water-colour and body colour, 15 × 18$\frac{1}{2}$. Collection Mr. and Mrs. Paul Mellon

Guildford, 1844
Water-colour and body colour, 4$\frac{3}{8}$ × 10$\frac{5}{8}$. Collection Mr. and Mrs. Paul Mellon

Pastoral Scene, 1844/5
Black chalk, water-colour and body colour, 16$\frac{1}{2}$ × 9$\frac{5}{8}$. Private Collection

Evening in Italy, 1845
Water-colour and gouache, 7$\frac{1}{2}$ × 16$\frac{1}{4}$. Private Collection

Farmyard near Princes Risborough, exhib. 1846 (*Plate 112*)
Water-colour, 15$\frac{7}{16}$ × 21$\frac{1}{4}$. Victoria and Albert Museum

Crossing the Ford, 1846
Water-colour and gouache, 20$\frac{1}{4}$ × 27$\frac{3}{4}$. Private Collection

Study of Dandelions, 1847/57
Water-colour and body colour, 7$\frac{1}{4}$ × 5$\frac{1}{4}$. Private Collection

Tintagel Castle, Approaching Rain, 1848 (*Plate 115*)
Body colour over pencil, 11$\frac{13}{16}$ × 17$\frac{5}{16}$. Ashmolean Museum

Farmyard near Princes Risborough, 1848 (*Plate 108*)
Water-colour and body colour over pencil, 10$\frac{9}{16}$ × 14$\frac{1}{2}$. Ashmolean Museum

At Redhill, 1848 (*Plate 109*)
Water-colour and body colour over black chalk, 10$\frac{3}{16}$ × 14$\frac{3}{4}$. Ashmolean Museum

Coast at Lynmouth, Devon, *c.*1848
Pencil and water-colour, 10$\frac{1}{8}$ × 7. Private Collection

Calypso's Island, *c.*1849
Water-colour, gouache and gold paint, 20$\frac{3}{4}$ × 29$\frac{1}{4}$. Whitworth Art Gallery, Manchester

The Watermill, 1848 (*Plate 111*)
Water-colour and body colour, 19$\frac{7}{8}$ × 27$\frac{3}{4}$. Ashmolean Museum

Coast Scene with passing Rain, 1848
Black and white chalk with wash, $7\frac{3}{8} \times 10\frac{7}{8}$. Private Collection

Landscape with Rain Cloud, 1848/50
Water-colour and pencil, heightened with white, $9\frac{1}{2} \times 13\frac{3}{4}$. Private Collection

Two Sketch Book Pages, Nos. 24 and 34: Cornish Coast, between 1848/58 (*Plates 113, 114*)
Black chalk, $4\frac{1}{8} \times 7$. Victoria and Albert Museum

Two Sketchbook Pages of Cornwall, between 1848/58
Black chalk, $4\frac{1}{8} \times 7$. Collection Mr. and Mrs. Paul Mellon

Study of Waves breaking over Sea Shore, 1848/58
Black chalk, $6\frac{5}{8} \times 9\frac{15}{16}$. National Gallery of Canada

Truro River, *c.*1850
Water-colour and pencil, $9\frac{7}{8} \times 5\frac{1}{2}$. Private Collection

The Willow, 1850
Etching, $3\frac{9}{16} \times 2\frac{5}{8}$. Victoria and Albert Museum

The Skylark, 1850
Etching, $3\frac{3}{4} \times 2\frac{7}{8}$. Victoria and Albert Museum

The Herdsman's Cottage, or **Sunset,** 1850 (*Plate 116*)
Etching, $3\frac{13}{16} \times 3$. Victoria and Albert Museum

Christmas, or **Folding the last Sheep,** 1850 (*Plate 117*)
Etching, $3\frac{7}{8} \times 3\frac{3}{16}$. Victoria and Albert Museum

Landscape and Dark Trees, 1850
Water-colour and body colour, $16\frac{5}{8} \times 11$. Private Collection

The Vine or **Plumpy Bacchus,** 1852
Etching, plate size $11\frac{7}{8} \times 8\frac{1}{2}$. British Museum

Old Cedar Botanic Gardens, Chelsea, 1854
Black chalk, $10\frac{9}{16} \times 14\frac{9}{16}$. Collection Mr. and Mrs. Paul Mellon

Foxgloves, 1855
Pencil, $6\frac{7}{8} \times 8\frac{3}{4}$. Collection Mr. and Mrs. Paul Mellon

The Dell of Comus, 1855
Water-colour, body colour and gum, $21\frac{1}{4} \times 29\frac{1}{2}$. Brighton Museum

Woodland Scene with Sheep, 1856
Black chalk, $6\frac{1}{2} \times 11\frac{1}{4}$. Private Collection

The Sunset, 1857
Water-colour, $7\frac{3}{4} \times 16\frac{1}{2}$. Private Collection

The Sleeping Shepherd: Early Morning, 1857 (*Plate 120*)
Etching, $3\frac{3}{4} \times 3\frac{1}{16}$. Victoria and Albert Museum

The Rising Moon or **An English Pastoral,** 1857 (*Plate 118*)
Etching, $4\frac{19}{32} \times 7\frac{1}{2}$. Victoria and Albert Museum

The Comet of 1858, 1858
Water-colour, n.a. Private Collection

The Weary Ploughman or **Tardus Bubulcus** or **The Herdsman,** begun 1858, published 1865 (*Plate 119*)
Etching, $5\frac{3}{16} \times 7\frac{15}{16}$. Victoria and Albert Museum

Pastoral, 1859
Water-colour and body colour, n.a. Laing Art Gallery and Museum

Open Ploughing at Sunset, after 1860
Water-colour, $13\frac{1}{2} \times 10\frac{1}{4}$. Private Collection

Evening, after 1860
Water-colour, $7\frac{1}{2} \times 16\frac{1}{8}$. Private Collection

Wooded Landscape with Stream, 1860
Water-colour and body colour, $15\frac{1}{4} \times 11$. Private Collection

After the Storm, 1861
Water-colour, $12\frac{3}{4} \times 27\frac{1}{2}$. Private Collection

The Streamlet, 1861
Water-colour, $7\frac{1}{2} \times 16\frac{3}{4}$. Private Collection

The Early Ploughman or **Morning Spread upon the Mountains,** begun before 1861 (*Plate 121*)
Etching, $5\frac{7}{8} \times 8\frac{1}{4}$. Victoria and Albert Museum

The Morning of Life, 1860/61 (*Plate 122*)
Etching, $5\frac{7}{8} \times 8\frac{1}{4}$. Victoria and Albert Museum

The Wooded Lane, after 1861 (*Plate 123*)
Water-colour and body colour, $14\frac{13}{16} \times 19\frac{15}{16}$. Ashmolean Museum

Landscape with Woman driving Sheep, after 1861 (*Plate 124*)
Water-colour and body colour, $10\frac{5}{8} \times 14\frac{15}{16}$. Victoria and Albert Museum

Tintern Abbey at Sunset, 1861
Water-colour and body colour, $12\frac{3}{4} \times 27\frac{1}{4}$. Collection Mr. and Mrs. Paul Mellon

The Furze Field, 1862
Water-colour, $7\frac{7}{16} \times 10\frac{5}{8}$. Victoria and Albert Museum

The Brother come Home from the Sea, 1863
Water-colour and gouache, $7\frac{7}{8} \times 17$. Private Collection

Going home at Curfew Time, 1864 (*Plate 125*)
Water-colour, $10\frac{3}{4} \times 15\frac{3}{8}$. Victoria and Albert Museum

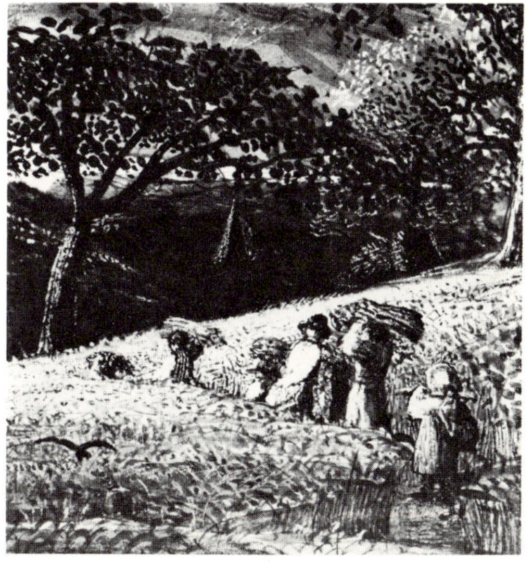

A Dream in the Apennine, exhib. 1864 (*Plate 134*)
Water-colour, 26 × 40. The Tate Gallery

Notebook, 1865/6?
Fifty leaves extant, $4\frac{7}{8} \times 2\frac{3}{4}$. Private Collection

ILLUSTRATIONS TO MILTON, BEGUN 1865

The Eastern Gate, finished 1879
Sepia, $10\frac{3}{4} \times 15$. Victoria and Albert Museum

Towered City
Sepia, $10\frac{1}{4} \times 16\frac{1}{4}$. Victoria and Albert Museum

Study for 'The Bellman', finished 1879 (*Plate 129*)
Chalk and Wash, $10\frac{7}{8} \times 14\frac{7}{8}$. Victoria and Albert Museum

The Waters Murmuring, finished 1879 (*Plate 127*)
Black chalk, $10\frac{3}{4} \times 15$. Victoria and Albert Museum

The Brothers under the Vine, finished *c.*1872
Sepia, heightened with white, $6\frac{7}{8} \times 9\frac{3}{8}$. Victoria and Albert Museum

Man and Woman seated by a Fire
Charcoal, $6\frac{11}{16} \times 5\frac{3}{16}$. Victoria and Albert Museum

View of Boxhill, 1868
Water-colour, $10\frac{1}{4} \times 14\frac{1}{2}$. Private Collection

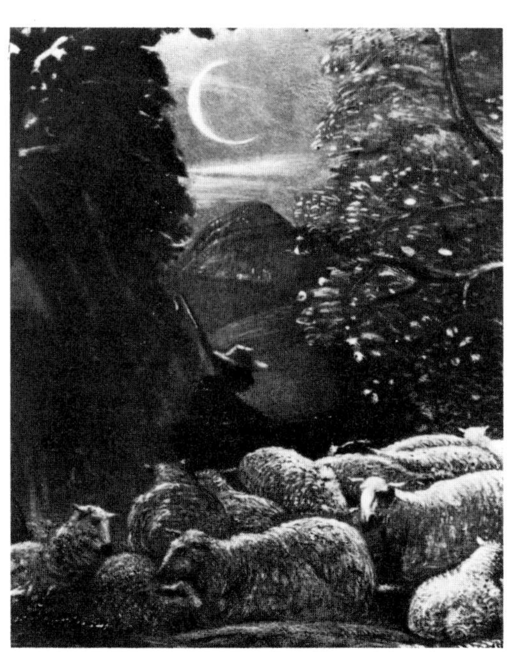

Boxhill, 1868
Black chalk and water-colour, $9\frac{3}{4} \times 12$. Collection Mr. and Mrs. Paul Mellon

View from Richmond Hill, 1872
Pencil, $7\frac{1}{4} \times 4\frac{1}{2}$. Private Collection

Landscape with Girl and Dog, 1875
Crayon and chinese white, $8\frac{3}{4} \times 10\frac{5}{8}$. Private Collection

The Bellman, completed 1879 (*Plate 131*)
Etching, $6\frac{9}{16} \times 9\frac{3}{16}$. Victoria and Albert Museum

The Lonely Tower, completed 1879 (*Plate 126*)
Etching, $6\frac{1}{2}$ to $6\frac{9}{10} \times 9\frac{3}{16}$
Victoria and Albert Museum

Opening the Fold or **Early Morning,** 1880 (*Plate 130*)
Etching, $4\frac{3}{8} \times 6\frac{15}{16}$. Victoria and Albert Museum

DESIGNS FOR VIRGIL'S 'ECLOGUES', begun about 1872 and continued until Palmer's death in 1881

First Eclogue, exhib. 1877
Pen, pencil and white, 4 × 6. Private Collection

First Eclogue, another version
Pen and wash, 4 × 6. Private Collection

Second Eclogue
Sepia, $4\frac{5}{8} \times 7$. Private Collection

Third Eclogue
Pen and sepia, 4 × 6. Private Collection

Third Eclogue, another version
Pen, pencil and white, 4 × 6. Private Collection

Third Eclogue, another version
Pen, pencil and white, 4 × 6. Private Collection

Fourth Eclogue
Pen, pencil and white, 4 × 6. Private Collection

Fifth Eclogue, The Cypress Grove
Pen, pencil touched with white, 4 × 6. Private Collection

Sixth Eclogue
Water-colour, 4 × 6. Private Collection

Sixth Eclogue, another version
Pen and sepia touched with white, $3\frac{3}{8} \times 5$. Private Collection

Sixth Eclogue, another version
Pen and wash, 4 × 6. Private Collection

Seventh Eclogue
Pen and charcoal touched with white, 4 × 6. Private Collection

Eighth Eclogue, The Sepulchre
Sepia, 4 × 6. Private Collection

Ninth Eclogue, Moeris and Galatea, 1880 (*Plate 139*)
Pen and pencil, 4 × 6. National Gallery of Canada

Ninth Eclogue, another version
Chalk and wash, 4 × 6. Private Collection

Tenth Eclogue
Pen and wash, 4 × 6. Private Collection

Tenth Eclogue, another version
Pencil and wash, $4\frac{3}{4} \times 7$. Private Collection

Tenth Eclogue, another version
Pencil and wash touched with white, 4 × 6. Private Collection

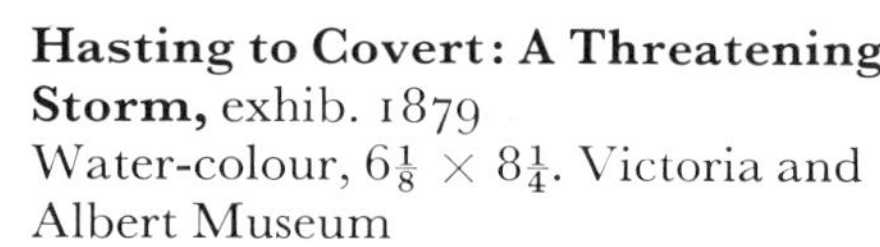

Hasting to Covert: A Threatening Storm, exhib. 1879
Water-colour, $6\frac{1}{8} \times 8\frac{1}{4}$. Victoria and Albert Museum

A Mountain Stream and an Ancient Fortress, 1879 (*Plate 132*)
Water-colour, $5\frac{7}{8} \times 7\frac{7}{8}$. Victoria and Albert Museum

The Western Shore, 1879 (*Plate 128*)
Water-colour, $5 \times 7\frac{1}{2}$. Victoria and Albert Museum

Going to Fold, 1879 (*Plate 136*)
Water-colour, 5×10. Victoria and Albert Museum

Church by a Mill, 1879/80?
Water-colour, $10\frac{1}{8} \times 14$. Private Collection

The Shadowy Stream, 1880 (*Plate 135*)
Water-colour and gouache, $4\frac{1}{4} \times 7\frac{1}{16}$. Victoria and Albert Museum

The Shining River, 1880 (*Plate 138*)
Water-colour, $4 \times 6\frac{15}{16}$. Victoria and Albert Museum

The Winding Stream, 1880 (*Plate 137*)
Water-colour, 4×7. Victoria and Albert Museum

Opening the Fold, 1880
Water-colour, $5\frac{3}{8} \times 8\frac{1}{4}$. Private Collection

ETCHINGS BEGUN BY SAMUEL PALMER AND FINISHED BY A. H. PALMER

The Homeward Star
Etching, $3\frac{15}{16} \times 5\frac{13}{16}$. Private Collection

The Cypress Grove
Etching, $3\frac{15}{16} \times 5\frac{15}{16}$. Private Collection

The Sepulchre
Etching, $3\frac{15}{16} \times 5\frac{15}{16}$. Private Collection

Moeris and Galatea
Etching, $3\frac{15}{16} \times 5\frac{15}{16}$. Private Collection

WORKS TO WHICH NO CERTAIN DATE CAN BE ATTRIBUTED

Mill at Trefiew, North Wales
No catalogue details available. Whitworth Art Gallery, Manchester

Trees in Blossom
Water-colour, body colour and graphite, $4\frac{1}{2} \times 7\frac{1}{4}$. National Gallery of Canada

Barn and Cottage among Trees
No catalogue details available. Collection Mr. and Mrs. Paul Mellon

Landscape with Cottage (Shoreham), Trees and Field
No catalogue details available. Collection Mr. and Mrs. Paul Mellon

The Travellers
Water-colour and gouache, $10\frac{1}{2} \times 17\frac{1}{4}$. Whitworth Art Gallery, Manchester

Box Hill
Water-colour, $9\frac{1}{2} \times 16\frac{1}{4}$. Courtauld Institute, Witt Drawings Collection

Rustic Contentment
Water-colour, $7\frac{1}{4} \times 15\frac{3}{4}$. Collection Mr. and Mrs. Paul Mellon

Kensington Gardens
Water-colour, $10 \times 14\frac{7}{8}$. Collection Mr. and Mrs. Paul Mellon

The Barns
Pen and water-colour, $10 \times 13\frac{1}{2}$. Collection Mr. and Mrs. Paul Mellon

Rocky Landscape in Wales
Water-colour, $15 \times 18\frac{1}{2}$. Collection Mr. and Mrs. Paul Mellon

The Valley of Dolwyddelan
Pen, black chalk and water-colour heightened with body colour, $7\frac{5}{8} \times 11$. Collection Mr. and Mrs. Paul Mellon

A Barn
Pencil, ink and wash. Collection Mr. and Mrs. Paul Mellon

The Rock Slip near Boscastle
Water-colour over black chalk, heightened with white, $9\frac{3}{8} \times 10\frac{3}{8}$. Collection Mr. and Mrs. Paul Mellon

Opening the Fold, Early Morning
Pen and pencil, heightened with white, $2\frac{1}{2} \times 3\frac{3}{4}$. Collection Mr. and Mrs. Paul Mellon

The Wayside Smithy
Brush and wash, 5×4. Collection Mr. and Mrs. Paul Mellon

Wimletts Hill, Kent
Water-colour and body colour over black chalk, $10\frac{3}{4} \times 14\frac{3}{4}$. Collection Mr. and Mrs. Paul Mellon

Brambles
Pencil, $6\frac{7}{8} \times 8\frac{3}{4}$. Collection Mr. and Mrs. Paul Mellon

Conway Castle
Black chalk, water-colour and gouache, $12\frac{3}{4} \times 17\frac{7}{8}$. Collection Mr. and Mrs. Paul Mellon

Waves
Water-colour, $5\frac{3}{4} \times 8\frac{7}{8}$. Collection Mr. and Mrs. Paul Mellon

Pistil Mawddach, North Wales
Water-colour, $17\frac{1}{4} \times 21$. Collection Mr. and Mrs. Paul Mellon

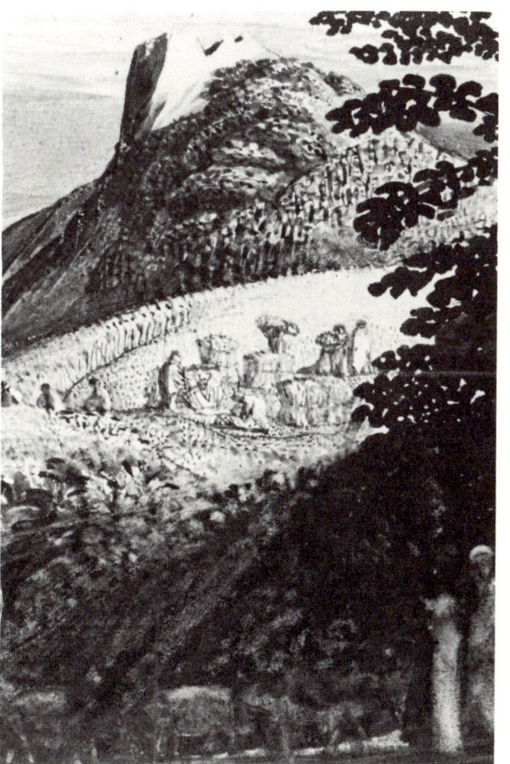

Evening, Cattle Watering
Water-colour and body colour, $4\frac{1}{4} \times 3$. Collection Mr. and Mrs. Paul Mellon

Dark Trees by the Side of a Pool
Sepia, $4\frac{1}{8} \times 2\frac{5}{8}$. Private Collection

A Path through a Cornfield
Sepia, $3\frac{1}{2} \times 5$. Private Collection

A Heath with a Shepherd and his Flock
Sepia, $3\frac{1}{2} \times 4\frac{3}{8}$. Private Collection

A Large Bare Tree
Sepia, $3\frac{1}{8} \times 4\frac{3}{16}$. Private Collection

A Thatched Cottage
Sepia, $3\frac{1}{8} \times 4\frac{3}{16}$. Private Collection

SECTION B

Sketch of a Windmill, 1812
Water-colour, $1\frac{5}{8} \times 2\frac{1}{16}$. G.

Landscape with Ruins, *c.*1819
G.

Cottage Scene: Banks of the Thames, Battersea, *c.*1819
G.

A Study, *c.*1819
G.

Bridge Scene: Composition, *c.*1819
G.

Landscape: Composition, *c.*1819
G.

Wood Scene: A Study from Nature, *c.*1820
G.

A Study from Nature, Battersea, *c.*1821
G.

Langley Locks, Hertfordshire, *c.*1821
G.

A Study from Nature, Battersea, *c.*1821
G.

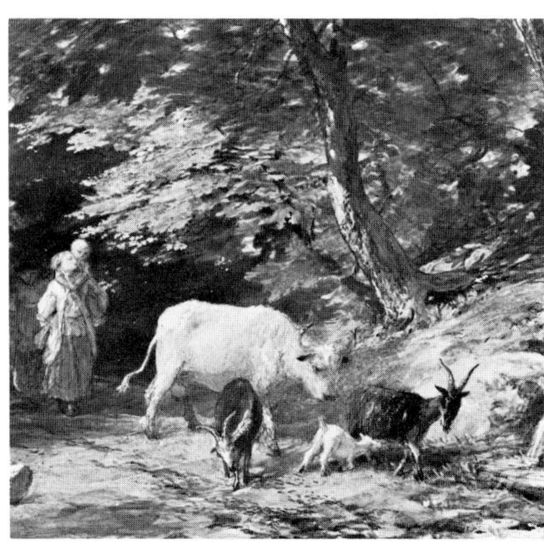

Maidstone Bridge, 1821
Pen and bistre, $7\frac{1}{2} \times 10\frac{1}{2}$. G.

Hailsham, Sussex: A Storm coming on, 1822
Water-colour, $8\frac{5}{16} \times 12\frac{1}{2}$.

A Lane Scene, Battersea, 1822
G.

Twilight, 1824/5
G.

Joseph's Dream, 1824
G.

Study of a Head, *c.*1824
G.

A Scene from Kent, 1825
G.

A Rustic Scene, 1825
G.

Windsor, 1825
G.

Harvest Moon, 1825
G.

Six Drawings, 1825
G.

A Biblical Subject, 1826
$17 \times 11\frac{1}{2}$. G.

Naomi before Bethlehem, 1826
$17 \times 11\frac{1}{2}$. G.

The Artist's Home, 1826
G.

A Young Man in a Landscape, *c.*1827/8
On ivory, $3\frac{1}{2}$ long. G.

The Shepherd, 1828
Engraving after Palmer. Welby Sherman. G.

The Valley Farm, *c.*1828
Pen, pencil, chalk and white, $8\frac{7}{16} \times$?. G.

The Village of Shoreham, near Sevenoaks, 1828?
Sepia and white, $9 \times 11\frac{3}{4}$. G.

The Deluge: A Sketch, 1828?
G.

A Cornfield, Shoreham, 1831/2
G.

The Sheepfold, 1831/2
G.

Scene near Shoreham, Kent, 1831/2
G.

A Pastoral Scene, Twilight, 1831/2
G.

A Pastoral Landscape, 1831/2
G.

A Harvest Scene, 1831/2
G.

Landscape Twilight, 1831/2
G.

Late Twilight, 1831/2
G.

Drawing for Scene at Underriver, *c.*1831/2
Pen. G.

The Skylark, 1831/2
Sepia. G.

A Valley with a Church, 1831/2
Sepia. G.

Still Life, 1832/4
Oil. G.

A Kentish Scene, 1833
G.

A Rustic Scene, 1833
G.

Landscape Twilight, 1833
G.

Study for 'The Shearers', 1833/4
A. H. Palmer *A Memoir*

Landscape Evening, 1834
G.

The Harvest Field, 1834
G.

The Flock, 1834
G.

The Cottage Window, 1834
G.

A Study from Nature, 1834
G.

Landscape, 1834
G.

The Reaper, 1834
G.

Evening, 1834
G.

Landscape, 1834
G.

Scene from Lee, North Devon, *c.*1835
G.

The Cornfield, *c.*1835
G.

A Scene near Shoreham, Kent, *c.*1835
G.

At Filston Farm, Kent, *c.*1835
G.

Cottage Window, *c.*1835
G.

The Lane Side, *c.*1835
G.

The Hop Pickers, *c.*1835
G.

Mount Siabod, 1835/6
Pen and water-colour, $14\frac{1}{2} \times 18$. G. Possibly the same picture as the **Mount Siabod** of the same year now in the collection of Mr. and Mrs. Paul Mellon. See Section A

An Italian Pifferaro, 1837/9
Water-colour, $11\frac{5}{8} \times 8\frac{11}{16}$. V.

The Burial Place of Keats, 1837
Pencil, $4 \times 5\frac{1}{2}$. V.

Papigno on the Nar between Terni and the Falls of Terni, 1837?
Water-colour, $12\frac{1}{4} \times 16\frac{5}{8}$. V.

Sketch of the town of Subiaco from the South-West, 1837/9
Water-colour, $10\frac{1}{8} \times 17\frac{1}{2}$. V.
Possibly the same picture as **Civitella di Subiaco** now in The Whitworth Art Gallery, Manchester. See Section A

Pompeii, 1837/9
Water-colour, $12\frac{7}{8} \times 16\frac{1}{2}$. V.

Harlech Castle, Twilight, exhib. 1843
Water-colour, $20\frac{1}{4} \times 27\frac{11}{16}$. V.

View in the Campagna, 1844/5
Pencil, $3\frac{1}{16} \times 4\frac{5}{8}$. V. Reproduced in Charles Dickens' *Pictures from Italy*, 1846, reprinted 1973

The Colosseum, Rome, 1844
Reproduced in Dickens, *op. cit.*

Villa d'Este, Tivoli, from the Cypress Avenue, 1844
Reproduced in Dickens, *op. cit.*

Vineyard Scene, 1844
Reproduced in Dickens, *op. cit.*

Street of the Tombs, Pompeii, 1844
Reproduced in Dickens, *op. cit.*

A Scene from 'The Mysteries of Udolpho', Jacob wrestling with the Angel, 1845
Water-colour, $20 \times 14\frac{1}{2}$. V.

Studies of Barley, Oats and Wheat, 1846/7
Water-colour and pencil, $10\frac{3}{4} \times 15$. V.

Backways, Tintagel, 1848/58
Water-colour, $7\frac{1}{4} \times 10\frac{1}{2}$. L.

Redstone Wood, 1849
Water-colour and gouache, $9\frac{7}{8} \times 15$. L.

The Château of Polignac, 1849
Water-colour, $9\frac{3}{4} \times 9\frac{1}{4}$. L.

The Skylark, 1850
Original design for etching, $7\frac{1}{8} \times 4\frac{1}{4}$. V.

The Rest on the Flight to Egypt, after 1850
Water-colour, $8 \times 10\frac{1}{2}$. L.

The Landing of St. Paul in Italy, exhib. 1850
Water-colour, $21 \times 29\frac{1}{2}$. L.

The Dip of the Sun, 1852
Water-colour and gouache, $10\frac{3}{8} \times 17$. L.

Study of Daisies and Dandelions, 1856
Chalk, $9\frac{3}{16} \times 11\frac{3}{4}$. V.

A Letter from India, 1859
10×17. L.

Welsh River Landscape, 1860
$13\frac{3}{8} \times 10$. L.

Crossing the Common at Sunset, after 1860
L.

The Good Farmer, exhib. 1865
Water-colour. L.

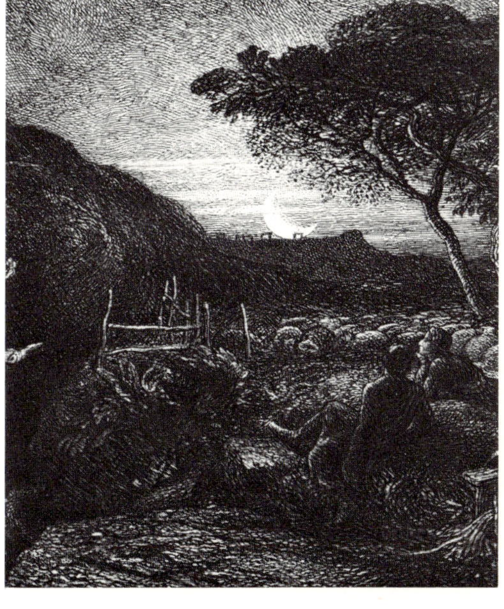

UNTRACED WORKS TO WHICH NO CERTAIN DATE CAN BE ATTRIBUTED

Emily and Valencourt at the Château Blanc
Water-colour, $9\frac{1}{2} \times 13\frac{1}{4}$. L.

Path through Trees
Water-colour and pen, $4\frac{1}{4} \times 5\frac{3}{8}$. Reproduced in *The Illustrated London News*, Nov. 4th, 1961

Trees
Water-colour, $9\frac{1}{2} \times 13\frac{1}{4}$. Reproduced in *The Illustrated London News*, Dec. 17th, 1949

The Barns
Water-colour. L.

Sunrise over the Sea
Black and white chalk heightened with white, $5\frac{1}{4} \times 7\frac{1}{4}$. L.

The Vintage
Pen and oil, $5\frac{1}{4} \times 3\frac{1}{8}$. L.

Landscape in the Campagna
Water-colour, $5\frac{1}{2} \times 15\frac{1}{2}$. L.

A Castle on a Hill
Water-colour heightened with white, $13\frac{1}{2} \times 10\frac{1}{4}$. L.

Golden City, Rome
Water-colour. L.

Landscape at Sunset
Water-colour, $11\frac{1}{2} \times 20\frac{1}{2}$. L.

Sheepfold at Sunset or **Eventide**
Water-colour heightened with body colour. L.

Sunset
Water-colour, $12\frac{1}{4} \times 21$. L.

The Full Moon
Water-colour, $7\frac{3}{8} \times 16\frac{3}{4}$. L.

Harvesting
Gouache, $7\frac{1}{2} \times 16\frac{1}{2}$. L.

Will o' the Wisp
Water-colour heightened with white, $4\frac{1}{2} \times 8\frac{1}{2}$. L.

Crossing the Common at Sunset
Water-colour. L.

The Sailor's Return
Water-colour and gum, $15\frac{3}{8} \times 27\frac{7}{8}$. L.

Landscape with Trees against a Setting Sun
Pencil, water-colour and gouache, $2\frac{1}{2} \times 5$. L.

The Ploughman Homeward Plods his Weary Way
Water-colour and gouache, $7 \times 15\frac{3}{4}$. L.

Moonlight Landscape, Brynderwan
Water-colour and pencil, $14\frac{1}{2} \times 22\frac{1}{8}$. L.

Harlech Castle
Water-colour and gouache. L.

Harvesting with Distant Prospect
Water-colour, $4\frac{15}{16} \times 6\frac{1}{8}$. V.

Wooded Landscape by Moonlight
Water-colour $7\frac{3}{4} \times 11\frac{3}{4}$. V.

Harlech Castle, Twilight
Water-colour, $20\frac{1}{4} \times 27\frac{11}{16}$. V.

The Distant Hills
Touched proof of a wood engraving by W. Meason after a design by Palmer for William Adam's *Sacred Allegories*, $14\frac{3}{4} \times 3\frac{3}{8}$. V.

Storm and Wreck on the North Coast of Cornwall
Water-colour, $5\frac{3}{8} \times 7\frac{7}{8}$. V.

The North Devon Coast
Water-colour, $7\frac{1}{4} \times 10\frac{1}{2}$. V.

Tombstones in Reigate Churchyard
Pencil, $4\frac{3}{16} \times 7\frac{1}{8}$. V.

Two Studies of a Windmill
Water-colour, $10\frac{5}{8} \times 14\frac{1}{4}$. V.

The Wayside Inn, Twilight
Water-colour, 5×6. V.

Yew Tree in Dolwyddelan Churchyard
Pencil, $9\frac{1}{8} \times 7\frac{1}{4}$. V.

Going to Sea
Water-colour, $7\frac{3}{8} \times 16\frac{7}{8}$. V.

Landscape with Windmill, Figures and Cattle
Water-colour, $21\frac{1}{8} \times 29\frac{3}{4}$. V.

NOTES TO THE TEXT

All unattributed quotations are from A. H. Palmer, *The Life and Letters of Samuel Palmer*, 1892.

1 G. Grigson, *Samuel Palmer – The Visionary Years.*

2 D. Cecil, *Visionary and Dreamer.*

3 Quoted in Grigson, *op. cit.*

4 A. Gilchrist, *The Life of William Blake.*

5 Grigson, *op. cit.*

6 A. H. Palmer, catalogue of the Victoria and Albert Museum Exhibition, 1926.

7 A pigment invented by William Blake, the recipe of which was given to Palmer.

8 See W. G. Archer, *Garwhal Painting.*

9 A. M. W. Stirling ed., *The Richmond Papers.*

10 Quoted in C. Peacock, *Samuel Palmer, Shoreham and After.*

11 A. H. Palmer, *op. cit.*

12 According to Peacock, *op. cit.*, there are letters in existence that hint of an incestuous relationship between Linnell and his daughter.

13 A. H. Palmer, *op. cit.*

BIBLIOGRAPHY

R. G. Alexander. *A Catalogue of the Etchings of Samuel Palmer*, Print Collector's Club Publication No. 16, 1937.

Mildred Archer. *Indian Miniatures and Folk Painting*, catalogue of an Arts Council Exhibition, 1967.

W. G. Archer. *Garwhal Painting*, 1954.

Ashmolean Museum. *Paintings and Drawings by Samuel Palmer*, Museum Handbook.

Laurence Binyon. *The Followers of William Blake*, 1925.

Martin Butlin, ed. *Samuel Palmer's Sketchbook: 1824*, 1962.

David Cecil. *Visionary and Dreamer: Two Poetic Painters, Samuel Palmer and Edward Burne Jones*, 1969.

Kenneth Clark. *Landscape into Art*, 1949.

John Commander. *Samuel Palmer and his Circle*, catalogue of an Arts Council Exhibition, 1957

Douglas Cooper. *Graham Sutherland*, 1961.

Alexander Gilchrist. *The Life of William Blake*, ed. Ruthven Todd, 1942.

Goeffrey Grigson. *Samuel Palmer – The Visionary Years*, 1947.

Geoffrey Grigson. *Samuel Palmer's Valley of Vision*, 1960.

Martin Hardie. *The Etched Work of Samuel Palmer*, Print Collector's Quarterly Vol. 3, 1913.

Geoffrey Keynes. *William Blake's Engravings*, 1950.

Twentieth Century British Watercolours, Victoria and Albert Museum, Handbook, 1958.

E. S. Lumsden. *The Art of Etching*, 1924.

Raymond Lister. *Edward Calvert*, 1962.

Raymond Lister, *Beulah to Byzantium: A Study of Parallels in the Works of W. B. Yeats, W. Blake, S. Palmer and E. Calvert*, 1965.

Raymond Lister. *Samuel Palmer and his Etchings*, 1969

Edward Malins. *Samuel Palmer's Italian Honeymoon*, 1968.

Robert Melville. *Samuel Palmer*, 1956.

Carlos Peacock. *Samuel Palmer, Shoreham and After*, 1968.

A. H. Palmer. *Samuel Palmer: A Memoir*, 1882.

A. H. Palmer. *The Life and Letters of Samuel Palmer*, 1892.

A. H. Palmer. *Drawings, Etchings and Woodcuts by Samuel Palmer and other Disciples of William Blake*, catalogue of a Victoria and Albert Museum Exhibition, 1926.

Edward Sackville-West. *Graham Sutherland*, 1943.

F. G. Stephens. *Notes on a Collection of Drawings, Paintings and Etchings by the late Samuel Palmer*, 1881.

A. M. W. Stirling, ed. *The Richmond Papers*, 1926.

Alfred Story. *The Life of John Linnell*, 1892.

R. H. Wilenski. *An Outline of English Painting*, 1946.

George Wingfield Digby. *Meaning and Symbol in Three Modern Artists*, 1950.

George Wingfield Digby. *Symbol and Image in William Blake*, 1957.

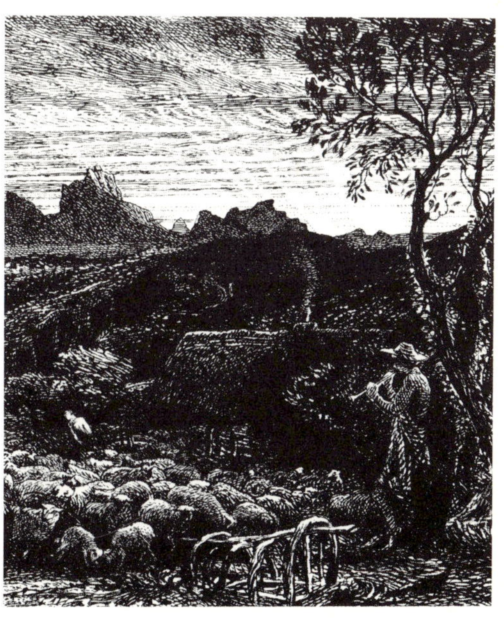

INDEX

Numbers in *italics* refer to pages on which illustrations will be found.